The Mobility of Displaced Syrians

The Mobility of Displaced Syrians

An Economic and Social Analysis

 WORLD BANK GROUP

Contents

Maps

Tables

Acknowledgments

This study was prepared by a multidisciplinary World Bank team led by Harun Onder (Task Team Leader and Senior Economist) and Haneen Sayed (Co-Task Team Leader and Lead Operations Officer). Inputs from the United Nations High Commissioner for Refugees (UNHCR) were prepared by a team led by Sima Kanaan (Senior Development Adviser, UNHCR). The project was implemented under the guidance of Kevin Carey (Practice Manager, World Bank). Contributing authors are from the World Bank Group unless otherwise indicated. They are as follows:

- **Introduction**: Harun Onder (Senior Economist), Georgia Christina Kosmidou (Consultant), Ray Salvatore Jennings (Consultant), Atsushi Iimi (Senior Economist), Mira Morad (Transport Specialist), Eyup Ozveren (Consultant, Middle East Technical University), and Sajjad Ali Shah Sayed (Manager)

- **Chapter 1**: Roger Zetter (Consultant, Oxford University), Ray Salvatore Jennings (Consultant), Sima Kanaan (Senior Development Adviser, UNHCR), Nina Schrepfer (Legal Adviser, UNHCR), Omer Karasapan (Senior Operations Officer), Dejan Bošnjak (Consultant), and Georgia Christina Kosmidou (Consultant)

- **Chapter 2**: Adam Stone Diehl (Operations Officer), Aiga Stokenberga (Transport Economist), Alan Moody (Lead Economist), Almedina Music (Junior Professional Officer), Amal Talbi (Lead Water and Sanitation Specialist), Anders Jagerskog (Senior Water Resources Management Specialist), Angela Elzir Assy (Labor Market Specialist), Annoula Rysova (Consultant), Asbjorn Wee (Senior Operations Officer), Ashok Sarkar (Senior Energy Specialist), Atsushi Iimi (Senior Economist), Bhavya Paliwal (Consultant), Carole Chartouni (Economist), Dhiraj Sharma (Economist), Dominick Revell de Waal (Senior Economist), Dorte Verner (Lead Agriculture Economist), Edinaldo Tebaldi (Consultant), Georgia Christina Kosmidou (Consultant), Guido Licciardi (Senior Urban Development Specialist), Hamzah Saif (Consultant), Ibrahim Dajani (Program Leader), Jae Kyun Kim (Consultant), Janet Minatelli (Senior Country Officer), John Morton (Senior Urban Environment Specialist), John Speakman (Adviser), Jonna Lundvall (Social Scientist), Joy Aoun (Disaster Risk Management Specialist), Kinley Clemens Salmon (Economist), Kurt Hagemann (Consultant), Lina Tutunji (Senior Procurement Specialist), Lina Fares (Senior Procurement Specialist), Luis Prada (Lead Procurement Specialist), Matthew Wai-Poi (Senior Economist), Maximilian Fischbach (Consultant), Mira Morad (Transport Specialist), Mohamed Ali Marouani (Consultant, Université Paris 1 Panthéon-Sorbonne), Nadwa Rafeh (Senior Health Specialist), Naila Ahmed

(Senior Social Development Specialist), Needa Arshad Malik (Consultant), Ola Hisou (Consultant), Omer Khan (Consultant), Pallavi Rai (Senior Cash-Based Interventions Officer, UNHCR), Paul Scott Prettitore (Senior Land Administration Specialist), Raja Arshad (Lead Disaster Risk Management Specialist), Roland Lomme (Senior Governance Specialist), Sally Zgheib (Water Supply and Sanitation Specialist), Samantha M. Constant (Consultant), Sepehr Fotovat (Senior Procurement Specialist), Simeon Sahaydachny (Consultant), Soraya El Khalil (Consultant), Syed Mehdi Hassan (Lead Financial Sector Specialist), Toni Joe Lebbos (Consultant), Venkatesh Sundararaman (Lead Economist), Ziad Nakat (Senior Transport Specialist), and Haneen Sayed (Lead Operations Officer)

- **Chapter 3**: Lori Beaman (Consultant, Northwestern University), Stefanie Onder (Adviser, American University), Georgia Christina Kosmidou (Consultant), Ola Hisou (Consultant), Luca Colombo (Consultant), Michael Morris (Consultant), Ahmed El Sayed Abo Kashaba (Regional Operation Data Management Officer, UNHCR), Anna Gaunt (Senior Livelihoods Officer, UNHCR), Edouard Legoupil (Senior Information Management Officer, UNHCR), Hania Sahnoun (Senior Economist, UNHCR), Magdalena Paddock (Intern, UNHCR), Yara Maasri (Vulnerability Assessment and Targeting Officer, UNHCR), and Harun Onder (Senior Economist)

- **Chapter 4**: Erhan Artuc (Senior Economist), Harun Onder (Senior Economist), Nicolas Gomez-Parra (Consultant), Jae Kyun Kim (Consultant), and Çağlar Özden (Lead Economist)

The team is grateful for guidance and support from Ferid Belhaj (Vice President), Saroj Kumar Jha (Regional Director), Anna M. Bjerde (Director of Strategy and Operations), Samia Msadek (Operations Director), and Amin Awad (Regional Director, UNHCR). The team received valuable comments and inputs from peer reviewers Eric Le Borgne (Adviser), Ganesh Kumar Seshan (Senior Economist), Nadia Piffaretti (Senior Economist), Randa Slim (Senior Fellow, Middle East Institute), and Raouf Mazou (Regional Director, UNHCR), and from advisers to the project, Claire Kfouri (Country Program Coordinator) and Ewen Macleod (Adviser to the High Commissioner, UNHCR). The following colleagues also provided thoughtful comments and inputs: Aaditya Mattoo (Manager), Abdallah Dardari (Senior Adviser), Emmanuel Gignac (Deputy Representative, UNHCR), Karolina Lindholm Billing (Deputy Representative, UNHCR), Lucia C. Hanmer (Lead Economist), Paolo Verme (Lead Economist), Rabie Nasr (Co-founder, Syrian Center for Policy Research), and Xavier Devictor (Manager).

This study was financed by generous financial contributions from the governments of Canada and Germany as well as from the State and Peacebuilding Fund and the Middle East and North Africa Multi-Donor Trust Fund. The team would also like to acknowledge numerous government officials, international community members, and civil society organization members who joined several rounds of consultations and shared their points of view.

The remote-sensing and survey data collection for this report was implemented by Ipsos Group S.A. Print design was provided by Design and Development Minds, and the art work was produced by Solara Shiha. Throughout the project cycle, excellent support was provided by Ekaterina G. Stefanova (Senior Program Assistant), Jihane Rached (Executive Assistant), Lana Kobeissi (Analyst), Mirvat Haddad (Program Assistant), Muna Salim (Senior Program Assistant), and Syviengxay Creger (Program Assistant).

Abbreviations

3RP	Regional Refugee & Resilience Plan
b/d	barrels per day
DOS	Department of Statistics (Jordan)
FAO	Food and Agriculture Organization of the United Nations
GDP	gross domestic product
ha	hectare
HNAP	Humanitarian Needs Assessment Programme
HRH	human resources for health (indicator)
IDP	internally displaced person
JD	Jordanian dinar
JLMPS	Jordan Labor Market Panel Survey
KRG	Kurdistan Regional Government
kV	kilovolt
LCRP	Lebanon Crisis Response Plan
LFP	labor force participation
LL	Lebanese pound
LS	Syrian pound
MEB	minimum expenditure basket
MOL	Ministry of Labor
MSNA	Multi-Sector Needs Assessment
NGO	nongovernmental organization
NRC	Norwegian Refugee Council
PEDEE	Public Establishment for Distribution and Exploitation of Electrical Energy

PEE	Public Establishment for Electricity
PEEGT	Public Establishment for Electricity Generation and Transmission
PPP	purchasing power parity
SCPR	Syrian Centre for Policy Research
UN Comtrade	United Nations International Trade Statistics Database
UN-Habitat	United Nations Human Settlements Programme
UNHCR	United Nations High Commissioner for Refugees
UNICEF	United Nations Children's Fund
UNOCHA	United Nations Office for the Coordination of Humanitarian Affairs
UNRWA	United Nations Relief and Works Agency
VAF	Vulnerability Assessment Framework
VASyR	Vulnerability Assessment of Syrian Refugees
WASH	water, sanitation, and hygiene
WDI	World Development Indicators
WFP	World Food Programme
WSS	water supply and sanitation

Key Messages

This report analyzes the spontaneous mobility of Syrian refugees in Iraq, Jordan, and Lebanon from an economic and social (not political) perspective. Main results are summarized in the Overview. The following is a list of 10 key messages built upon those results:

Conditions faced by Syrians inside and outside the Syrian Arab Republic

1. Despite the generosity of host countries and the best efforts of the international community, the sheer scale and pace of the conflict in Syria have resulted in persistent hardships for Syrians both inside and outside Syria.

2. Taking refuge is not always a "win–win" situation (that is, with both better security and better economic opportunities) for Syrian refugees. On the contrary, access to security is often counterbalanced by a decrease in the quality of life.

3. The security and quality of life trade-off often takes an intergenerational form: short-term security comes at the expense of lower human capital accumulation that will disproportionately affect Syrian children and youth going forward.

Returns so far

4. Conditions on the ground affect both the scale and the composition of returns in different ways. With persistent concerns regarding insecurity in Syria, the return of Syrian refugees has been infrequent and selective so far, which does not represent a large-scale return.

5. Conditions in Syria have rather predictable and monotonic effects on the return of refugees, that is, better security and service access in Syria consistently increase returns.

6. Host country conditions affect returns in more complex ways. A lower quality of life in exile does not always increase returns—for example, more education increases return at the primary education level but not at secondary or tertiary education levels.

Return simulations

7. The international community has a diversified policy tool kit—including subsidies (return assistance), transfers, and service restoration in Syria—to help refugees, their hosts, and Syrians in Syria.

8. This policy tool kit should ideally be used in an adaptive manner. "Corner solutions" (for example, using all resources through one tool only) are inefficient. The optimal allocation of resources across the policy tools is shaped by the conditions on the ground.

9. Insecurity in Syria is a major deterrent to return, and it reduces the effectiveness of service restoration efforts. Thus, with improvements in security, which would include the cessation of arbitrary detainment, forced conscription, and other violations of human and property rights, more resources can effectively be allocated to restoring services.

10. Maximizing refugee returns at any cost is a poorly defined policy target. Maximizing the well-being of refugees, including those who return and those who do not return; of their hosts; and of Syrians in Syria should be considered.

Overview

This report analyzes the spontaneous mobility of Syrian refugees in Iraq, Jordan, and Lebanon. To do so, it follows a five-step integrated analytical strategy. First, a review of international experience helps identify factors that contribute to mobility (push and pull factors); then, the conditions faced by Syrians inside and outside the Syrian Arab Republic with respect to these factors are investigated. Next, the relative importance of each factor is estimated by using actual returns to Syria that have taken place so far. Finally, potential roles that can be played by these factors going forward are simulated with a scenario-based approach.

Overview

In its eighth year, the Syrian conflict continues to take its toll on the Syrian people. Even though the incidence of armed conflict and forced displacement diminished to a certain degree in the first half of 2018, persistent effects from the brutal conflict continue to unfold. Over one-half of the population of Syria remains displaced (as of September 2018), with more than 5.6 million registered as refugees outside of the country and another 6.2 million displaced within Syria's borders.[1] The internally displaced include 2 million school-age children, with less than one-half enjoying full access to education. Another 739,000 Syrian children are out of school in five neighboring countries that host Syria's refugees.[2] The loss of human capital is staggering. The combined effects of displacement and forgone investments in human development will create permanent hardship for generations of Syrians going forward.

Although cessation of hostilities within Syria is conducive to the return of displaced Syrians, it may not, by itself, be a sufficient condition. Despite the tragic prospects for renewed fighting and large-scale displacement in certain parts of the country, parties to the multiple-strand peace process continue to push for deescalation, and overall reduction in armed conflict is possible going forward. International experience shows, however, that the absence of fighting is rarely a singular trigger for return. Although strict causality is difficult to assign, return experiences such as those in Afghanistan, Angola, Bosnia and Herzegovina, Iraq, Liberia, Somalia, and South Sudan demonstrate that numerous other factors—including improved security and socioeconomic conditions in origin states, access to property and assets, the availability of key services, and restitution in home areas—play important roles in shaping the scale and composition of returns. Overall, refugees have their own calculus of return that considers all these factors and assesses available options.

This study sheds light on the "mobility calculus" of Syrian refugees. In complete adherence to international norms governing issues related to refugees, and in strict repudiation of any policies that imply wrongful practices involving forced repatriation, this study analyzes factors that may be considered by refugees in their decision to relocate. By doing so, it aims to provide a conceptual framework, supported by data and analysis, to facilitate an impartial conversation about refugees and their return choices. To this end, the study follows a five-step integrated analytical strategy (figure O.1):

- *The first step considers international experience*, which helps identify important factors in analyzing refugee movements (that is, push and pull factors). Given the lack of data and empirical research about the drivers of refugee returns, the analysis adheres to descriptive findings that rely on case studies.

Figure O.1. Five-Step Integrated Analytical Strategy

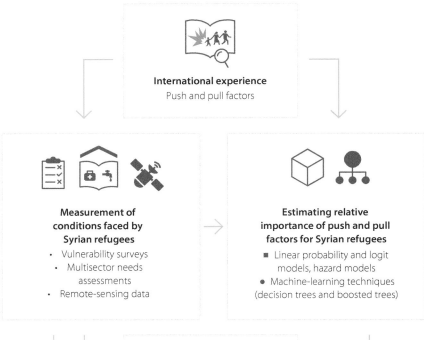

International experience
Push and pull factors

Measurement of
conditions faced by
Syrian refugees
• Vulnerability surveys
• Multisector needs
  assessments
• Remote-sensing data

Estimating relative
importance of push and pull
factors for Syrian refugees
■ Linear probability and logit
  models, hazard models
● Machine-learning techniques
(decision trees and boosted trees)

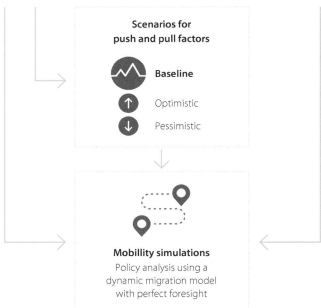

Scenarios for
push and pull factors

Baseline

↑ Optimistic

↓ Pessimistic

Mobillity simulations
Policy analysis using a
dynamic migration model
with perfect foresight

• ***The second step measures these factors*** in Syria (using previous United Nations surveys and remote-sensing techniques) and for refugees in host countries (using official data, vulnerability surveys led by the United Nations High Commissioner for Refugees [UNHCR], and a World Bank verification survey).

- **The third step estimates the relative importance of each factor** in explaining the spontaneous returns that have taken place so far in the Syrian context by using various econometric approaches (for example, linear probability and logit models) and machine-learning specifications such as decision trees.

- **The fourth and fifth steps** use a simulation model that builds on *The Toll of War: The Economic and Social Consequences of the Conflict in Syria* (World Bank 2017) to analyze the role that can be played by several factors in influencing spontaneous return of refugees in the medium term. Because this model is prone to significant uncertainty, a scenario-based approach, where factors that can affect refugees' decisions can vary, is adopted.

The analysis in this study focuses solely on the rational choices of refugees themselves. It is important to emphasize that refugees are not people who are "misplaced and to be returned." They are fully capable of assessing their options and act rationally given their resources and constraints, except for facing extreme circumstances and, sometimes, posttraumatic complications. Other parties, including the international community, host country governments and communities, and the government of the source country, can influence those resources and constraints by means of rules, regulations, and assistance; but they cannot prevent refugees reassessing the situation and acting according to their own perceived best interest just like any other human being. In technical terms, it is the refugee who undertakes the optimization decision, not other parties. Thus, an analysis of the potential implications of any policy action primarily entails understanding how refugees may react to the proposed changes. This concept constitutes the core of the analysis in this report. The remainder of this executive summary discusses key findings of the study.

Given the immense complexity surrounding the refugee mobility issue, the report leaves several equally, if not more, important topics for future work. The analytical complexity of refugee situations forced the report to narrow its focus to be able to provide some real value added in improving understanding. For instance, issues pertaining to the security sector and the cultural, ethical, and political dimensions of the conflict are beyond the scope of this report. In addition, data shortages were more daunting in areas such as internally displaced persons (IDPs) in Syria and refugees in Turkey. Thus, this analysis focuses on the refugee mobility issue through the five described steps in Iraq, Jordan, and Lebanon; it leaves the study of IDPs in Syria and refugees in Europe and Turkey for the future. Finally, the highly pertinent topic of how the host communities are affected by the arrivals of refugees, and more broadly by the Syrian conflict, is scheduled to be analyzed in a forthcoming study "The Regional Economic and Social Impact of Syrian Conflict," which will benefit from the methodology and findings of this report.

International Experience

An overview of international experience highlights four major groups of factors that drive the mobility of refugees, although these factors work together in a complex manner. Refugee return is not a monotonic event: it often includes an iterative, staggered, or cyclical process. In the case of iterative return processes, there may also be temporary return movement. Evidence from Iraqi refugees hosted in Syria (before the war in Syria) and Somali refugees in Kenya, points to the idea that refugees follow complex strategies in spontaneous returns: a few members of refugee households may return informally for short periods to, among other things, assess the scope for more permanent return, safeguard and reestablish entitlements to property, or assist family members who have remained behind. Nevertheless, trends in spontaneous returns point to a few structural factors that are commonly considered by refugees when considering their decision to move:

- *Peace, security, and protection*, including the scope of peace and reconciliation measures, adequate rights protection, access to justice, and trust in local actors

- *Livelihoods and economic opportunities*, including economic and social absorption capacity of return areas and access to resources including financial resources, with intangible economic aspects, such as human capital and social networks, playing an important role

- *Housing, land, and property*, including the ownership of assets in countries of asylum and origin, likelihood of asset restitution, prevailing conditions of appropriation, and property rights

- *Infrastructure and access to services*, including the scale of physical and infrastructure destruction; strategies and funding for reconstruction/restoration; and access to adequate services and housing, social programs, education, and health services.

The specific role played by each of these four categories of factors varies from case to case. International experience shows that each refugee situation is different. For many of the individual factors that fall into one of these four broad categories, the magnitude and direction of their impact on returns may not be consistent across refugee situations depending on various other conditions. For instance, poverty in countries of asylum may be a driver of return—as in the case of Iraqi refugees from Syria in 2007–10—but, perhaps counterintuitively, the opposite may also be true. Refugees from higher socioeconomic groups may have a greater propensity than others to return earlier, as in the case of Liberian displacement. Similarly, after a protracted period of exile, the loss of skills or the lack of skills to meet new economic conditions may constrain return or it may propel returnees to urban areas with better livelihood opportunities.

All refugees are not alike: each person in exile faces a different configuration of constraints and capabilities. The role played by the four major factor groups also varies across individuals within a given refugee situation. This is true because each person who is in exile faces a different combination of these factors, based on his or her economic and social background. The most obvious case in this regard is refugee women. They often have fewer opportunities than men to acquire new skills or capital savings in exile; they generally have less power and influence than men about the decision to return. Upon return, women may face additional difficulties in securing livelihoods; reclaiming house, land, and property; and accessing other essential services. The experience of Chilean women returning home from exile at the end of the Pinochet dictatorship in the 1990s provides a poignant example of such impact of changing domestic power structures. Overall, such differences across subgroups of refugees necessitate a granular approach to understanding the determinants of refugee mobility. It is important to account for a large set of characteristics before any causal relationship is attributed to the role played by any specific factor. To this end, the next step assesses the conditions faced by Syrians inside Syria and in host communities.

UNHCR's policy on return is predicated on refugees' right to go back to their country of origin at a time of their choosing. Their decisions and choices are to be respected and enabled. In cases where refugees choose to return, UNHCR provides counseling and assesses that the decision is voluntary, and then works to make the return dignified, but without incentivizing other refugees to return. UNHCR also works actively to find solutions for refugees from the beginning of the crisis. In the context of Syria, through consultations with refugees, UNHCR identifies the obstacles to their return in safety and dignity and is working with all parties to remove obstacles to return, including through discussing a legal framework with the government of Syria, addressing gaps in civil documentation and legal status, and expanding operations and humanitarian programs in places of return. UNHCR is engaged with the government of Syria and other stakeholders to ensure that everyone is aware and applies international protection standards and principles to return planning. UNHCR advocates for the application of international protection standards to ensure that returns are safe and dignified and no one is forced to return prematurely. While protecting individual rights, this approach also means returns are more likely to be sustainable and the risk of further displacement will be reduced in the longer term.

Conditions Faced by Syrians Inside and Outside Syria

This study combines numerous data sources to assess the conditions faced by Syrians along the four categories distilled from international experience. In the absence of comprehensive administrative or survey data, this report pays special attention to combining disparate sources of information that are not immediately comparable otherwise. For conditions in countries of asylum, this analysis uses refugee registration data and vulnerability surveys from UNHCR; official data from governments of Iraq, Jordan, and Lebanon; and a new World Bank survey for return intentions and verification of other large-scale surveys. For conditions in Syria, the Humanitarian Needs Assessment Programme (UNOCHA 2018), the UNHCR-led Multi-Sector Needs Assessment (UNHCR 2017a), and the Urban Community Profiling Surveys from the United Nations Human Settlements Programme (UN-Habitat 2016) are used. Additionally, a novel database of physical damage and functionality of facilities was created for the purposes of this study, reflecting conditions as of May 2018. To this end, optical imagery at 30–50 centimeters resolution from Digital Globe and Airbus satellite platforms and the visible infrared imaging radiometer suite of the U.S. National Aeronautics and Space Administration were employed to generate a series of physical damage and human activities around facilities in 15 cities and six sectors. These city-level assessments were then extrapolated to the 14 governorates by using conflict intensity and baseline asset inventories.

In Syria, access to publicly provided services is determined by displacement, destruction, and disorganization. Conditions in a given location, especially those related to services like education and health, are driven by displacement, physical destruction, and organizational factors such as availability of skilled personnel and supplies. Whereas some Syrian governorates like Ar-Raqqa, Deir-ez-Zor, and Al-Hasakeh have lost large shares of their inhabitants (53 percent, 28 percent, and

Map O.1. Change in Population, Syrian Arab Republic, 2011–18

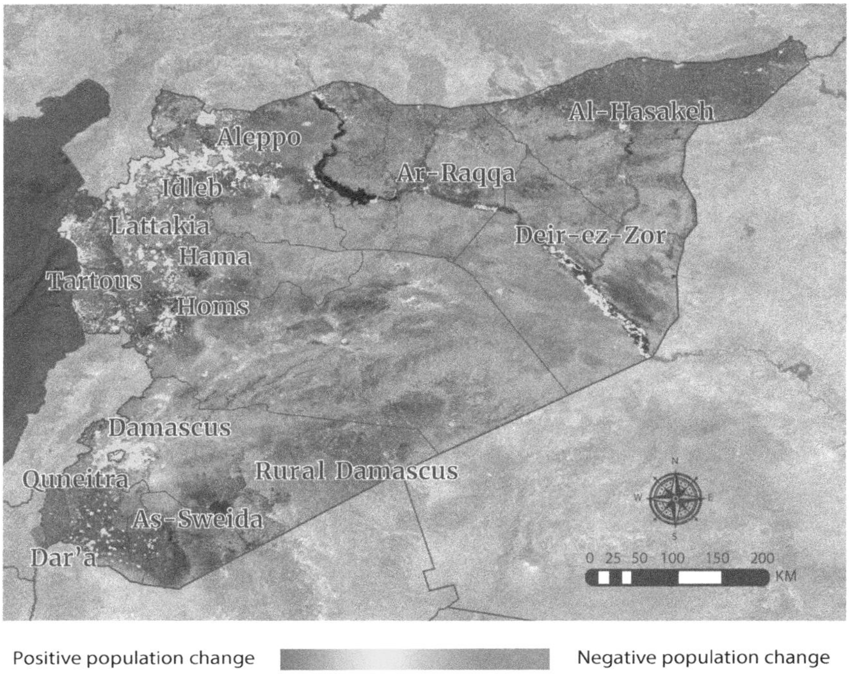

Positive population change ▮▮▮▮▮▮▮▮▮ Negative population change

Source: WorldPop, https://www.worldpop.org/; World Bank staff calculations.

27 percent, respectively) over the course of the conflict, others have increased their populations, such as Idleb (39 percent) and Rural Damascus (15 percent) (map O.1). This pattern, by itself, can lead to unexpected conclusions if other factors, especially disorganization, are not taken into consideration. In proportionate terms, more Syrians moved away from conflict-hit areas than the share of infrastructure damage in those areas. In addition, conflict has been relatively more intensive in areas with historically low infrastructure availability, such as Ar-Raqqa and Deir-ez-Zor. As a result, the share of population with 30-minute access to health facilities in 2018 (about 73.8 percent) was only marginally lower than that in 2010 (about 74.5 percent) (map O.2). The picture is, however, completely different when human resources are taken into consideration. From 2010 until 2018, the number of physicians in Syria fell from 0.529 per 1,000 persons to 0.291 per 1,000. Household and community surveys (such as the Multi-Sector Needs Assessment) confirm that access to infrastructure alone does not guarantee access to service. A summary of the findings regarding the conditions faced by Syrians inside and outside Syria is discussed in the four broad categories in the next section.

Peace, security, and protection

More than any other factor, what worries Syrians, especially refugees, is that persecution and the lawlessness in the country may endure well into the future. UNHCR's fourth regional survey on Syrian refugees' perceptions and intentions on return to Syria found that safety and security in Syria were by far their most important concern regarding return: among refugees not intending to return to Syria within

Map O.2. **Change in Proximity to a Functioning Hospital, Syrian Arab Republic, 2010–18**

30-minute proximity to a functioning health facility

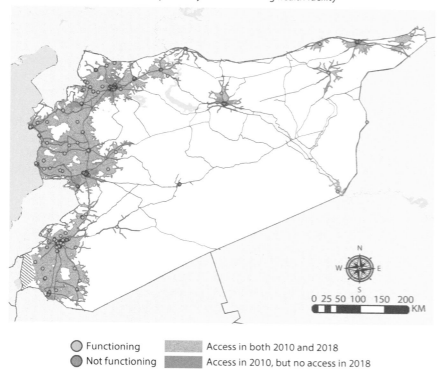

| Functioning | | Access in both 2010 and 2018 |
| Not functioning | | Access in 2010, but no access in 2018 |

12 months, 45 percent of the reasons provided to explain their intentions were related to the prevalence of indiscriminate violence or the risk of targeted reprisals (UNHCR 2018). Refugee apprehension over security conditions includes other dimensions of security as well. As of June 2018, mandatory military conscription for men ages 18–42 remained a major deterrent against returns; as governed by Decree No. 18, conscription also pertains to those who came of age following the crisis and who now technically qualify as "draft-dodgers" rather than deserters. Lack of civil documentation and insecurity seem to reinforce each other. About 40 percent of the Syrians surveyed by the Humanitarian Needs Assessment Programme reported a lack of some official civil document, such as birth certificate or national identification card, with higher percentages in opposition-controlled areas (for example, 80 percent in Idleb) (UNOCHA 2018). Syrians primarily attribute the marked lack of documentation to insecurity during travel (63 percent). Finally, about 45 percent of Syrians reported that their inability to obtain official documentation curtailed their freedom of movement, and 9 percent claimed that it led to arrest (UNOCHA 2018).

Employment and livelihood opportunities

Syrians have better access to livelihood opportunities in countries of asylum than in Syria, but poverty prevails among Syrians everywhere. Unemployment rates in Syria are not known exactly; estimates vary up to 57.7 percent (Syrian Center for Policy

Research at end-2014) (SCPR 2015). In comparison, the UNHCR vulnerability surveys report a 20.5 percent unemployment rate for Syrian men in Jordan and 12.7 percent in Lebanon (2017 estimates) (UNHCR 2017b; UNHCR, UNICEF, and WFP 2018). The labor force participation rate of Syrian men is higher in Syria (79.1 percent) than in Lebanon and Jordan (68 percent and 63.3 percent, respectively), whereas female labor force participation is similarly low in all three locations (between 10 and 13 percent). These rates do not account for underemployment where the employed may not be necessarily engaged in full-time activity. In Jordan, Syrian men are employed largely in the informal sector where they work without work permits or formal contracts and are concentrated in the manufacturing, construction, and agriculture sectors—the only sectors open to refugees for employment.[3] The pattern of labor market outcomes is approximately the same in Lebanon; whereas more than two-thirds of Syrian men is active, only one in 10 women is active in the labor force. Employment restrictions in sectors where Syrians can work, costs of obtaining a work permit, and regulatory barriers to hiring refugees lead to informality, lack of job security, underemployment, and subpar wages. The government of Jordan has, however, relaxed the rules that restricted the economic activities of Syrian refugees: more work permits are being issued, and nongovernmental organizations are supporting home-based businesses inside camps, with the scope widening for the operation of home-based businesses outside the camps. Finally, despite the efforts of host governments and the international community, extreme poverty rates of Syrian refugees in Jordan (51–61 percent), and to a lesser extent in Lebanon (37–50 percent), remain close to those in Syria (55–67 percent).

Housing, land, and property

The top housing-related concern for Syrians is looting and expropriation, followed by concerns over damage. In conflict-affected Syrian cities, physical destruction along with the exodus of people is extensive. About one-fifth of all residential buildings in the 15 cities covered in this study suffered damage. With both conflict-driven damage and large inflows of IDPs, the worst housing conditions are in Idleb (48 percent housing deprivation). The least deprivation is in Quneitra (11 percent) and Tartous (18 percent). Most Syrians see looting as the primary housing-related concern in As-Sweida (80 percent), Ar-Raqqa (42 percent), and Deir-ez-Zor (41 percent). Damage to land and property is also a significant concern in Ar-Raqqa, Idleb, and Dar'a. The lack of documents is an important concern in Ar-Raqqa (24 percent), Deir-ez-Zor (15 percent), and Aleppo and Homs (10 percent). Returnees are more likely to face this problem (9 percent) compared to IDPs (4.4 percent) and the host community (5 percent). Refugees, if and when they return, are likely to face even more challenges than the IDP returnees—results captured by surveys in Syria may not fully reflect the challenges faced by Syrian refugees. Several recent legislative actions (for example, Law No. 10 in 2018, Law No. 33 in 2017, and Legislatives Decrees No. 40, No. 63, and No. 66 in 2012) seem to facilitate further confiscation and expropriation of property, especially that of refugees.

Access to services

Refugees have better access to services, such as health, education, and water in countries of asylum than in conflict-intensive regions of Syria, but this is not always true for other regions. To assess the health care access of Syrians, this study has built a health accessibility index, comprising infrastructure, human resources, and financial coverage indicators. Using this tool, the overall health care accessibility index within Syria (0.390) is lower than that of Jordan (0.436) and Lebanon (0.462) but higher than that of Iraq (0.304), with conflict-intensive Syrian governorates faring much lower: Idleb (0.267), Rural Damascus (0.318), and Dar'a (0.319). In contrast, despite efforts by host countries and the international community, refugee children are generally worse off in education. The average school enrollment ratio in Syria dropped from 82 percent before the crisis to 61 percent currently. In comparison, school-age enrollment of Syrian children in Lebanon is only 42 percent (the enrollment rate for Lebanese children is 77 percent), and in Jordan it is 56 percent (the enrollment rate for Jordanian children is 90 percent). Overall, for many displaced families, the cost of education for their children is too high, and attending school also has high opportunity cost for youth. Teenage males often drop out of school to work and support their families, and an increasing share of girls gets married under the age of 18. Finally, water deprivation faced by Syrians is lower in Syria (index: 25 percent) than Lebanon (index: 33 percent), but not Jordan (index: 14–22 percent, depending on uncertainty about water quality).

Overall, the economic and social context analysis shows that most refugees face a trade-off between security and other aspects of quality of life. For Syrians, one factor is unambiguously better outside Syria: security. The analysis shows that a multidimensional sense of insecurity (including violence, prosecution, and social tensions) is the primary concern among refugees regarding potential future returns. The countries hosting Syrian refugees also provide better access to services and livelihood opportunities when compared to the war-torn regions of Syria. However, this finding is not always true, especially in education and water, when compared to those Syrian locations with lower conflict intensity. This distinction leads to a conjecture about the "revealed preferences" of Syrians: in exile, refugees gain access to better security, yet they face additional hardships that may lower the quality of life for current generations (lower living standards) and future generations (lower education). In other words, taking refuge in neighboring countries is not necessarily a win–win situation (better security and better quality of life), but is sometimes a win–lose situation involving a difficult trade-off (better security but in some respects a lower quality of life).

With increased economic responsibilities, decreased access to economic and social life, and deepening gender-based violence, Syrian women face additional challenges. The conflict has exacerbated an already restrictive environment for women in Syria, reinforcing patriarchal traditions and attitudes. With weak to no enforcement and limited effective protection of women against violence, cases of domestic violence, rape (including marital rape), forced marriage to armed group fighters, trafficking, and sexual enslavement have all increased in scale and scope. The fear of sexual violence and its consequences is one of the leading causes of displacement. This is particularly challenging because more women are now required to replace disappeared, killed, or displaced males to provide for their families: female-headed households have increased from 4.4 percent in 2009 to 12–17 percent in 2015. Syrians cope with this dilemma by either migrating or resorting to negative coping mechanisms, including child marriages. The share of marriages among female minors is reported to have surged from 7 percent in 2011 to about 30 percent in 2015, with an estimated 60 percent of child marriages going unreported. For most of these children, human capital accumulation ceases with their early marriage.

The Anatomy of Returns to Date

In this step, the analysis estimates the importance of the four broad factors distilled from international experience in shaping the mobility of Syrian refugees so far. Returns to Syria have been low relative to the total refugee population but significant nevertheless (103,090 UNHCR-verified returns between 2015 and 2018). These returnees (and nonreturnees) provide an opportunity to investigate the factors that have contributed to the return decision so far. To do this, the report uses empirical tests including linear probability and logit models to identify generalized (population-wise) effects of each factor on return behavior and uses machine-learning techniques like decision trees and boosted trees to capture localized (group-wise) effects, which enables better capture of the complexity of return. Finally, the study employs novel surveys of refugees, including nonregistered ones, to analyze the willingness to return. The use of vignette scenarios (that is, not asking refugees directly about their own return, but presenting them with scenarios about hypothetical refugee profiles, and randomizing the scenarios across participants) lessens some important biases that often plague return-intentions surveys, such as cognitive problems (for example, responses being shaped by social or political pressure).

The analysis shows that the actual returns to date are of a special kind, in both their scale and composition, and are generally different from large-scale returns. Overall, the estimations of generalized effects show that demographic characteristics like family ties, age, and marital status are important determinants of return. Empirical results in this study confirm the findings from international experience that refugee return is a complex process. Although this analysis is not able to verify the cyclical and transitory nature of some return behavior (because these data do not lend themselves to such an exercise), the nuances of who returns and under what conditions are shown.

- Refugees who are single, or male, or not members of a nuclear family have been more likely to return. Generalized results (applicable to the entire Syrian refugee population in Iraq, Jordan, and Lebanon) show that singles are 2.7 percentage points more likely to return than married refugees, male members are 0.6 percentage point more likely to return than female, and extended family members are 12 percentage points more likely to return than nuclear family members. This pattern varies greatly, however, across countries of asylum with individual returns being very common in Lebanon (89 percent of all returns). In contrast, case-level returns are much more common in Iraq and Jordan, making up more than 85 percent of all returns. "Case" here refers to UNHCR's registration system of "refugee case" in which a group of refugees, often a family with relatives, is headed by the case-head. It should also be noted that frequent back-and-forth movements of refugees between Lebanon and Syria have been reported, which may not be completely captured by the official return statistics.

- With intensive conflict in home locations in Syria, returnees are more narrowly selected from a specific profile of refugees. Using the machine-learning algorithm with a return-augmented sample (by randomly choosing a smaller sample from nonreturnees) elaborates on more complex dynamics. In this biased sample, overall, only 14 percent of nuclear family members return, whereas 74 percent of non-nuclear-family members return in this specific sample; however, the returns of nuclear family members become even less likely under high-intensity conflict. For instance, only 3 percent of nuclear family members return when the dread factor (tank, artillery, and air strikes) has been high in the district of origin in Syria. In comparison, among those in the non-nuclear-family member group, 88 percent return when the dread factor is low and 67 percent return when the dread factor is moderate and the non-nuclear member is older than 55 years of age. These findings provide some support for the anecdotal evidence that suggests that, despite an active conflict, senior relatives go back for family reunification, to identify return conditions, or to guard property against appropriation risk.

Results show that, whereas "pull" factors in Syria have unambiguous effects on return behavior, "push" factors in countries of asylum have mixed implications. Findings confirm international lessons regarding dominance of country of origin effects; however, this study finds no evidence for any suggestion that bad living conditions in host communities always make refugees go back. The relationship between host community living conditions and return is complex, as shown below.

- Security in Syria, along with demographic trends, is one of the most important determinants of return as shown in figure O.2. Refugees are found to be less likely to return to districts with a history of intensive conflict. A one-standard-deviation increase in the dread factor reduces the likelihood of return by 4.5 percentage points. By itself, however, the absence of violence is not sufficient, and the party in control is equally critical. Estimations show that refugees are 3.6 percentage points more likely to return if the district of origin is not controlled by the government of Syria. Similarly, a takeover of control (by any group) increases the likelihood of return by 18 percentage points. Thus, security is not only a backward-looking factor (conflict history) but also a forward-looking one (future exposure to violence and possible tensions).

Figure O.2. Most Important Factors in Explaining Returns So Far, Case versus Individual Levels

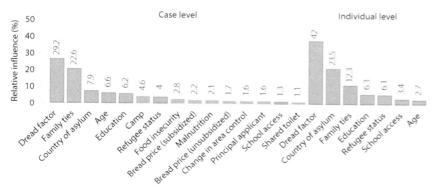

Note: Estimations show boosted tree results. Case-level estimations feature both pull (country of origin) and push (country of asylum) factors, in addition to demographic characteristics, using a limited sample size of about 43,000 refugees. Individual-level estimations feature only pull factors and demographic characteristics of refugees with a sample size of about 2.2 million refugees.

15

- Low provision of education, health, and basic services in Syria provides an effective deterrent against return. Other things being equal, concerns about access to basic services, education, and health provide a consistently negative effect on the likelihood of return across all specifications. Refugees are 2.2 percentage points less likely to return if access to basic services (electricity, fuelwood, and so forth) is a primary concern in their home district. Similar results are obtained for limited access to public health and education, but the coefficients are smaller.

- Better living conditions and access to services in countries of asylum do not reduce the likelihood of return on the low end of the distribution. Results regarding living conditions (such as food security) and access to services (such as education) show that refugees' living conditions and access to services in countries of asylum have nonlinear effects on the likelihood of return. For instance, refugees are 15 percentage points more likely to return if they consume an extra meal per day (Jordan and Lebanon dataset with geographical aggregation). Similarly, a one-standard-deviation increase in food insecurity decreases the likelihood to return by 1.8 percentage points. Although higher education has been associated with lower likelihood of return at secondary and tertiary levels (for example, having a university degree reduced the likelihood of return by 2.5 percentage points, and having a secondary degree by 1.7 percentage points), having a primary education increased this likelihood by 0.3 percentage points relative to having no education.

Surveys detected a complex nexus of human psyche and economic factors: refugees do not embrace financial issues in discussing mobility, but those issues still matter. Responses to vignette surveys provided predictable results regarding the role of assets in returns. About 38 percent of respondents indicated that their family would likely return to Syria if they find out from their neighbors in Syria that their house is intact, but the destruction of the family's house reduces the likelihood of return by 22–23 percentage points. Responses to hypothetical scenarios of financial assistance, however, were rather unexpected. Positive responses to a fictional return scenario decreased from 50 percent to 46 percent when a hypothetical amount of US$2,000 cash assistance was introduced into the scenario.[4] Interestingly, a scenario with less money (US$1,000) is still associated with a lower likelihood to return to Syria by about 8 percentage points as compared to the more money (US$2,000) scenario. Thus, somewhat paradoxically, cash assistance reduced the positive return responses, but more assistance still triggered more positive responses than less assistance.

The future mobility of Syrian refugees could be different from their past mobility. In many ways, the return that has taken place so far has been undertaken in specific circumstances—that is, during an active conflict—with specific motives like protecting property. Going forward, however, both the circumstances and motives are likely to be different. To capture these concerns, the analysis next considers scenario-based simulations.

Mobility Simulations

To study the responsiveness of refugee movements to shifting conditions in Syria, a bottom-up scenario-based approach is developed. To avoid making strong, top-down assumptions regarding the complex and unpredictable political economy dynamics surrounding the Syrian conflict, the analysis described here pursues a pragmatic microapproach. This microapproach involves building scenarios for two prominent pull factors: security and infrastructure. To do this, eight underlying conditions are analyzed for every governorate in Syria (14 overall): political influence/control, administrative capacity, social tensions, reconstruction priority, rule of law, legal/procedural complexity of return, financial capacity, and the region's connectivity with other regions. By using observations and expert assessments regarding these conditions, three possible future paths for security and infrastructure are generated for each location:

- *Baseline environment*: The insecurity index decreases from 1.40 in 2017 to 0.15 in 2023. In the meantime, 16 percent of the currently damaged infrastructure is rebuilt or fixed in the entire country, but the reconstruction ratio varies from 3 percent to 32 percent in different areas.

- *Optimistic environment*: The insecurity index decreases from 1.40 to 0.07 between 2017 and 2023, and about 30 percent of the currently damaged infrastructure is rebuilt or fixed during that period. With a greater amount of rebuilding, the reconstruction ratio is more divergent across different locations than the baseline: 5 percent in the lowest case and 48 percent in the highest.

- *Pessimistic environment*: The insecurity index decreases from 1.40 in 2017 to 0.54 in 2023. The average reconstruction ratio remains at 5 percent of the current damages across the country, with significant disparities between the highest reconstruction at 14 percent and the lowest at 2 percent.

Simulations confirm the importance of security and service provision for mobility. If the insecurity index is reduced from 1.40 now to 0.07 (optimistic environment) in five years, instead of 0.15 (baseline environment), and if 30 percent of the infrastructure is rebuilt (optimistic environment) instead of 16 percent (baseline environment), then returns would be 4.9 percentage points higher than in the baseline environment by the fifth year. In contrast, if the insecurity index decreases to only 0.54 and only 5 percent of the infrastructure is rebuilt (pessimistic environment), then returns would be about 9.8 percentage points less than the baseline.

Service restoration is more effective in mobilizing refugees when security is less of an issue. To better understand the distinct roles played by improving security conditions and service restoration, these effects were introduced separately. When only security improvements are considered, the optimistic path features 1.9 percentage points more returns than the baseline environments in five years (figure O.3). This ratio more than doubles to reach 4.9 percentage points when service restorations are involved (second blue group in the figure). In comparison, the gap between "security only" and "security + service restoration" cases is smaller when the pessimistic scenario is compared to the baseline scenario. The pessimistic insecurity path, by itself, reduced returns by 5.3 percentage points as compared to baseline path. When differences between service restoration rates are also accounted for, this gap widens to 9.8 percentage points, nearly double. Thus, the difference-making potential of service sector restoration goes together with improvements in security.

Figure O.3. The Effect of Service Restoration on Returns (Relative to the Baseline, Percentage Points)

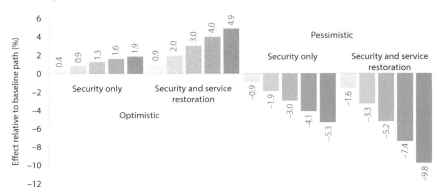

To further analyze the mobility responses of refugees, alternative resource allocation scenarios are considered. Because refugees' mobility decisions may also be influenced by other policy-driven conditions, this report analyzes the relative effectiveness of alternative uses of financial resources. More specifically, each of the three environments specified above (baseline, optimistic, and pessimistic) is investigated to determine if certain ways of allocating resources other than service restoration may be more conducive to return. To this end, the following options are used:

- *Transfers*: In each environment, the estimated environment-specific cost of service restoration is distributed equally on a per capita basis within Syria, in the form of cash transfers, including to the returnees. This distribution continues for five years until the money is depleted; no service restoration is performed.

- *Subsidies*: In each environment, the estimated environment-specific cost of service restoration is used to subsidize the return of refugees to Syria, in the form of reductions in mobility costs and cash transfers including to the returnees. Because the Syrians inside Syria are not subsidized, the returned receive a larger transfer in this case. This distribution continues for five years until the money is depleted; no service restoration is performed.

Finally, maximizing returns and maximizing Syrians' welfare may be different objectives, and trade-offs between the two are likely. Simulations show that, on average, mobility subsidies are the most effective in mobilizing refugees, but the least desirable from a welfare perspective (table O.1). Returns under the subsidy scheme can exceed those under the service restoration scheme by about 29 percentage points, 45 percentage points, and 60 percentage points under pessimistic, baseline, and optimistic environments, respectively. Intuitively, for refugees, subsidies provide a more direct, exclusive, and thus larger benefit associated with returns. In comparison, the benefits of service restoration are shared by all Syrians and, thus, diluted from the refugee's perspective. The difference between

Table O.1. Returns and Welfare under Transfers and Subsidy Schemes (Compared to the Service Restoration Case, Percentage Points, Cumulative)

Returns and welfare (% deviation from service restoration case)						
		RETURN				
		1 year	2 years	3 years	4 years	5 years
Baseline environment	Transfers	−0.1	−0.7	−1.6	−2.9	−4.8
	Subsidies	9.1	17.9	26.6	35.5	45.0
Optimistic environment	Transfers	0.7	0.4	−0.7	−2.6	−5.2
	Subsidies	14.0	26.6	38.3	49.3	60.3
Pessimistic environment	Transfers	−0.1	−0.4	−0.7	−1.1	−1.7
	Subsidies	5.6	11.1	16.6	22.5	28.8
		WELFARE				
		1 year	2 years	3 years	4 years	5 years
Baseline environment	Transfers	−4.1	−4.6	−5.1	−5.6	−6.2
	Subsidies	−6.9	−7.1	−7.4	−7.6	−7.8
Optimistic environment	Transfers	−4.0	−4.8	−5.7	−6.5	−7.4
	Subsidies	−8.6	−9.0	−9.2	−9.5	−9.7
Pessimistic environment	Transfers	−2.5	−2.7	−3.0	−3.2	−3.5
	Subsidies	−4.0	−4.1	−4.2	−4.4	−4.5

the two schemes is the most prominent in the optimistic environment, where a larger financial resource is either shared among returnees (subsidies) or diluted by means of service restoration.

Overall, the analysis in this report does not attempt to generate policy solutions, but it provides important reminders about the design of such policies. The simulation exercise developed here shows that the international community has access to diversified policies to help refugees, their hosts, and the Syrians in Syria. These include, but are not limited to, subsidies (return assistance), transfers, and service restoration in Syria. Although simulations do no attempt to solve for the "optimal allocation of resources" across these tools, it is still possible to infer key insights from them. First, "corner solutions" (for example, using all resources through one tool only) are inefficient because the problems addressed by these tools reinforce each other. Second, these policy tools should ideally be used in an adaptive manner, responding to changes in conditions on the ground. For instance, insecurity in Syria is a major deterrent to return, and it reduces the effectiveness of service restoration efforts. Thus, with improvements in security—which would include the cessation of arbitrary detainment, forced conscription, and other violations of human and property rights—more resources can effectively be allocated to restoring services. Third, while allocating resources across these policies, the objective should be maximizing the welfare of refugees, including those who return and who do not return, of their hosts, and of Syrians. Maximizing refugee returns comes at a cost in terms of welfare losses; accordingly, it is a poorly designed policy objective.

Notes

1. This figure includes Syrians registered in the Arab Republic of Egypt, Iraq, Lebanon, Jordan, North Africa, and Turkey. It does not include the nearly 800,000 Syrians who entered Europe between 2011 and December 2016, because many of these individuals have not been removed from registration lists in their first country of refuge. The figure also does not include an estimated 0.4 to 1.1 million unregistered Syrian refugees in Iraq, Jordan, Lebanon, and Turkey.

2. From the United Nations Development Programme/United Nations High Commissioner for Refugees "Regional Refugee and Resilience Plan (3RP)" (December 2017). For more information on the 3RP, visit http://www.3rpsyriacrisis.org/.

3. Circular 98/2017 dated March 16, 2017, (Ref. No. TM/1/1/481) clarifies the open professions in the agriculture sector, and a letter dated June 14, 2017, clarifies the open professions in the manufacturing sector.

4. Please note that enumerators emphasized the fictional nature of this question.

References

SCPR (Syrian Center for Policy Research). 2015. "Alienation and Violence: Impact of Syria Crisis Report." SCPR, Damascus, Syria. https://www.unrwa.org/sites/default/files/alienation_and_violence_impact_of_the _syria_crisis_in_2014_eng.pdf.

UN-Habitat (United Nations Human Settlements Programme). 2016. "Urban Community Profiling Survey." UN-Habitat, Nairobi.

UNHCR (United Nations High Commissioner for Refugees). 2017a. "Multi-Sector Needs Assessment: Syria." UNHCR, Geneva.

———. 2017b. "Jordan Vulnerability Assessment Framework: 2017 Population Survey Report." UNHCR, Geneva.

———. 2018. "Fourth Regional Survey on Syrian Refugees' Perceptions and Intentions on Return to Syria: Egypt, Iraq, Jordan, and Lebanon." UNHCR, Amman, Jordan.

UNHCR, UNICEF (United Nations Children's Fund), and WFP (World Food Programme). 2018. "Vulnerability Assessment of Syrian Refugees in Lebanon—VASyR 2018." Geneva: UNHCR.

UNOCHA (United Nations Office for the Coordination of Humanitarian Affairs). 2018. "Humanitarian Needs Assessment Programme: Syrian Arab Republic." UNOCHA, New York and Geneva.

World Bank. 2017. *The Toll of War: The Economic and Social Consequences of the Conflict in Syria.* Washington, DC: World Bank.

Introduction

The forced displacement crisis resulting from the conflict in the Syrian Arab Republic remains the largest in the world. By September 2018, over one-half of Syrians had been forcibly displaced, with over 5.6 million registered as refugees outside of their country and another 6.2 million displaced within Syria's borders. Refugee returns to Syria have been relatively low: from 2015 until mid-2018, about 103,090 Syrian refugees were verified to have returned to Syria by the United Nations High Commissioner for Refugees (UNHCR).

This introduction first describes the nature of the Syrian displacement and refugee returns in more detail and then summarizes how the remainder of the report analyzes the complex issue of refugee mobility. Special attention is paid to the report's five-step integrated analytical strategy, which provides a fact-based and transparent framework to support a concerted dialogue among concerned parties.

Introduction

As the war in Syria enters its eighth year, the forced displacement crisis resulting from the conflict remains the largest in the world. Although recent population movements are comparatively smaller in size than in previous years, the numbers of forcibly displaced persons both inside and outside the country remain unprecedented. Over one-half of the population of Syria has been displaced, as of September 2018, with over 5.6 million Syrians now registered as refugees outside of their country and another 6.2 million persons displaced within Syria's borders.[1] Of the number of refugees, 3.5 million are registered in Turkey, with another 2.1 million registered in the Arab Republic of Egypt, Iraq, Jordan, and Lebanon (table I.1). About 35,000 refugees are registered in North African countries. These totals do not account for those refugees who are not registered or those who have migrated outside of the Middle East and North Africa region.[2]

A reduction in hostilities has finally become possible going forward; however, the effects of war continue to unfold. Although tragic prospects for renewed fighting and large-scale displacement are still ongoing in certain parts of the country, such as Idleb, parties to the Astana talks and the Geneva process continue to push for deescalation. Even in the absence of a negotiated settlement, the trajectory of the war has consolidated territorial control under forces loyal to the Syrian government, although that consolidation today may be best described as fragmented. The war has reversed development gains and compromised prospects for stability, peace, and prosperity for future generations in the country and across the region.[3]

A previous World Bank (2017a) report, *The Toll of War: The Economic and Social Consequences of the Conflict in Syria*, estimated a 27 percent damage ratio in the country's housing stock, and more in education and health facilities. More than 400,000 people died because of the war. Life expectancy declined dramatically, especially for males ages 15–39, from 69.7 years in 2010 to an estimated 48.4 years in 2016.[4] Over 2 million school-age children inside Syria have been displaced, with less than one-half enjoying full access to education. Another 739,000 Syrian children are out of school in the five neighboring countries that host Syria's refugees (table I.1).[5] The loss of human capital is staggering. The combined effects of casualties, displacement, and forgone investments in human development will create permanent hardship for generations of Syrians.

Some believe that a less violent landscape within Syria should serve as a preamble to large-scale return. Rarely, however, is the absence of fighting a singular trigger for return. Although strict causality is difficult to assign, return experiences such

Table I.1. Total Number of Registered Syrian Refugees, by Host Country

Country of asylum	Number of registered refugees	Percentage of total caseload	Data date
Turkey	3,564,919	63.4	September 21, 2018
Lebanon	976,002	17.3	July 31, 2018
Jordan	671,428	11.9	September 24, 2018
Iraq	248,696	4.4	August 31, 2018
Egypt, Arab Rep.	131,019	2.3	August 31, 2018

Source: UNHCR Operational Data Portal on Refugee Situations, Syrian Refugees Regional Response (accessed September 2018), https://data2.unhcr.org/en/situations/syria.

as those in Afghanistan, Angola, Bosnia and Herzegovina, Iraq, Liberia, Somalia, and South Sudan serve as a reminder that numerous other factors are required to precipitate return.[6] These factors include improved security and socioeconomic conditions in origin states, access to property and assets, and the availability of key services and restitution in home areas. Overall, refugees have their own calculus of mobility that considers all these factors and assesses available options before return is considered.

This study analyzes that "mobility calculus" of Syrian refugees. In complete adherence to international rules and norms governing issues related to refugees as practiced by UNHCR, and in strict repudiation of any policies that may involve wrongful practices like forced repatriation, this study analyzes the factors that are likely to be taken into consideration by refugees in their rational decision to relocate. This introduction will first describe the nature of displacement and returns, focusing on the demographic side of the problem, and then will explain how the remainder of the report will analyze the complex issue of refugee mobility.

The Nature of the Syrian Displacement

In only seven years, the conflict has changed the demographic map of Syria dramatically. In the absence of official census data, especially during an active conflict, knowledge of the scale and composition of Syrian demography comes from estimates performed by different agencies. Nevertheless, all estimates suggest that, during the conflict, massive and rapid movements of Syrians took place, both internally and in the direction of other countries. Overall, the population within Syria is estimated to have decreased from 20.8 million in 2011 to an estimated 19.4 million in 2017 (UNOCHA 2018). By May 2018, the population estimate was revised up to 20.2 million, still falling short of what it could be without conflict, especially when the high fertility rate (about 3.5 births per woman) before the conflict is considered.

Some governorates experienced dramatic displacement of population. In nominal terms, Aleppo lost the most residents over the past seven years, about 1.3 million inhabitants. It was followed by Ar-Raqqa (500,000), Homs (400,000), and Al-Hasakeh (400,000). In relative terms, however, Ar-Raqqa presents the biggest displacement case—with its population decreasing by more than 53 percent—followed by Aleppo, Al-Hasakeh, and Deir-ez-Zor, all with a 27 percent decline (see figure I.1).

Figure I.1. Population Change by Province and Refugee Outflows, Syrian Arab Republic

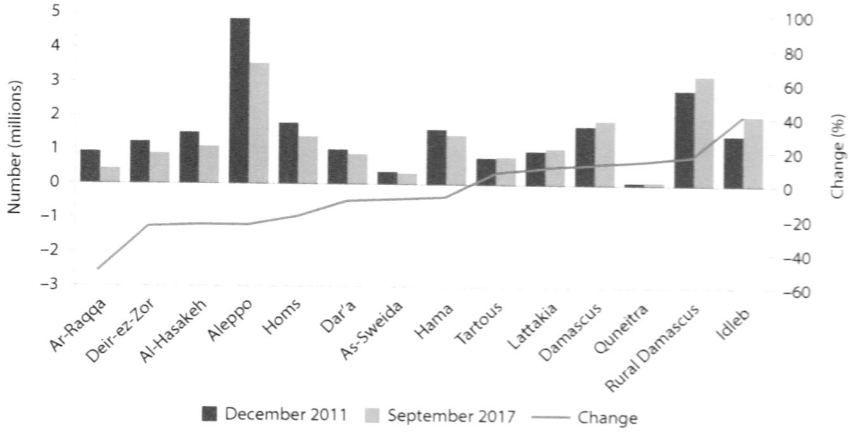

Sources: UNOCHA 2017.

The governorates that lost inhabitants at a smaller scale include As-Sweida, Dar'a, and Hama. Intergovernorate displacement is not the only type of internal displacement; in fact, it is not even the largest one. Most displacement takes place near the original settlement, that is, within the same governorate. These numbers are in net terms; the actual displacement numbers are higher because cross movements of internally displace person (IDPs)—for example, simultaneous inflows and outflows—reduce the net population differentials over time.

Other governorates witnessed a large influx of people. Idleb governorate registered the highest numbers of population inflows, both nominally and relatively, with a population increase of about 600,000 between 2011 and 2018, a 40 percent increase. Other governorates, including Damascus, Quneitra, and Rural Damascus, received more than 10 percent new inhabitants, in net terms. Although some of these increases can be explained by the fact that these governorates provided a relatively safer environment, in certain cases the arrivals and safety are not correlated. For instance, although Idleb is far from being a safe location for civilians, even in relative terms, it admitted internal population shifts because of several reconciliation agreements between the Syrian government and opposition groups.

The exodus of Syrians from some places, and influx in others, changed the population density of Syrian cities dramatically. As a result, there is a marked difference between the precrisis and current population distribution at a micro scale. To show this, the analysis uses population distributions at about 100-meter resolution from WorldPop.[7] Because the latest data available from this source are for 2015, those were extrapolated by using 2018 district-level data from UN agencies. Map I.1 shows the results of this exercise. The reductions along the highway in Deir-ez-Zor and around Ar-Raqqa are particularly visible. In contrast, intensification in Idleb and northern Aleppo, especially along border areas with Turkey, is remarkable. Numerical measurements of these changes are discussed in more detail in box I.1.

The arrival times of Syrians in countries of asylum were highly correlated with the intensity of conflict until 2015, but tightened border controls broke this parallelism

Map I.1. Geographic Distribution of Population (100-meter resolution), Syrian Arab Republic, 2010 vs. 2018

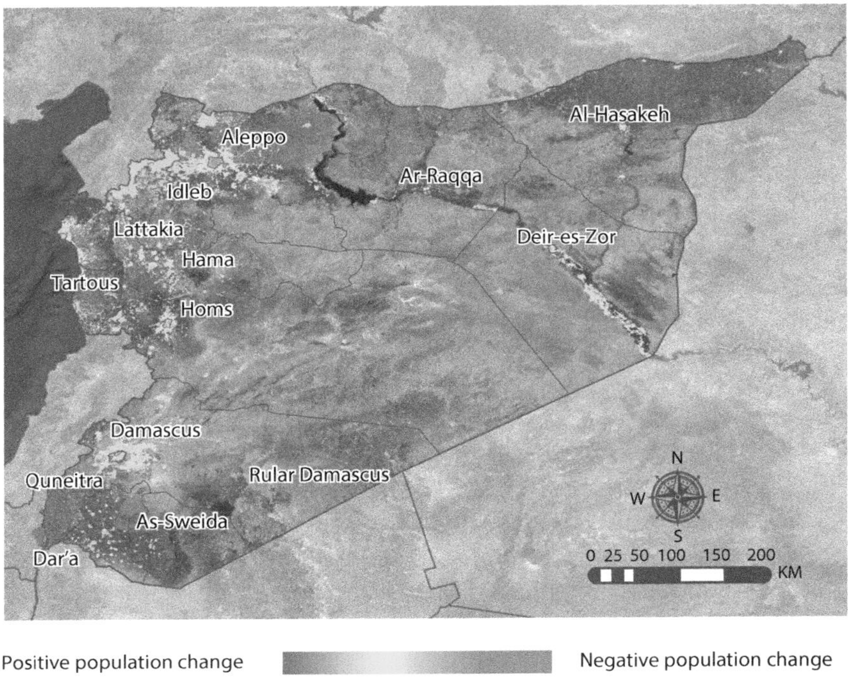

Positive population change   Negative population change

Source: WorldPop, https://www.worldpop.org/; World Bank staff calculations.

BOX I.1.

Displacement in the Syrian Arab Republic: A Granular View

No single indicator can capture all dimensions of displacement in Syria by itself. Thus, interpreting several indicators together is often the best way to understand the true nature of displacement. To this end, figure BI.1.1 shows four displacement indicators that use granular data and calculate percentage changes between 2010 and 2018:

1. Populated surface area for each governorate

2. Population density using total surface area of each governorate

3. Population density using only the inhabited area of each governorate

4. Population dispersion using standard deviation divided by the governorate's surface area

(box continues next page)

BOX I.1. *(continued)*

To generate these indicators, high-resolution data from WorldPop were used.[a] Statistics are calculated for each zone defined by the official administrative boundaries for the Syrian governorates, based on the values from a value raster dataset (in this case a geolocated population dataset for 2010 and 2018 with a resolution of 84 by 84 meters per pixel). Then the mean and standard deviation by governorate for the population datasets of 2010 and 2018 are calculated. These are scaled with governorate surface areas to get the density and dispersion values. For inhabited area statistics, areas with zero population are removed.

As figure BI.1.1 shows, except for Quneitra the inhabited surface area decreased for all Syrian governorates between 2010 and 2018 (panel d). The largest decreases are observed in Lattakia, where the newly unpopulated areas are up by 25 percent, and in Aleppo and Hama, with an 11 percent increase in the desolate areas. Panel a (change in dispersion of population) shows the change in the dispersion of the population within each governorate, and it follows the pattern of the change in density indicator to a large extent. Panel b (change in population density) shows directly the net population movements because the denominator (surface area) is fixed. The largest proportionate influx of people is observed in Idleb and Quneitra, and the largest outflow is observed in Deir-ez-Zor, Aleppo, and Al-Hasakeh (panel c). Density in inhabited areas increased in all governorates except in Deir-ez-Zor, Homs, Quneitra, and Tartous. Notably, the density of the inhabited areas in Idleb and Lattakia increased by almost 70 percent.

Figure BI.1.1. Population Change Indicators by Governorate between 2010 and 2018

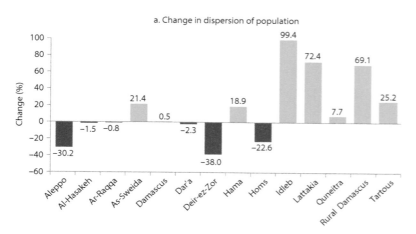

a. Change in dispersion of population

(figure continues next page)

(box continues next page)

27

BOX I.1. *(continued)*

Figure BI.1.1. *(continued)*

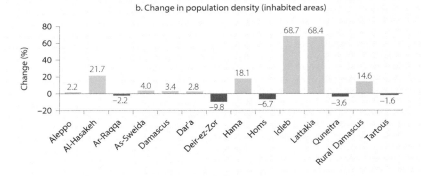

b. Change in population density (inhabited areas)

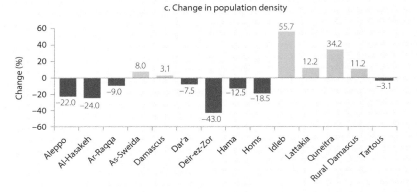

c. Change in population density

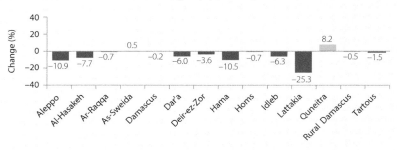

d. Change in populated surface area

Source: WorldPop, https://www.worldpop.org/; World Bank staff calculations.

Overall, Idleb and Lattakia had reductions in populated surface areas but increases in density and dispersion. These, together, imply that both the local population and those coming from elsewhere moved toward relatively more urban areas, including both large and medium-size ones, over the course of the conflict.

a. For more information on the WorldPop project datasets, visit https://www.worldpop.org/.

after that. Figure I.2 shows the monthly series of verified casualties and refugee arrivals in Iraq, Jordan, and Lebanon. From 2011 until the end of 2014, these two series were highly correlated (coefficient of contemporaneous correlation 0.71). Following tightened border controls in Jordan and Lebanon, however, this correlation disappeared until the end of the series (coefficient of contemporaneous correlation –0.08). This change is also clearly visible in the 2017 values of the figure. Although casualties spiked in early 2017 and remained elevated throughout the year, refugee arrivals exhibited a downward trend.

Syrians were often displaced toward the nearest neighboring country, but proximity was not the only determinant for the selection of destination. An analysis of the UNHCR's registration systems for Iraq, Jordan, and Lebanon shows that 19 percent of the Syrian refugees in these countries came from Aleppo governorate (figure I.3).[8] Homs registered the second-largest outflow of refugees, representing 17 percent of the overall refugee population, followed by Dar'a (16 percent). At the source, almost 70 percent of the refugees from Homs fled to Lebanon and about 78 percent of the refugees from Dar'a fled to Jordan. In these cases, proximity is an important explanation: Homs is near the border with Lebanon, and Dar'a is near the border with Jordan. In other cases, the explanation is less obvious. Although Ar-Raqqa is located closer to the border with Iraq, about 82 percent of Syrians from Ar-Raqqa in these three countries relocated to Lebanon. This indicates a more sophisticated displacement pattern, possibly determined by ethnic-sectarian factors, networks, access to information, and economic opportunities. For instance, for many years after the war in Lebanon and until 2011, the Lebanese construction sector relied on Syrian workers for the reconstruction process. Many Syrian farmers worked in the Jordanian agriculture sector before 2011. These economic ties probably provided some predictability when these workers and their families had to move.

Syrian refugees are generously hosted by the communities in Iraq's Kurdistan Region, in Jordan, and in Lebanon. The sizes of the refugee populations in Lebanon

29

Figure I.2. Verified Casualties in the Syrian Arab Republic and Refugee Arrivals in Iraq, Jordan, and Lebanon

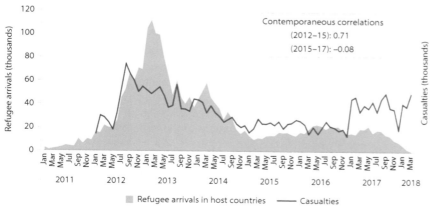

Source: UNHCR 2018.

Figure I.3. Refugee Flows from Syrian Governorate of Origin to Selected Country of Asylum

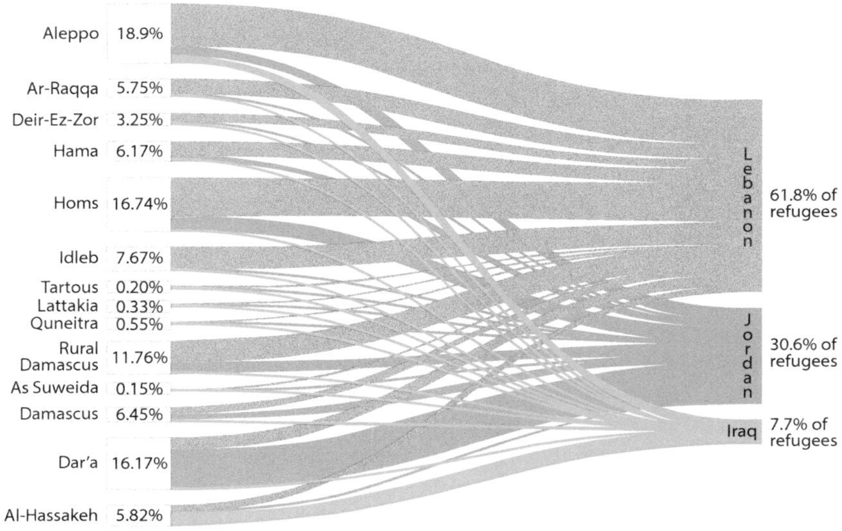

Source: UNHCR registration data (April 2018); World Bank staff calculations.

and Jordan relative to host country populations are among the greatest in the world. In Lebanon, the Beqaa province hosts the largest number of refugees, 351,252 (36 percent); with another 255,424 refugees in Beirut; 251,619 in North Lebanon; and 117,770 in South Lebanon.[9] Informal settlements are spread across much of Lebanon, with concentrations near the Syrian border and in Beqaa. In Jordan, Amman governorate hosts the largest number of refugees (194,958, or 29.3 percent), followed by the Mafraq and Irbid governorates (162,213 and 139,945, respectively). Close to 20 percent of Syrian refugees stay in three camps (Zaatari in Mafraq governorate and Azraq and Mrajeeb Al Fhood in Zarqa governorate). In Iraq, the number of refugees is small compared to the country's total population (about 0.7 percent) but constitutes 5 percent of Iraq's Kurdistan Region population, where almost all refugees reside.

The age distribution of Syrians inside and outside Syria demonstrates clearly the age-biased displacement effects of the conflict. Before the conflict (2010), the Syrian population was already very young, with about 80 percent under the age of 40 (figure I.4). The conflict seems to have pushed away younger people disproportionately. Currently, about 87 percent of refugees in Iraq, Jordan, and Lebanon are under the age of 40, compared to 77 percent of Syrians in Syria. Almost one in two (47 percent) of the refugees is a child under the age of 14. This proportion brings them in sharp contrast with the populations of the host countries. Lebanon has a youth-dependency ratio of 46.2, and Jordan's is 58.5, whereas the ratio for Syrian refugees is higher than 63.5. This creates a unique set of challenges both for the refugees and the host countries, which shoulder the responsibility of meeting the needs of this predominantly young population.

Figure I.4. Population Pyramids for the Syrian Arab Republic, Host Communities, and Syrian Refugees, 2010 vs. 2017

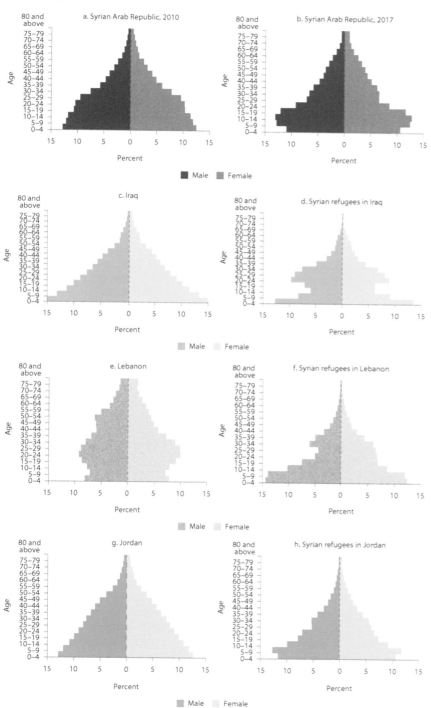

31

Source: World Bank 2010, 2017b; UNHCR ProGres data, https://undatacatalog.org/dataset/progres.

Despite minor differences, the demographic profiles of refugees across Iraq, Jordan, and Lebanon are remarkably similar. In the three countries examined in this study, the percent of female refugees is slightly higher (51 percent) than the share of men, except for Iraq where women represent about 47 percent of the refugee population (figure I.5). About 85 percent of refugee cases (a case is a group of refugees, often a household with relatives, who are registered together by UNHCR) have children, with that number being slightly higher for Lebanon (89 percent) and lower for Iraq (76.5). Syrian refugees in Iraq are more likely to be single-person cases than those in Lebanon and Jordan. The average case size in these three countries is 5.3 persons, with bigger families more likely to be in Lebanon. Most refugees (about 60 percent) are under the age of 14. In terms of education, over a quarter of the refugees in Iraq, Jordan, and Lebanon are not educated (29 percent); more than one-half received some elementary education (1–6 years) (59 percent), less than 10 percent received preparatory and secondary education (7–12 year), and only 3 percent have university education.

Returns to Syria have been relatively low but have reached to tens of thousands every year since 2015. Although UNHCR keeps a record of registered refugees who returned to Syria, access constraints and the spontaneous nature of returns make it impossible to systematically trace these returnees; it is not known if they returned to their original places or whether they were arrested, killed, or became displaced again. From 2015 until 2018, however, UNHCR verified that 103,090 Syrian refugees have returned to Syria (map I.2). About 40,000 of those returned from Turkey (about 1.1 percent of the total Syrian refugee population in the country). In relative terms, the highest return from the three countries covered in this study took place from Iraq: about 26,000 refugees (10.8 percent of all registered Syrian refugees in the country) have returned so far. About 17,000 Syrian refugees (6.6 percent) have returned from Jordan, and about 19,000 Syrian refugees (1.5 percent) have returned from Lebanon. In all three cases, return numbers in 2017 were higher than those in 2016, with the greatest increase (twofold) recorded in Lebanon.

About This Report

It is not easy to talk about refugees. The issue is highly politicized, and facts and fiction are sometimes indistinguishable in a polarized public view. Although nations often act to help refugees on the basis of moral and legal imperatives, their actions may not always be sufficient, despite the best efforts of host country governments, nongovernmental organizations, international organizations, and donor countries. Kushner and Knox (2012) suggest that "people feel that the country should maintain asylum for genuine asylum seekers, but they're always in the past, never today." In the Syrian case, neighboring countries have suffered massive inflows of refugees, the largest in the world in proportion to host populations. Absorbing such an extreme shock is not easy. Even if international assistance helped offset some direct costs associated with refugee arrivals, it is impossible to mitigate the impact on host societies in all dimensions. The issue is open to political exploitation, and policy makers often adopt an increasingly conservative approach, willingly or by means of political calculus. This dynamic can be effective in host countries and advanced economies alike.

Against this background, this study aims to provide a fact-based and transparent framework to support a concerted dialogue among concerned parties. The main objective of this report is to provide a conceptual framework, supported by data and

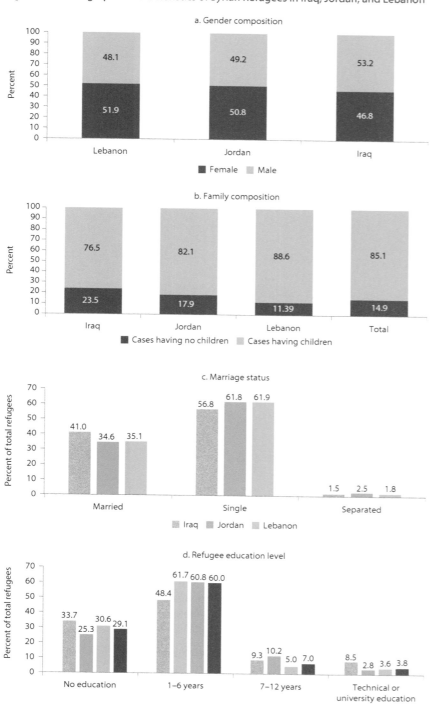

Figure I.5. Demographic Characteristics of Syrian Refugees in Iraq, Jordan, and Lebanon

Source: UNHCR ProGres data, https://undatacatalog.org/dataset/progres; World Bank staff calculations.

Map I.2. Return Statistics

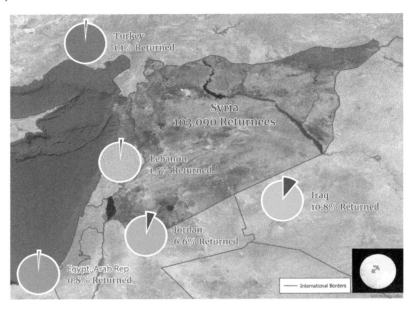

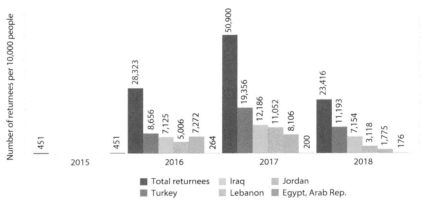

Source: Based on data from UNHCR 2018.

analysis, to facilitate an objective conversation about refugees. To this end, the study sheds some light on conditions faced by Syrians inside and outside Syria, analyzes their patterns of mobility based on these conditions, and provides reasoned conjectures about possible future patterns of such mobility in a scenario-dependent manner. More specifically, a five-step integrated analytical strategy is adopted (figure I.6).

- *The first step (chapter 1)* considers international experience, which helps to identify important factors in analyzing refugee movements, that is, push and pull factors. Given the paucity of data and the lack of empirical research in this area, the analysis adheres to descriptive findings that rely on case studies.

- *The second step (chapter 2)* provides measurements of these factors in the case of Syria and host communities (Iraq, Jordan, and Lebanon). Conditions inside Syria

Figure I.6. A Five-Step Integrated Analytical Strategy

International experience
Push and pull factors

**Measurement of
conditions faced by
Syrian refugees**
- Vulnerability surveys
- Multisector needs
  assessments
- Remote-sensing data

→

**Estimating relative
importance of push and pull
factors for Syrian refugees**
- Linear probability and logit
  models, hazard models
- Machine-learning techniques
  (decision trees and boosted trees)

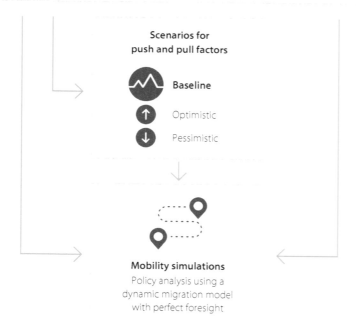

**Scenarios for
push and pull factors**

Baseline

↑ Optimistic

↓ Pessimistic

Mobility simulations
Policy analysis using a
dynamic migration model
with perfect foresight

are measured by means of on-the-ground surveys by partner UN agencies and remote-sensing techniques (such as satellite images and radar sensors), with social and traditional media verification in Syria. Conditions outside Syria are measured by using UNHCR-led vulnerability surveys—the Vulnerability Assessment of Syrian Refugees in Lebanon and the Vulnerability Assessment Framework in Jordan—as well as a verification survey conducted by the World Bank.

- **The third step (chapter 3)** estimates the relative importance of the above-men-tioned factors in explaining the spontaneous returns that have taken place so far in the Syrian context. Estimations employ various econometric approaches (such as linear probability and logit models), and machine-learning specifica-tions such as decision trees.

- **The fourth and fifth steps (chapter 4)** analyze the role that several factors can play in increasing or decreasing the spontaneous return of Syrian refugees in the future. Because this approach is prone to significant uncertainty, a scenario-based approach, where factors that can affect refugees' decisions can vary, is adopted to present the range of outcomes. The results are produced by using a simulation model that builds on *The Toll of War* (World Bank 2017a) and empha-sizes a rational, forward-looking decision-making procedure that guides the mobility of all Syrians.

This report focuses solely on voluntary mobility of refugees. The analysis presented in this report adheres strictly to international norms and practices of refugee returns, which put the voluntary movements of refugees at the center. Any forms of policies that may involve actions against refugees' will and safety are renounced and not analyzed in this report. In fact, both the empirical analyses and the simulation work are firmly grounded in this principle. The former considers only the spontaneous returns that have taken place from 2012 until March 2018. The latter employs a mobility model with perfect foresight, where agents make mobility decisions given their constraints—border policies, economic conditions, and security conditions. This approach also provides more useful policy implications because the incentives of refugees, and their rational responses, are captured in a bottom-up manner.

Given the immense complexity surrounding the refugee mobility issue, the report leaves several equally, if not more, important topics for future work. The analytical complexity of refugee situations forced the report to narrow its focus to be able to help dissect the complexity around the return of refugees. In addition, data short-ages were more daunting in areas such as IDPs in Syria and refugees in Turkey. Thus, this analysis focuses on the refugee mobility issue through the five steps described in Iraq, Jordan, and Lebanon; it leaves the study of displaced Syrians in Syria, Turkey, and Europe for the future. Similarly, the highly pertinent topic of how the host communities are affected by the arrivals of refugees, and more broadly by the Syrian conflict, is scheduled to be analyzed in a forthcoming study, "The Regional Economic and Social Impact of Syrian Conflict," which will benefit from the methodology and findings of this report.

Notes

1. This figure includes Syrians registered in the Arab Republic of Egypt, Iraq, Jordan, Lebanon, North Africa, and Turkey. This figure does not include the nearly 800,000 Syrians who entered Europe between 2011 and December 2016 because many of these individuals have not been removed from registration lists in their first country of refuge. The figure also does not include an estimated 0.4 million to 1.1 million unregistered Syrian refugees in Iraq, Jordan, Lebanon, and Turkey.

2. Data from the UNHCR Operational Data Portal on Refugee Situations, Syrian Refugees Regional Response (accessed September 2018), https://data2.unhcr.org/en/situations/syria.

3. From the United Nations Development Programme/United Nations High Commissioner for Refugees "Regional Refugee and Resilience Plan (3RP)" (December 2017). For more information on the 3RP, visit http://www.3rpsyriacrisis.org/.

4.   Data retrieved from World Bank Open Database, World Bank Group, https://data.worldbank.org/ (accessed September 2018).

5.   From the United Nations Development Programme/United Nations High Commissioner for Refugees "Regional Refugee and Resilience Plan (3RP)" (December 2017). For more information on the 3RP, visit http://www.3rpsyriacrisis.org/.

6.   A typical example can be found in the case study of Liberian refugees in Ghana in Omata (2013).

7.   For more information on the WorldPop project datasets, visit https://www.worldpop.org/.

8.   Additionally, most refugees in Turkey are from Aleppo, making the Aleppo governorate the main governorate of origin for Syrian refugees in the entire region.

9.   Data from the UNHCR Operational Data Portal on Refugee Situations, Syrian Refugees Regional Response, http://data2.unhcr.org/en/situations/syria/location/71.

References

Kushner, Tony, and Katharine Knox. 2012. *Refugees in an Age of Genocide: Global, National and Local Perspectives during the Twentieth Century*. Routledge.

Omata, Naohiko. 2013. "The Complexity of Refugees' Return Decision-Making in a Protracted Exile: Beyond the Home-Coming Model and Durable Solutions." *Journal of Ethnic and Migration Studies* 39 (8): 1281–97.

UNHCR (United Nations High Commissioner for Refugees). 2018. "Global Trends: Forced Displacement in 2017." UNHCR, Geneva. http://www.unhcr.org/5b27be547.pdf.

UNOCHA (United Nations Office for the Coordination of Humanitarian Affairs). 2017. "Humanitarian Needs Overview: Syrian Arab Republic." UNOCHA, New York and Geneva.

———. 2018. "Humanitarian Needs Assessment Programme: Syrian Arab Republic." UNOCHA, New York and Geneva.

World Bank. 2010. *World Development Indicators 2010*. Washington, DC: World Bank.

———. 2017a. *The Toll of War: The Economic and Social Consequences of the Conflict in Syria*. Washington, DC: World Bank.

———. 2017b. *World Development Indicators 2017*. Washington, DC: World Bank.

CHAPTER 1

Refugee Returns through a Global Lens

The overview of international experience points to key areas of concern for analyzing refugee returns and shows the complexity of the problem. The discussion in this chapter focuses on providing general trends in return experience globally and categorizing factors that may influence decision making regarding returns. Overall, the complex nature of the problem and absence of empirical evidence, two factors that reinforce each other, limit understanding of the mechanisms that drive return decisions. Nevertheless, several key observations provide the necessary guidelines for analyzing the mobility of refugees from the Syrian Arab Republic.

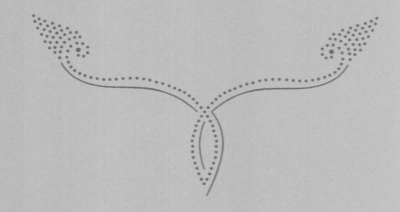

Artwork Credit: Solara Shiha

CHAPTER 1

Refugee Returns through a Global Lens

The return of refugees, when feasible and undertaken under the right conditions, is often supported by all who are involved in a refugee situation. Of the three durable solutions to refugee displacement—refugee return, third-country resettlement, and local integration—"voluntary return in safety and dignity" has always been pursued by the United Nations High Commissioner for Refugees (UNHCR), intergovernmental organizations, and governments as the preferred and, in some respects, the optimum durable solution for all stakeholders. When refugees return home under the right conditions, first and foremost, a durable solution for refugees is reached. In addition, host states are relieved of the responsibility of hosting them; likewise, the international community and donors are relieved of long-term funding commitments to assist them. The country of origin is also, in principle, content to have its citizens return and to reconcile pending issues that may threaten peace and stability.

Return is not an end in itself, but it can provide an effective resolution to a refugee situation if implemented properly. Return programs are predicated on a general presumption that refugees will mostly return voluntarily, either in an organized manner or spontaneously, once the conditions of violence or persecution precipitating their flight have ended. Realistically, however, many refugees may not return home and others require near-term solutions when circumstances in the country of origin are not yet conducive to voluntary repatriation. In such instances, the other durable solutions, along with interim measures, may be necessary. Return is the preferred solution because it reduces the pressure for both third-country resettlement, which is politically more complex and usually costlier, and local integration, which often occurs informally in conditions of protracted exile.

Despite their importance, refugee returns have not been comprehensively studied. A systematic analysis of global refugee returns is hampered by the complexity of the problem and the paucity of data.[1]

Just like any other groups of individuals, refugees are rational (and emotional) actors who use available information to frame return decisions as comparisons of conditions in exile and in their country of origin. Movements are calibrated accordingly, with refugees and their families sometimes choosing to stage their return, engage in cyclical back-and-forth movements, or move where social networks and livelihood prospects are best—even if this means settling in areas within their country of origin, yet away from their homes of record. Given vastly differing profiles of refugees—a factor that is driven by the fact that violence displaces all types of people, not only specific segments of the society—these factors generate further heterogeneity of mobility patterns among refugees, which is difficult to aggregate and compare. Additionally, the complexity of such behaviors, and the fact that often they take place in "gray areas" where monitoring and record keeping are often not possible, translates into an acute absence of data. Together, these two factors have limited the understanding of return phenomena to often anecdotal and descriptive analyses, which are not usually comparable across cases.

This chapter provides a summary of the key findings from international practice of return. The first section describes the legal and normative context adopted by the international community to limit adverse practices and promote mechanisms aligned with protection of refugees' well-being. The next section provides an overview of aggregate return statistics in the context of broader displacement trends. The third section analyzes the factors that are associated with return (for example, push and pull factors) by using findings from case studies and descriptive evidence. The fourth and final section of this chapter discusses the asymmetries in terms of destination of returnees and the distribution of burden among men and women.

Unless otherwise stated, all references to refugees in this report refer to those under UNHCR's mandate. UNHCR's mandate applies to all persons outside their country of origin for reasons of feared persecution, conflict, generalized violence, or other circumstances requiring international protection, and who cannot return because of that fear. It includes asylum seekers, stateless persons, and returnees, and applies to emergency and nonemergency situations as well as camp and non-camp refugee populations. UNHCR does not have a general or exclusive mandate for internally displaced persons and shares complementary functions with the United Nations Relief and Works Agency (UNRWA) regarding Palestinian refugees.[2]

The Legal and Normative Context for Returns

Since the end of the Second World War, the principle of "voluntary return" has been at the core of international norms and regulations regarding refugees. The principle international legal instruments dealing with refugees, the 1951 Convention Relating to the Status of Refugees and its 1967 Protocol, do not directly address the question of refugee repatriation except in terms of the overriding principle of *non-refoulement* (not forcing refugees or asylum seekers to return to a country in which they are liable to be subjected to persecution) and in relation to the conditions over which *cessation* of refugee status is warranted. Article 1C of the Convention defines the situations and conditions that trigger the withdrawal or cessation of refugee status, among which are voluntary return to and reestablishment in an origin state,[3] centering attention thereafter on the importance of determining whether such return movements are truly voluntary.[4] The 1950 Statute of the Office of the UNHCR also charges the Office with "seeking permanent [that is, durable] solutions" to the problem of refugees by, among other things, calling on governments to cooperate with the High Commissioner by "assisting the High Commissioner in (her/his) efforts to promote the voluntary repatriation of refugees."[5] It is worth noting that "return" within this legal context refers to reentry into the country of origin and not return to a specific home of record.

The parameters of return practice evolved over decades. UNHCR's role and responsibilities with regard to voluntary repatriation have been developed over decades through texts, instruments, and practice. As early as 1961, the UN General Assembly passed Resolution 1672 (XVI) requesting the High Commissioner to "use the means at his disposal to assist in the orderly return of Algerian refugees in Morocco and Tunisia to their homes and [to] consider the possibility, when necessary, of facilitating their resettlement in their home land."[6] In 1980, UNHCR's special competence for refugee return was reaffirmed and codified as part of the Executive Committee (ExCom) that year (UNHCR 1980). Five years later, ExCom 1985 significantly developed the doctrine of voluntary repatriation, reiterating and further detailing the basic principles (UNHCR 1985). In 2003, the UNHCR's "Framework for Durable Solutions for Refugees and Persons of Concern" further articulated the international commitment to UNHCR's mandated responsibility to facilitate return (UNHCR 2003).

Although returns can take place spontaneously, large-scale voluntary returns are often assisted. The current international approach distinguishes between three types of returns: (a) self-organized or unassisted returns, (b) facilitated large-scale voluntary returns, and (c) promoted returns, as a potential last stage of a returns process. In the first case, which is often called "spontaneous return," return movements are driven by the planning and initiatives of refugees themselves. UNHCR does not provide direct assistance but sometimes offers counseling to returning refugees wherever possible, available, or desired. The largest unassisted returns movements include those since 1989 in Afghanistan, Rwandan returns from Eastern Zaire in 1997, Angolans returning after the 2003 Luena Accords, and most of the returns to date in South Sudan. Overall, about 33 percent of all returns between 2006 and 2014 were unassisted (World Bank 2017). At times, refugees return unassisted because they lack information on available programs, or they may be pressured to move urgently back to home areas, or they fear losing refugee status and prefer to move to their origin countries outside of official channels. They may also choose to return unassisted when UNHCR elects not to facilitate return because of concerns that refugees are "pushed" out of asylum countries or when conditions remain insecure in origin countries.

"Voluntary assisted returns" refers to repatriation with the voluntary agreement of refugees, organized by UNHCR and usually assisted by international support. Examples of large assisted return movements include Cambodians returning from Thailand in 1992–93, Mozambicans returning in 1992–96, and Afghans returning from Pakistan in 2002. In comparison, promoted return involves logistical and other support to refugees who are encouraged to return by various factors. In these cases, and when UNHCR judges the return environment to be free of the conditions that prompted forced displacement initially, UNHCR will proactively assist prospective and actual returnees with information and logistical support. Examples include not only Cambodian refugees in the 1980s but also those from Bosnia and Herzegovina after the 1995 Dayton Peace Accord, some of the Burundi refugees from Tanzania after 2002, and Liberian refugees after 2015.

The complex logistics of large-scale voluntary repatriations are organized within the framework of tripartite agreements. As reaffirmed in the Conclusions of UNHCR's ExCom 1985, large-scale voluntary returns have been managed by means of agreements between UNHCR, under whose aegis the agreements are made, and

43

the country of origin and host country (or countries). Refugees are also consulted. The most coherent example of coordinated voluntary return was the International Conference on Central American Refugees (CIREFCA). This process, which ran from 1987 until 1994, developed wide-ranging action plans and included tripartite agreements for reintegration and political dialogue that facilitated the voluntary repatriation of almost 135,000 Guatemalan, Nicaraguan, and Salvadoran refugees. Since the early 1990s, UNHCR has assisted in over 17 major voluntary repatriations, supporting millions of refugees during their voluntary return to their countries of origin.

Tripartite agreements outline specific responsibilities for all signatories to ensure the voluntary nature, safety, and dignity of the repatriation. Designated responsibilities of the governments (host and origin) often include facilitation of the repatriation; refugees' rights to return to their former places of residence or a choice to return elsewhere within the origin country; the physical, legal, and material safety of refugees and returnees; unhindered access by humanitarian and development actors to refugee populations before, during, and after the repatriation process; continued provision of protection and assistance to those refugees who choose not to repatriate; establishment in the country of origin of administrative and judicial measures to support reintegration; and logistical arrangements (such as security escorts, exemption of refugee goods from customs duties, and establishment of repatriation commissions).[7]

The Numbers of Returns

Although refugee returns can provide a durable solution, statistics reveal relatively low aggregate numbers of returns over time compared with the total number of refugees. According to UNHCR, however, 2016 and 2017 were exceptional years for refugee returns, compared to preceding years, with unusually large numbers of refugees returned to their countries of origin—552,200 in 2016 and 667,400 in 2017

Figure 1.1. Slowdown in Refugee Returns

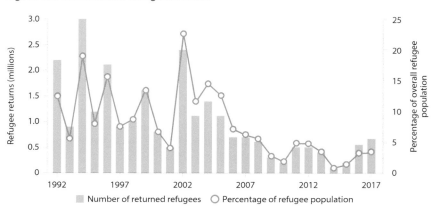

■ Number of returned refugees ○ Percentage of refugee population

Source: UNHCR 2018.

(UNHCR 2017a, 2018; figure 1.1). The largest returns comprised 384,000 returnees to Afghanistan in 2016 and 282,800 returnees to Nigeria, mainly from Cameroon and Niger, in 2017. More than 80 percent of the returnees over this period received UNHCR assistance for the return, although support varied widely from the provision of information to more substantive packages of reintegration support. The number of countries or areas to which refugees returned included 40 countries in 2016 and 43 in 2017. However, overall numbers of refugees climbed to historic levels over the period. Moreover, returns averaged about 400,000 per year over the past decade (2008–17), compared to an annual average of 970,000 in the preceding decade and over 1 million per year in the 1990s—the so-called decade of repatriation (UNHCR 1997).

The number of newly displaced refugees has dwarfed that of returnees. In 2017, about 2.9 million people, nearly 4.4 times the number of returnees, became refugees (figure 1.2). By the end of the year, the global refugee population was 25.4 million, the highest known total to date and an increase of 2.9 million from 2016.[8] The number of refugees under UNHCR's mandate increased for the sixth year in a row, to a total population at the end of the year just shy of 20 million. The corollary of the low return rates and the high displacement rates is ever longer protracted refugee situations. An estimated 11.6 million refugees (65 percent of those under UNHCR's mandate) are currently in protracted displacement, driven by a combination of lengthened civil conflicts, an inability (or unwillingness) of states to afford protection for returnees, and enduring state fragility in key refugee-producing

Figure 1.2. Refugee Stocks and Flows, Syrian vs. Non-Syrian, Millions

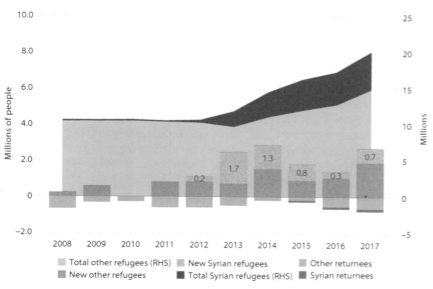

Source: UNHCR 2018.
Note: RHS = Right-hand side; Data for "New Syrian refugees" and "New other refugees" were missing for 2010, so the values may not necessarily be zero.

areas (Long 2011). A recent World Bank study estimated that the average duration of exile for current refugees is 10.3 years. (World Bank 2017)

From 2012 onward, the conflict in the Syrian Arab Republic became a major driver of displacement, and quickly led to the world's largest refugee population. The number of refugees under UNHCR's mandate nearly doubled after 2012, and more than half of this increase was generated by the conflict in Syria. In 2013, the number of newly registered Syrian refugees (1.7 million) was more than double the total number of registrations in the rest of the world, and 2014 and 2015 saw comparable new refugee numbers. Given the active conflict situation, however, the return of Syrian refugees back home has been negligible compared to returns elsewhere. The following section will analyze characteristics of returns by looking at refugee populations other than Syrian.

The Determinants of Return

Refugee return is not a monotonic or linear event: it often includes an iterative, staggered, or cyclical process. Evidence of Iraqi refugees hosted in Jordan and Syria (before the war in Syria), and Somali refugees in Kenya, points to complex strategies followed by refugees in spontaneous returns. The behavioral patterns are by no means random or unorganized, which the term "spontaneous" misleadingly suggests. One or two members of refugee households return informally from host countries for short periods to, among other things, assess the scope for more permanent return of the household or community, which will permit the reestablishment of livelihoods and housing where this is possible, safeguard and reestablish entitlements to property pending more permanent return, or assist family members who have remained behind.

Just like any other groups of individuals, refugees act rationally, facing a set of constraints, to ensure the well-being of themselves and their families. As rational actors, refugees use available information to frame decisions to stay or return as comparisons of security, kinship and social networks, and socioeconomic conditions in exile and in the country of origin.[9] Movements are calibrated accordingly, with refugees and their families sometimes choosing to stage their return, engage in cyclical back-and-forth movements, or move where social networks and livelihood prospects are best—even if this means settling in areas within origin countries that are away from their homes of record (Jeffery and Murison 2011). South Sudanese and early Afghan returns reveal patterns of staged and cyclical movement. Angolan, Cambodian, Liberian, Tamil, and later Afghan returns exhibit aspects of refugees attempting to synchronize movements with extended social networks and tendencies to gravitate toward urban centers.[10] All things being equal, these behaviors are part of the sophisticated repertoire of responses refugees deploy when considering return (Christensen and Harild 2009).

Adverse conditions can lead to unconventional coping strategies. When conditions are not ripe, refugees may remain in exile, despite an increasing "push" from host countries, or from international donors, for refugees to leave. In parallel, refugees may develop coping strategies such as family subdivision. South Sudanese and, in earlier times, Afghan refugees used a strategy of temporary or permanent geographical dispersal of family members between exile and return locations (and sometimes resettlement countries as well) to maximize and diversify access to livelihoods and services and enhance remittance income to support priorities for household well-being (Liuhto 2018). Moreover, in many refugee situations ongoing mobility or circular movements are key livelihood strategies that contribute to sustainable solutions and reconstruction and often draw on transnational networks that predate the conflicts that caused the displacement. The case of the Somali refugee diaspora and their use of remittances to support both refugees and returnees is well documented (Norwegian Refugee Council 2016; UNHCR 2017b). Similarly, Tamil refugees from Sri Lanka also used their diasporic networks as a risk-sharing mechanism.

Trends in spontaneous returns point to a few structural factors that are commonly considered by refugees in optimizing their return decision. The pace and scale of return primarily depend on how refugees perceive structural conditions such as security, livelihoods, property rights, access to basic services, and the potential for survival in exile or reintegration in the country of origin in a comparative sense—that is, they continuously compare conditions in countries of asylum and the country of origin at the same time. Although there is little evidence on how the porosity of borders and ease of cross-border movement affect these trends, additional factors often facilitate the process. The following subsections study these factors in more detail because the success of any voluntary repatriation model relies on its ability to consider such rational decision making from refugees.

Peace, security, and protection

Assisted voluntary return schemes are usually predicated on political agreements and peace accords that are expected to end the conflicts. In the case of Bosnia and Herzegovina, the Dayton Peace Accord was constructed on the principle of reversing ethnic cleansing and was essential to the return of refugees. In most cases, however, the international political imperatives that drive many return programs are often conceived without regard to history, and in a technocratic way that ignores the national and local political realities. Nonetheless, these realities may have precipitated displacement and certainly govern the scope for successful return.[11] There is often an imposed urgency on return—by donors, the host countries, and sometimes also the country of origin (for example, the desire to expedite return for elections in the newly established South Sudan)—that does not always allow time for violence to fully cease or peacebuilding measures to gain a foothold. The cases of Afghanistan and Iraq, two countries that closely mirror conditions for return to Syria, as well as South Sudan, illustrate how protracted conflict continues alongside the push for return, with appalling consequences for the returnees as well as for those who remained—conflict, continuing instability, human rights violations, secondary displacement, and fragile governance and development. The divergent political aspirations of returning communities that may have precipitated conflict and the rival interests of local political leaders and militias highlight the need for effective peacebuilding processes, stability, rule of law, reconciliation, compensation, and restitution as the means to facilitate return. Left unaddressed in settlement talks, these aspects of physical, material, and legal security for refugees will continue to constrain voluntary return and immiserate those who do repatriate.

Spontaneous returns can also take place to areas or countries that are far from peaceful and stable or are in postconflict recovery. On average, spontaneous and unassisted returns take place in security conditions that are inferior to those under voluntary and assisted programs (Harild, Christensen, and Zetter 2015). Spontaneous returns still involve substantial numbers of returnees. Afghanistan, Angola, Liberia, South Sudan, and to a lesser extent Iraq, provide examples where early spontaneous returns have taken place, usually preceding the enactment of assisted voluntary return schemes under tripartite agreements, and where the overall number of spontaneous returns, at least initially, exceeded those assisted through such return programs. This is, however, not always the case. For Bosnians returning to Bosnia and Herzegovina from Germany, the United Kingdom, and other European countries of refuge, there was little spontaneous return. Refugees themselves did not consider it safe to return before the introduction of the voluntary repatriation program. The additional role of information flows about conditions and return options, as well as the behavior of social networks among the displaced, is just now becoming clear as a precipitant to return movements or decisions to remain in exile (Lloyd et al. 2013).

A sense of security requires not only the absence of an active conflict but also the absence of explicit or implicit threats from government, militias, and other social groups. The fear of persecution and retribution is an effective deterrent to return, which may not be obvious during a small-scale spontaneous return phase but becomes apparent in episodes of large-scale returns. Returnees may experience resentment from those who remained, or conversely returnees may exhibit disparagement toward those who stayed. These attitudes may be played out in job discrimination, create obstacles to restitution of land and property, add to social marginalization, and affect the emergence of local power brokers. Overall country-level trends in return may obscure the way that local social, ethnic, and religious conditions affect the modalities of reception and the effectiveness of livelihood restoration strategies and reintegration. These dynamics highlight the role of everyday diplomacy and "vernacular reconciliation." Overall, social factors, social networks, and local civil society organizations play a prominent role in the ability of returnees to reintegrate and reestablish livelihoods and make sure conflict-related grievances do not escalate into a new round of violence. Refugee apprehension over security conditions is broader than fears of being caught in the cross fire of active conflict. Anxieties over the presence of gangs, remnants of militias, capricious treatment by authorities, and a loss of control over their lives constitute powerful economic, social, and physical considerations for those deciding whether to return. Assuming that a cessation of hostilities will assuage refugee concerns over security overlooks these other trenchant aspects of well-being.

Livelihoods and access to employment

Other things being equal, refugees prefer to live in locations that present better livelihood opportunities, just as other rational individuals do. Refugees consider alternative actions (for example, migrate, and search for jobs) and make decisions that are best for themselves and their families and friends. In practice, they face more constraints, such as the absence of formal work permits; and, given the poor conditions they live in, access to information may be more limited than that for an average person. Therefore, they may not be fully informed about their legal rights and limitations. Such comparison of alternatives applies directly to job market conditions as well. At the margin, a better livelihood opportunity in the host country or in the country of origin should tilt refugees' mobility decisions in favor of that country to some extent.

Simplistic extrapolations of this abstract comparison mechanism do not hold well when reaching policy conclusions. It is sometimes assumed that a general deterioration of living conditions and declining economic opportunities in countries of asylum, reduction or withdrawal of international assistance, and the diminishing quality of rights protection, all of which result in increased insecurity for refugees, can induce repatriation. The negative stance of many host countries, it is argued, may also be a significant lever on spontaneous refugee return and organized voluntary repatriation. All these factors play a part in some return cases (for example, the case for Afghan refugees in the Islamic Republic of Iran and Pakistan). Factors vary from case to case, however, and there is a lack of rigorous analytical research of the cause–effect relationships either in correlations between individual factors and return or in multivariate investigation.

Many international return experiences suggest a more nuanced relationship between livelihoods and return. One perspective on how host country treatment affects the potential for return concerns the extent of adaptation into the host society. Perhaps counterintuitively—though not definitive—local adaptation does not necessarily work against the decision of refugees to repatriate. Even where large-scale local integration appears to have occurred, most refugees may still return home if the conditions are right—even after decades in exile. Cases in point are the more than 300,000 apparently settled and integrated Angolan refugees returning from Zambia; the large numbers of Afghan refugees returning from the Islamic Republic of Iran and Pakistan, where they were well adapted to the local economy in Peshawar, for example, in the 1990s and later (albeit not permanently as we now know); and South Sudanese refugees returning from Sudan and Uganda prior to and after independence.

The incidence of poverty among refugees can be critical in stimulating or constraining return. However, the relationship between poverty and return is not straightforward. Among Liberian refugees returning from Ghana, those from higher socioeconomic groups, many of whom had maintained a foothold in Liberia even in exile, more easily accomplished repatriation and economic recovery than those from poorer socioeconomic groups and those whose household units had become fragmented during displacement. For the more well-off socioeconomic groups, remittances from the diaspora population provided initial capital for new income-generating activities; and a returnee's personal contacts often played a crucial role in access to shelter, food, employment, and financial assistance. Poverty may constrain return for poorer groups: there appears to be a correlation between their poor socioeconomic status, their limited livelihood strategies in exile, and concerns about establishing a new economic basis upon return where their vulnerability is exacerbated as a consequence of their repatriation. It is important to note, however, that in some cases poverty may also be a driver of return, a feature of Iraqi refugees' spontaneous return from Syria in the period 2007–10. There is evidence from many return situations, for example, Somalia and South Sudan, that refugee households plan a gradual process of

49

return to minimize risks: not all family members return at the same time, and they use kinship networks to facilitate remittances.

The very same factors that empower refugees in host countries can also enable them to return to their countries of origin. Education, employment, and training in the country of asylum, all of which may be perceived to facilitate local integration, may actually help equip refugees to undertake sustainable return. The case of Cambodian refugees returning from Thailand provides evidence to this effect. Those who had been employed by nongovernmental organizations and international organizations or who had engaged in trade with local Thai traders, as well as other camp residents, had amassed some assets and had learned technical and organizational skills that they could use upon their return. Similarly, those who had benefitted from vocational training programs were better placed to develop their livelihoods upon return. Interestingly, all these groups had been among the longest residents in camps, suggesting that the duration of stay may have helped them to acquire skills and assets. What is also clear is that opportunities for integration in the host country strengthen the ability of refugees to make adaptations involving either a staggered return or the geographical dispersal of household members that diversifies access to livelihoods, services, or other priorities when the main household unit does return. These opportunities contribute both to undertaking a return if and when refugees deem that conditions in the country of origin are conducive and to ensuring household well-being in the medium term after return.

Housing, land, and property rights

Asset restitution is an important and often necessary condition for return, yet it is also one of the most daunting postconflict problems to resolve. The extent to which life in exile affects the propensity to return segues to wider considerations of the reception and treatment refugees receive when they return home. Access of refugee households to livelihood opportunities back home is often intertwined with their ability to restore their documentation and reclaim assets such as property and agricultural land. The prospect for recovering these assets is a key factor that influences the refugee decision to return to the country of origin. The exact relative importance of asset restitution is, however, also determined by several other factors including, where relevant, access to financial resources (for example, small and medium enterprise funding), the scope to diversify economic activity, the level of ethnic or sectarian tensions, and the degree of development in housing and land markets.

Restitution of assets is also central to reconstruction programming and to a just return. For refugees returning to both urban and rural areas, the ability to reclaim their land or obtain access to land elsewhere or receive compensation where their restitution is impossible or limited (the situation in Bosnia and Herzegovina), lies at the crux of return decisions and is crucial to prospects of reestablishing livelihoods. These conditions appear to have been an incentive for both substantial "spontaneous" and assisted returns by Afghan refugees in the early 1990s, for Angolan refugees reclaiming their land on return from Zambia from 2002 onward, and for refugees returning after the Comprehensive Peace Agreement in 2015 to what became South Sudan—although, as noted, the situation in South Sudan quickly unraveled. In Bosnia and Herzegovina, these conditions were also vital, supplemented by a very extensive program of reconstruction of war-damaged housing. Beyond the restitution of land as a material and productive asset, restoration of land entitlements may also help to underpin the principle of a "just return."

Infrastructure and services

Like livelihoods, access to infrastructure often has complex implications for return. The legacy of war is most evident in the destruction of infrastructure and services, which may be a deterrent to the timing of return (if not to the principle of return itself), for example, in Bosnia and Herzegovina. There are, however, examples of refugees spontaneously returning to countries after the cessation of hostilities where destruction is widespread—Angola and Liberia, for example. Experience suggests that reconstruction and rehabilitation of infrastructure, public buildings such as schools, repair of services (such as roads, water supply, and irrigation systems), and housing are critical but often take years to accomplish—well after refugees have returned spontaneously or through voluntary assisted repatriation. Such was the case in Bosnia and Herzegovina, which parallels Syria in terms of levels of economic development, urbanization, and the scale of displacement and destruction. Large-scale, voluntary, and assisted repatriation from western European countries was rapidly implemented after the Dayton Accords, even though postwar destruction remained widespread and there was no "precondition" of long-term commitment by donors to heavily invest in reconstruction. Conversely, to kick-start this process, community-driven quick impact projects are a useful tool in parallel with a focus, in the early phases of return, on a few transformative programs that can be delivered at scale and that have impact and durability.

Discerning a pathway to autonomy is a foundational underpinning to successful recovery and the motivation to repatriate. Becoming forcibly displaced is a profoundly disempowering and disenfranchising experience. As part of the comparative measure of push and pull factors that characterize repatriation decisions, refugees often cite agency as a critical enabling factor for return movements. Community-driven quick impact projects that employ localized decision-making processes have been used to increase autonomy among refugees contemplating return and among those that have recently arrived in origin countries. The twin goals of such programs are to deliver community-level infrastructure and services and to allow residents and refugees within a community to decide on the use of public and donor funds to improve their lives.

Postconflict reconstruction and service restoration cannot be reduced to a mere technical process; they have important political and distributional relevance. Where reconstruction and service restoration tackle the grievances of social and economic exclusion, which often contribute to conflict and refugee exodus, they may help to mitigate further conflict. If unaddressed, economic and social exclusion can be important contributors, not only to livelihood failure but also to governance and political fragility after return, as observed in countries such as Afghanistan and South Sudan. It may also lead to secondary displacement or failed return. Conversely, in the case of Bosnia and Herzegovina, these grievances were addressed, albeit through a very contrived power-sharing constitutional arrangement that took place alongside a reconstruction process. This process largely acceded to the physical separation of ethnic communities whose previous inter-mixing had been destroyed by the conflict. As such, the political overlay of the Dayton Accords consolidated a new demographic reality that halted active conflict while creating difficult return conditions for the displaced.

Coordination among donors and implementing partners is essential for a success-ful return and reintegration program that is driven by reconstruction and service restoration. Both local and large-scale regional development programs can be vehicles to assist return and reintegration. At the same time, they can provide a common approach for donors and nongovernmental organization implementing partners. These programs can be effective if designed with a clear focus on rein-tegration of the displaced, in response to the demand and with the involvement in planning of both returnees and populations that remained, and with adequate funding. Useful examples include the Seila Program in Cambodia and the National Solidarity Program in Afghanistan, both in the early 2000s, and, at least for the first few years after its inception in 2012, the Local Governance and Service Delivery Project in South Sudan.

The role of international assistance in return

The record of international assistance for refugee return is not uniform—either within countries at different periods or across countries. Each situation of return is characterized by a unique array of complex factors that must be resolved. Key pol-icy, strategic, and operational factors that transpire from international assistance for refugee return are as follows:

- **The political economy of peacebuilding**

  ○ Assisting the recovery of countries emerging from conflict and the return of refugees by adopting a broad "political economy" analysis of fragility, the drivers of conflict and forced displacement, and issues related to the return and reintegration of the displaced.

  ○ Sustaining long-term investment in the politically complex strategies for conflict reduction, reconciliation, and peacebuilding.

- **Programming and coordination of return and reconstruction**

  ○ Ensuring that the operationally driven focus of repatriation programs does not divert attention and funding from the long-term processes of recovery, reconstruction, and reintegration, as well as the creation of a sustainable development environment.

  ○ Coordinating return with the macro- and microeconomic and spatial devel-opment planning strategies of countries of return.

  ○ Securing stakeholder partnerships with development partners including international financial institutions and the World Bank, regional bodies, and civil society, among others.

  ○ Ensuring logistical and operational coordination, joint programming, and partnership and donor alignment around reconstruction and reintegration strategies. This factor is part of the emergent value of "nexus" approaches to displacement crises among humanitarian and development actors found, most notably, in Ukraine at present (Benner 2018).

○ Anticipating the likelihood of early and large-scale spontaneous returns, which can derail carefully planned voluntary assisted return programs.

○ Recognizing the importance that returnees place on information about the conditions in areas of return.

○ Giving due attention to monitoring indicators that provide disaggregated data on the implementation and impact of return and reintegration strategies and programs.

- **Urban planning and land and property restitution**

○ Addressing the thorny issue of land rights and property restitution.

○ Recognizing the reality that returnees increasingly settle in urban environments.

Even before they are signed, internationally assisted peace accords influence the return of refugees in a complex manner. Peace accords—the cessation of conflict, demilitarization, and the formation of functioning postwar government—play an important part in reestablishing the international legitimacy of countries that have been engulfed by war. Their role in the dynamics of refugee return and the associated tripartite voluntary repatriation programs is, however, plagued with complexity. In the case of the Luanda Accord ending the Angolan Civil War (1975–2002), several hundred thousand refugees returned in advance of the Accord. In the case of the Rome General Accords ending the Mozambican Civil War (1977–92), refugees gradually returned in anticipation of the ending of the war.

Refugee displacement is often a regional phenomenon, but agreements that lead to return are not. Many recent and contemporary refugee crises, such as the Afghan refugee situations, result in regional displacement across several neighboring countries rather than one host country. Although this problem has been the focus of much promising discussion as part of the New York Declarations Comprehensive Refugee Response Framework, there are only two instances in the past 40 years where regional agreements have underpinned refugee return. The 1989 Comprehensive Plan of Action for Indo-Chinese Refugees was established as an international regional framework for cooperation at a time when asylum conditions for Vietnamese and Cambodian refugees in Southeast Asia were in crisis. In the same year the International Conference on Central American Refugees, known by its Spanish acronym CIREFCA, was agreed as a regional framework to establish a peace process and to tackle the similarly large crisis of refugee (and in this case also internally displaced person [IDP]) displacement in Central America resulting from civil wars in Guatemala and Nicaragua. These comprehensive agreements principally reflect national and international interests in establishing peace, the status quo ante, and the return of displaced populations. The complexity of establishing a common nexus of interests among many diverse stakeholders inevitably militates against such regional agreements, hence their limited use. Table 1.1 summarizes the information in this subsection.

Table 1.1. Determinants of Return and Lessons from International Experience

Determinant	Lessons from international experience
1. Peace, security, and protection	• Assisted voluntary return programs work well (especially if they follow peace agreements). • Some refugees return spontaneously while conflict is receding but not necessarily ended or if return programs are regarded as inadequate. • Refugees need to be enabled to return to places of origin. • Family reunification needs to be facilitated. • Freedom of movement eases access to employment. • Local protection capacities need to be enhanced. • Community-driven development needs to be promoted to resuscitate local social networks and social capital.
2. Livelihoods and access to employment	• Returning refugees increasingly head for urban areas. • Reconstruction, a leading sector in recovery, absorbs informal labor and regenerates livelihoods. • Reinforcing entrenched inequities through development investments needs to be avoided. • Supply chains can be crucial. • Regulatory apparatus needs to be sped up. • Employment for women needs to be promoted.
3. Housing, land, and property (HLP)	• Fast-track mechanisms for identifying ownership are needed to facilitate recovery and restitution of property and assets. • Protection of HLP rights for women needs to be ensured.
4. Infrastructure and services	• Investments need to benefit residents as well as the recently returned. • Local urban services (schools and health centers) need to be restored. • Quick impact projects for key urban services need to be implemented. • Reconnaissance and information systems should be used to profile local needs and assets. • Block grants should be used to fund community-level projects. • Neighborhood capacity building and partnership with projects should be implemented by civil society and nongovernmental organizations.
5. The role of international assistance	• Assistance needs to support the political economy of peacebuilding and international funding. • Assistance needs to support programming and coordination of return, funding streams, and postconflict reconstruction.

Asymmetries in Return

The complexities that render return difficult to predict are aggravated by the fact that "refugees" comprise a vastly heterogeneous group of human beings. International experience shows that return is neither a finite event nor a fixed destination but is better understood as an often long and drawn out process of mobility and adaptation. Refugees are purposive and rational (and emotional) actors; their decisions and modalities of return are better understood as a process of adaptation and optimization strategies, not necessarily an end-state solution. For returning refugees, the aim is to accomplish their own versions of durable (that is, sustainable), but not necessarily permanent, solutions to the different circumstances in which they find themselves. Return is typically enacted after comparing information about conditions and prospects in the host country—security, economy, services, and housing/land—with those in the country of origin. Each person faces a different combination of these factors and has a different set of priorities.

The following subsection focuses on two asymmetries that elaborate on this complexity. First, refugees may not necessarily return to where they came from. Second, the burden of return is not equally distributed across genders, with women facing distinct challenges.

Destinations of return: Where is home?

Refugees decreasingly return to their places of origin, even when accompanied by reintegration assistance, but rather go to cities, which often triggers further urbanization. Returning refugees, particularly younger refugees, increasingly head for the cities in their countries of origin, irrespective of the level of urbanization. Although growing numbers of refugees have fled from cities and towns and might logically be expected to return to them, significant numbers also come from rural areas. However, many rural refugees do not—as anticipated in assisted voluntary return schemes and reintegration strategies—go back to the rural communities they hailed from. If and when they do return, it is mainly to urban locations. Examples of cities whose growth is significantly driven by the influx of returnees, IDPs, or both are Kabul in Afghanistan (where some 70 percent of the population may be returnees or IDPs), Juba in South Sudan, Monrovia in Liberia, Luanda in Angola, and Abidjan in Côte d'Ivoire. Some estimates suggest that the substantial majority of the 330,000 returning refugees and 1 million IDPs settled in Juba, almost doubling the city's population from an estimated range between 400,000 and 600,000 (Martin and Mosel 2011). Kabul's urban population increased from a high estimate of 2 million in 2001 to a conservative estimate of 4.5 million in 2010—again mostly fueled by refugees and IDPs although there is no breakdown of the figures (Metcalfe, Haysom, and Martin 2012).

Refugee returns accentuate substandard urban conditions. Increasing numbers of IDPs/returnees to cities and towns are attracted by the following factors: familiarity with urban environments in exile as most refugees now live in urban areas not camps; the expectation of better security; and, likewise, the expectation of better access to services and economic opportunities than in rural areas, even with assisted return. With an accelerated process of permanent urban settlement, the unsatisfactory urban conditions in many countries of return are compounded because most of those returning to urban areas live alongside the urban poor in slums and informal settlements. In these settlements, housing is frequently substandard and tenure insecure, services inadequate and overstretched, livelihood opportunities few and marginal, and the physical environment often vulnerable to natural hazards. Although many of the problems that affect returnees (refugees and IDPs) also affect the urban poor more generally, additional challenges often confront returnees to urban environments. They can be further disadvantaged by a lack of required documentation, limited social support networks that assist with return and access to labor markets, and a lack of access to land. They may often face harassment or discrimination for several reasons: their ethnicity, competition for scarce resources, the fact that they fled rather than remained to endure conflict, or a weak rule of law in the early stages of peace and reconciliation.

"Returnee displacement" is an increasingly common phenomenon. Large numbers of refugees returning to Bosnia and Herzegovina, Iraq, and South Sudan have gone back to their homes and towns and attempted to reintegrate where they previously lived in ethnically mixed communities. But the legacy of ethnic cleansing in Bosnia and Herzegovina, and fresh conflict, sectarian, and interethnic violence in Iraq and South Sudan, has severely diminished security conditions, subjecting returnees (and co-ethnic stayees) to secondary displacement to mono-ethnic enclaves and regions in ostensibly (re)united countries. Over 1.9 million IDPs in South Sudan exemplify this pattern of secondary displacement of returnees following the postindependence power struggle and conflict (UNOCHA 2018a). In Afghanistan, refugees returning to their rural areas of origin have also subsequently migrated to cities primarily to seek better protection from ongoing violence and severe human rights violations, as well as to enhance their livelihood opportunities. Nearly 1 million Afghans, including returnees, became internally displaced between mid-2016 and end-2017 (UNOCHA 2018b). In Iraq, internal conflict and violence have also precipitated very large-scale internal secondary migration of both returning refugees and those who remained, totaling some 2.6 million IDPs from December 2013 to January 2018 (UNOCHA 2018c). In the case of Iraq, it is conflict between ethnic and religious groups rather than generalized violence and human rights violations, as in Afghanistan, that has produced, in effect, mono-ethnic and sectarian cities and regions replacing previously mixed localities. In Bosnia and Herzegovina, a similar but slower, nonviolent separation of ethnically remixed Bosniak, Croat, and Serbian returning refugees has taken place.[12] This experience presages a potentially similar outcome for refugee return in Syria, where not only ethnicity but also political orientation may play a role in repatriation patterns.

Gender and return: A double burden

Return entails new and additional hardships and challenges for women. They may have had fewer opportunities than men to acquire new skills or capital savings in exile; they generally have less power and influence than men about the decision to—and modalities of—return. With fewer resources and lower social status, women and female-headed households may find it difficult to secure livelihoods upon return; ensure the restitution of or access to housing, land, and property; and access other essential services.

Changes in household roles and social structures in exile also complicate women's experience of return. The case of Chilean women refugees returning home at the end of the Pinochet dictatorship in the 1990s provides a poignant example of the impact of changing domestic power structures. Women were often more adaptable in exile and engaged more readily in new livelihoods; these roles were reflected in the changing balance of household roles and power between men and women. On return, the households reverted to more traditional, male dominated social and family structures and roles, which placed significant social and psychological pressure on how refugee women adapted to return.

Gender concerns highlight the importance of distinguishing the needs of different demographic and social groups within the returning populations. Returnees are not homogeneous. Different communities and households have different needs, and varying levels of social and economic vulnerability and coping capacities, often conditioned by where they return to. They will achieve satisfactory thresholds of economic self-sufficiency, social well-being, protection, and human rights, if at all, through different means and at different times.

Concluding Remarks

The overview of international experience so far points to key areas of concern for analyzing refugee returns, and it also shows the complexity of the problem. The discussion in this chapter focuses on providing general trends in return experience globally and categorizing factors that may influence the decision making regarding returns. Overall, the complex nature of the problem and absence of empirical evidence, two factors that reinforce each other, limit understanding of the mechanisms that drive return decisions. Nevertheless, key observations provide the necessary guidelines for analyzing Syrian refugees' mobility. These observations are the following:

- Four broad categories of conditions are identified to shape return significantly. *Peace, security, and protection*: scope of peace and reconciliation measures, adequate rights protection, access to justice, and trust in local actors. This may also include the ability to enjoy administrative and legal security, freedom from arbitrary arrest and conscription, and equal effective access to administrative services and documentation (identity) restoration. *Livelihoods and economic opportunities*: economic and social absorption capacity of areas of return, and access to resources including land, land rights and financial resources. This includes intangible aspects like human capital and social networks. *Housing, land, and property*: ownership of assets in country of asylum or home country, the likelihood of asset restitution, prevailing conditions of appropriation, and property rights. *Infrastructure and access to services*: scale of physical and infrastructure destruction, strategies and funding of reconstruction/restoration, access to adequate services and housing, social programs, education, and health services.

- Although formal peace agreements provide the context for large-scale refugee returns, spontaneous returns to places that are far from peaceful and in post-conflict recovery are not uncommon. Experiences in Afghanistan, Angola, Iraq, Liberia, and South Sudan show that trends in spontaneous return depend on how refugees perceive structural conditions such as security, livelihoods, and the potential for reintegration. Evidence of Iraqi and Somali refugee return shows that the process is not unilineal but often iterative, staggered, and cyclical. Conversely, peace agreements that "settle" conflicts are sometimes not enough to catalyze large-scale returns.

- Poverty in the country of asylum may be a driver of return, but, perhaps counterintuitively, the opposite may also be true. The incidence of poverty in exile, and (broadly) standards of living, and the extent to which refugees have pursued livelihoods and built up skills, capital, and assets can be critical in stimulating or constraining return. Inclusion of refugees in the economic life of host countries can provide the basis for a more durable and flexible repertoire of responses to return movements. Poverty may be a driver of return as, for example, with Iraqi refugees from Syria in 2007–10. However, refugee groups with higher socioeconomic status may have a greater propensity to return earlier than groups impoverished by displacement (for example, Liberian refugees). In a related fashion, after protracted exile the loss of skills, or the lack of skills to meet new economic conditions, may constrain return or propel returnees to urban areas with better livelihood opportunities.

- Returning refugees decreasingly return to their places of origin, even with reintegration assistance. Two characteristics are evident in many contemporary return processes. First, refugees from rural origins increasingly return to the cities in their countries of origin because of better access to services and economic opportunities and increasing familiarity with urban environments in exile. Examples include Juba, Kabul, Luanda, and Monrovia. Second, sizable secondary (internal) displacement of returning refugees is the legacy of the factors that precipitated refugee displacement, for example in Bosnia and Herzegovina, Iraq, and South Sudan.

- Return entails new hardships and additional challenges for women. They may have had fewer opportunities than men to acquire new skills or capital savings in exile, and they generally have less power and influence than men about the decision to return. Upon return women may find it difficult to secure livelihoods; ensure the restitution of, or access to housing, land, and property; and gain access to other essential services.

The next chapter analyzes the conditions faced by Syrian refugees using these guidelines. The complexity described by the overview of international experience shows that each refugee situation is different. Thus, effective programming of international assistance to refugees entails a careful analysis of each situation separately. The next chapter provides a description of conditions, to the extent possible in an empirical manner, in the four broad categories described. These categories will then be used in the following chapters to assess their relative importance, as revealed by the return of Syrian refugees so far, by using a suite of statistical techniques.

Notes

1. One of the most comprehensive chronicles of voluntary repatriation is "Voluntary Repatriation throughout the Years: A Compilation of Selected Extracts from UNHCR Document (1953–2012)" (UNHCR 2013). Few other sources take such an inclusive view of voluntary returns. A second source that regards returns through a sustainability lens is Harild, Christensen, and Zetter (2015).

2. See UN doc. A/AC.96/830, 7 September 1994, paras. 8, 10–11, 31–32, at https://www.refworld.org/docid/3f0a935f2.html. UNRWA has a specific mandate over a particular category of refugees residing in five areas of operation (Gaza, Lebanon, Jordan, Syria, and West Bank). This complementarity is acknowledged in the Statute, para. 7(c), and also in Art. 1D of the 1951 Convention. There are additional exclusions for those with nationality in the asylum state, those under the protection of other UN offices, and those suspected of serious nonpolitical crimes, war crimes, or crimes against humanity.

3. For more information, see UNHCR, *Interpreting Article 1 of the 1951 Convention Relating to the Status of Refugees*, April 2001, available at http://www.refworld.org/docid/3b20a3914.html (accessed November 16, 2018).

4. UNHCR, Interpreting Article 1, 13.

5. See the full General Assembly Resolution, A/RES/428 (V) at https://www.refworld.org/docid/3ae6b3628.html.

6. See "UN Archive Gallery for Algeria 1952 to 1964" at http://www.unhcr.org/en-us/research/archives/4a3272846/unhcr-archive-gallery-algeria-1954-1962.html.

7. See UNHCR's sample template for tripartite agreements at http://www.unhcr.org/50aa07929.pdf.

8. This number includes the 5.4 million Palestine refugees under UNRWA's mandate.

9. See, for example, Harild, Christensen, and Zetter (2015); Morris and Salomons (2013); and discussions of emplacement in, for example, Pedersen (2003).

10. The phenomenon of migrating toward urban centers is sometimes called "urbanization" and will be described later in more detail (see Martin and Mosel 2011, 4; Metcalfe, Haysom, and Martin 2012).

11. A typical example can be found in the case study of Liberian refugees in Ghana by Omata (2011).

12. A controversial paper modeled a variety of social and population data and estimated that the population of 48.4 percent Bosniaks, 32.7 percent Serbs, and 14.6 percent Croats had largely separated out in the 20 years since the Dayton Agreement (Bochsler and Schläpfer 2015).

References

Benner, Holly Wellborn. 2018. "Scoping Study: Conflict in Ukraine: Coordinating Peacebuilding, Recovery, and Development Response Efforts." World Bank, Washington, DC.

Bochsler, D., and B. Schläpfer. 2015. "An Indirect Approach to Map Ethnic Identities in Postconflict Societies." *Ethnopolitics* 15 (6): 467–86.

Christensen, Asger, and Niels Harild. 2009. "Forced Displacement: The Development Challenge." Conflict, Crime & Violence Issue Note, Social Development Department, World Bank, Washington, DC.

Harild, Niels, Asger Christensen, and Roger Zetter. 2015. "Sustainable Refugee Return: Triggers, Constraints, and Lessons on Addressing the Development Challenges of Forced Displacement." GPRD Issue Note Series, World Bank, Washington, DC.

Jeffery, Laura, and Jude Murison. 2011. "The Temporal, Social, Spatial, and Legal Dimensions of Return and Onward Migration." *Population, Space and Place* 17 (2): 131–39.

Liuhto, Maija. 2018. "Afghanistan: Where Home Is a Battlefield." *The New Humanitarian* (formerly IRIN News), May 1. https://www.irinnews.org/feature/2018/05/01/Afghanistan-Pakistan-returnees-refugees-conflict.

Lloyd, Annemaree, Mary Kennan, Kim Thompson, and Asim Qayuum. 2013. "Connecting with New Information Landscapes: Information Literacy Practices of Refugees." *Journal of Documentation* 69 (1): 121–44.

Long, Katy. 2011. "Permanent Crises? Unlocking the Protracted Displacement of Refugees and Internally Displaced Persons." Policy Overview, Oxford Department of International Development Refugee Studies Centre, Oxford, U.K.

Martin, Ellen, and Irina Mosel. 2011. "City Limits: Urbanisation and Vulnerability in Sudan: Juba Case Study." Humanitarian Policy Group, Overseas Development Institute, London.

Metcalfe, Victoria, Simone Haysom, and Ellen Martin. 2012. "Sanctuary in the City? Urban Displacement and Vulnerability in Kabul." HPG Working Paper, Humanitarian Policy Group, Overseas Development Institute, London.

Morris, Helen, and Machiel Salomons. 2013. "Difficult Decisions: A Review of UNHCR's Engagement with Assisted Voluntary Return Programmes." Policy Development and Evaluation Service, United Nations High Commissioner for Refugees, Geneva.

Norwegian Refugee Council. 2016. "Dadaab's Broken Promise: A Call to Reinstate Voluntary, Safe and Dignified Returns for the Dadaab Refugee Community." Position paper, Norwegian Refugee Council, Oslo, October. https://www.nrc.no/globalassets/dadaabs-broken-promise-an-nrc-report-10.10.16.pdf.

Omata, Naohiko. 2011. "The Complexity of Refugees' Return Decision-Making in a Protracted Exile: Beyond the Home-Coming Model and Durable Solutions." *Journal of Ethnic and Migration Studies* 39 (8):1281–97.

Pedersen, Marianne Holm. 2003. "Between Homes: Post-war Return, Emplacement and the Negotiation of Belonging in Lebanon." New Issues in Refugee Research, Working Paper No. 79, Evaluation and Policy Analysis Unit, United Nations High Commissioner for Refugees, Geneva.

UNHCR (United Nations High Commissioner for Refugees). 1980. "Note on Voluntary Repatriation EC/SCP/13." UNHCR, Geneva. https://www.unhcr.org/en-us/excom/scip/3ae68cce8/note-voluntary-repatriation.html.

———. 1985. "Voluntary Repatriation No. 40 Executive Committee 36th session." Contained in United Nations General Assembly Document No. 12A (A/40/12/Add.1), UNHCR, Geneva. https://www.unhcr.org/en-us/excom/exconc/3ae68c9518/voluntary-repatriation.html.

———. 1994. "Note on International Protection, A/AC.96/830." UNHCR, Geneva. https://www.refworld.org/docid/3f0a935f2.html.

———. 1997. *The State of the World's Refugees: A Humanitarian Agenda*. Geneva: UNHCR.

———. 2003. "Framework for Durable Solutions for Refugees and Persons of Concern." Core Group on Durable Solutions, UNHCR. https://www.unhcr.org/en-us/partners/partners/3f1408764/framework-durable-solutions-refugees-persons-concern.html.

———. 2013. "Voluntary Repatriation Throughout the Years: A Compilation of Selected Extracts from UNHCR Document (1953–2012)."

———. 2017a. "Global Trends: Forced Displacement in 2016." UNHCR, Geneva. http://www.unhcr.org/5943e8a34.pdf.

———. 2017b. "UNHCR Operational Update—Dadaab, Kenya, 16–30 September 2017." UNHCR, Geneva. https://targeting.alnap.org/system/files/content/resource/files/main/30-September-Dadaab-Bi-weekly-Operational-Update.pdf.

———. 2018. "Global Trends: Forced Displacement in 2017." UNHCR, Geneva. http://www.unhcr.org/5b27be547.pdf.

UNOCHA (United Nations Office for the Coordination of Humanitarian Affairs). 2018a. "Humanitarian Needs Overview: South Sudan." UNOCHA, New York and Geneva. https://reliefweb.int/sites/reliefweb.int/files/resources/South_Sudan_2018_Humanitarian_Needs_Overview.pdf.

———. 2018b. "Humanitarian Needs Overview: Afghanistan." UNOCHA, New York and Geneva. https://reliefweb.int/sites/reliefweb.int/files/resources/afg_2018_humanitarian_needs_overview_1.pdf.

———. 2018c. "Humanitarian Bulletin: Iraq." UNOCHA, New York and Geneva. https://reliefweb.int/sites/reliefweb.int/files/resources/DRAFT_OCHA%20Iraq%20Humanitarian%20Bulletin%20%28January%202018%29_final.pdf.

World Bank. 2017. *The Forcibly Displaced: Toward a Development Approach to Supporting Refugees, the Internally Displaced, and Their Hosts*. Washington, DC: World Bank.

CHAPTER 2

Economic and Social Context for Syrians

This chapter assesses the conditions faced by Syrians inside and outside the Syrian Arab Republic along the four dimensions distilled from international experience (peace, security, and protection; livelihoods and employment; housing, land, and property rights; and access to basic services). For each of these four dimensions, several narrower categories are identified and analyzed using multiple sources of data including needs assessments and vulnerability assessments organized by United Nations agencies, official sources of data, and World Bank assessments of damage and functionality. Data sources lend themselves to comparison between conditions within Syria and those outside Syria in some cases—especially in vulnerability- and needs-related issues because they were covered by surveys both in Syria and in host communities, albeit not identically. The data, however, do not always support such comparisons, forcing the analysis to pursue second- or third-best approaches for some issues, such as monetary poverty.

Economic and Social Context for Syrians

International experience suggests four broad categories of factors, at origin or in countries of asylum, that can influence refugees' mobility decisions. Chapter 1 distills these four categories of factors—from many sources—that shape the return calculus of refugees: (a) peace, security, and protection; (b) livelihoods and access to employment; (c) housing, land, and property rights; and (d) infrastructure and publicly provided services. For many of the individual factors that fall into one of these four broad categories, the magnitude and direction of impact on returns is complex; their effect may not be monotonic depending on various other conditions. It is important, therefore, to account for a large set of factors before any causal relationship is attributed to the role played by any specific factor.

This chapter provides an assessment of the conditions faced by Syrians in the four designated categories of factors in the Syrian Arab Republic and in Iraq, Jordan, and Lebanon. Unlike previous World Bank reports on Syria (for example, World Bank 2017a), the starting point of the analysis here is the nature of a specific factor as directly observed by a Syrian citizen. For instance, for a core service like education, the first layer of the analysis is about the availability of the service (that is, a functional and accessible school that can reasonably admit students). Only in the second layer are other factors investigated (for instance, identification of the reason that a school is not functional, including but not limited to physical damage to infrastructure, absence of teachers, or absence of supplies). Although it is not always supported by data, when possible, special attention is paid to provide a three-way comparison of conditions faced by Syrians: conditions in Syria before the conflict, conditions in Syria currently (latest available), and conditions faced by Syrian refugees in countries of asylum.

Data and Methodology

There are considerable data constraints in assessing conditions faced by Syrians, especially in relation to the current situation within Syria. In the absence of comprehensive household survey data, this analysis relies on disparate sources of information, some based on surveys, others collected for programming purposes by humanitarian agencies, and yet others relying on data collected for sectoral damage assessments. More specifically, the following sources of information from partners and official sources are used:

- For conditions in countries of asylum, numerous sources are used. For Jordan: the Vulnerability Assessment Framework (VAF) led by the United Nations High Commissioner for Refugees (UNHCR), UNHCR registration data of Syrians in Jordan (2018), Jordan Labor Market Panel Survey (JLMPS) (2016), Jordan Department of Statistics (DOS) Job Creation Surveys (2016), and Employment and Unemployment Surveys (first quarter 2018). For Lebanon: Vulnerability Assessment of Syrian Refugees (VASyR), UNHCR registration data of Syrians in Lebanon (2018). For Iraq: UNHCR Multi-Sector Needs Assessment (MSNA) III report (2017), which is based on the survey conducted in September 2017 and the UNHCR registration data of Syrians in the Kurdistan Region of Iraq (2018) and a representative socioeconomic survey of all of its residents (2018).

- For conditions in Syria, it was not possible to acquire a comparable and geographically comprehensive time series. Aggregate tabulations for preconflict and most recent labor market indicators are from Syrian labor force surveys (2007 and 2009) from the Central Bureau of Statistics, the Syrian Center for Policy Research, and the World Development Indicators (2017). For living conditions and vulnerability assessments, the following resources are used: United Nations Office for the Coordination of Humanitarian Affair's (UNOCHA) Humanitarian Needs Assessment Programme (HNAP) (2018); UNHCR-led MSNA (2017); United Nations Children's Fund (UNICEF) water, sanitation, and hygiene (WASH) survey (2017); Urban Community Profiling Surveys from the United Nations Human Settlements Programme (UN-Habitat) (2016); market prices from the World Food Programme (WFP) (2018); Education Management Information System (EMIS) from the Syrian Ministry of Education for the school year 2009–10; trade statistics from the United Nations International Trade Statistics Database (UN Comtrade) (2016); agriculture surveys from the Food and Agriculture Organization of the United Nations (FAO) (2017); and water supply statistics from the Needs Population Monitoring round 5 (2016) conducted by UNOCHA.

A novel database of physical damage and functionality of facilities was created for the purposes of this study. Remote-sensing techniques were used to assess physical damage to infrastructure and housing and facility damage. To this end, optical imagery at 30–50 centimeters from Digital Globe and Airbus satellite platforms and the U.S. National Aeronautics and Space Administration's visible infrared imaging radiometer suite were employed to generate data series of physical damage, and human activity around facilities in 15 cities and six sectors (table 2.1). Traditional and social media were also used to confirm these damage and functionality assessments. These city-level assessments were then extrapolated to 14 governorates by using conflict intensity and baseline asset inventories.

The damage estimates based on remote-sensing techniques are second-best solutions. The damage assessment is based on actual physical conditions as of July 2018. The actual damage inflicted by the conflict may be higher, because there may be some reconstruction in areas of these cities. In addition, the analysis presented here does not capture variations in the quality of the housing units and considers all building categories mostly identical across cities, based on the limited available data. Similarly, the satellite imagery used in this analysis relies on vertical damage and cannot capture lateral damage. Nevertheless, when combined with

Table 2.1. Studies' Coverage Comparison

	DNA phase III (2017)	*Toll of War* (World Bank 2017)	This study
Methodology	Damage assessment: Facility-level	Damage assessment: Area-based	Damage assessment: Area-based Functionality assessment: Facility-level
Geographic coverage	3 cities: Aleppo, Hama, Idleb	10 cities: Aleppo, Ar-Raqqa, Dar'a, Douma, Deir-ez-Zor, Homs, Hama, Idleb, Tadmor, Kobani. Extrapolated to 8 governorates	15 cities: Afrin, Al-Bab, Aleppo, Al-Qusayr, Ar-Raqqa, Dar'a, Deir-ez-Zor, Douma, Homs, Idleb, Kobane, Menbij, Qamishli, Tadmor, Yabroud. Extrapolated to 14 governorates
Sector coverage	6 sectors: Education, energy, housing, health, transport, water and sanitation	6 sectors: Education, energy, housing, health, transport, water and sanitation	6 sectors for damages and functionality: Education, energy, housing, health, transport, water and sanitation Additionally: Agriculture, housing, land and property, governance and security

Source: World Bank 2017b. documents.worldbank.org/curated/en/530541512657033401/pdf/121943-WP-P161647-PUBLIC-Syria-Damage-Assessment.pdf
Note: DNA = damage and needs assessment.

cross-verification through traditional and social media, this approach provides a systematic approach to taking stock of damage, which does not suffer from differences between focal point reporting or surveyor judgment. In subsequent sections these data sources will be used to provide a comparison of conditions faced by Syrians in Syria and in Iraq, Jordan, and Lebanon.

Peace, Security, and Protection

The Syrian conflict, now in its eighth year, has gone through a series of political, diplomatic, and military transformations over time. The early phases of the Syrian conflict, from March 2011 to June 2012, comprised typically moderate to severe clashes between the Syrian army and locally organized small group formations within major urban environments. Increasingly, tanks, artillery, and air force bombings were used within highly populated urban environments, including some of the largest Syrian cities. Although fighting had intensified, the period from June 2013 to January 2014 witnessed a mostly strategic stalemate between the opposing forces. The year 2015 saw new Syrian government offensives, involving a heavy use of armor, artillery, and air force as well as open intervention by the Russian Federation. The intensity of conflict reached new heights in 2017 as the Syrian Arab Army aimed to reconsolidate territory by means of new offensives, which continued in 2018 (figure 2.1).

For the first time since the onset of the crisis, there are expectations of a reduction in hostilities. Although the tragic possibility of renewed fighting and large-scale displacement in certain areas cannot be ruled out, the incidence of large-scale violence is expected to decrease within the next 12 months. Parties to the Astana talks

Figure 2.1. Conflict Events and Verified Casualties

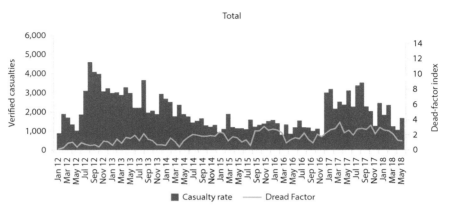

Total

Source: World Bank staff calculations based on multiple data sources.
Note: Dread factor comprises the monthly weighted sums of tank, artillery, and air strikes at light, medium, and heavy incidence levels.

and a United Nations–sponsored Geneva process continue to push for deescalation. Even in the absence of a negotiated settlement, the trajectory of the war has consolidated territorial control under forces loyal to the Syrian government, though that consolidation today may be best described as fragmented.

Rarely, however, is the absence of fighting a sufficient condition for people to feel safe. A negative peace, or the simple absence of violence, is inadequate to engender a feeling of safety, especially for refugees. Fears over conscription; an inability to regain access to homes, land, and property; the lack of justice mechanisms that ensure accountability for past transgressions and future threats; and vetting procedures by security forces are among the reasons that delay return. Necessary improvements in such pull factors, factors with direct bearing on the decision to return, are frequently ignored in political settlements, as they were after conflicts in Bosnia and Herzegovina, Burundi, Cambodia, Iraq, and South Sudan. These factors can also be easily overlooked by international technical assessments of physical damage and the economic impacts of war.

In this section, the analysis will focus on the security perceptions of Syrians. To put the current conditions into perspective, refugees' own assessments about their safety and freedom of movement once they return are analyzed. The underlying survey data are provided by UNOCHA's 2018 HNAP and perception surveys of refugees by UNHCR. Refugees also worry that legal obstacles could make it extremely difficult to resume their lives. Special attention is paid to the disproportionately adverse conditions faced by Syrian women and children.

Status quo: The absence of a positive peace

Syrians, especially refugees, are worried about persecution and the lawlessness that may endure well past any moderation of the conflict. Most refugees anticipate arbitrary arrests, frequent document checks, and active discrimination against those who opposed the current government if they reenter areas of the country controlled by Damascus. The 2017 VASyR survey of Syrian refugees in Lebanon, for instance, found safety and security in Syria was by far the most important pull factor in the return decision, cited by 63 percent of respondents; no other factor had a response rate exceeding 16 percent (figure 2.2) (UNHCR, UNICEF, and WFP 2018). More recently, the "Fourth Regional Survey on Syrian Refugees' Perceptions and Intentions on Return to Syria," which covers refugees in Egypt, Iraq, Jordan, and Lebanon, found that safety and security in Syria was by far their most important concern regarding return: among refugees not intending to return to Syria within 12 months, 45 percent of the reasons provided to explain their intentions were related to the prevalence of indiscriminate violence or the risk of targeted reprisals (UNHCR 2018a). Refugee apprehensions over security conditions are broader than fears of being caught in the cross fire of active conflict. Concerns over military service, conscription, or recruitment and fear of arrest and detention or retaliation upon return are among the frequently reported obstacles to return. Assuming that a cessation of hostilities will assuage refugee concerns over security overlooks these other trenchant aspects of well-being.

Concerns about the mandatory military conscription for men ages 18–42 remained in place by mid-2018. This policy not only drove the departure of many young men and their families from Syria in the first place but also actively discouraged their return. Recent legislation has further complicated this issue. As of 2017, fines of up to US$8,000 could be levied on male youth who do not register for military service within three months of turning 18. The law is retroactive, and those who fled Syria before 2017 may be fined and required to fulfill their service obligation. Those who refuse military service may be imprisoned for one year and pay the equivalent of US$200 for each year after the starting date of their original conscription period as a penalty. If returnees are unable to pay these fines, assets may be seized until payments are made in full. The prospect of military service, large fines, and the seizure of assets is one of the key obstacles keeping many young men and their families in exile.

Figure 2.2. Considerations for Return to the Syrian Arab Republic (Syrian Refugees in Lebanon)

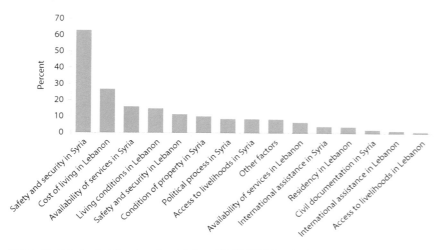

Source: World Bank calculations based on data from UNHCR, UNICEF, and WFP 2018.

By the time of this report's preparation, some amendments to these policies were anticipated but had not yet been announced or implemented.

In Syria, lack of civil documentation and insecurity feed each other. About 40 percent of the Syrians surveyed as part of the 2018 HNAP lack some official civil document, such as a birth, marriage, or death certificate; national identification card; family booklet; or passport (figure 2.3) (UNOCHA 2018). This condition varies drastically across governorates. Whereas more than 8 out of 10 residents lack some official document in Idleb, almost the entire population in the governorates of As-Sweida and Homs was able to obtain the desired documentation (about 99 percent). Lack of access to civil documentation was also grave for the populations of Lattakia, Tartous, and Ar-Raqqa (about 75 percent for all three governorates). In addition to geography, a person's displacement status also affects the ability to obtain civil documentation.

Figure 2.3. Security and Civil Documentation Nexus, Syrian Arab Republic

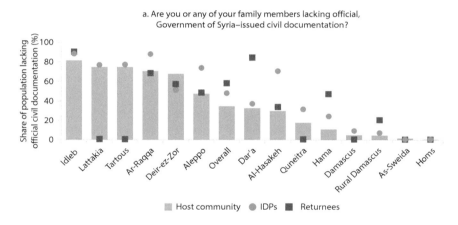

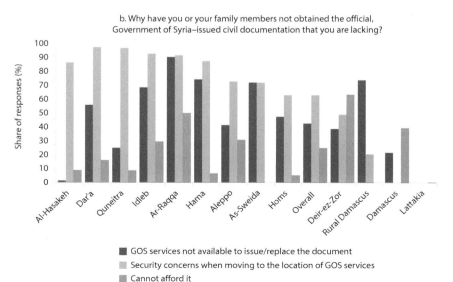

(figure continues next page)

Figure 2.3. *(continued)*

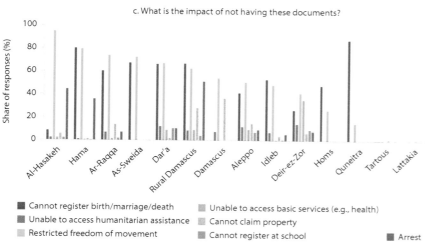

c. What is the impact of not having these documents?

Source: World Bank staff calculations based on data from UNOCHA 2018.
Note: Returnees refer to IDP returnees in this case. GOS = government of Syria; IDP = internally displaced person.

Almost 60 percent of the returnees and half of the internally displaced persons (IDPs) reported that they could not acquire at least one civil document, whereas for the host communities the figure drops to 35 percent. Additionally, a significant difference in outcomes for these three population groups can be observed within the same governorate. Notably, almost 85 percent of the returnees in Dar'a lack some form of civil documentation, whereas the figure for both the host community and the IDPs in the same governorate is about 35 percent. Similarly, IDPs in Aleppo and Al-Hasakeh are affected to a far greater extent (74 and 71 percent, respectively) than the other two groups in their governorate (about 30 and 48 percent, respectively).

Syrians attribute the marked lack of access to documentation to insecurity during travel (63 percent), unavailability of government services (43 percent), and prohibitive cost of the documents (25 percent). About 10 percent report that the process is too lengthy, 10 percent mentioned that they did not attempt to obtain the documentation at all, and about 5 percent report that discrimination or officials' abuse prevented them from obtaining documentation. Except for Damascus and Rural Damascus, security concerns during the travel required to acquire the official documentation ranked consistently as the top reason for its lack for every governorate. In fact, more than 90 percent of the respondents in Al-Hasakeh, Ar-Raqqa, As-Sweida, Dar'a, Hama, and Quneitra mentioned it as a constraint. Unavailability of government services is particularly important in Ar-Raqqa (90 percent), As-Sweida (72 percent), Hama (74 percent), Idleb (69 percent), and Rural Damascus (74 percent). The inability to afford the fee for the documentation appears to be an important factor for the residents of Deir-ez-Zor, Ar-Raqqa, Damascus, and Aleppo.

At the same time, the absence of civil documents makes Syrians more insecure. Official documents play important roles in the everyday lives of Syrians: absence of a document could mean restriction of movement, lack of access to basic services or humanitarian aid, and even arrest. Overall, about 45 percent of Syrians reported that their inability to obtain official documentation curtailed their freedom of movement, 36 percent stated that it led to inability to register a life event (birth, marriage, or death), an unexpected 9 percent claimed that it led to arrest, and about 7 percent mentioned it affected their ability to claim property or get access to humanitarian aid. The highest impact to the freedom of movement was experienced in Al-Hasakeh (95 percent), Hama (79 percent), Ar-Raqqa (74 percent), and As-Sweida (72 percent). In Quneitra and Hama 7 out 10 of those who were missing at least one official document were subsequently unable to register a life event. Notably, 35 percent of the affected residents of Deir-ez-Zor could not access health care as a result; however, this effect is not observed in any of the other governorates. Similarly, significant numbers of respondents attributed their arrest to lack of documentation in the governorates of Rural Damascus (51 percent), Al-Hasakeh (44 percent), and Hama (36 percent), whereas for the rest of the country this outcome is mentioned far more rarely.

Syrian women face greater risks and restricted mobility

Syrian women are disproportionately affected by insecurity. The conflict has exacerbated an already restrictive environment for women in Syria, reinforcing patriarchal traditions and attitudes. Syrian women face greater risks in access to livelihoods as well as in personal and family security. In particular, women's already legally restricted mobility has been further affected by rising concerns for safety and honor in the existing fragile and conflict-affected environment (figure 2.4). This restricted mobility is particularly challenging in an environment that also requires women to access services and markets or support systems at a greater

Figure 2.4. Groups Perceived to Have the Greatest Restrictions to Movement in the Syrian Arab Republic, 2016

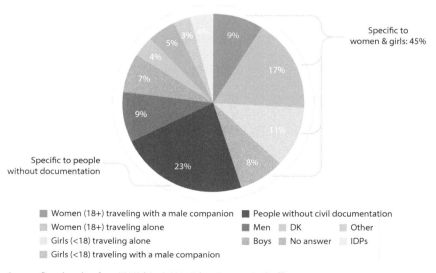

Source: Based on data from UN-Habitat's 2016 Urban Community Profiling survey.
Note: DK = Do not know; IDPs = internally displaced persons.

rate than before the conflict because men mostly engage outside the home, are on the frontlines, or have become victims of armed conflict. Assessments from inside Syria show that 12–17 percent of households are headed by women, up from 4.4 percent in 2009, with men in the family away or missing, injured, or perished in combat (CARE 2016). This has provided new channels of empowerment, albeit at a high cost as the shift in roles adds to the continuous responsibilities related to household and childcare.

The lack of security, economic and social opportunities, and protection measures has intensified exposure to gender-based violence among women and girls. Reports point to a major surge in the number of reported rape cases against women in Syria, from 300 in 2011 to 6,000 in 2013 (Euro-Mediterranean Human Rights Network 2013). These numbers reflect only the known cases claimed, and the crime is likely to be underreported. Forced abductions of young women and girls at checkpoints to spread shame and stigma upon their release (as weapons of war along with sexual violence) have also been reported. As a result, the fear of sexual violence and its consequences is one of the leading causes of displacement of many families. With weak to no enforcement and no legislation protecting women against violence (including domestic violence and marital rape), cases of gang rape, forced marriage to armed group fighters, trafficking, and sexual enslavement have all increased in scale and scope. Exacerbating the situation is the lack of services for survivors of violence, and few opportunities to overcome the stigma and alienation. An overwhelming majority of those surveyed (70 percent) across the country agree that there is a lack of clinical care for rape survivors. Only in Damascus is that figure below 50 percent.

Many families resort to negative coping mechanisms that have specific implications for women and girls. Syrian families adopt many mechanisms to cope with conflict. Among the most frequent—after reliance on aid and nongovernmental organization (NGO) support—is child marriage. Historically, child marriage was higher in Syria than its neighboring countries. Thirteen percent of girls were married by age 18 and 3 percent by age 15, compared to 6 and 1 percent, respectively, in Lebanon and 8 and 0 percent, respectively, in Jordan (UNICEF 2006, 2009, 2012). Adolescent fertility rates were high at approximately 45 births per 1,000 women age 15–19 in 2010 and have dropped only to 40 births in 2016, which is still higher than the regional average of 39 for 2012. To date, and according to internal reporting, the share of marriages among female minors surged from 7 percent in 2011 to about 15 percent a year later, hovering at 30 percent in 2015, with many of the forced marriages among girls to armed men to protect their families (SCLSR 2018). It is further estimated that about 60 percent of child marriages go unreported (Syrian Center for Legal Studies and Research 2018). Getting married earlier curtails a girl's education, minimizes her opportunities to access decent work, and increases her risk of domestic violence including spousal rape (HRGJ 2016). Moreover, the mortality rate of infants increases by 60 percent when mothers are under the age of 18.[1] As before the conflict, women and girls have no effective legal protections against domestic violence or criminalization of rape or marital rape and limited to no mechanisms available to file complaints. Generally, there is a lack of services to support survivors of domestic violence, although the first official shelter for battered women was opened in 2008 (World Bank 2009).

In the absence of adequate safety conditions, Syrians endure protracted displacement both inside and outside the country. The context for hosting Syrians in Iraq, Jordan, and Lebanon continues to include limited and unbalanced growth, heavy burdens on public services, and high unemployment rates among host populations and refugees, particularly among youth and women. Exhaustion of financial means and spirals of negative coping strategies for refugees are increasing, with most refugees living in poverty. Constraints on residency, employment, and freedom of movement in Jordan, Lebanon, Turkey, and increasingly in Iraq have increased Syrian refugees' vulnerability to exploitation. By July 2018, however, 85 percent of Syrian refugees surveyed as part of UNHCR's "Fourth Regional Survey on Syrian Refugees' Perceptions and Intentions on Return to Syria" reported that they have no intention to return within 12 months (UNHCR 2018a).

Livelihoods and Access to Employment

International experience shows that economic opportunities at origin can influence returns positively, but the effects of conditions in host countries are more complex. Chapter 1 argued that, other things being equal, refugees prefer to live in locations that present better livelihood opportunities. However, simplistic extrapolations of this observation are often misleading. A general deterioration of living conditions, declining economic opportunities in countries of asylum, and reduction or withdrawal of international assistance do not always induce repatriation. The factors that empower refugees in host countries can also enable them to return to their countries of origin. Education, employment, and training in the country of asylum, all of which could be perceived as supporting local integration, may help equip refugees to undertake sustainable return.

This section provides an overview of current economic conditions in Syria and in host countries. The analysis investigates the livelihood conditions in three dimensions: first, an analysis of the evolution of broad economic activities in Syria and Syrian refugees' business opportunities in host communities. Next, the job market conditions faced by Syrians in Syria and in host communities are analyzed. In this case, special attention is paid to institutional factors, such as labor market regulations. Finally, an attempt is made to compare poverty statistics within Syria with those of Syrians in Jordan and Lebanon. The analysis of these issues is constrained by data limitations, which bind at different degrees in different issues; therefore, some aspects are discussed in detail, whereas others are not.

Economic activity

In addition to public or philanthropic actions, the livelihoods and economic well-being of most Syrians depend on the level of broad economic activity. The ability of Syrians to find jobs and make a living largely depends on the extent to which economic systems can operate to connect producers with consumers and other producers. This section assesses these conditions by using currently available data, which lack up-to-date national and fiscal accounts and microdata on economic activity but include trade statistics from UN Comtrade and comprehensive agriculture surveys from WFP and FAO.

Conditions in Syria

The Syrian economy suffered heavy losses that were inflicted through multiple channels during the conflict. The destruction of physical capital, casualties, forced migration, and breaking up of economic networks have had devastating consequences for Syria's economic activity. By using data available in early 2017, the World Bank (2017) report *The Toll of War: The Economic and Social Consequences of the Conflict in Syria* estimated that Syria's gross domestic product (GDP) contracted by 63 percent between 2011 and 2016. Oil GDP declined by 93 percent during the same period, whereas the nonoil economy contracted by 52 percent because of the severe destruction of infrastructure, reduced access to fuel and electricity, low business confidence, and disruption in trade. Estimates of economic activity within Syria are hampered by the paucity and low quality of data, which are driven by the difficulty of measuring highly informal transactions. Relatively better-quality data are available for trade statistics because mirror records from trade partners can be used. A more detailed discussion of this topic follows.

Transportation statistics clearly reveal the collapse in economic activity. Syrian railways carried about 3.5 million people per year with more than 8.5 million tons of freight in 2010. The war exacted a heavy toll on the rail infrastructure, and only very limited operations have been resumed, with 3,294 passengers on the Hijaz Railway, and 600 thousand tons of goods carried in 2017 (figure 2.5).[2] Passenger traffic (and numbers of flights) had seen significant growth in the years preceding the crisis, reaching a maximum of about 2.5 million arrivals (and a similar number of departures) in 2010. With the onset of violence, passenger traffic fell to less than half a million in 2013, with modest growth in the years following (figure 2.6).

Although naval infrastructure remains undamaged, Syria's shipping sector has been dramatically impacted by reduced demand. Syria is served by two primary ports along its Mediterranean coastline, in Lattakia and Tartous. These ports served as gateways into the Syrian economy, and as hubs for the transit of goods onward into Iraq and other neighboring countries. Although the conflict has not touched either port, both have seen steep declines in total activity, with

73

Figure 2.5. Merchandise Transported through Railway, Syrian Arab Republic

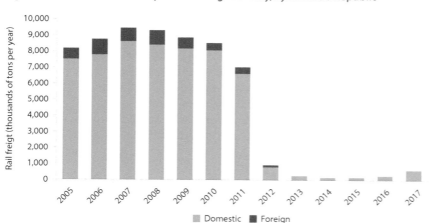

Source: Based on data from the Syrian Ministry of Transport, http://www.mot.gov.sy/web/main.php.

Figure 2.6. Aviation Passengers, Syrian Arab Republic

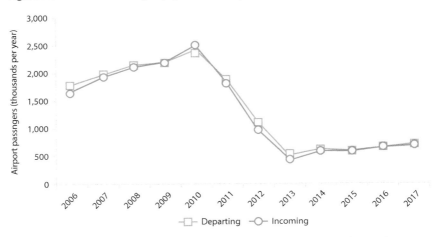

Source: Based on data from the Syrian Ministry of Transport, http://www.mot.gov.sy/web/main.php.

current activity at only about one-third of precrisis levels (figure 2.7). The use of the ports for transit has practically ceased, while exports and imports are at only 23 percent and 40 percent of their 2010 levels, respectively. Additionally, the Tartous port was affected by the collapse in phosphate exports due to the conflict and the destruction of the rail network. It is now used as a military naval facility.

Trade statistics confirm the extent of the economic collapse: Syria's exports have crashed since the commencement of the conflict. The latest UN Comtrade data show that Syrian receipts from exports fell from a value of US$19 billion in 2010 to US$745 million in 2016—just over 10 percent of the earlier level (figure 2.8)

In 2010, Syrian exports were highly concentrated within two main sectors: travel and tourism (32.5 percent basket share) and crude petroleum (22.3 percent basket share) (figure 2.9). In that year, the crude oil destination markets were mainly Italy and Germany. By 2014, crude oil exports had dropped to US$52 million and Syria was exporting crude oil only to India. By 2016, there were no official crude or refined oil exports, which resulted in the drop of Syria's total export value by almost 10-fold. Not all sectors suffered a collapse in exports, though. Syria's exports of virgin olive oil increased from US$57.8 million (0.3 percent basket share) in 2010 to US$65 million (9 percent basket share) by 2016. The exports of anise, fennel, and the like have also slightly increased, from US$73 million (2.8 percent basket share) in 2010 to US$78.6 million (17.5 percent basket share) in 2016.

The conflict slashed Syrian exports to all destinations, but some were slashed more radically. In 2010, the top five destinations for Syrian exports of mer-chandise were Iraq (19.6 percent), Germany (12.5 percent), Italy (12.3 percent), Turkey (5.4 percent), and Saudi Arabia (4.6 percent). Together, they accounted for about US$6.4 billion in export revenues. By 2016, however, they totaled less

Figure 2.7. Shipping Activity at Primary Ports, Syrian Arab Republic

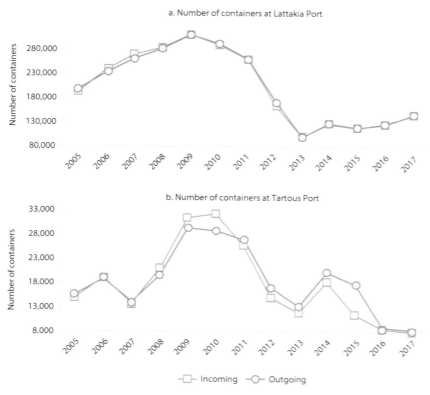

a. Number of containers at Lattakia Port

b. Number of containers at Tartous Port

—□— Incoming   —○— Outgoing

Source: Based on data from Syrian Ministry of Transport, http://www.mot.gov.sy/web/main.php.

than US$0.2 billion. Some other markets shrank less dramatically. The exports to Egypt fell from US$374 million in 2010 to US$122 million in 2016. The latter comprised mainly agricultural products such as apples and pears (27 percent), spices and other oily seeds (25 percent), pitted fruits (11 percent), and natural resources like refined copper (8 percent) and nonretail pure cotton yarn (7 percent) (see figure 2.9).[3] It is important to note that these outcomes could be driven by necessity (for example, the result of economic forces) or by choice (for example, policy decisions like procurement restrictions; see box 2.1).

Syria's oil production was particularly hit by conflict. Since 2011 the oil sector has been in disarray, with the country facing a shortage of refined products and with oil exports all but ceasing. Despite averaging roughly 400,000 barrels per day (b/d) from 2008 to 2010, as of May 2015 Syrian oil production was less than 25,000 b/d because of the ongoing conflict, a drop of over 90 percent in production. In 2002, the all-time peak production stood at 677,000 b/d and fell to a nadir of 15,000 as of February 2018 (figure 2.10). In total, Syria has 2.5 billion barrels of proven crude oil reserves. Daily petroleum consumption in 2013 stood at 224,000 b/d. Before the conflict, the oil and gas sector accounted for roughly one-fourth of government revenues, revenues that have largely dissipated with the collapse of production and exporting. Although the country exported a

Figure 2.8. Dynamics of Syrian Trade before and during Conflict

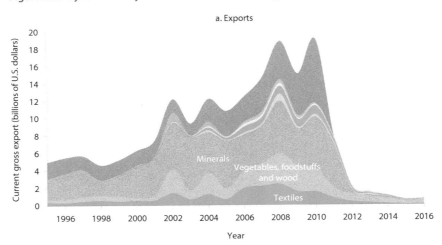

a. Exports

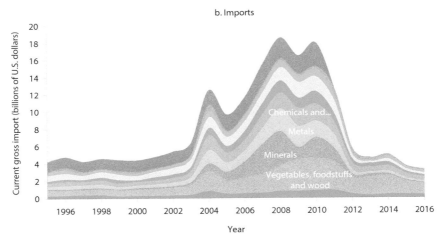

b. Imports

Source: Atlas of Economic Complexity, Center for International Development at Harvard University (accessed September 2018), http://atlas.cid.harvard.edu/.

modest 36,000 b/d in 2010, by 2012 domestic demand outpaced supply, and Syria became a net oil importer.

The country's refining capacity was already less than adequate before the conflict; during the conflict, half its refining capacity was lost. Syria has two state-owned oil refineries, one in Homs and the other in Baniyas—overseen by the Syrian Petroleum Company, the country's largest state-owned enterprise—with a combined capacity of roughly 240,000 b/d as of 2015. This capacity met only roughly three-fourths of preconflict Syria's refined products demand. With damage resulting from the conflict, the country's actual refining capacity stands closer to 120,000 b/d, roughly

Figure 2.9. The Composition of Syrian Exports, by Type and Destination, 2010 vs. 2016

a. Main export destination in 2010 (US$11.7 billion)

b. Main export destination in 2016 (US$745 million)

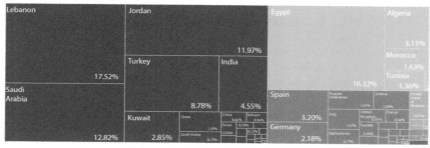

c. Main export in 2010 (US$19.0 billion)

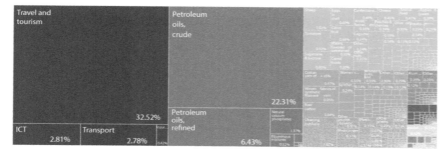

d. Main export in 2016 (US$745 million)

Source: Atlas of Economic Complexity, Center for International Development at Harvard University (accessed in September 2018), http://atlas.cid.harvard.edu/.

BOX 2.1.

Public Procurement in the Syrian Arab Republic

In theory, public procurement can shape trade and economic activity during conflict; however, access to meaningful and comprehensive information on public procurement has been limited. This study reviewed relevant laws and regulations enacted after 2011 and analyzed 1,511 tenders from different areas (Aleppo, Al-Hasakeh and Kobani, Damascus, Homs, and Qamishli) published in 2017 and 2018 through government and United Nations agencies procurement websites, as well as relevant published articles. Although more procurement/tender notices are published through government websites, tender documents, evaluation results, and contract award notices are often not published.

Ninety-six percent of the tenders were controlled by the Syrian government at the subcentral/municipal level. The available data do not include estimated costs or contract values, so it is not possible to assess whether the latter distribution would change for larger contract values. Figure B2.1.1 shows a distribution of the 1,511 tenders/contracts by geographic area and service delivery sector. The distribution of tenders by sector did not vary significantly over geographic locations. Health and power had the highest shares of tenders in most areas followed by education; however, in the absence of information on estimated costs/contract values, such distribution could be misleading.

The analyzed tenders were mostly competitive, with some explicitly containing nationality-based limitations. Twenty-eight contracts were awarded on a single-source basis in Aleppo, Damascus, and Homs primarily in the

Figure B2.1.1. Distribution of Tenders, Syrian Arab Republic, 2017–18

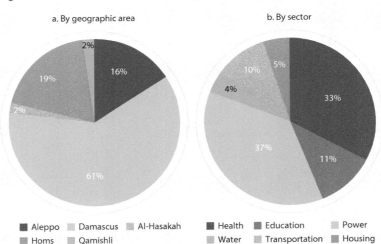

a. By geographic area

b. By sector

Aleppo   Damascus   Al-Hasakah   Health   Education   Power
Homs   Qamishli   Water   Transportation   Housing

(box continues next page)

power sector but also in the health and water sectors. The awards were mainly directed to companies from China, the Islamic Republic of Iran, and the Russian Federation; but awards to companies from the Arab Republic of Egypt, Lebanon, and Turkey were also noted. When competitive methods were used, it was not possible to assess to what extent there was obvious favoritism through directing the procurement opportunities to certain companies or countries. In a few instances, however, the tender notices specifically mentioned that participation is restricted to Iranian companies and others that excluded goods manufactured in Turkey.

The core procurement legislation (Law No. 51) has not changed, but several related laws have been enacted. An important step in the wider procurement legal framework is the enactment of the Public–Private Partnership Law No. 5 of 2016, which addresses some key issues regarding public–private partnerships in a comprehensive manner. It may play a role in reconstruction operations, whenever that may happen. Also, the enactment of Law No. 107 of 2011 (Local Administration, which authorizes procurement of certain projects at the local level and enacts decentralization) and Law No. 10 of 2018 (which governs the allocation of land, including possibly for development projects) are important developments; the latter is analyzed in more detail later in this chapter.

Figure 2.10. Oil Production, Syrian Arab Republic, 2006–17

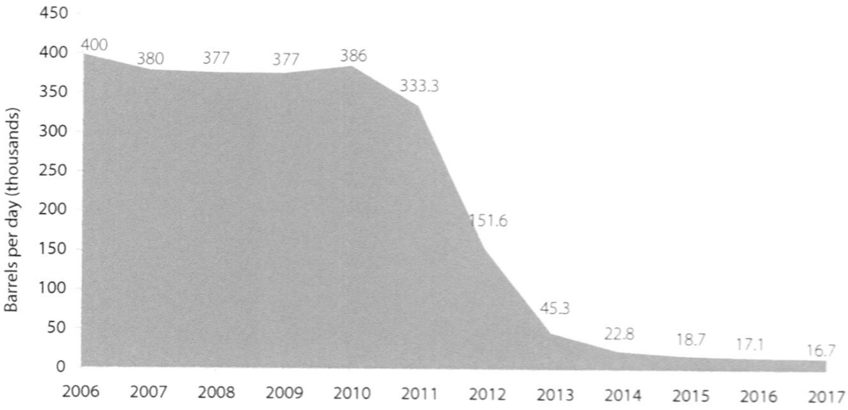

Source: Based on data from the CEIC database, https://www.ceicdata.com/en/indicator/syria/crude-oil-production.

50 percent of its prewar capacity. "Artisanal," or improvised, oil refining in the vacuum left by defunct oil refineries has caused significant environmental degradation and public health crises in regions of Syria. In late January 2018, the government of Syria signed an energy cooperation framework giving Russia exclusive rights to produce oil and gas in Syria, also stipulating rehabilitation modalities for damaged

oil sector infrastructure, serving as an energy advisory, and training a new generation of Syrian oil workers. In addition to repairing the substantial damage to Syria's
two existing refineries, the Islamic Republic of Iran announced plans to construct a
US$1 billion oil refinery with a capacity of 140,000 b/d in Homs after the war.

Conflict shaped agricultural activity in multiple ways, including effects through
land-use change, market prices, and availability of inputs and labor. The reduction in agricultural activity has been widespread and affected crops (particularly
barley and wheat), vegetables, and fruit production. Cultivated land decreased
from an average area of 4.7 million hectares (ha) (85 percent of the total cultivated land) between 2005 and 2010 to an average of 4.2 million ha (64 percent
of the total cultivated land) between 2011 and 2015. Fallow land increased by
56 percent in the same period, reaching 1.5 million ha between 2011 and 2015.
The production of barley and wheat, which together account for approximately
60 percent of the cultivated land in Syria, dropped significantly since 2011. The
cultivated area of wheat declined from 1.6 million ha in 2010 to 1 million ha
in 2017, a decline of 38 percent (figure 2.11). This caused a reduction in wheat
production of approximately 1.3 million tons. Wheat yield also declined from
1.93 tons/ha in 2010 to 1.79 tons/ha in 2017. The decline in the cultivated area
accounts for approximately 60 percent of the decline in wheat production, and

Figure 2.11. Decline of Cereal Production, Syrian Arab Republic, 2008–17

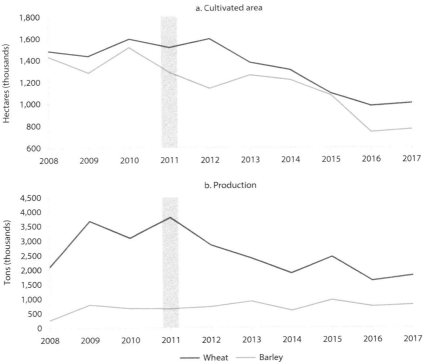

Source: World Bank staff calculations using data from the Food and Agriculture Organization of the United
Nations (www.fao.org/faostat/en/#country/212).

the reduction in yields accounts for approximately 40 percent of the decrease in wheat production since the start of the Syrian conflict. These declines indicate that the sector's infrastructure and capability in areas where wheat production takes place were significantly affected by the conflict. Limited access to basic inputs including seeds and fertilizer and damaged/reduced collection centers significantly affected barley production in Syria.[4]

Vegetable production was also affected by the conflict, but the reduction in cultivated area was relatively smaller compared to the impact on crop land. The total area used to grow lentils, chickpeas, fava beans, and peas declined from a peak of 235,000 ha in 2011 to 203,000 ha in 2017, a reduction of 14 percent. The production of lentils declined significantly from 2011 to 2016 but experienced an increase of 25 percent from 2016 to 2017. Chickpea production continues to decline, from 74,000 ha in 2011 to 56,000 ha in 2017. It is worth noticing, however, that the area used to grow fava beans and peas increased from 17,000 ha and 4,000 ha in 2011 to 19,000 ha and 5,000 ha in 2017, respectively. The cultivated area of summer crops and vegetables including cotton, sugar beet, watermelon, and tomato was also significantly affected by the war. The area used to grow cotton declined from an average of 193,129 ha between 2005 and 2010 to an average of 104,677 ha between 2011 and 2015, a reduction of 46 percent (table 2.2). During the same period, the decline in cultivated area was 57 percent for sugar beets, 27 percent for tomato, 37 percent for watermelon, 19 percent for maize, and 11 percent for potato.

Cultivation of fruit trees increased despite the conflict. The cultivated area of fruit trees increased by 12 percent from 2005–10 to 2011–15, reaching 1.05 million ha or 18 percent of the total cultivated land in Syria. Among the main fruit trees, olives, grapes, apples, and pistachios experienced the most significant increase

Table 2.2. Average Cultivated Area of Main Summer Crops, Vegetables, and Fruit Trees, Syrian Arab Republic

	Summer crops and vegetables	Average 2005–10 (hectares)	Average 2011–15 (hectares)	Percentage change 2005–10 vs. 2011–15
Summer crops and vegetables	Cotton	193,129	104,677	−46
	Sugar beet	26,540	11,493	−57
	Tomato	14,365	10,479	−27
	Watermelon	28,416	17,962	−37
	Maize	52,580	42,384	−19
	Potato	32,282	28,891	−11
Fruit trees	Olive	601,716	693,920	15
	Grape	54,544	38,626	−29
	Apple	47,708	52,084	9
	Pistachio	56,444	60,114	7
	Almond	62,990	71,591	14

Source: World Bank staff calculations using data from the Food and Agriculture Organization of the United Nations (http://www.fao.org/faostat/en/#country/212).

81

in cultivated area since the conflict started. Total average surface area of olive trees increased by 15 percent, reaching 693,920 ha on average between 2011 and 2015, which represents 66 percent of total surface area cultivated with fruit trees. From 2005–10 to 2011–15, the area used for apple production increased by 9 percent, pistachio by 7 percent, and almond by 14 percent. The total average surface area allocated for grapes, however, decreased by 29 percent during this period.

There has been a significant change in yields for crops, including vegetables and fruit trees, since the war started in Syria. Average annual yields for maize, chickpeas, lentils, sugar beets, watermelon, and olives increased from 2005–10 to 2011–15. For instance, maize average yield increased from 4,930 kg/ha during 2005–10 to 5,648 kg/ha during 2011–15, an increase of 15 percent. In contrast, there was a significant decline in yields for cotton, tomatoes, grapes, almonds, and pistachios during this period. For instance, cotton average yield decreased from an average of 3,641 kg/ha during 2005–10 to 3,041 kg/ha during 2011–15, and tomato yield decreased from 43,228 kg/ha during 2005–10 to 35,034 kg/ha during 2011–15, a decrease of 19 percent. The significant decline in yield for key crops is related to the damage to agricultural infrastructure as well as to out-migration from rural areas, which reduced labor availability.

Livestock production, like agriculture, has been affected by the conflict, but the changes in the size of the herd and production differ by animal type. From 2005–10 to 2011–15, Syria saw a decline in the total number of cattle and sheep raised, and in milk production from both cattle and sheep. During the same period, however, cattle meat production increased about 6 percent compared to a decline of 12 percent in sheep meat production. Conversely, the number of goats raised increased 40 percent, goat milk production increased 38 percent, and goat meat production increased 52 percent. In addition, poultry farming decreased 20 percent and fish production collapsed, falling from 15,799 metric tons in 2005–10 to 5,802 metric tons in 2011–15, a reduction of 63 percent in production. The number of beehives and amount of honey production stayed about the same during this period.

Conditions in countries of asylum

Although no official information is available, anecdotal evidence points to a remarkable tendency among Syrian refugees to establish businesses wherever they are. Displaced Syrians' entrepreneurship potential can be categorized into three basic groups: (a) entrepreneurs (including those with a social capital orientation) with capital and a viable firm, (b) potential investors with capital but not presently operating a business, and (c) investors who may have had a business but have very little capital and if operating are doing so in a very constrained manner. Within this framework, most of the action to date has been in the first category. There have been some very modest efforts in the last category, and no more than talk in the second category.

Some Syrian firms simply relocated to their markets. In terms of entrepreneurs with capital and a viable firm, there are many examples in the Arab Republic of Egypt, Jordan, and Turkey of firms originally based in Syria that have relocated their existing markets and capital they have been able to preserve through monetary or physical means. In Turkey it is estimated there are 10,000 such formal and informal firms. Similar movement took place in Egypt and Jordan, proportionate to the number of refugees. For example, the small Jordanian border town of Mafraq has 160 Syrian merchants. Official 2013 data showed 499 businesses with Syrian shareholders (Freihat 2014). This kind of entrepreneurial behavior is found often with refugees and economic migrants. For example, recent work by Aston University notes that in the United Kingdom ethnic minorities and economic migrants have double the rate of entrepreneurship compared with the residual population (Shami 2019).

Syrian diaspora businesses face distinct challenges. In 2017 the World Bank conducted a survey of the Syrian diaspora business community, with 185 responses from investors, business owners, or those who belonged to senior management, asking them about the major challenges they faced.[5] Figure 2.12 shows the results for Jordan and Lebanon, and other countries are included for comparison purposes. Overall only 29 percent felt they were treated the same as host country firms. Leveling the regulatory playing field is an important area they identified. These issues range from getting a business license to getting a driver's license, and they vary across countries. In Jordan, 35 percent of respondents reported the hiring quota for Syrians to be a major obstacle. In both Jordan and Lebanon, registering a business was reported to be one of the most important obstacles (29 percent and 30 percent, respectively). Mobility issues for businesspeople are also an important challenge. In every country, most respondents indicated that obtaining visa and travel documents was a problem. This problem is especially challenging for firms engaged in exports, which need to connect with their markets.

In Jordan, Syrians are not allowed to register a standalone enterprise without a Jordanian partner and are prohibited from owning businesses in several sectors. According to instructions issued on behalf of the Prime Minister's office in March 2018, as with other businesses, Syrians are not allowed to register a home-based business without a Jordanian partner; an exception is camp residents, who are able

Figure 2.12. Obstacles to Business

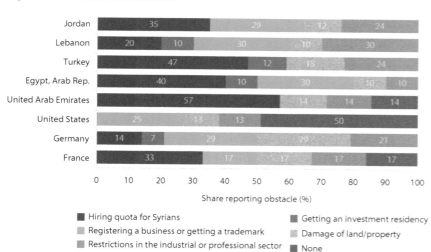

Source: Competitive Industries and Innovation Program 2017, https://www.theciip.org/content/jordan.

to register their businesses independently but are prohibited from selling their products outside the camp. Additionally, Syrian-owned home-based businesses are not allowed to receive small business grants from NGOs. The Jordan Investment Commission's instruction prohibits foreigners from owning businesses in key areas including food preparation, handicrafts, tailoring, and hairdressing (areas where women are traditionally active).

The financial sector generates several specific challenges. The displaced are often caught up in a complex web of financial rules and regulations designed to prevent money laundering and antiterrorist financing: banks are required to "know their customers." In some cases, displaced people find it hard to comply with these requirements, which makes it difficult for them to open bank accounts, make international payments for goods, or obtain trade financing or any other form of credit. In Lebanon, 67 percent of respondents reported opening a bank account as a major obstacle against their businesses. In Jordan, this obstacle was limited to 38 percent of respondents. In comparison, making an international transfer is the second-most important problem in Jordan (31 percent), and is somewhat less problematic in Lebanon (17 percent). See figure 2.13.

Despite these obstacles, the diaspora firms survive, and many are successful. Many of them are interested in making further investments in host countries either directly (24 percent) or through some form of intermediary (52 percent). The diaspora is equally willing to invest in Syria. About 70 percent of those who had businesses in Syria indicated a willingness to return if conditions change. With a gradual easing of some of these constraints faced by Syrian entrepreneurs, potential investors with capital who are not currently operating a business and those investors who may have had a business but now have little capital can also become active investors again.

Figure 2.13. Obstacles around Financial Transactions

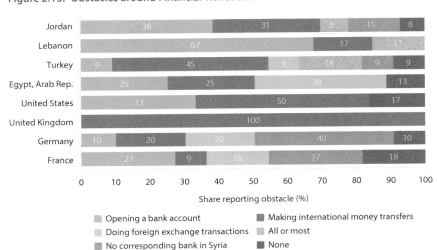

Source: Competitive Industries and Innovation Program 2017, https://www.theciip.org/content/jordan.

Employment

A systematic analysis of job market conditions is hampered by the absence of comprehensive data in both Syria and in host communities for Syrian refugees. In Syria,
the latest official statistics regarding aggregate employment trends are from 2015
and lack granularity. Thus, the analysis uses HNAP surveys to complement official
statistics. In host communities, informality of refugee work is the main problem. To
cope with this problem, multiple sources of data have been used. For Jordan, these
include UNHCR Vulnerability Assessments, the JLMPS (JPRSC 2016), Jordan DOS
Job Creation Surveys (2016), and Employment and Unemployment Surveys (first
quarter 2018). The data for Iraq are extracted from the UNHCR-led MSNA III report
(UNHCR 2017c), which is based on the survey conducted in September 2017 and
the UNHCR registration data of Syrians in the Kurdistan Region of Iraq (2018).

Conditions in Syria

Forced displacement and economic collapse have translated into dramatic
changes in scale and composition of employment opportunities in Syria.
An estimated 2.4 million net jobs were lost from 2010 to 2015 (Central Bureau of
Statistics 2017). The figure accounted only for government-controlled regions
and was therefore a lower estimate for destroyed jobs.[6] Construction and industry were the sectors that suffered the greatest loss: 8.5 percent and 10.7 percent
of workers were employed in these two industries in 2015, respectively, compared to 16 percent in 2010. This decline corresponded to a total of about
1.15 million lost jobs in construction and industry, accounting for 47 percent of
total net jobs destroyed between 2010 and 2015. Agriculture also decreased its
employment share from 14.3 percent in 2010 to 9.5 percent in 2015, accounting
for a loss of 19.5 percent of net jobs. Services in contrast increased its employment share from 25 percent to 46 percent but still shed about 41,000 jobs
(1.67 percent of total net jobs destroyed).

Since the onset of the conflict, the unemployment rate has increased despite significant reductions in the labor force. In the decade preceding the conflict, Syria
had a large (and increasing) share of the population entering working age, and
thus the size of the labor force would have continued to increase in absolute
terms. According to World Development Indicators (WDI), however, between 2010
and 2015 the working-age population decreased by about 1.8 million, leading
to a decrease of about 930 thousand individuals in the labor force. Despite such
a dramatic decrease in potential job seekers, and as employment opportunities
shrank more dramatically, unemployment increased. Estimates varied widely for
unemployment rates. The Syrian Centre for Policy Research estimated it at about
57.7 percent at the end of 2014 (SCPR 2015). Using WDI labor force figures and
employment figures from the Central Bureau of Statistics, unemployment was
estimated to be also about 46 percent.[7] Conversely, an International Labour
Organization estimate of the overall unemployment rate reported in the WDI data
was only 15 percent in 2015. Further, recent employment-to-population ratios from
HNAP (UNOCHA 2018) data suggest that unemployment rates are in the low range,
which is partly due to the significant presence of underemployment or occasional
work. Because of the large variation in estimates, the exact figure on the extent
of the increase in unemployment rates remains unknown. Nonetheless, it is clear
from the data that unemployment has become a bigger challenge since 2010, and
that it has primarily affected females, especially female youth (figure 2.14).

85

Figure 2.14. Unemployment Rate, Syrian Arab Republic, by Gender and Age, 2010, 2014, and 2017

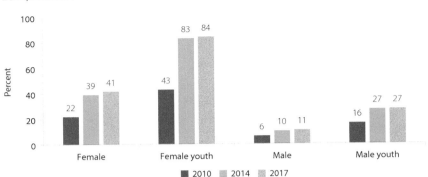

Source: Based on data from World Development Indicators. https://datacatalog.worldbank.org/dataset/world -development-indicators.
Note: Youth are individuals ages 15 to 24 years.

By 2018, the uneven incidence of conflict across the Syrian land has been fully manifested in a spatial translation of employment dynamics. With the displacement of people, economic activity was also displaced, although at a slower scale because economic activity often has inputs that are less mobile, such as land and networks. Overall, conflict led to lower employment and high unemployment in high-conflict-intensity areas as security concerns dominated other economic considerations. In the meantime, it led to somewhat higher employment in relatively safer areas as displaced people poured in. However, unemployment also soared in those IDP-receiving areas because many displaced people could not find employment rapidly. According to 2018 HNAP data, Rural Damascus, Aleppo, and Damascus had the highest employment shares at about 15 percent, whereas Quneitra, As-Sweida, Ar-Raqqa, and Deir-ez-Zor had the lowest at about 2–3 percent (figure 2.15) (UNOCHA 2018).

In Syria, women's participation in the economy was extremely low and deteriorating in the years before the conflict. By 2010, the female labor force participation (LFP) rate in Syria was 13 percent (the second-lowest rate in the world; the lowest rate was in Yemen), having dropped from about 20 percent a decade earlier (according to data from WDI). For young women, the LFP rate dropped to 9 percent in 2010. Although the LFP rate was also declining for men, their share was significantly larger at 73 percent for men above 15 years of age and 50 percent for young men (ages 15–24).

Conflict has had different and nuanced effects on the economic participation of women. The recent HNAP numbers show that the ratio of employment to working-age population of women (those who remained within Syria) increased to 21.4 percent by 2018. But this aggregate number hides an interesting nuance. In areas with lower incidence of conflict, women have become relatively more active economically, filling in for the missing men. Damascus, Rural Damascus, and Lattakia retained an important share of the employed Syrian women among the governorates in 2018. In contrast, in areas with high incidence of conflict, women were further isolated from economic participation. Al-Hasakeh had one

Figure 2.15. Syrian Arab Republic Governorates' Shares in Total Employment, 2011 and 2018

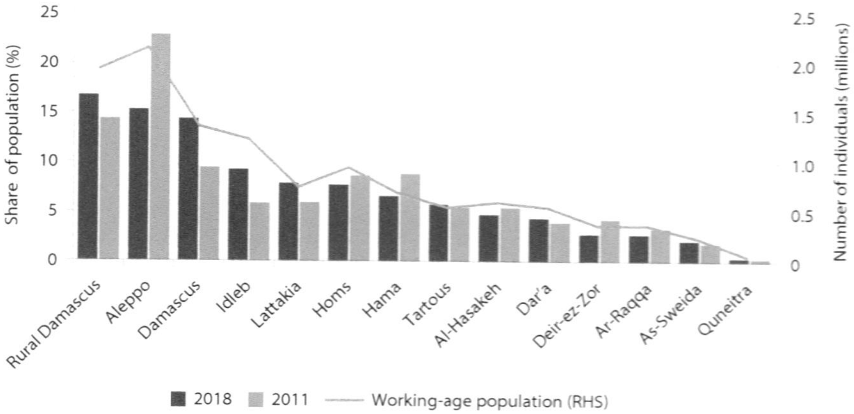

Sources: Based on 2011 data from the Central Bureau of Statistics 2011 and data from UNOCHA 2018.
Note: Employment includes the underemployed, defined as occasional work.

of the highest LFP rates for women among the governorates at 31 percent in 2010, mainly engaged in services and agriculture industries. In 2018, however, its share in the overall employment of Syrian women was only 3 percent (figure 2.16). Ar-Raqqa, Idleb, Dar'a, Deir-ez-Zor, As-Sweida, and Quneitra also employed less than 3 percent of the working women in Syria.

The conflict has further exacerbated the high unemployment rates among young women, and women in general. Overall, the female unemployment rate increased from 22 percent in 2010 to 41 percent in 2017, which compares to men at 6 percent in 2010 and 11 percent in 2017 (figure 2.14). Massive lay-offs and closures of a significant number of factories and firms, high informality as a coping mechanism, and significant movement of people and economic activities from conflict zones into relatively stable and safer ones resulted in increased joblessness and high regional inequality in labor market outcomes. Women were particularly affected in the agriculture sector, where the share of female employment dropped an average of 60 percent from 2001 to 2017.

Conditions in countries of asylum

Multiple sources of data have been used to compare the labor market outcomes of Syrian refugees in host countries with the citizens of that country, their preconflict situation in Syria, and, to the best extent possible, the current status quo in Syria. Because of such differences between the datasets, labor market indicators are calculated differently for the three host countries: Jordan, Lebanon, and the Kurdistan Region of Iraq.

Jordan

The Jordanian Labor Law prioritizes hiring Jordanian nationals over foreigners unless the required skill is not found among national job seekers. Foreign workers who meet this condition must obtain permission to work from the Ministry of Labor (MOL), at the risk of being deported or detained.[8] As of June 2015, however,

Figure 2.16. Syrian Arab Republic Governorates' Shares in Total Employment, by Gender, 2018

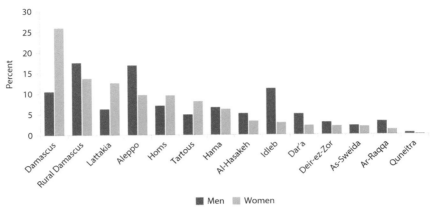

Source: Based on data from UNOCHA 2018.

Figure 2.17. Ratios of Employment to Working-Age Population, by Governorate and Gender, 2018

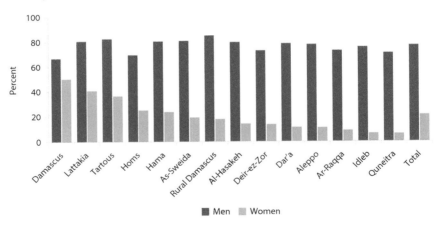

Source: Based on data from UNOCHA 2018.

Syrian refugees found without work permits are no longer being deported.[9] Under these circumstances, the benefits to Syrians of holding a work permit consist of protection under the Jordanian Labor Law (including the right to a work contract and minimum wage) and avoiding detention (ILO 2017a).[10]

In the context of the refugee crisis, closed occupations and sector quotas are used to promote "Jordanization" of the labor force. Although these mechanisms were developed during the crisis, they apply to all foreign workers regardless of refugee status. Occupations closed to non-Jordanians are laid out in an MOL

Figure 2.18. Time Line of Labor Regulations, Jordan

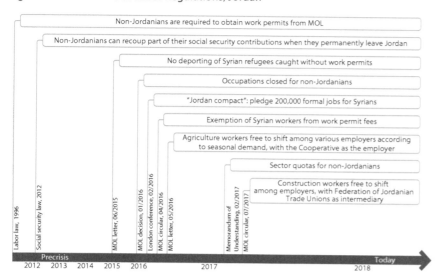

Sources: Jordan Labor Code, 1996; Ministry of Labor (MOL) letter dated June 7, 2015 (Ref. No L/1/6868) and MOL letter dated March 1, 2016 (Ref. No. L/1/2389); Circular 98/2017 dated March 16, 2017 (Ref. No. TM/1/1/481); Circular 126/2017 dated April 10, 2017 (Ref. No. TM/1/1/6486); Jordan Social Security Law of 2012, Article 11; MOL letter dated February 8, 2016 (Ref. No. L/1/1449); MOL letter dated April 14, 2016 (Ref. No. L/1/4945); MOL letter dated May 22, 2016 (Ref. No. L/1/6751); Circular 249/2017 dated July 23, 2017 (Ref. No. TM/1/1/13997).

decision dated January 4, 2016. Open sectors include manufacturing, construction, and agriculture; closed sectors include sales, education, hairdressing, and most professional sectors such as engineering and medicine.[11] In addition, sector quotas are delineated in a series of memoranda of understanding and range from 5 percent of foreign workers in the curative industries, to 85 percent in semiautomated bakeries. In closed occupations and beyond specified quotas, employers are prohibited from hiring qualified Syrians or other non-Jordanians even when qualified Jordanians are not available. Employers, however, find ways to evade these regulations by hiring workers informally, by obtaining permits for them under an "open" occupation, or by adding Jordanian "ghost workers" to the payroll (ILO 2017b).

Besides quotas and closed occupations, the government has taken measures to ease access of Syrian refugees to formal employment. In February 2016, as part of the "Jordan Compact," the government of Jordan pledged to provide formal work opportunities to 200,000 Syrian refugees. To facilitate the work permit application process, most financial costs associated with work permits for Syrians have been temporarily waived, and Syrian workers are exempted from a series of medical checkups.[12] Although prior to the initiative documentation was a serious barrier to work permit access for Syrians (work permits require a passport to register), Syrian refugees are now able to use their identity card from the Ministry of Interior. An estimated 105,404 work permits were issued from January 2016 to June 2018. Of these permits, 29 percent were issued in the agriculture sector, 43 percent in construction, and 11 percent in manufacturing. Syrian women have obtained only 4 percent of the total permits issued nationwide to Syrians as of August 2018 (Syrian Ministry of Labour 2018).

Despite the government's efforts to increase the number of work permits as part of the Jordan Compact, many Syrians in Jordan preferred to work informally. Costs associated with social security contributions are frequently a motivation for this preference and are also behind the high informality rate of Jordanian workers.[13] Another obstacle to formal employment is the standard work permit system, which ties the worker to a single employer/sponsor (ILO 2017b). Regulations laid out in the Instructions of 2012 prohibit workers from leaving their employer without explicit agreement from the latter, leaving workers vulnerable to exploitation.[14] Furthermore, agriculture and construction, the sectors in which Syrian workers are most active, are both inherently short term and informal.

The MOL has adapted work permit regulations to address the short-term and informal nature of jobs in agriculture and construction. As of May 2016, Syrian agricultural workers no longer need a contract with an individual employer/sponsor and can submit their own application and work permit fees through an Agricultural Cooperative.[15] Under this scheme, workers are free to move among various employers, with the Cooperative listed as the employer on the work permit. In 2017, a similar scheme was established for construction workers, using the General Federation of Jordanian Trade Unions as the intermediary between workers and the MOL.[16] However, workers shift across sectors on a seasonal basis (for example, between agriculture and construction), which is not possible under the existing schemes.[17]

The authorities' efforts to amend work permit regulations seem to have had a positive impact on Syrian refugees' employment. Sources on employment estimates vary widely for Syrian refugees in Jordan, ranging from 20 percent to 50 percent depending on the year the surveys were conducted. The most recent data from the 2017 VAF survey estimate that one-half of Syrian refugee working-age men were employed in the last seven days, 13 percent wanted to work but could not find a job, 9 percent were registered as full-time students, and the remaining 13 percent did not wish or were unavailable to work (UNHCR 2017b).[18] Unemployment, though, is still relatively high for Syrian refugee men. In 2017, it reached 20.5 percent, higher than Jordanian men's unemployment rate of 16 percent. Syrian men prior to the conflict in 2009 had a much lower unemployment rate of 5.8 percent nationally and even lower in Dar'a (3.5 percent) where a large share of Syrian refugees come from.

Data do not provide evidence for greater economic participation of refugee women in Jordan. The refugee workforce in Jordan consists largely of men, and the small share of women joining the labor force face high unemployment rates. In 2017, about 78.5 percent of UNHCR-registered Syrian refugee women did not want to or were unavailable to work in the past seven days and were not students.[19]

Only 5 percent of UNHCR-registered Syrian refugee women were employed, 8 percent wanted to work but could not find employment, and 8.5 percent were full-time students. Out of the 13 percent of women who joined the labor force, about 60 percent were unemployed (figure 2.19). This share is in contrast to men, of whom 63 percent participated in the labor force and 20.5 percent were unemployed; however, it is similar to the rate that was prevalent in preconflict Syria in 2009 at 13 percent and the estimated current rate in Syria (12 percent). It is also only slightly lower than the current rate of Jordanian women (15.2 percent in the first quarter of 2018; see table 2.3).

A large share of Syrian refugee men remains employed informally without obtaining work permits or without contracts. Estimates from the VAF showed that only 34 percent of employed Syrian men have a work permit, which they obtained mostly through employers or unions depending on the sector and regulations (figure 2.19). The JLMPS estimated a higher share of 43 percent (for both genders), which still suggested that 57 percent of employed Syrian refugees did not have

Figure 2.19. Work Status of Preconflict Syrians, Syrian Refugees in Jordan, and Jordanians

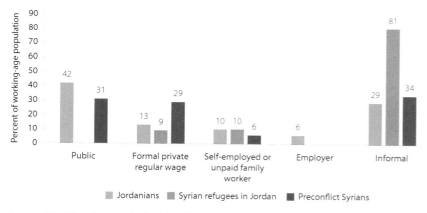

Source: Calculations based on Jordan Labor Market Panel Survey 2016 data; Central Bureau of Statistics 2007.

Table 2.3. Labor Force Participation and Unemployment Rates, Estimates from Various Sources

	Syrian Arab Republic (2009)	Syrian Arab Republic (2017 or latest)	Dar'a (2009)	Syrian refugees in Jordan (2017)	Jordanians (2018)
Men's LFPR	71	79.1	67.8	63.3	57.4
Women's LFPR	13.3	11.9	6.91	13.1	15.2
Men's UR	5.78	11	3.48	20.5	16
Women's UR	23.7	41	9.9	59.9	27.8

Sources: Data for Syria 2009 come from Central Bureau of Statistics 2009; Syria 2017 or latest data come from World Bank World Development Indicators 2017 (https://datacatalog.worldbank.org/dataset/world-development-indicators); data for Syrian refugees in Jordan come from UNHCR 2017b; 2018 data for Jordanians come from the Jordan Department of Statistics (dosweb.dos.gov.jo/labourforce/employment-and-unemployment).
Note: LFPR = labor force participation rate; UR = unemployment rate.

a work permit despite the ease of regulations (Jordan Department of Statistics 2016). Indeed, the JLMPS data showed that 81 percent of Syrians were informal (meaning they did not have a contract or were not registered with Social Security), either with private regular wages (53 percent) or with irregular wages (28 percent). By contrast, 42 percent of Jordanians were formally employed in the public sector, in formal employment with private regular wages (13 percent) or self-employed or an employer (16 percent). About 29 percent of Jordanians were informally employed or working in irregular wage jobs. Prior to the conflict, in 2007, the situation was similar to present day Jordan, where Syrians were also employed in the public sector (31 percent), formally employed (29 percent), or informally employed (34 percent), with the remaining few employed by family, self-employed, or employers (figure 2.19). Informality, however, was much higher in Dar'a at 50 percent.

The construction sector employs the largest share of working Syrian refugee men in Jordan, as was prevalent in Dar'a before the conflict. According to the VAF, 26 percent of employed Syrian refugees in Jordan were working in construction, with the others spread out in agriculture (11 percent), accommodation (11 percent), transportation (10 percent), manufacturing (9 percent), and other activities (figure 2.20). In comparison, only 10 percent of Jordanian men were employed in construction in 2018. In Dar'a, prior to the conflict in 2007, Syrian men also worked largely in the construction industry (37 percent), suggesting that Syrian men were able to transfer their work skills to the country they sought refuge in when they had the chance to do so. A quarter of Syrians in Dar'a were also working in services.

Syrian refugee women who work are mostly engaged in domestic services, followed by agriculture, with neither sector desired by Jordanian workers.

Figure 2.20. Sector Share of Employed Male Syrian Refugees and Jordanians

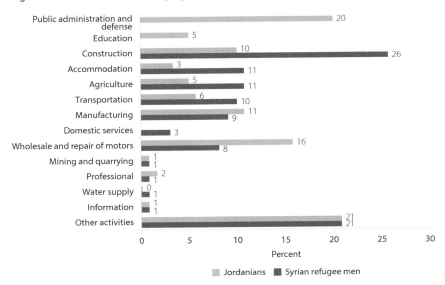

Source: Calculations based on data from the Jordan Department of Statistics (dosweb.dos.gov.jo/labourforce /employment-and-unemployment) and UNHCR 2017b.

About 44 percent of Syrian refugee women worked in domestic services and 15 percent in agriculture (figure 2.21). Conversely, in 2018, Jordanian women mostly worked in education (41 percent) and human health and social work activities (15.4 percent). Almost none were working in agriculture (0.9 percent). Overall, net job creation in the agriculture sector in 2016 in Jordan was negative although its economic growth in the first quarter of 2018 was positive at 6.4 percent.

Lebanon

Before the outbreak of the conflict, the Syrian workforce was in high demand in Lebanon, especially in specific sectors facing labor shortages. In 1993, Lebanon and Syria implemented a bilateral Agreement for Economic and Social Cooperation, where nationals of both countries were granted the freedom to stay, work, and carry out economic activities in both countries (figure 2.22).[20] In practice, this agreement allowed many Syrians to work in sectors for which there was little or no supply of Lebanese labor.

Following the onset of the Syrian conflict, Lebanese authorities closed a growing number of sectors to foreign labor.[21] Article 9 of Decree No. 17561 issued in 1964, regulating foreign labor in Lebanon, stipulates that each year the Minister of Labor issues a decision specifying the jobs and professions that are restricted to Lebanese nationals. In February 2013, the MOL issued Resolution No. 1/19, which restricts a number of fields to Lebanese nationals—including all kinds of administrative and banking jobs, jobs in the education sector, engineering, nursing, pharmacy, medical laboratories, liberal professions (for example, medicine and law), and others—basically limiting Syrian nationals to professions in construction, electricity, carpentry, blacksmithing, and sales (a work permit would still be necessary to work in these sectors). Exceptions were granted for candidates who (a) have

Figure 2.21. Sector Share of Employed Female Syrian Refugees and Jordanians

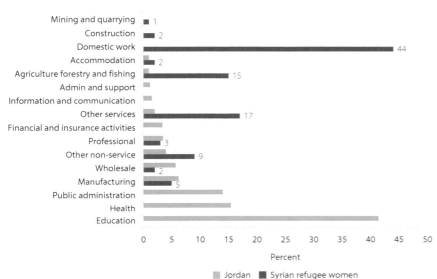

Source: Calculations based on first quarter 2018 data from the Jordan Department of Statistics (dosweb.dos .gov.jo/labourforce/employment-and-unemployment) and UNHCR 2017b.

Figure 2.22. Time Line of Labor Regulations, Lebanon

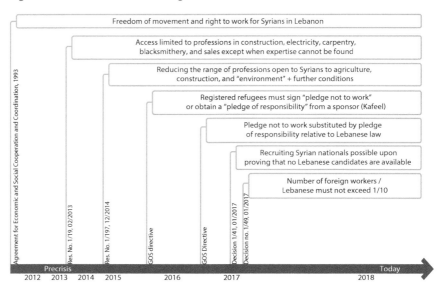

Sources: Agreement for Economic and Social Cooperation and Coordination between the Lebanese Republic and the Syrian Arab Republic (1993); Res. No. 1/19, 02/2013; Res. No. 1/197, 12/2014; Decision 1/41, 01/2017; Decision no. 1/49, 01/2017.

Note: The requirement regarding the number of foreign workers per Lebanese exempts domestic workers, Palestinian refugees, and agricultural workers who work for individuals on the basis of one worker per 5,000 square meters; modified ratios apply to cleaning companies, where there is a maximum ratio of 10 foreigners to 1 Lebanese, and construction or equivalent work where there can be 1 foreign worker per Lebanese worker. GOS = Government of Syria.

expertise that cannot be found among Lebanese applicants, (b) have resided in Lebanon since birth, (c) are born to a Lebanese mother, or (d) are managing a company registered in Lebanon. Although Syrians and other foreign nationals are still able to set up and run their own business activities (even under full foreign ownership), anecdotal evidence points toward a recent government crackdown on Syrian businesses (Howden, Alfred, and Patchett 2017).

Sector limitations were adjusted over time. In December 2014, the MOL issued Res. No. 1/197, which further reduced the range of professions open to Syrians to agriculture, construction, and cleaning. Displaced Syrians in Lebanon have largely worked in construction, agriculture, and environmental sectors, where they are allowed to work. Given difficulties in monitoring such a large workforce, however, many Syrian refugees work without contracts or other work agreements, with occasional crackdowns. In January 2017, Decision No. 1/49 was put in place, stipulating that the number of foreign workers per company must not exceed 1 foreigner per 10 Lebanese workers. Domestic workers, Palestinian refugees, and agricultural workers who work for individuals on the basis of one worker per 5,000 square meters, are exempt from these restrictions. Modified ratios apply to cleaning companies (maximum 10 foreigners for each Lebanese) and construction or equivalent work (maximum 1 foreign worker for every Lebanese worker). Decision No. 29/1 issued in 2018 removed previously adopted exemptions for Syrian nationals.

Although Syrian refugees can obtain work permits at a reduced fee, they often remain informal for other reasons. Syrians can obtain work permits at the reduced fee of 120,000 Lebanese pounds; however, because they often work in highly informal environments, obtaining a work permit is not always desirable. In addition, paying full contributions to the National Social Security Fund, while receiving only limited social security coverage, further reduces the appeal of formal work. According to the MOL, in 2017, only 1,775 work permits were issued to Syrian nationals (366 new permits and 1,409 renewals), whereas 42,717 work permits were issued to other nonnationals (12,398 new permits and 30,319 renewals).

Most Syrian refugee men in Lebanon are either employed or looking for a job (68 percent of the working-age population), compared to only 10 percent of Syrian refugee women. Although low participation of women is characteristic of most labor markets in the Middle East and North Africa (MENA) region, it should be noted that the LFP rate of Syrian refugee women in Lebanon (10 percent) is lower than that of their Lebanese counterparts (18 percent). It is also slightly lower than that of Syrian women before the crisis (13 percent), but higher than what was prevalent in Aleppo and Homs prior to the conflict (table 2.4). Reported reasons for nonparticipation vary for Syrian refugee men and women. For women, the primary reasons cited for not working were cultural (29 percent), followed by the need to take care of children and other dependent family members (24 percent and 23 percent, respectively), and lack of skills and experience (19 percent). For men the primary reasons cited were having dependent family members and children (21 percent and 25 percent, respectively), the absence of employment opportunities (19 percent), lack of skills or experience (17 percent), and medical conditions or injuries (15 percent) (figure 2.23). Unemployment rates for Syrian refugee women were also extremely low at 2.7 percent as compared to their Lebanese counterparts (18 percent) and the preconflict rate of 23.7 percent.

Table 2.4. Labor Force Participation and Unemployment Rates

	Preconflict, Syrian Arab Republic (2009)	Preconflict, Homs (2009)	Preconflict, Aleppo (2009)	Current, Syrian Arab Republic (2017 or latest)	Syrian refugees in Lebanon (2017)	Lebanese (2010)
Women's LFPR	13.3	5	9	11.9	10	18
Men's LFPR	71	70.2	70.3	79.1	68	71
Men's UR	5.8	3.2	3.6	11	12.7	9
Women's UR	23.7	12.3	9.85	41	2.7	18

Sources: Preconflict data for Syria come from the Central Bureau of Statistics (cbssyr.sy/index-EN.htm); data on Syrian refugees in Lebanon are from UNHCR 2017a; data for Lebanese are from the 2010 Employer-Employee Survey; data for current Syria come from World Bank 2017a.

Note: LFPR = labor force participation rate; UR = unemployment rate.

Figure 2.23. Main Reported Reasons for Economic Inactivity for Syrian Refugees in Lebanon, by Gender

Source: UNHCR 2017a.

Unemployment for Syrian refugee men in Lebanon is lower than what is prevalent in Syria because of the conflict but is higher than the precrisis rate. Unemployment for Syrian men in Lebanon is estimated at 12.7 percent (defined as the number of individuals ages 15–64 who were seeking a job in the past 30 days but did not find one). It is slightly higher than the observed rate for Lebanese men (9 percent). As noted earlier, Syrian men prior to the conflict in 2009 had a much lower unemployment rate of 5.8 percent nationally; the rate was even lower in Homs and Aleppo (3.2 and 3.6 percent, respectively), where a large share of Syrian refugees come from (table 2.4).

Most Syrian refugees in Lebanon are involved in construction and agriculture. Employed men (ages 15–64) are mainly involved in construction (33 percent), agriculture activities (22 percent), and services (16 percent) (including hospitality, restoration, transport, domestic work, hairdressing, and so on), with some engaged in manufacturing activities (8 percent), according to data from the 2017 VASyR. In comparison, the sectoral distribution of employment for Lebanese workers is very different: nearly one-half (46 percent) work in services, followed by about one-third (27 percent) working in trade (Central Administration of Statistics 2010). The sectoral distribution, however, is not very different from the regions where Syrian refugees lived prior to the conflict. As for women, Syrian refugees in Lebanon are mainly involved in agriculture (55 percent), followed by services (24 percent), with a small number (8 percent) employed in professional services.

Syrian employment in Lebanon is also characterized by underemployment and low wages, especially in the case of female refugees. On average, employed individuals ages 15–64 work 14 days per month, with a small difference between women and men (13 days for women versus 14 days for men), which indicates significant underemployment when compared to the standard 22 working days per month. Average monthly income for working adult refugees is estimated at US$193, which represents about 43 percent of the minimum wage in Lebanon (US$450 per month). Despite being employed for nearly the same number of working days, men earn US$206 per month (46 percent of minimum wage), whereas their female counterparts earn as little as US$158 per month

(35 percent of the minimum wage). Men working in agriculture earned more than double the amount of their female counterparts (US$12.4 per day versus US$6 per day). Figure 2.23 shows that female Syrian refugees list cultural reasons as the top reason for economic inactivity, followed by having dependent children or family members.

Kurdistan Region of Iraq

The Kurdistan Regional Government (KRG) has issued no restrictions on Syrian refugees' LFP. Syrian refugees can work in the private sector if they have official residency issued by the Ministry of Interior. The KRG's official policy is that Syrians registered with UNHCR, or who have a residency card, have free access to employment (WANA 2017). Similarly, no official employment ratios are imposed on Syrian refugees relative to Kurdish Iraqis. Instead, the Ministry of Labor and Social Affairs observes workplaces and the level of Kurdish Iraqi national hiring on an ad hoc basis: if the ratio of foreigners to locals becomes too skewed in any business or organization, the ministry may issue an informal warning concerning foreign hires (WANA 2017).

Employment of Syrian refugee men in the Kurdistan Region of Iraq is slightly higher than in Jordan and Lebanon, but women's employment remains low. This higher employment is consistent with the less-strict labor regulations in effect in the Kurdistan Region of Iraq. In about 74 percent of households, a male member between the ages of 15 and 59 was reported to work during the last seven days of the survey. The share of employed men in all regions in the Kurdistan Region of Iraq is above 50 percent, with Sulaymaniyah city district having the highest employment rate at 82 percent. The high employment rate of Syrian men is corroborated by the representative survey data collected in mid-2018, according to which almost 90 percent of economically active men are employed. This contrasts with women: only 5 percent of women between the ages of 15 and 59 are currently working. In the Kurdistan Region of Iraq, women's LFP rate in general is low at 15 percent irrespective of nationality (Kurdistan Regional Statistics Office 2016). The representative data also show Syrian women's LFP rate at 14 percent. Further, prior to the conflict, in Aleppo, where most Syrian refugees came from, the LFP rate of women was also low at 9 percent in 2009. Their unemployment rate (10 percent) was relatively lower than in other regions. Men's unemployment rate was also low in Aleppo (about 3.6 percent).

The main economic activity Syrian refugees in the Kurdistan Region of Iraq are engaged in is agriculture, followed by construction. About 38 percent of Syrian refugee households rely on agricultural labor wages, and 24 percent on construction labor wages. About 47 percent in Dahuk are involved in agricultural activities, whereas that share is 31 percent in Irbil and 29 percent in Sulaymaniyah.[22] As such, even though employment rates are relatively high for Syrian refugee men, these men are mostly engaged in low-skill or manual jobs. In comparison, prior to the conflict, Syrian men in Aleppo worked in many industries. In 2007, 25 percent of Syrian men in Aleppo were employed in manufacturing, 22 percent in hospitality and restaurants, 15 percent in agriculture, 14 percent in construction, and 13 percent in services. In the Kurdistan Region of Iraq, male employees are also involved in many economic activities, but mainly in public administration and defense and compulsory social security (29 percent), followed by wholesale and trade (14 percent) and construction (11 percent); agriculture's share is only about 6.5 percent (Kurdistan Regional Statistics Office 2016).

Monetary poverty

Although the well-being of Syrians and Syrian refugees is a multidimensional concept, monetary poverty provides a simple and intuitive indicator of welfare. Household welfare is assessed along both monetary and nonmonetary dimensions. In Syria, precrisis monetary poverty was estimated using several standard methods, but current estimates often follow a second-best or third-best approach in the absence of microdata. This lack creates a problem of comparability between the poverty assessments for Syrians in Syria and Syrian refugees in neighboring countries. This section considers these issues in more detail.

Conditions in Syria

Lack of data within Syria limits the ability to measure the poverty rate for the country, but all indicators point to a significant deterioration in living standards. Years of conflict have taken a toll on household welfare through a variety of channels such as displacement, injury to working-age adults, loss of employment, disruption of basic services, inflation and lack of basic goods, and disorganization of markets. Recent microdata on per capita expenditure, the usual measure of household welfare, are not available from Syria, which makes it difficult to definitively know the current level of poverty within the country. In a previous exercise, the 2016 poverty rate was extrapolated using a simple method that linked known historical information on the relationship between GDP per capita growth rate and poverty. It suggested a drastic increase in extreme poverty, as high as 66 percent in some scenarios (World Bank 2017a). This section provides a fresh update of the poverty level of Syrians seven years after the onset of the conflict.

Before the conflict, the extreme poverty rate in Syria was on average relatively low but exhibited large regional variation, the Northeast being significantly poorer (UNDP 2005, 2011).[23] In 1996–97 the national extreme poverty rate was 14.3 percent, declining to 11.4 percent by 2003–04. In 2006–07 poverty rose slightly to 12.3 percent, partially reversing the gains between 1997 and 2004.[24] Underneath the aggregate poverty rate, there was a large variation in the headcount ratio across regions and between urban and rural areas. Rural areas are consistently poorer than urban centers, and the urban–rural divide had grown since 1997. Poverty was concentrated in the Northeastern region, especially in rural areas.[25] The poorest part of the country in 2007 was the rural Northeast with a headcount ratio of 19.7 percent, 7 percentage points higher than the next area (12.8 percent in rural areas of the Southern region). Although only 44 percent of the total population lived in the Northeast, that region accounted for 56 percent of the extreme poor. The least poor area in 2007 was the Coastal region with an extreme poverty rate of 7.7 percent (figure 2.24).

The gap among regions was also widening prior to the conflict: poverty was increasing in poor regions. The Southern and Central regions enjoyed significant declines in poverty between 1997 and 2004, which drove overall poverty rates in Syria in 2003–04. The rural Northeast was the only area that experienced an increase in poverty between 1997 and 2004. Only the Southern region (the urban South in particular) and the rural Northeast experienced increases in the poverty rates between 2004 and 2007, which explains the increase in poverty in Syria as

Figure 2.24. Syrian Extreme Poverty Rate, by Region, 1997–2007

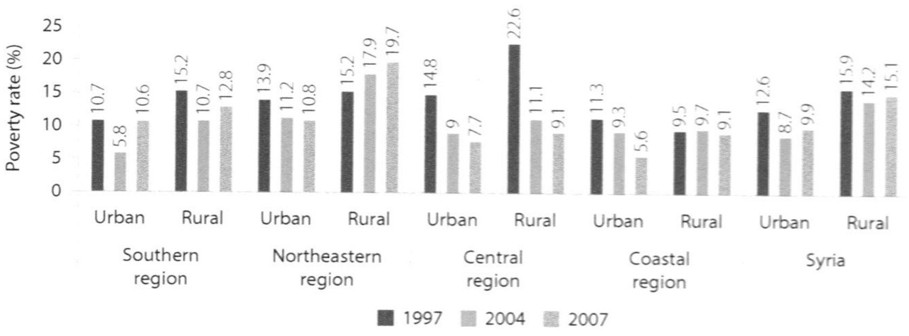

Source: UNDP 2005, 2011.

Table 2.5. Current Extreme Poverty in the Syrian Arab Republic and for Refugees in Host Countries

Location	Extreme poverty rate (percentage living below the Syrian extreme poverty line)
Syrian Arab Republic (2007)	6–20
Syrian Arab Republic (2016)	55–67
Syrians in Jordan (2017)	51–61
Syrians in Lebanon (2017)	37–50

Sources: UNHCR 2017b; UNHCR, UNICEF, and WFP 2018; World Bank calculations.

a whole. The most plausible explanation for this increase is the drought that pre-dominantly affected the rural Northeast region and the resulting out-migration from these areas to the Southern urban region, compounded by the large influx of Iraqi refugees to the urban South (Kelley et al. 2015).

The current conditions in Syria are much worse. A 2017 exercise placed the extreme poverty rate in Syria in 2016 between 55 and 67 percent depending on various growth scenarios, while an independent estimate suggested 69 percent of Syrians were living in extreme poverty in 2015 (SCPR 2015; World Bank 2017a).[26] Table 2.5 summarizes national extreme poverty estimates for precrisis Syria, for present day Syria, and for Syrian refugees living in Jordan and Lebanon. Precrisis poverty ranged from 6 percent in the urban areas of the Coastal region to 20 percent in the rural areas of the Northeastern region. Although the comparability of the esti-mates is somewhat limited, under all assumptions and sensitivities, it is clear that poverty for Syrians everywhere is higher today than it was before the crisis. Box 2.2 provides a more detailed discussion on food insecurity, a clear correlate of extreme poverty, in Syria. There are some suggestions that poverty in Lebanon might be slightly lower (37–50 percent) than in Jordan (51–61 percent) or Syria currently (55–67 percent), but limitations on comparability mean this conclusion cannot be reached definitively; it remains the case that at least 40 percent of refugees in Lebanon—and possibly closer to half—are poor.

BOX 2.2

Food Insecurity in the Syrian Arab Republic

About 5.5 million Syrians are food insecure and require some form of food assistance according to World Food Programme (WFP). Food insecurity is one of the most critical issues facing Syria today. The displacement of more than 6 million people is a large contributor to food insecurity together with high food prices, reduced land access, limited jobs and income, and increasing climate variability. Internally displaced persons, female-headed households, and returnees are the most food insecure. About a quarter of Syrian households cope with limited access to food by purchasing poor-quality and low quantities of food. Nearly one-half of households reduced the number of meals consumed in a day.

The problem is not only that food is lacking but also that nutritious foods are not being consumed. Iron, vitamin A, and zinc deficiencies together with limited protein intake have long-term human development impacts for today's children. Data show that 27.5 percent of Syrian children under 5 years of age were stunted in 2012. Also, the prevalence of anemia among women of reproductive age (15–49) increased by 2 percentage points from 2012 to 33.6 percent in 2016.

Food prices are very high but slowly falling because of better market integration across Syria as supply routes and roads are reopening and because of improved security. Commodity prices are more than seven times higher than before the conflict erupted. According to WFP, the average price of a WFP-equivalent standard food basket has fallen by 40 percent since it was at its highest in 2016.

At a time when security is improving, agriculture production has been hit by severe climate variability. This variability includes hail, reduced rain, and elevated temperatures at a time when more than 800,000 internally displace persons and 23,000 refugees have been returning to their home governorates. Many of the returnees have a background in farming. Cereals, such as wheat, have been especially hard hit this year, and the 2018 production was only 1.2 million tons compared to preconflict production of 4.1 million tons average per year (the drought in Al-Hasakeh, the region that produced 45 percent of the country's cereals, was severe during much of that time). Industrial crop production such as sugar beet, cotton, and tobacco is also low compared to preconflict years; and horticulture has been hard hit by the conflict, sanctions on imports, and climate variability. Livestock and tree crops are very slowly being revived.

Food- and agriculture-related infrastructures—for example, food factories, irrigation structures, machinery and factories, silos, and warehouses—have still not been rehabilitated. There is also a need to increase access to quality inputs, everything from seeds to fertilizers—many farmers are not even

(box continues next page)

BOX 2.2. *(continued)*

using fertilizers. Given the low harvest in 2018, there will likely be less seed available for planting in 2019. The loss of infrastructure and machinery also reduces employment and job generation opportunities. The limited livelihood options result in low disposable income. Finally, many more households are female-headed as men are less present because of forced migration or mortality.

The Ministry of Agriculture estimates that agriculture accounts for 60 percent of Syrian gross domestic product, roughly three times more than before the conflict. The 2019 outlook is more promising because the rain collected in the reservoirs in early summer of 2018 can be used for supplementary irrigation of crops in spring of 2019.

Source: FAO et al. 2018.

Conditions in countries of asylum

Assessing the degree of refugees' impoverishment in a manner that is comparable to that of current or preconflict Syria is a challenging task. The sources of the recent data for Syrian refugees are the 2017 VAF in Jordan collected by UNHCR and the 2017 VASyR in Lebanon collected by UNHCR, UNICEF and WFP.[27] To compare the poverty rates in Jordan and Lebanon, and to make them somewhat comparable to the last known national poverty estimates for Syria (2007–08), this analysis makes several adjustments: First, the 2007 Syrian extreme poverty line is converted to local currencies of Jordan and Lebanon using purchasing power parity (PPP) exchange rate. Next, the lines are expressed in 2017 prices by applying the consumer price index series of the respective countries. These are purchasing power equivalent poverty lines in local currency in 2017. Per capita expenditure data from the 2017 VASyR and VAF surveys are compared against these poverty lines to estimate the poverty rate for Syrian refugees. These poverty rates can be compared, with some caveats discussed later, to the 2007 poverty rate of Syrians in Syria.

The extreme poverty rate of Syrian refugees is significantly higher than in precrisis Syria. In 2007, the poverty line in Syria was 2,183 Syrian pounds per person per month in local currency,[28] and the share of people living below the poverty line was 12.3 percent (the extreme poverty rate). In PPP terms, the poverty line was US$95.45 (2011 PPP exchange rate of 22.8866). The purchasing power equivalent poverty lines in 2017 were PPP US$118.43 in Jordan and PPP US$119.8 in Lebanon (Atamanov et al. 2018).[29]

Two-fifths of refugees living in Lebanon and almost three-fifths of refugees in Jordan are poor by the precrisis Syrian standard (table 2.6). Refugees in Jordan appear to be poorer than those in Lebanon, consistent with an analysis of 2013 data, which also found a higher poverty rate in Jordan, albeit with a different poverty line (Verme et al. 2016).

Table 2.6. Poverty Rate of Syrian Refugees Compared to Precrisis Syrian Arab Republic, by Host Country, 2017

	Precrisis Syrian Arab Republic (2007)	Jordan (2017)	Lebanon (2017)
Poverty line (LCU)	LS 2,183	JD 52.8	LL 99,374
Poverty line (US$PPP)	95.5	118.4	119.8
Poverty rate (%)	12.3	55.8	42.5
Poverty rate (90% of per capita expenditure)		60.6	49.6
Poverty rate (107% of per capita expenditure)		51.9	38.6
Poverty rate (110% of per capita expenditure)		50.5	36.9

Sources: World Bank calculations using data from United Nations Development Program, UNHCR 2017b, and UNHCR, UNICEF, and WFP 2018.
Note: JD = Jordanian dinar; LCU = local currency units; LL = Lebanese pound; LS = Syrian pound; PPP = purchasing power parity.

Even after adjusting for prices between countries and across time to estimate a purchasing power equivalent poverty line, there are other issues that make comparing poverty estimates between precrisis Syria and the host countries difficult. First, there are concerns about whether refugees in host countries are truthfully reporting their consumption. It is not obvious which direction any bias will go; refugees may understate their expenditures to demonstrate that they are in poverty and in need of assistance, or they may overstate consumption to demonstrate the high cost of living and a shortfall in their ability to meet it.

Second, the expenditure questions in VASyR and VAF are less detailed than those in the original questionnaire in the Syrian national survey. Research has shown that, when a survey asks about a fewer number of items or uses fewer groups of items, total aggregate expenditure is lower than when the survey asks for expenditures on items one by one or from a longer list (Beegle et al. 2012).

To address these concerns, this analysis performed sensitivity checks. To account for the ambiguities specified above, poverty rates were calculated for cases with total expenditures being 7 percent and 10 percent higher (to account for difference in survey questionnaires and possible underreporting), and if total expenditure was 10 percent lower (to account for possible exaggeration of living costs). If many households are clustered just below or above the poverty line, these adjustments will have a large impact on poverty rate. With these adjustments, estimates of refugees living in poverty ranged from 51 percent to 61 percent in Jordan and 37 percent to 50 percent in Lebanon. Although these estimates are sensitive to the assumptions and methodological choices discussed before, the standard of living of Syrian refugees living outside their country is clearly worse than it was in preconflict Syria. The war has forced a significant proportion of Syrians to live under material conditions that would have been deemed unacceptable by earlier

Syrian standards. Moreover, the lowest rate of the likely range in Jordan remains slightly higher than the highest rate of the likely range in Lebanon, suggesting that refugee poverty is indeed lower in Lebanon than in Jordan, although to what extent is less clear.

Social assistance

The assistance offered to the refugees through UNHCR and its partner organizations has evolved with the scale and duration of displacement. What began as predominantly an emergency response has morphed into a long-term program focused on building resilience and fostering stabilization. The first phase of the response, lasting from the beginning of 2012 to mid-2013, focused largely on protection and emergency response to the increasing refugee population. The initial plans focused only on the registration of the people crossing the border and on providing the core set of basic needs.

As the scale of the crisis ballooned, UNHCR launched the first Regional Response Plan (2013 RRP) in 2012, which allowed it to coordinate the needs of the United Nations (UN) and other partner agencies. While the first phase of the Regional Response Plan centered on protection, the scope was broadened in the second phase to address the impact on host governments and communities, promoting social stability and supporting local infrastructure and institutions (such as waste management and health service delivery).

The third phase of the response, from 2015 onward, marked a departure in how the response was formulated. UNHCR, jointly with the United Nations Development Programme (UNDP), developed the Regional Refugee & Resilience Plan (3RP), which kept the focus on international protection while aiming to build resilience and address the stabilization needs of affected communities.[30] The inclusion of a "durable solution" in the 2018 3RP marks a strategic shift, not only highlighting the need to meet immediate protection and assistance needs but also ensuring a pillar toward finding a long-term, durable solution to protracted displacement—a solution intended not toward local integration but toward dignity in exile and voluntary return.

The 3RP is the largest organizing platform in the international community's response to the regional refugee crisis. The 3RP is a nationally led process, incorporating in full the Lebanon Crisis Response Plan (LCRP) and Jordan Response Plan. It is implemented by UN agencies, NGOs, and host country governments. The two co-leads of the 3RP—UNDP and UNHCR—together coordinate the activities of more than 270 implementing partners. In each country, assistance is provided in eight sectors: protection, health, WASH, shelter, livelihoods, food security, basic needs, and education. The type of assistance provided in each sector also varies by whether the refugee is in a camp or outside of a camp.

The type and volume of assistance has increased in line with the increase in the registered refugee population and their needs. Those receiving food assistance increased from nearly 1.4 million in 2013 to over 2.5 million in 2017, and the number of Syrian children enrolled in formal education rose from 215,000 to 930,000. The numbers of health care consultations, child protection services, employment programs, sanitation facility upgrades, and other services provided by 3RP partners have also increased as the needs have grown.

There has also been a gradual shift from in-kind assistance toward cash transfers (conditional or unconditional). The number of individuals receiving cash assistance increased to 1.85 million individuals in 2017 from just over 400,000 in 2014. In 2018, 582,000 families, approximately 2.9 million people, were targeted for cash assistance, while 2.3 million were targeted to receive food assistance (cash, voucher, or in-kind). There has been a corresponding decrease in the provision of in-kind support, such as basic relief items (a standardized set of daily household and other items often provided to refugee populations in many contexts, particularly where refugee camps exist). The 2017 plan aimed to provide core relief items in-kind to over 200,000 households across the region, but this figure dropped to 90,000 vulnerable households in 2018. Furthermore, specific support to households during the winter period has increasingly moved from in-kind to cash-based assistance.

Although the response has continued to evolve, the relative share of funding across sectors has remained relatively constant. Figure 2.25 shows that food assistance, usually in the form of cash vouchers, accounted for almost a quarter of the allocated funds between 2015 and 2017. The second-largest sector is education, typically accounting for just under 20 percent of the response. The percentage of received 3RP funding allocated to livelihoods increased significantly in 2017, from 3 percent in 2016 to 9 percent in 2017. This change reflects a shifting priority among donors and implementers to focus more on sustainable solutions for refugees, with access to employment being a key component.

The exact composition of the sectors varies from country to country. The response across the 3RP countries has evolved according to the political, economic, and social context and other factors affecting the operating environment in each country, including resources and the capacity of agencies. Although differences exist across contexts, refugees are generally facing a high degree of vulnerability arising from the cumulative effects of poverty, unemployment, limited access to quality basic services such as health and education, and in many cases a tenuous legal situation.

Figure 2.25. Sector as percent of 3RP Funding in Jordan

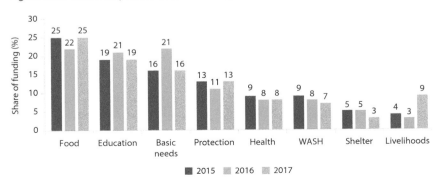

Source: Based on data from the United Nations High Commissioner for Refugees, http://www.3rpsyriacrisis.org.
Note: 3RP = Regional Refugee & Resilience Plan; WASH = water, sanitation, and hygiene.

Conditions in Jordan

The bulk of the assistance in Jordan is directed to food assistance to mitigate food insecurity or vulnerability to food insecurity of Syrian refugees (figure 2.26). WFP provides regular, unconditional food vouchers and, less often, in-kind food assistance. In 2017, in-kind food assistance was provided to over 260,000 Syrians and vulnerable Jordanians; cash-based assistance was provided to over 500,000 people (JPRSC 2018, 18–19, 66). Basic-needs support takes the form of winterization assistance, cash assistance, and basic needs kits to refugees and vulnerable Jordanians. In 2017, monthly multipurpose cash assistance reached an average of 143,000 Syrians and 5,800 Jordanians (JPRSC 2018, 33). Livelihoods and social cohesion were added as an individual sector in 2017, reflecting the evolution of the response toward a more sustainable model.

Cash assistance has become a regular part of humanitarian assistance in Jordan. UNHCR supports only the most vulnerable families (approximately 23 percent of the noncamp population) as defined by the VAF. This group includes 32,800 families, mostly Syrian but also refugees of other nationalities. From February 2015 to May 2017, UNICEF distributed unconditional Child Cash Grants to assist approximately 15,000 of the most vulnerable Syrian refugee families with children under the age of 18 living in host communities. The WFP voucher program was introduced for those living in host communities in 2012 and later in Zaatari camp, allowing them to shop in certain supermarkets for their preferred foods (Luce 2014).

Eligibility for UNHCR assistance is determined by the vulnerability score defined by the VAF. The VAF is a comprehensive framework consisting of a set of common indicators of vulnerability, a standardized data collection tool (Home Visit form), agreed "thresholds" of vulnerability (low to severe), and a central database to capture and securely share vulnerability data. VAF indicators are collected at UNHCR registration and during home visits by UNHCR and VAF data collection partners. Data are

Figure 2.26. Share of Total 3RP Funding in Jordan, by Sector

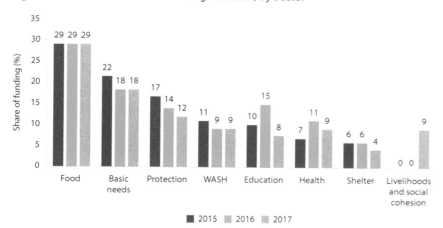

Source: Based on data from the United Nations High Commissioner for Refugees available at http:// www.3rpsyriacrisis.org.

Note: 3RP = Regional Refugee & Resilience Plan; WASH = water, sanitation, and hygiene.

regularly updated, creating a "vulnerability profile" for each refugee household. Once eligibility is established on the basis of an initial home visit, it is verified every two years.

A survival minimum expenditure basket and family size are used to determine the value of the cash transfers. For example, in 2018, the minimum expenditure basket (MEB) for a family of four is estimated at 387 Jordanian dinars (JD) per person per month, and the total size of the transfers (UNHCR and WFP combined), was JD 196. Winterization support is also provided to eligible cases determined by the MEB, VAF eligibility criteria, and the assessed shelter needs. In 2017, the full standard level of assistance was US$277 for family size of up to three and a top-up, capped at US$453, for households with seven or more members.

Conditions in Lebanon

The education sector absorbs a larger share of the 3RP funding in Lebanon. The Ministry of Education and Higher Education has waived school fees for all Lebanese and non-Lebanese children attending public school, while partner organizations have assisted school rehabilitation and curriculum development. Between 2016 and 2017, there was a significant increase in the share of funding allocated by the LCRP for food, which is mostly given in the form of cash transfers (figure 2.27 and figure 2.28)

In Lebanon, UNHCR uses the Proxy Means Test targeting methodology to determine eligibility for cash assistance. It is derived from VASyR-reported expenditure data and applied to the UNHCR registration data. The model is updated annually with the most up-to-date data and a refinement of methods. UNHCR also conducts validation of beneficiaries with an aim to ensure that the right person is in possession of the right card.

Figure 2.27. Share of Total 3RP Funding in Lebanon, by Sector

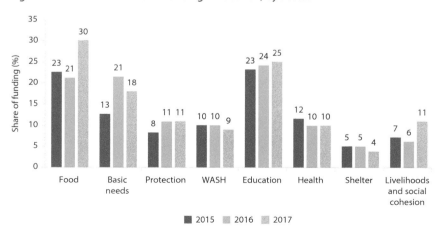

Source: Based on data from the United Nations High Commissioner for Refugees available at http://www.3rpsyriacrisis.org.

Note: 3RP = Regional Refugee & Resilience Plan; WASH = water, sanitation, and hygiene.

Figure 2.28. Sector Funding, Percentage of Total

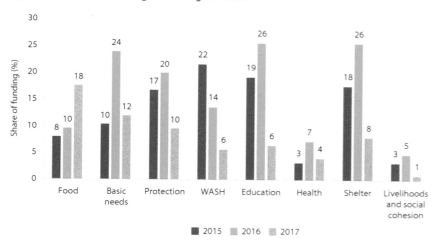

Source: Based on data from the United Nations High Commissioner for Refugees available at http://www.3rpsyriacrisis.org.

Note: 3RP = Regional Refugee & Resilience Plan; WASH = water, sanitation, and hygiene.

The transfer amount is determined by the estimated MEB that captures what a Syrian refugee household in Lebanon requires to cover basic needs for a dignified way of living. The MEB stands at US$517 for a household of five members. The MEB consists of food, water, sanitation, health, nonfood items, shelter, education, transportation, and other services. However, the size of the cash grant is largely set by the amount of resources available. Winterization support is also provided to highly vulnerable refugees. The amount of assistance is tiered, with the largest support flowing to refugees who are not receiving any other assistance.

Conditions in the Kurdistan Region of Iraq

International organizations and humanitarian agencies are the most common source of assistance for Syrian refugees in Kurdistan. Almost one-third of Syrian refugees in Kurdistan are covered by cash assistance from these sources, and one-fifth have received cash or in-kind transfers. Cash or in-kind transfers from friends and relatives, both within and outside Iraq, constitute the next most important sources of support, with approximately one-fifth of Syrian refugees relying on informal networks for support.

There is no information on the size or the frequency of the transfers, so it is difficult to determine their relative contribution to the overall household budget. Subjective assessment suggests, however, that the level of support received is inadequate. Only 4 percent of refugees agree that the support received during the past 12 months was sufficient to meet the household's basic food needs.

Housing, Land, and Property Rights

International experience shows that refugees' ability to reclaim their properties is crucial for return, yet it is also one of the most challenging problems to resolve. Assets like houses and land often underlie the sense of "belonging." In addition,

107

livelihood opportunities are often linked to access to such assets, especially in rural areas. Thus, the prospects for recovering these assets can be a key driver of return for refugees. This issue is also a daunting one to resolve because such assets are usually damaged, looted, or occupied by others, often by people with a differ-ent ethnic or sectarian profile; and proving ownership may not always be possi-ble because of informality or destroyed records. In this section, the analysis will focus on the accessibility of assets in two dimensions: first, the prospects of having access to housing shelter regardless of ownership issues and, second, the property rights issue surrounding housing and land ownership.

Housing and shelter conditions in Syria

Syria is a highly urbanized country. Prior to the conflict, Syria was rapidly urban-izing, with 56 percent of the population living in urban areas, most of which are rain-fed agricultural regions, including the basin of the Euphrates River, or along interior trade routes. The two largest cities, Damascus and Aleppo, accounted for nearly 37 percent of the urban population and 20 percent of the total population. According to 2010 Syrian census data, there were 4,128,941 conventional dwelling units across 14 governorates.

The conflict further intensified rural–urban migration. Starting from the mid- to late 1990s, Syria experienced rural–urban migration spurred by drought and envi-ronmental degradation. About 40,000 to 60,000 families migrated from rural to urban areas each year because of droughts. The conflict provided a major boost to urbanization. Today, it is estimated that about 72.6 percent of the population (13.7 million people) lives in urban areas in Syria, and these urban areas have undergone dramatic demographic change as a result of the conflict. Those areas directly impacted by the conflict, like eastern Aleppo and Homs, have been expe-riencing an exodus of residents fleeing violence, destruction, and the collapse of basic services. Other areas, with promising relative security and consistency of services, have experienced large influxes, with the net result being a significant concentration of population (IDPs and hosts) in urban areas.

In conflict-affected cities, physical destruction has been extensive. The conflict in Syria has severely impacted the housing sector, with a significant share of residen-tial units partially damaged or fully destroyed, housing investment disrupted, qual-ity of living space deteriorated, and land and property rights severely challenged. At the city level, data have been collected through algorithm-based analysis of satellite imagery. Table 2.7 provides the total number of buildings affected by the conflict, both partially and totally damaged. On average, about one-fifth of all res-idential buildings in the 15 cities covered in this study suffered damage, about a quarter of which were fully destroyed. The overall damage was highest in Al-Qusayr (29.4 percent) and Dar'a (29.0 percent).

Housing damage reported here suggests some reconstruction activity, unevenly distributed across cities. In Aleppo, approximately one-third of housing areas have undergone possible reconstruction operations (including debris removal) since August 2016. Still, as of June 2018, at least 20.9 percent of housing remains unimproved across the city, requiring further investment of time, equipment, and materials. Of note is the large area within the Old City, which suffered 100 percent damage of housing structures during the conflict. Although 15 percent of that

Table 2.7. Total Number of Buildings Affected by the Conflict, by City in the Syrian Arab Republic

	Baseline # of buildings	No damage	Partially damaged	Destroyed	Damage ratio (%)
Afrin	1,195	1,192	0	3	0.3
Al Bab	1,196	1,067	104	25	10.8
Aleppo	88,360	69,882	14,785	3,693	20.9
Al-Qusayr	1,315	928	310	77	29.4
Dar'a	9,348	6,634	2,172	542	29.0
Deir ez-Zor	5,712	4,395	1,058	259	23.1
Douma	5,578	4,047	1,228	303	27.4
Homs	41,941	31,322	7,911	2,708	25.3
Idleb	5,896	4,959	736	201	15.9
Kobani	5,673	5,111	450	112	9.9
Menbij	3,402	3,178	180	44	6.6
Qamishli	8,341	8,341	0	0	0
Ar-Raqqa	6,409	5,817	478	114	9.2
Tadmur	1,364	1,067	239	58	21.8
Yabroud	727	727	0	0	0
Total (15 cities)	186,457	148,667	29,651	8,139	20.3

Source: World Bank 2017.

109

area has been cleaned up, 85 percent still awaits repair or reconstruction. It is estimated that more than 18,000 buildings (out of approximately 88,360) remain damaged, with 3,693 (medium estimate) destroyed. In contrast, the damage ratio in Homs has remained practically unchanged when compared with 2014 data—in part because of additional destruction that has occurred during this period, and also because of very recent bulldozing of heavily damaged structures to make room for new construction. Of note are the neighborhoods of Karm Shamsham and Deir Ba'alba, both of which suffered 100 percent damage of housing structures during the conflict. Although 3 percent and 22 percent, respectively, of those neighborhoods have been cleaned up, 97 percent and 78 percent, respectively, still await repair and reconstruction.

Conflict-driven physical damage has been translated into significant restrictions for Syrians' access to housing and shelter. The available data from household surveys and community focal points paint a picture that is similar but more nuanced compared to the remote-sensing-based damage assessments. Overall, most of the dwelling stock in more than one-third of neighborhoods is reported to have sustained some damage. As a result, houses are not available for rent in most communities. Thus, only in a few communities can households afford the rent, even though they are living in structures that have sustained some damage, that do not provide adequate protection from weather, and that are not served well by public services.

Figure 2.29. Housing Deprivation Index, Syrian Arab Republic, 2017

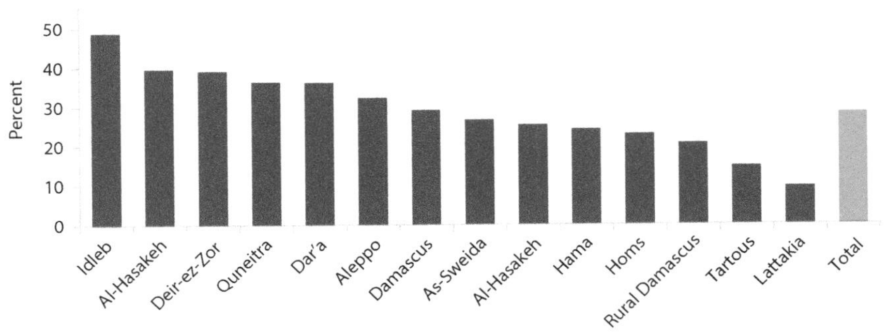

Source: UNHCR 2017d and World Bank analysis.
Note: Deprivations surveyed included lack of insulation from the cold, leaking during rain, limited ventilation, overcrowding, lack of internal privacy, inability to secure house, lack of cooking facilities, lack of bathing facilities, lack of lighting, lack of heating, and existence of any other common inadequacy. The Index is the average number of deprivations (out of 10) in each governorate.

The conditions for access to housing reflect not only supply-side problems (such as damage), but also demand-side problems (such as IDP inflows or outflows). The Housing Deprivation Index shown in figure 2.29 uses the 2017 MSNA focal points data to summarize the average deprivation on 10 different housing dimensions, such as lack of heating or leaking during rain (UNHCR 2017d). Implicitly, damage done to housing stock will be reflected in these amenities, although it will only indirectly capture insufficiency of the overall housing stock. Across the country, the average deprivation is 28 percent. The worst conditions are in Idleb (consistent with its being one of the governorates most affected by both damage and IDP inflows), where houses on average lack 6 of the 10 amenities surveyed. Other governorates with the most deprivation include Ar-Raqqa (40 percent), Dar'a (36 percent), and Deir-ez-Zor (39 percent). The least deprivation is in Lattakia (10 percent) and Tartous (15 percent).

Access to housing and shelter in countries of asylum

A clear majority of Syrians in Jordan, the Kurdistan Region of Iraq, and Lebanon live in rented dwellings. A quarter or so who do not live with friends or relatives or in temporary structures like tents and abandoned buildings (UNHCR, UNICEF, and WFP 2018). In Kurdistan, more than 90 percent of Syrian refugees live in rented dwellings. Even those who live in rented houses or apartments are not well served by public services. Unreliable electricity supply and lack of access to piped drinking water and sanitation facilities among renters is common in Jordan and Lebanon, as well as in Kurdistan.

There may be, however, some differences in refugee housing quality between Lebanon and Jordan. Figure 2.30 shows the number of housing problems for Syrian refugees living in each Jordanian governorate, out of a possible total of

Figure 2.30. Number of Housing Problems for Syrian Refugees in Jordan, by Location

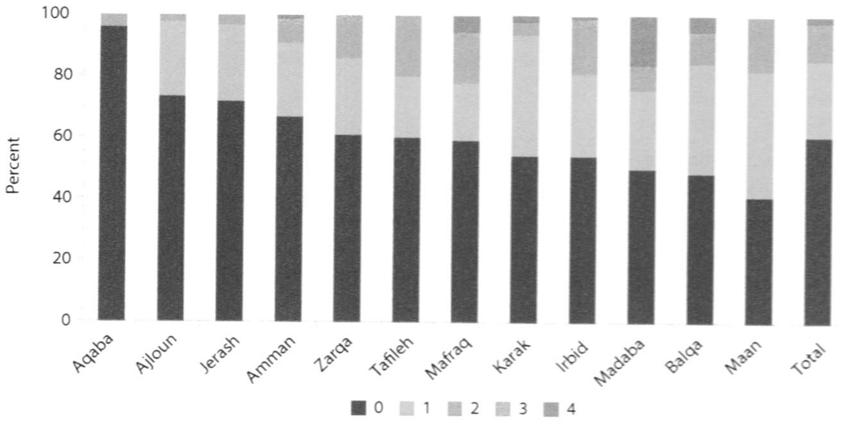

Source: UNHCR 2017b.
Note: Number of problems from substandard roofing (yes/no), substandard electrical features (yes/no), poor-quality wall materials (taken as neither brick nor reinforced concrete), and poor-quality roofing (taken as tarp or wood).

four (substandard roofing, substandard electrical features, poor-quality wall materials, and poor-quality roofing materials). Outcomes vary by location, but in all but two governorates most households report no housing problems, while relatively few households report more than one problem. Across all governorates the average share of households reporting housing problems is 15 percent. The data for refugees living in Lebanon are not exactly the same, but refugee households report an average of 44 percent from eight different housing problems (unsealed windows, leaking roof, rot, damaged walls, damaged plumbing, unusable toilet, unusable bathroom, and lack of electrical features) (UNHCR, UNICEF, and WFP 2018). Although these percentages may suggest that housing quality for refugees in Jordan is better than for those in Lebanon, it might also be the case that a higher percentage of possible problems in Lebanon reflects more potential problems to report, or that some of the problems in the Lebanon list are less severe and not contained in the Jordan list. As such, it is difficult to make a confident comparison.

It is difficult to compare housing conditions across countries where Syrians reside. Common indicators are not available, and the total number of potential housing problems differs across surveys (table 2.8). On average, however, those still living in Syria report 28 percent of possible housing problems (out of 10), refugees living in Lebanon report an average of 44 percent of possible problems (out of 8), and those in Jordan report only 15 percent (out of 4). Syrian and Lebanese data are most comparable, in terms of both the number of potential problems and the overlap of problems. The results suggest that, although housing conditions are not ideal in Syria, they are likely worse on average for refugees living in Lebanon, comparable to the worst conflict-affected areas in Syria (49 percent in Idleb, 40 percent in Ar-Raqqa, 39 percent in Deir-ez-Zor, and 36 percent in Dar'a).

Table 2.8. Percentage of Housing Problems in Syria and for Refugees in Host Countries, 2017

	Residents in Syrian Arab Republic	Refugees in Lebanon	Refugees in Jordan
Number of housing problems in data	10	8	4
Percentage of housing problems reported (%)	28	44	15

Sources: UNHCR 2017b, 2017d; UNHCR, UNICEF, and WFP 2018.

Institutional aspects of house and land ownership in Syria

Before the conflict, a large portion of the Syrian population lived under informal housing arrangements recognized in effect but not legally guaranteed by the state. This tacit consent to informal housing arrangements was expressed through the provision of basic services to residents. The Central Bureau of Statistics estimated the percentage of informal housing units at roughly 38 percent nationally and about 40 percent in the Damascus governorate in 2004. An estimated 32 percent of the total urban population resided in informal settlements in 2013, with the percentages rising to 40 percent in Damascus and 46 percent in Aleppo (UN-Habitat 2013).

Preconflict land administration was characterized by unfulfilled policies, administrative neglect, and elite capture. With roughly 62 percent of land classified as state land (Forni 2001), the state had a strong role in land administration. The government of Syria had no single, comprehensive land policy, but land administration was a feature of a number of other policies. Such policies included public land distribution and ceilings on ownership of agricultural land, the latter of which resulted in roughly 22 percent of cultivable land being confiscated and partially redistributed to farmers (Sarris 1995). These policies proved unable to prevent the growth of landlessness (Forni 2001). Despite formal recognition of a diverse land tenure system in law, the continuation of informal practices complicated security of tenure.

Low levels of private land registration and use of parallel systems of transactions persisted in part because of administrative neglect. According to unofficial estimates by the Ministry of Local Government in 2011 only about 50 percent of land was officially registered. Plans for automation and simplification of registration procedures were interrupted by the conflict. Public services related to private land transactions were characterized by corruption. Only about 20 percent of state land was registered, and inventories were outdated (UN-Habitat 2013), providing considerable opportunity for disputes over ownership and usage. Considerable amounts of land remained administered under customary norms, including dispute resolution (Cunial 2016; UN-Habitat 2013).

Land administration practices had no overt confessional overtones but exclusion from land ownership resulted from other polices. A census taken in 1962 in the Al-Hasakeh area of northeastern Syria led to an estimated 120,000 ethnic Kurds being stripped of Syrian citizenship. The loss of citizenship made these citizens legally stateless. This legal status effectively prevented those affected from registering land in the land registry (HLRN 2011), pushing many transactions into the informal sector and subsequently undermining security of tenure. About 500,000 Palestinians refugees, many of whom lived in camps with unclear land tenure rights, were also registered as refugees in Syria.

Popular practices at times undermined the accuracy of the land registries and weakened the security of land tenure. Land passed through inheritance was not always registered after subdivision among heirs, undermining the accuracy of the private land registries. Land transactions were sometimes facilitated through powers of attorney without being recorded in the land registry. Married couples did not routinely register land titles jointly, though joint registration with numerous shares spread among family members was common. Pressure on agricultural lands was at the root of illegal occupations and conflicts between landowners and would-be cultivators, which were complicated by unclear tenure rights due at least in part to the emerging problem of squatters on private land (Forni 2001).

Elite capture affected both public and private lands. Prior to the conflict, political and economic power was concentrated in a group of elites who benefitted from access to land through a number of mechanisms, including nontransparent management of public lands; expropriation of land for military and security purposes; allocation of agricultural land then converted to construction land; and construction of housing in periurban areas. Rural land was at risk of takeover by elite private interests through the designation of areas as military or government zones leading to expropriation without adequate compensation (Unruh 2016). Since the start of the conflict, governance indicators linked with elite capture, based on a relatively weak starting point, have generally declined (figure 2.31).

Measures of protection of property, basic administration, and combatting corruption have declined during the conflict. Security of tenure has declined during the conflict through several channels. Paper land registries have reportedly been damaged or destroyed. For example, the land registry for the Homs governorate was destroyed by fire in 2013; possible similar destruction occurred to the one in Menbij (PAX and TSI 2013). There are allegations that deliberate destruction of land records has become an objective of some military forces as has demographic reengineering along confessional lines (Unruh 2016). Destruction of land registries could be used as a tool for preventing return of displaced persons because it would create legal confusion over land tenure rights.

The conflict has led to distress sales of land, particularly by individuals fleeing violence. This effect has led to a market for purchase and sale of land and property of displaced persons, which has been accompanied by a proliferation of fraudulent sales based on fake documentation (Unruh 2016). Both good-faith and bad-faith transactions take place involving land of displaced persons, with the fraudulent sometimes formalized in land records (Cunial 2016). Disputes over property occupied by armed groups are also becoming more common (Cunial 2016).

Confiscation of private land and housing has been widespread throughout the conflict. Such action normally targets land and housing belonging to minorities and displaced persons. Confiscation of property was a regular stream of revenue

113

Figure 2.31. Governance Indicators during Conflict

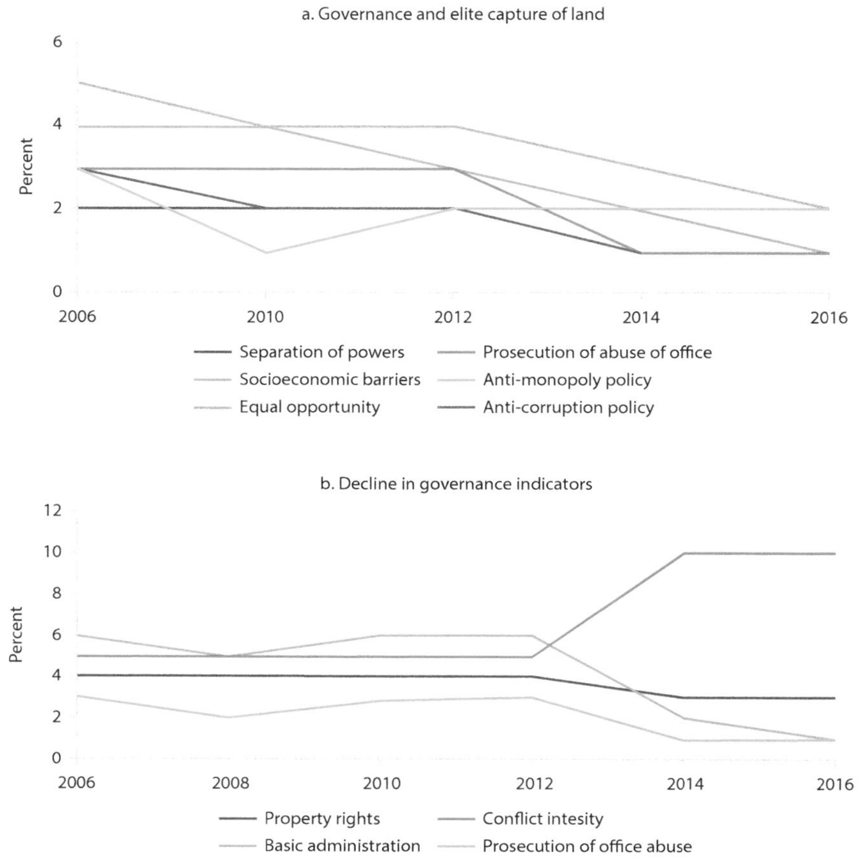
a. Governance and elite capture of land
Percent
6
4
2
0
2006
2010
2012
2014
2016
Separation of powers
Prosecution of abuse of office
Socioeconomic barriers
Anti-monopoly policy
Equal opportunity
Anti-corruption policy
b. Decline in governance indicators
Percent
12
10
8
6
4
2
0
2006
2008
2010
2012
2014
2016
Property rights
Conflict intesity
Basic administration
Prosecution of office abuse

Source: Bertelsmann Stiftung's Transformation Index, https://www.bti-project.org/en/data/rankings/governance-index/.

for Islamic State (IS), and helped fill the void in revenue due to losses of oil production and sale. Confiscation of property accounted for a relatively large part of IS revenues. For example, IS documents from Deir ez-Zor governorate showed that 44 percent of revenues came directly from confiscation of private property (Al-Tamimi 2015).

In most governorates, the top housing-related concern for Syrians is connected to looting, followed by concerns over damage. The 2018 HNAP surveys show that most Syrians see looting as the primary housing-related concern in As-Sweida (80 percent), Ar-Raqqa (42 percent), Deir ez-Zor (41 percent), Idleb, and Dar'a (both 34 percent) (UNOCHA 2018). Damage to land and property was a concern for more than one-third of the respondents in Ar-Raqqa and more than one in four respondents in Idleb and Dar'a (figure 2.32). In contrast, for Damascus, Rural Damascus, As-Sweida, Tartous, and Lattakia, war-related damage did not feature prominently in the responses, garnering percentages in the low single digits. The primary issue for the respondents in Damascus is rental problems (20 percent). Another problem

Figure 2.32. Concerns Related to Housing, Land, and Property, by Governorate, Syrian Arab Republic

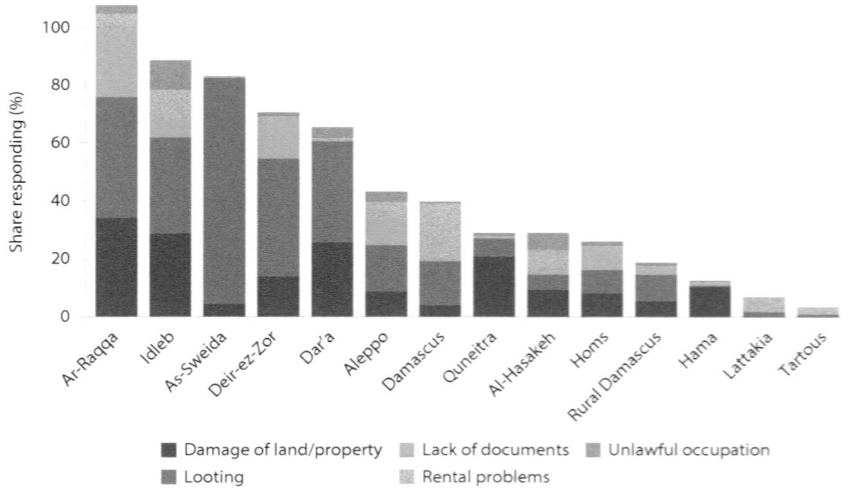

Source: Based on data from UNOCHA 2018.

that seems to have a strong geographic component is lack of documents. This problem features as an important concern in Ar-Raqqa (24 percent), Deir ez-Zor (15 percent), and Aleppo and Homs (10 percent each).

Concern about looting appears to affect returnees most. About 43 percent of all returnees mentioned looting as a significant problem, whereas only 19 percent of IDPs and 15 percent of the host communities brought it up (figure 2.33). Looting is the primary concern for As-Sweida, where two-thirds of the host communities, 90 percent of the IDPs, and virtually all the returnees who mentioned a concern chose this one. This issue seems to be very salient for Ar-Raqqa, Dar'a, Deir ez-Zor, and Idleb (about 35 percent for each governorate), and to a lesser extent for Aleppo and Damascus. The most striking disparity between returnees and host communities is observed in Rural Damascus and Dar'a, where more than 90 percent of the returnees report concerns over looting.

Lack of documentation related to land and property appears to be a regionally concentrated concern. Concerns about lack of land and property related documentation come out strongly in the governorates of Ar-Raqqa (21 percent) and Deir ez-Zor (20 percent) and, to a lesser extent, Aleppo, Idleb, and Homs (11 percent, 8 percent, and 5 percent, respectively). Respondents in the rest of the governorates seldom brought up this issue. On average returnees were more likely to face this problem (9 percent compared to 4.4 percent of IDPs and 5 percent for the host community); however, the IDPs in Ar-Raqqa and Homs fared worse compared to the other two population groups in their governorate (see figure 2.34).

Refugees, if or when they return, are likely to face more challenges than the IDP returnees captured by the surveys in Syria. Surveys within Syria may not fully reflect the challenges faced by Syrian refugees for several reasons. First, the number of refugee returnees is relatively small compared to Syrians inside and outside Syria.

Figure 2.33. Concerns Related to Looting of Private Property, by Governorate, Syrian Arab Republic

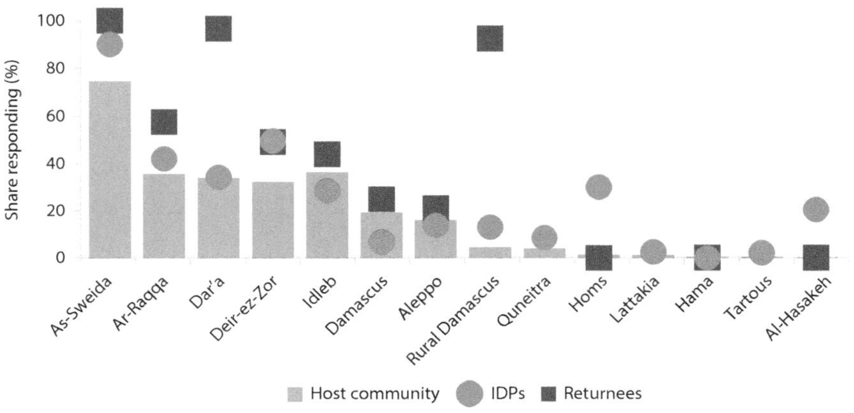

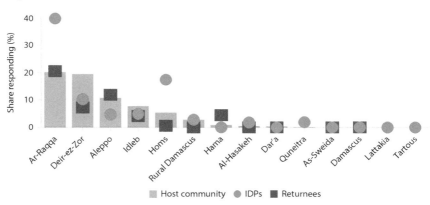

Source: Based on data from UNOCHA 2018.

Figure 2.34. Concerns Related to Lack of Documents, by Governorate, Syrian Arab Republic

Source: Based on data from UNOCHA 2018.
Note: IDP = internally displaced person.

Second, the refugee returnees often do not prefer to be identified as such for security reasons. Third, those who have returned are likely to be a self-selected group of people with different characteristics than those who have not yet returned. Fourth, reported land ownership is relatively high among refugees. According to a Norwegian Refugee Council (NRC) survey, over two-thirds (70 percent) of refugee households in Lebanon and the Kurdistan Region of Iraq reported ownership of residential dwellings, while 83 percent of surveyed households in Jordan reported ownership of land and other property (NRC 2017).

Providing documentary evidence of ownership is likely to be a challenge for many refugees. Lack of documentary evidence proving land rights puts land tenure at particular risk. Over 80 percent of refugee household respondents reported having formal evidence of ownership or other rights to property, including land title and lease contracts, but only 50 percent of respondents from the NRC survey reported possessing title documents. Other reported proof of tenure included sales contracts, notarized documents, and utility bills. Of those reporting the existence of ownership documents, however, more than 80 percent do not have access to the documents (figure 2.35). In the Kurdish Region of Iraq, over 70 percent of surveyed refugee households reported their documents are with someone else. Furthering confusing tenure rights, roughly 70 percent of the respondents in the NRC Survey stated that documents proving their ownership were actually in the name of another person, such as extended family members. Missing and unclear documentation is likely to lead to competing claims for property in the postconflict setting (see figure 2.35).

Land tenure security may be further weakened through changes to the legislative and regulatory framework applicable to land (table 2.9). Numerous changes have been made to the legislative and regulatory framework governing land administration (Cunial 2016). Roughly one-third of Syrian legislation and regulations have been adopted during the conflict, with implications for land in areas within, and outside of, Syrian government control. Changes cover land registration, tenancy, zoning, and planning. Clearance from security services is now required for private land transactions, and the government of Syria can suspend transactions in conflict areas, effectively shifting them to temporary registries located in government–controlled territory. The government of Syria has also signaled an initiative to digitize existing land registries. In Homs, residents received notices that objections to the accuracy of digitization would need to be received in person at service centers within four months. These changes may, in particular, undermine tenure security for displaced persons. They also may further complicate any attempt at postconflict land restitution, and thus reconciliation.

Figure 2.35. Status of Land Tenure Documentation of Syrian Refugees

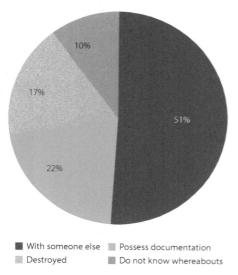

Source: Based on data from the 2017 Norwegian Refugee Council Refugee Household Survey.

Table 2.9. Syrian Legislation with Potential Implications for Refugees and IDPs, as of June 2018

Legislation number and name	Summary of potential concerns for refugees and IDPs
Law No. 10 issued on April 2, 2018, "Permitting the Establishment of New Development Areas Within the General Organizational Plan of Administrative Units"	Law No.10 Year 2018 allows for the establishment of one or more urban development zones within the general organizational plan of administrative units (the governorate, the city, the village, and the municipality as defined in the Local Administration Law LD#107 Year 2011) in all Syrian departments. The new law is based on controversial LD# 66 Year 2012, which created two urban development zones in Damascus because its scope of application is in Damascus only, whereas the scope of application of law No.10 Year 2018 is the rest of the Syrian Arab Republic. Concerns over law No.10 Year 2018 arise from the following points: • Short and inadequate period for landowners (whose property is not listed in the real estate record) in the area to be redeveloped to prove their ownership in the urban development zones (30 days from notification—Article 2 2). GOS has promised to extend it to one year, but this has not yet been done. • Difficulties in proving ownership in some areas because several of Syria's local land registries have been destroyed during the war and only 50 percent of Syrian land was officially registered even before the war. • Relatives of absent landowners up to the fourth degree or their legal representatives could submit proof of ownership to local authorities on behalf of absent landowners; however, 70 percent of refugees lack basic identification documentation, according to the Norwegian Refugee Council. Moreover, appointment of a local agent to submit the land ownership documents requires the use of a proxy or a power of attorney to be sent by refugees from abroad, which is subject to screening and security clearance of several security agencies in Syria (often denied for people in the "black list" or those from certain areas). GOS has promised to waive the requirement of security clearance for the power of attorney, but it has yet to happen. • The law does not adequately deal with the right to adequate housing for the residents of informal settlements in the area to be redeveloped. No certainty in the law about substitute houses to be offered to informal residents of the developed area, which frustrates the objective of an urban development project, which is to provide adequate housing for all formal and informal residents of the area to be redeveloped, a right guaranteed by several international instruments (International Covenant on Economic, Social, and Cultural Rights, Pinheiro principles, and many others). There are serious concerns that urban planning is used to justify the eviction and demolition of informal settlements.
Law No. 33 of October 26, 2017, "Reconstitution of Damaged or lost Cadastral Records"	The law regulates the restructuring of lost or partially damaged property documents or records, through a set of administrative and judicial procedures that lead to the issuance of a replacement of the damaged or lost real estate document. Concerns regarding the implementation of Law No.33 Year 2017 are as follows: • The administrative reconstitution of the lost or damaged property document is done by the directorate of cadastral affairs alone without supervision of the judiciary. • The judicial reconstitution of the land document requires, in case of complaint, the presence of the objector or a legal representative before the real estate judge. This is impossible for many Syrian IDPs and refugees considering the constraints on legalization of power of attorney and the relatively short term (six months) for recording the objection against the initial reconstitution decision of the real estate judge. • Moreover, it will be nearly impossible to reconstitute destroyed land documents and land registries in destroyed areas considering the large-scale destruction. The possibility of reconstructing social verification mechanisms to reestablish property rights in the future will be very difficult because individuals will have to be located and their property information triangulated with individuals from the same location. Consequently, refugees will not return if they have lost their houses or became unable to prove their property rights and recover them.

(table continues next page)

Table 2.9. *(continued)*

Legislation number and name	Summary of potential concerns for refugees and IDPs
Legislative decree No. 66 issued on September 18, 2012, "Master Planning of Two Areas in Damascus" as amended by Law No. 10 Year 2018	The declared objective of the decree is to "redevelop areas of unauthorized housing and informal settlements [slums]" inside Damascus. Legislative Decree 66/2012 enables local government to expropriate land, change the allowed land use, and develop it through a public private partnership. Within a certain time frame, original owners can apply for compensation, which is based on the original value of the property, without benefitting from the value increase. Moreover, because of their absence, many IDPs and refugees have missed the application deadline for claims and lost their property rights. There are serious concerns that residents of informal housing in the area will not be granted any substitute houses nor would they be compensated. They do not have a formal title, and therefore they will not be considered as formal owners having a right to compensation but may rather be treated as renters. Renters will receive compensation equivalent to two years of rent only. Many refugees are unlikely to return without a house or property to return to.
Legislative decree No. 63 issued on September 16, 2012, related to "Police Powers"	This legislative decree provides that during its investigations of crimes against the state's internal or external security and offenses set forth in Act No. 19 of July 2, 2012 (the counterterrorism law), security agencies may request in writing to the Syrian Minister of Finance to take the necessary precautionary measures against the movable and immovable property belonging to the accused. Many IDPs are unlikely to return if their property is confiscated during their absence or if they face the significant risk of persecution, restricted freedom of movement, or arbitrary arrest.
Legislative decree No. 40 of May 20, 2012, "Construction Violations Removal" also known as "Informal Settlement Law"	The main objective of the legislative decree 40/2012 is to prohibit further construction in destroyed informal settlements. It ordered the destruction of all unauthorized buildings after its publication and provided for fines and prison sanctions to be imposed on all persons convicted of involvement in illegal construction, including officials who failed to prevent the violation of the law. The main concern regarding law # 40/2012 is that it has primarily sanctioned displaced informal house owners whose houses were partly damaged or fully destroyed during the war. They will not be able to return, reconstruct their homes, and regularize them, because they would be severely punished if they do so; and their rights, if any, will be restricted to financial compensation. This constitutes a significant hurdle to the return of refugees if they are not allowed to reconstruct their destroyed informal homes. Additionally, new urban development legislation does not properly address housing needs and rights of informal owners.

Note: GOS = government of Syria; IDP = internally displaced person.

Private property remains at risk of expropriation and confiscation. Government forces are alleged to have confiscated property of displaced persons (U.S. Department of State 2015). The government of Syria has targeted land supporting illegal (unregistered) housing, long tolerated by the government, for expropriation, particularly in those areas with populations deemed supportive of the opposition. Urban planning codes have been changed to allow replacement of informal housing in rebellious areas with high-value real estate projects (Sayigh 2016). Areas in which conflict has occurred, such as As-Sweida and Dar'a, have also been subjected to large-scale state expropriations. The government of Syria now has the power to confiscate agricultural land holdings over established limits, without compensation or adequate appeal procedures, including through a Counterterrorism Court established in 2012; and the power to seize the property and assets of persons detained on charges of terrorism.

Infrastructure and Publicly Provided Services

International experience suggests a complex and nuanced relationship between refugee returns and access to services and infrastructure. Other things being equal, better access to services and repaired infrastructure should provide additional incentives for return. Other things, however, are usually not equal. There are cases where damage to infrastructure and lacking services delayed return, for example in Bosnia and Herzegovina; there are also examples of refugees spontaneously returning to countries after the cessation of hostilities where destruction is widespread—for example in Angola and Liberia. In any case, it is important to take stock of service availability and infrastructure damage, either for return or for assessing the well-being of the populations that are affected by those conditions. In this section the analysis will investigate such conditions faced by Syrians inside and outside Syria in several categories: health, education, water, solid waste management, energy, and transportation.

Health

Syria's health indicators have noticeably deteriorated during the conflict and stand currently below their precrisis values as well as below levels in peer countries. Although life expectancy in the country had increased since the 1960s, this trend was reversed by the onset of armed conflict. Life expectancy in Syria stands at about 70 years, well below its precrisis figure of 75 years and below comparative countries and the MENA average of 73 years (figure 2.36). Similarly, improvements in infant mortality, estimated at 14 infants per 1,000 live births, have stagnated.

The crisis imposed a disproportionate cost on women's health. The maternal mortality rate in Syria, for instance, is 68 deaths per 100,000 live births in 2016—significantly worse than the precrisis rate of 49 deaths per 100,000 live births in 2010 (figure 2.37).[31] Maternal mortality in conflict areas is particularly exacerbated by limited access to maternal health services due to safety, financial, and geographical restrictions, as well as the general collapse of the health system and disruption of routine health service delivery. The leading direct causes of maternal mortality were identified as hemorrhage, thromboembolism, preeclampsia/eclampsia, maternal sepsis, and obstructed labor.

Figure 2.36. Life Expectancy, 1960–2016

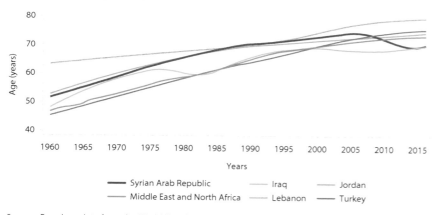

Source: Based on data from the World Development Indicators (https://datacatalog.worldbank.org/dataset /world-development-indicators).

Figure 2.37. Maternal Mortality Rate, 1990–2016

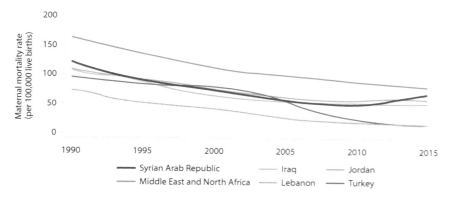

Source: Based on data from the World Development Indicators (https://datacatalog.worldbank.org/dataset /world-development-indicators).

Women are also at a disadvantage in refuge. Data from Lebanon show significant setbacks in neonatal and maternal mortality indicators (the data exclude deliveries outside the hospitals). As of 2017, the neonatal mortality rate had increased from 3.4 per 10,000 in 2012 to 4.9 per 10,000, with the rate among displaced Syrians (7.0 per 10,000) almost double that among Lebanese (3.7 per 10,000). Similarly, the maternal mortality rate increased from 12.7 per 100,000 in 2012 to 21.3 per 100,000, with the rate among displaced Syrians (30.4 per 100,000) double that among Lebanese (15.8 per 100,000).

The most direct impact of the war has obviously been the conflict-driven loss of lives. According to the latest Institute of Health Metrics and Evaluation (IHME) assessment, conflict and terrorism have become the leading cause of death in Syria in 2016, compared to being the 145th cause of death in 2005.[32] Indirect death due to war injuries and lack of medication is reported to have increased because of the conflict—with estimates ranging between 200,000 deaths to 300,000.[33] Despite the ongoing conflict, Syria is in the delayed degenerative diseases stage of epidemiological transition, with noncommunicable diseases (NCDs) such as ischemic heart disease and cerebrovascular diseases remaining the leading causes of death. The World Health Organization indicates that approximately 46 percent of mortality in 2014 was attributed to NCDs. Chronic kidney disease, leukemia, chronic obstructive pulmonary disease, and diabetes are among the top 10 causes of mortality in Syria (figure 2.38). This finding is in line with the prewar epidemiological profile of Syria where 77 percent of all mortalities were caused by NCDs (Kherallah et al. 2012). Although NCDs are manageable, they can be deadly if appropriate medications and treatment are not available—which highlights the need to consider the needs of the Syrian population beyond direct injuries due to war.

Figure 2.38. Top 10 Causes of Death, Syrian Arab Republic, 2005–16

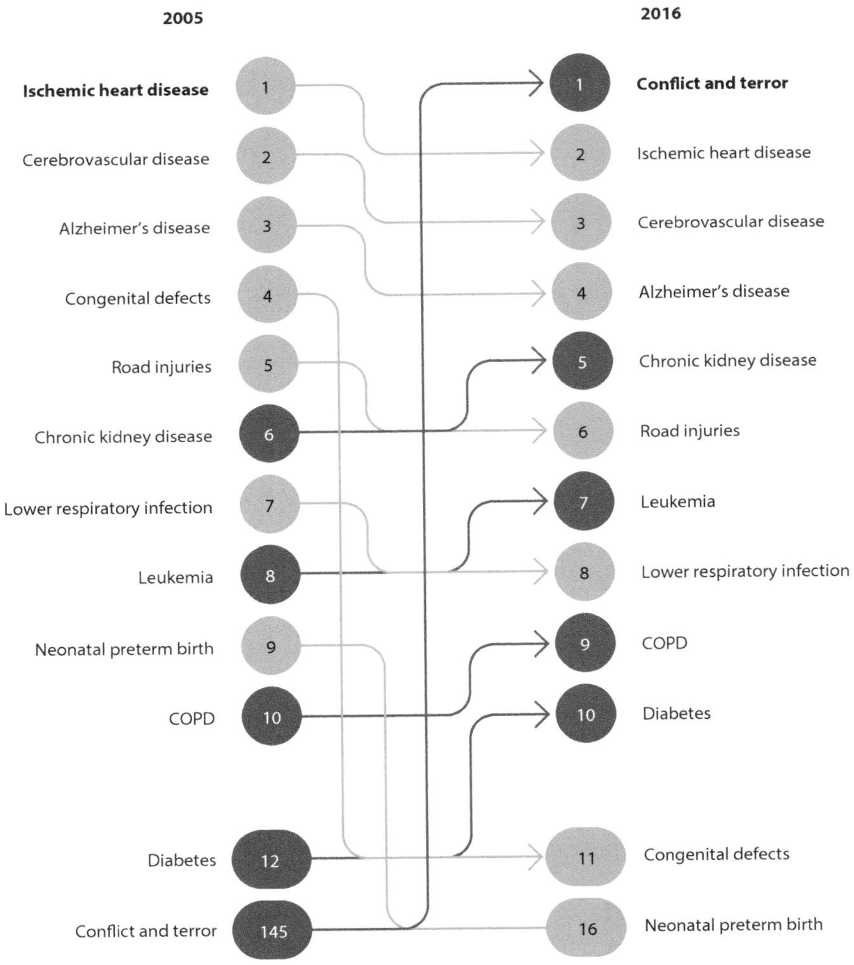

2005			2016
Ischemic heart disease	1	1	Conflict and terror
Cerebrovascular disease	2	2	Ischemic heart disease
Alzheimer's disease	3	3	Cerebrovascular disease
Congenital defects	4	4	Alzheimer's disease
Road injuries	5	5	Chronic kidney disease
Chronic kidney disease	6	6	Road injuries
Lower respiratory infection	7	7	Leukemia
Leukemia	8	8	Lower respiratory infection
Neonatal preterm birth	9	9	COPD
COPD	10	10	Diabetes
Diabetes	12	11	Congenital defects
Conflict and terror	145	16	Neonatal preterm birth

Source: Institute of Health Metrics and Evaluation 2018.
Note: COPD = chronic obstructive pulmonary disease.

In terms of morbidity, NCDs accounted for 8 of the 10 top causes of years lived with disability in the latest IHME assessment. In fact, in 2016 low back pain, sense organ disease, migraine, skin disease, depressive disorder, and anxiety disorder accounted for the top six causes of disability in Syria along with diabetes and other musculoskeletal diseases respectively occupying the eighth and ninth top causes of disability.

The conflict has also led to the reemergence of some preventable communicable diseases such as measles, mumps, polio, and leishmaniasis. Latest figures from May 2018 show high incidences of leishmaniasis (770 new cases in May alone mostly concentrated in Idleb, Aleppo, Deir ez-Zor, and Hama), measles (182 new cases), brucellosis (136 new cases), pertussis (47 new cases), mumps (24 new cases), and tuberculosis (11 new cases).[34]

This study has developed a novel approach to compare the accessibility of health care services to Syrians inside Syria with that of Syrian refugees in host countries. To this end, access to health care services is defined in terms of three factors: (a) access to health care infrastructure, (b) access to human resources for health, and (c) access to financial coverage for health care services. More specifically is as follows:

- **Access to health care infrastructure** is measured in terms of both the ratio of hospital beds per 1,000 persons and the ratio of health units per 1,000 persons (figure 2.39). Both ratios are then normalized and added to form an *infrastructure access indicator* where ratios are weighted equally.

- **Access to human resources for health** is measured in terms of the ratio of physicians per 1,000 persons and the ratio of nurses/midwives per 1,000 persons. Like the infrastructure indicator, both human resource ratios are normalized and added to form a *human resources access indicator* where ratios are weighted equally.

Figure 2.39. Hospitals per 1,000 Persons, 2010 vs. 2018

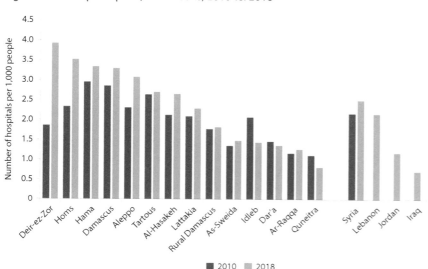

Source: Urban Community Profiling (UCP) surveys by UN-Habitat.

- **Access to financial coverage** is measured in terms of the availability of financial resources to cover the cost of care for Syrians inside and outside Syria. For regions inside Syria, it is assumed that the controlling group will maintain the precrisis national policy of providing coverage for health care service. Coverage is therefore considered to be 100 percent in regions inside Syria. For host countries, financial coverage is determined according to local policies toward refugee coverage.[35]

The three access indicators listed above are then combined and weighted to form a *health accessibility index*. The index represents overall access to health services for Syrians. The weights attributed to each indicator in the index have been determined based on the latest Urban Community Profiling (UCP) surveys by UN-Habitat, which highlight the main barriers to health care for Syrians inside Syria. According to the results of the UCP survey, 50 percent of respondents listed lack of availability of health infrastructure as the main barrier to accessing health care, followed by 25 percent of respondents listing lack of human resources. The remaining respondents (25 percent) listed lack of financial coverage in Syria as the main barrier to accessing health care.

In the absence of comprehensive microdata, multiple sources of data were used in a second-best fashion. This analysis relies on several sources of data including official data from the Ministry of Health in Syria, as well as Urban Community Profiling, VAF, and VASyR survey data from UN agencies for studies conducted inside Syria and in host countries. The figures are also quality-checked using satellite imagery, social media data, and phone usage data. It is important to note as well that the ratios depend on population size, which varies between 2010 and 2018. In fact, population size, which is used as a denominator in the access ratios, is seen to have decreased in many governorates between the years 2010 and 2018. This factor implies that, even in cases where a nominal decrease in asset numbers is seen, the access ratio might still increase or remain constant because of decreases in population.

Results show that the conflict-driven reduction in functioning infrastructure was somewhat overshadowed by conflict-driven displacement. In general, the ratio of hospital beds per 1,000 persons in Syria in 2018 remains almost the same (1.368) as the precrisis level in 2010 (1.236), but it remains lower than access ratios in Lebanon (1.839) and Jordan (1.504), and is similar to that in Iraq (1.232). A simple ratio of hospital beds to population is misleading, however, because both factors—hospital beds and population size—are affected by the crisis, which indicates that decreases in the nominal values of hospital beds might be compensated for with a decrease in the population served. The governorate-level analysis, conducted to get a better understanding of the situation, shows a wide variation in access to hospitals among the different regions with the governorates of Ar-Raqqa, As-Sweida, Idleb, Quneitra, and Rural Damascus witnessing the largest drop in hospital beds per population served (figure 2.40). Other governorates that witnessed severe violence such as Aleppo, Dar'a, and Deir-ez-Zor, show an increase in access to hospitals primarily due to a decrease in the size of their population.

There has been a clear reduction in access to health units in Syria. The ratio of health units per 1,000 persons in Syria has decreased from 0.085 in 2010 to 0.078 in 2018. This ratio is lower than the values observed in Lebanon (0.132) and Jordan (0.120), but higher than Iraq (0.073). At the governorate level in Syria, there is wide variation

Figure 2.40. Hospital Beds per 100,000 Persons, 2010 vs. 2018

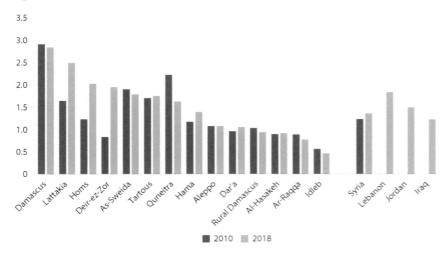

Source: Urban Community Profiling (UCP) surveys by UN-Habitat.

Figure 2.41. Health Units per 1,000 Persons, 2010 vs. 2018

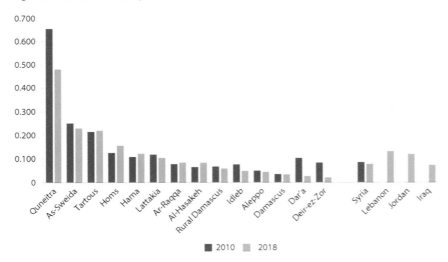

Source: Urban Community Profiling (UCP) surveys by UN-Habitat.

in access to health units, with the most significant decrease observed in Dar'a (0.103 to 0.026), Quneitra (0.656 to 0.481), and As-Sweida (0.251 to 0.230) (figure 2.41).

Overall, standard indicators like beds or unit per person, by themselves, do not provide a convincing assessment of health care access. Combining hospital and health unit indicators, the results of the analysis show that the overall health infrastructure accessibility remained almost the same in Syria between 2010 (0.209) and 2018 (0.230). Governorates like Deir ez-Zor, Lattakia, Homs, and Hama show an increase in access to health care infrastructure whereas Quneitra, Idleb, As-Sweida, and Dar'a show a decrease in access to infrastructure. When compared to host countries in 2018, Syria still has lower access to infrastructure than Lebanon (0.369) and Jordan

(0.291), but higher than Iraq (0.199). (figure 2.42). These findings show that standard indicators, where the numerator (population) tends to remain rather stable, cannot be relied upon when analyzing cases where there are discrete changes in population, like conflict and forced displacement. Next, this challenge can be offset by considering the human capital dimension, which follows.

The impact of conflict on human resources for health has been dramatic. Data show that the conflict has halved the number of physicians in Syria, from 11,305 in 2010 (0.529 per 1,000 persons) to 5,889 physicians (0.291 per 1,000 persons) in 2018 (figure 2.43). Similarly, the number of nurses and midwives dropped from 29,126 (1.362 per 1,000 persons) in 2010 to 12,915 (0.639 per 1,000 persons) in 2018 (figure 2.44). Comparatively, Iraq, Jordan, and Lebanon have much larger ratios of

Figure 2.42. Infrastructure Access Indicator, 2010 vs. 2018

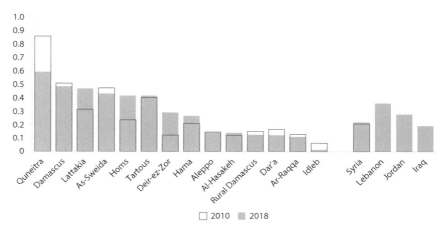

Source: World Bank calculations based on multiple sources.

Figure 2.43. Physicians per 1,000 Persons, 2010 vs. 2018

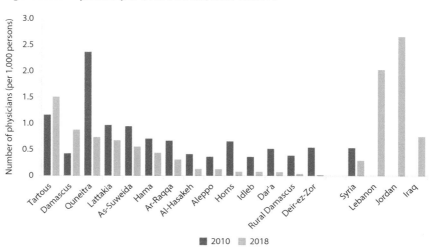

Source: World Bank staff calculations based on multiple sources.

physicians per 1,000 persons (0.748, 2.648, and 2.023, respectively) as well as nurses and midwives per 1,000 persons (1.727, 1.506, and 2.356, respectively). The human resources for health (HRH) indicator normalizes and combines the number of physicians per 1,000 persons and the number of nurses and midwives per 1,000 persons. When combined, the indicator places current Syria (0.095) well below its HRH availability values in 2010 (0.198). The most notable decreases in the HRH indicator are seen in Dar'a (from 0.168 to 0.025), Homs (0.289 to 0.063), Aleppo (0.095 to 0.027), As-Sweida (0.675 to 0.296), Rural Damascus (0.723 to 0.214), Quneitra (0.723 to 0.214), and Deir ez-Zor (0.227 to 0). Furthermore, according to this indicator, Syria (0.095) is comparatively well below Iraq (0.269), Jordan (0.612), and Lebanon (0.562). All governorates show a significant decrease in physicians except for Damascus and Tartous, while the number of nurses dropped in all governorates (figure 2.44).

Financial coverage for health care in host countries (averaging about 55 percent) is volatile and below that of Syria (if assumed at 100 percent given existing financial coverage policies). The lower coverage in host countries is likely due to insufficient donor funding to cover all the health needs of Syrian refugees. Results from the latest UN surveys, including the VASyR in Lebanon and the VAF in Jordan, are used to estimate the extent to which financial coverage is provided to Syrian refugees in host countries. Responses from the surveys indicate that approximately 65 percent of respondents did not see financial coverage as a barrier to accessing primary health care services. In contrast, 45 percent of respondents did not indicate financial coverage as a barrier to accessing hospital care services. Financial coverage for primary care and hospital care, weighted equally, form the financial coverage indicator that holds the values of 1.00 for Syria and 0.55 for Iraq, Jordan, and Lebanon. This finding indicates that Syrians have less access to financial coverage for health care in host countries than in Syria and that financial coverage is perceived more as a barrier to health care by refugees than inside Syria.

Figure 2.44. Nurses and Midwives per 1,000 Persons, 2010 vs. 2018

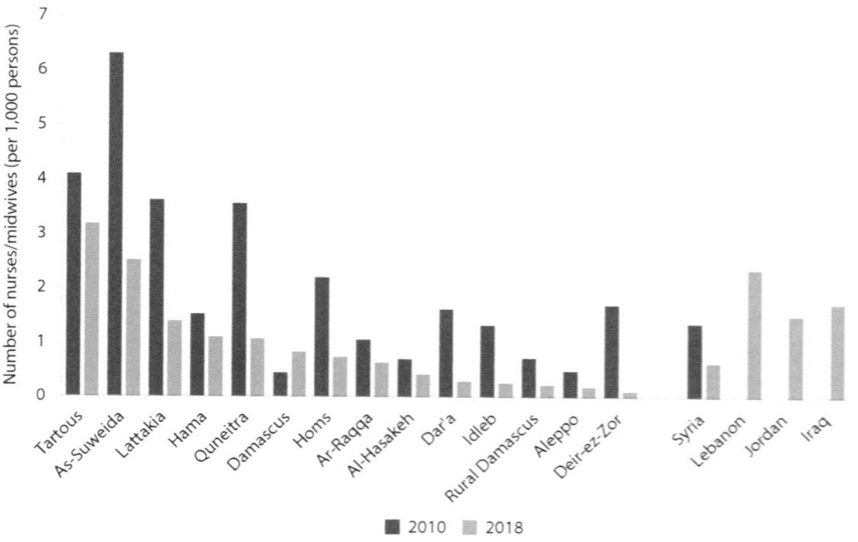

Source: World Bank staff calculations based on multiple sources.

Figure 2.45. Human Resources for Health Indicator, 2010 vs. 2018

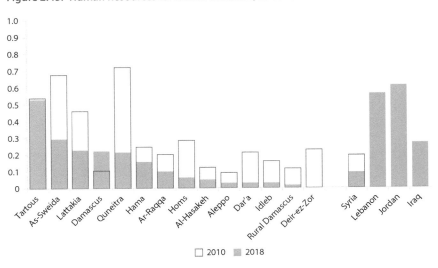

□ 2010   ■ 2018

Source: World Bank calculations based on multiple sources.

The health accessibility index exhibits large variations across governorates. As indicated earlier, the health accessibility index combines the three indicators—infrastructure, human resources, and financial coverage—to come up with a unified access index. Tables 2A.1 and 2A.2 in annex 2A provide the accessibility indexes for all governorates for 2010 and 2018, respectively. At the national level, the overall health care accessibility index within Syria remained relatively constant, standing at 0.39 in 2018 compared to 0.4 in 2010, mainly because of the decrease in the size of the population served. The population of Syria dropped from 21,377,000 in 2010 to 20,226,627 in 2018. There is still, however, a wide variation in the health accessibility index between governorates—with As-Sweida, Quneitra, Dar'a, Idleb, Ar-Raqqa, and Rural Damascus showing a decrease in their health accessibility index compared to other governorates (figure 2.46). When compared to host countries, Syria today has a lower accessibility index (0.389) compared to Jordan (0.436) and Lebanon (0.462) but higher than Iraq (0.304). At the governorate level, governorates that witnessed the highest levels of conflict show a lower health accessibility index than host countries, namely Idleb (0.267), Rural Damascus (0.318), Dar'a (0.319), Ar-Raqqa (0.319), Aleppo (0.330), and Al-Hasakeh (0.334).

Household and community surveys suggest that having access to infrastructure alone does not always translate into having access to service. The 2017 MSNA survey shows that health care facilities are within relatively easy reach for most households, with almost 80 percent of households living within 30 minutes of a facility. Almost one-third of households did not seek treatment when one family member was sick, and several did not use the facilities because they were not functional or they lack qualified personnel. Only in Damascus and Rural Damascus are less than one-half of the surveyed health services available on average in communities (figure 2.47). Health service deprivation was particularly bad in Al-Hasakeh (70 percent of services not available on average), Ar-Raqqa (77 percent), Dar'a (77 percent), Deir-ez-Zor (84 percent), Idleb (74 percent), and Quneitra (84 percent).

Figure 2.46. Health Accessibility Index, 2010 vs. 2018

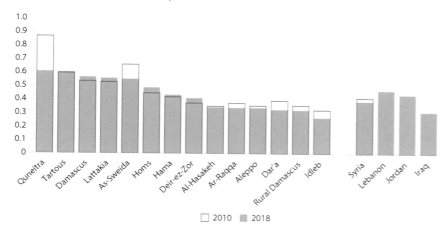

□ 2010   ■ 2018

Source: World Bank staff calculations based on multiple sources.

Figure 2.47. Health Services, Outcomes and Deprivation, Syrian Arab Republic, 2017

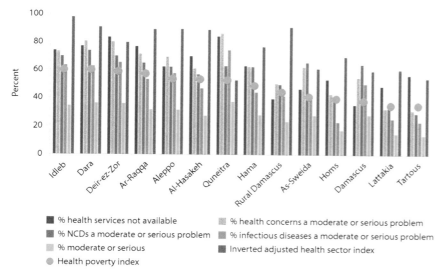

■ % health services not available   ▦ % health concerns a moderate or serious problem

■ % NCDs a moderate or serious problem   ■ % infectious diseases a moderate or serious problem

▧ % moderate or serious   ■ Inverted adjusted health sector index

● Health poverty index

Source: UNHCR 2017d and World Bank analysis.
Note: Health services include prosthetics, family planning, skilled birth delivery, antenatal health, surgery, mental health, pharmacy of essential drugs, psychosocial support, dialysis, treatment for malnutrition, integrated management of childhood illnesses, leishmaniasis disease care, management of chronic diseases, elderly health services, noninfectious disease care, clinical care for rape survivors, physical rehabilitation, and other health services. Health concerns include war-related injuries, non-war-related injuries, pregnancy or delivery complications, malnutrition, communicable diseases, noncommunicable diseases (NCDs), war-related burns, non-war-related burns, dog bites, scorpion and snake bites, long-term impairments, mental health disorders, post-traumatic stress disorder, lack of medical staff, and lack of medical supplies. Infectious diseases include watery and bloody diarrhea, typhoid, upper and lower respiratory infections, influenza, tuberculosis, sexually transmitted diseases, diphtheria, tetanus, rabies, meningoencephalitis, hepatitis, skin infections, eye infections, and other infectious diseases. The inverted and adjusted Health Sector Index is two-thirds the infrastructure (hospitals and beds) and one-third human resources (nurses and doctors), inverted (1 minus this positive index). The aggregate Health Accessibility Index is 0.50 times the average health concerns, infectious diseases and NCD rates, 0.25 times the inverted and adjusted Health Sector Index, and 0.25 times the percentage of health services not available.

Many communities report moderate to serious problems in terms of health concerns, infectious diseases, and NCDs. Figure 2.47 shows a Health Accessibility Index, which is based on 50 percent of the average health outcomes deprivation (from surveys), 25 percent of the service availability deprivation (from surveys), and 25 percent of the infrastructure and resource adversity (from the above analysis). Only Lattakia and Tartous (both 35 percent) and Damascus (38 percent) are below 40 percent of aggregate deprivation. Deprivation is highest in Dar'a and Idleb (60 percent).

Education

Less than a decade ago, Syria was on the verge of achieving the education targets under the Millennium Development Goals. Primary net enrollment rates in school year 2009–10 were at 93 percent, the same as the MENA region average and higher than that of middle-income countries (90 percent). Similarly, the net enrollment rate at the secondary level was 67 percent for the same year, above the MENA regional average of 60 percent. The gender parity index was 0.98 at the primary level and 1.01 at the secondary level. Student learning outcomes in Syria were below international averages, but higher than those in most MENA countries.

The conflict has had a devastating effect on Syrian children. It has claimed the lives of tens of thousands of children in addition to depriving millions of them an education. The number of children killed since the start of the conflict has been estimated at a quarter of all deaths (Guha-Sapir et al. 2018). A whole generation of children has received inadequate education: at least one-third of school-age children are out of school (UNOCHA 2018). About 150,000 teachers have left the formal education system, representing more than one-third of prewar education employees. In addition, about 40 percent of education facilities have been damaged, destroyed, or occupied by parties to the conflict or serve as shelters to IDPs. There are about 5.8 million school-age children within Syria, or about 28 percent of the overall population currently residing in country.

Host countries continue to make a significant contribution by opening their national education systems to refugee children and removing barriers to access. Of the 1.9 million refugees who have sought shelter in Iraq, Jordan, and Lebanon, nearly one-half are school-age children. Trends show stability in enrollment since 2014–15 inside Syria and progress in host countries—a positive course considering the unprecedented magnitude of the Syrian crisis and the extremely difficult and ever-shifting circumstances. Still, there is a long way to go before all education needs are met. About 2.5 million school-age Syrian children remain out of school in Syria and in the host countries. Barriers to access and effective learning for Syrian children and youth are complex and extend beyond the education sector to a wide range of economic, social, and cultural issues. For many displaced families, the financial cost of education for their children is too high. School fees, transportation, and expenses for learning material accumulate; and school quickly becomes unaffordable for households. Attending school also implies high opportunity cost for youth. Teenage males often drop out of school to work and support their families, while an increasing share of girls get married under age 18 (UNICEF 2018). Cumulative psychosocial effects and protracted trauma and a lack of safety at home and in school are also key concerns.

Conditions in Syria

The conflict has altered the demographic distribution of Syrian children and their school enrollment ratios alike.[36] The total number of 5- to17-year-old Syrians currently residing in Syria is estimated to be between 5.3 million and 5. 8 million, about 31 percent of the population in 2018. Almost one-half of all children in that age group live in Aleppo, Idleb, and Rural Damascus (figure 2.48). About 30 percent of school-age children are internally displaced within Syria. In Damascus city (192,000 internally displaced children), rural Damascus (390,000), Idleb (292,000), and Lattakia (126,000), more than 40 percent of all children are internally displaced. In Syria, the conflict has significantly decreased enrollment rates in most governorates. Overall, between 2010 and 2018 the enrollment rate for the 5–17 age group decreased from 85 percent to 61 percent.[37]

There is a large heterogeneity in enrollment rates by governorate but not by gender. Figure 2.49 shows enrollment rates of school-age children by governorate in 2010 and in 2018. Aleppo, Ar-Raqqa, Deir-ez-Zor and Idleb governorates faced the largest decreases in enrollment between 2010 and 2018. At the same time, Lattakia, Tartous, Damascus City, and As-Sweida have remained relatively stable. Overall, enrollment of boys and girls seems equally affected by the conflict. Girls have lower enrollment rates in Ar-Raqqa and Al-Hasakeh, Homs, and Lattakia; but differences in enrollment do not exceed 3 percentage points. The largest difference in enrollment by gender is in Damascus City, which has a 6-percentage-point difference in favor of girls (UNOCHA 2018).

Internally displaced children are particularly affected by the conflict. As of September 2018, an estimated 2 million out of 5.76 million school-age children were displaced inside Syria (UNICEF estimates). Although enrollment rates specifically for internally displaced children are not available, qualitative reports suggest that their enrollment rates are significantly lower. Internally displaced children are at a particularly high risk of dropping out of education, and they typically face

131

Figure 2.48. Number and Share of Syrians Ages 5 to 17, by Governorate, 2018

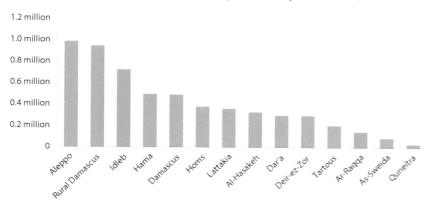

Source: UNOCHA 2018.
Note: The reference population used in UNOCHA 2018 is 19.2 million.

Figure 2.49. Enrollment Rate of School-Age Population, by Governorate, Syrian Arab Republic, 2010 and 2018

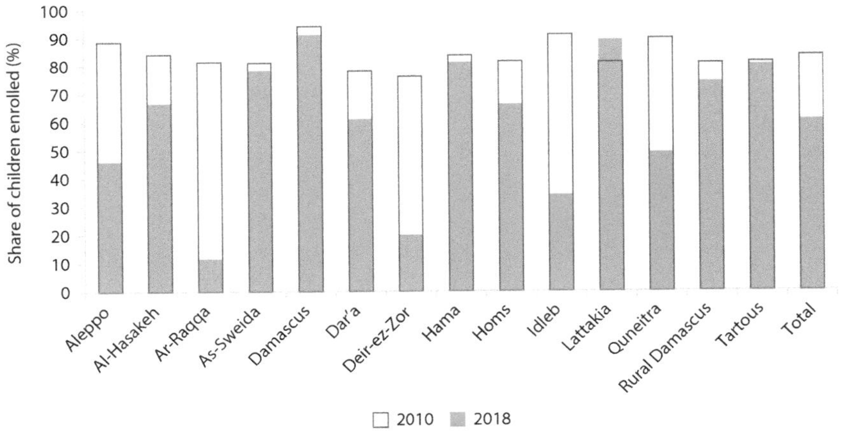

Source: Estimates for 2010 rely on the Ministry of Education's Education Management Information System. Estimates for 2018 rely on United Nations Children's Fund estimates for the 2016–17 school year (https://www.unicef.org/syria/reports/education-section-facts-and-figures).

higher hurdles to access education services. Displaced children are often required to take official placement examinations determining their education levels before being allowed to register in school. Because of the large number of IDPs, some schools are unable to accommodate displaced children even when those children provide all necessary documentation.

The quality of teaching has suffered drastically as well. The Early Grade Reading Assessment and Early Grade Mathematics Assessment conducted in Idleb, Rural Damascus, Rural Aleppo, and Deir-ez-Zor in 2016 found that less than 10 percent of grade 3 students can read and perform basic mathematical tasks at the corresponding grade level. Trends in national examinations for grades 9 and 12 inside Syria reveal a significant decline in both access and quality of education. The number of grade 9 examination candidates decreased by 34 percent between 2011 and 2017, and grade 12 candidates decreased by 42 percent over the same period. The number of candidates who passed the grade 9 and 12 exams also decreased by 39 percent and 23 percent, respectively. These results illustrate the massive quality challenges facing the education sector, in addition to the challenge of ensuring access to education for all school-age children.

School destruction and nonfunctioning schools are the primary drivers of low enrollment rates. Education facilities have been targets during the conflict. Schools have also been used as military quarters and informal shelters for displaced households. Figure 2.50 shows that, in cities like Tadmur, Douma, Deir-ez-Zor, and Ar-Raqqa, most schools are not functioning. In many cities about one-third of education facilities are not operational, whereas cities such as Yabroud, Idleb, Kobani, and others are less affected, with most education facilities still functional. MSNA focal point surveys from 2017 confirm significant disruptions to educational facilities (figure 2.51), particularly in Ar-Raqqa, where 95 percent of community focal points report less than three-fourths are functional and 89 percent report less than

Figure 2.50. Share of Nonfunctioning Education Facilities in the Syrian Arab Republic, by City

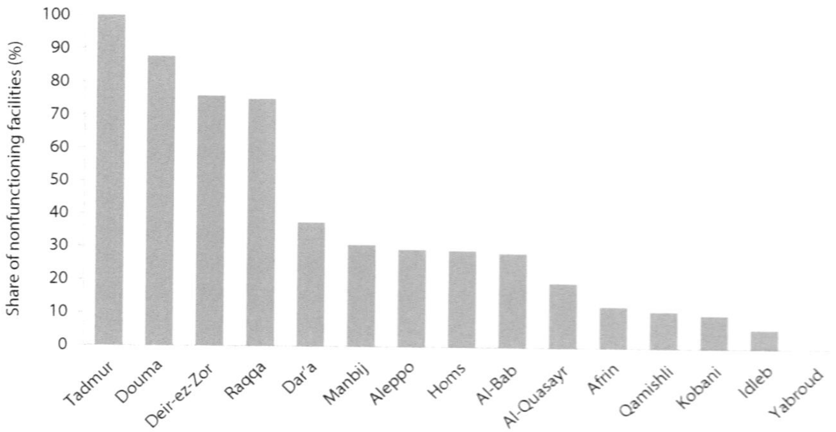

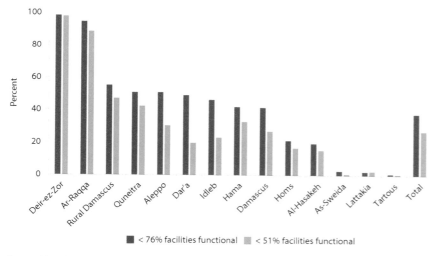

Figure 2.51. Survey Responses to Educational Facility Functionality, 2017

Source: UNHCR 2017d.

one-half are functional. In Deir-ez-Zor almost all communities report that less than one-half of the facilities are functional.

Additional drivers of education service delivery problems in Syria include teacher shortage and lack of learning materials. The number of teachers in the formal education system has decreased since 2011–12 by more than one-half, to less than 200,000 teachers in 2017. An additional 300,000 education personnel need assistance in Syria. In the 2017 MSNA conducted by the UNOCHA, 45 percent of communities in Syria indicated teacher-related needs as the priority educational need. Teacher stipends/incentives are often insufficient to meet their families' basic needs, and thousands of teachers continue to work voluntarily, particularly in contested areas. Children often learn without textbooks or learning materials; in very poor learning spaces, especially in UN-declared besieged and hard-to-reach areas; and for only few hours a day. The prolonged conflict extends into the classroom as part of the contest for legitimacy. Depending on the spheres of influence, education services are provided by the government, opposition groups, or NGOs and international organizations. In areas controlled by the government, students follow the prewar curriculum, whereas facilities overseen by opposition groups implement revised versions of the Syrian curriculum. Both the government and the opposition groups operate a large share of their schools on a double-shift model (WES 2016).

Children also drop out because of child labor, child marriage, and violence. Over 2,100 communities (40 percent) surveyed in Syria consider the need for children to work or help the family one of the key reasons for being out of school (UNICEF 2018). In 82 percent of surveyed communities, respondents reported that child labor was an issue of concern. Boys are more likely to be involved in hazardous forms of labor and girls in domestic work. Also, children, particularly boys, often get involved in frontline combat roles, military training, and support roles. Verified cases of the recruitment and use of children in combat increased by 13 percent compared to 2016, with 961 cases (872 boys, 89 girls) verified. Ninety percent of the children served in combat roles (861) and 26 percent (254) were below the age of 15 (United Nations 2018). Children and their families may resort to child marriage as a negative coping strategy to respond to economic difficulties and protection concerns. In 69 percent of assessed communities, respondents reported child marriage as an issue of concern, with 20 percent reporting it as a common or very common issue (UNICEF 2018). Psychosocial trauma and violence are additional reasons for school dropout. Teachers and students suffer from stress and psychosocial disorders due to the protracted nature of the crisis. Both children and teachers demonstrate psychosocial distress inflicted by conflict, including depression, anxiety, and panic attacks, which increases their vulnerability and exposure to risks, including negative coping strategies.

Overall, physical damage, functionality status of schools, and ratio of children out of school provide a consistent picture across governorates. An aggregate Education Deprivation Index has been constructed for each governorate based on 0.7 times the average percentage of communities with more than a quarter of children ages 5–11 years out of formal education, 0.2 times the percentage of communities with less than three-quarters of educational facilities functioning, and 0.1 times the physical damage index. With school functionality and out of education indicators correlating so closely, the aggregate Education Deprivation measure ranks governorates in a very similar manner (figure 2.52).

Conditions in countries of asylum
Despite substantial efforts to include refugee children in the education system, Syrian children are enrolled at low rates in host countries. Lebanon has almost doubled the size of its national public education system in five years to accommodate non-Lebanese children. As a result, a remarkable 264,970 non-Lebanese children were enrolled in public schools in the 2017–18 school year. In Iraq, too, most public schools opened registration for refugee children for first grade at the beginning of the school year in October 2017. However, 43 percent of school-age refugee children in Lebanon do not have access to either formal or nonformal education. The corresponding shares are 31 percent and 4 percent in Jordan and Iraq, respectively. In Iraq, outside of camps, only 46 percent of school-age children attend school, with the share reaching 71 percent in camps. In 2014, only about 5 percent of Syrians ages 15–17 were registered in formal secondary school in Iraq.

Figure 2.52. Education Deprivation Index, 2017

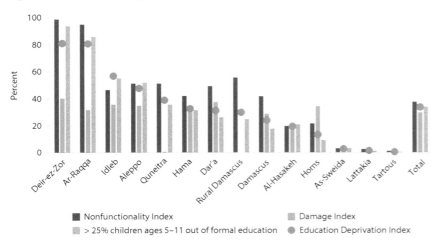

Legend:
- Nonfunctionality Index
- Damage Index
- > 25% children ages 5–11 out of formal education
- Education Deprivation Index

Source: World Bank staff calculations based on data from UNHCR 2017d.
Note: Education Deprivation Index = 0.7 × Children Out of Formal Education + 0.2 × facilities functional + 0.1 × Damage Index.

School enrollment rates of Syrian refugee children in Jordan and Lebanon are even lower than the enrollment of Syrian children inside Syria. Two-thirds of refugee children in the Mashreq live in Lebanon where their school-age enrollment is only 42 percent, considerably lower than the 77 percent enrollment rate for Lebanese children. Refugee children living in Jordan have a slightly lower enrollment rate than currently in Syria, at 56 percent, which is also significantly lower than for Jordanian children (90 percent). Only in Iraq are refugee enrollment rates both higher than currently in Syria (70 percent) and close to the local nonrefugee enrollment rate (74 percent). The enrollment rate of Syrian children in Iraq only includes in-camp children; out-of-camp children have a significantly lower enrollment rate (figure 2.53).

Like the situation for children inside Syria, child labor and marriage are prevalent in host communities. Attending school implies high opportunity cost for youth, and sending children to work is often a necessity to guarantee a household's survival (Basu and Van 1998).[38] Teenage males often drop out of school to work and support their families (UNICEF 2017a). In Lebanon, 20 percent of children between the ages of 15 and 17 reported working (9.9 percent for girls and 30 percent for boys), compared to 2.3 percent for children 5–14 years old (0.7 percent for girls and 3.8 percent for boys) (UNHCR, UNICEF, and WFP 2018).[39] Also, child marriage, defined as a formal marriage or informal union before age 18, is a reality for both boys and girls, although girls were disproportionately affected. In Lebanon, 22 percent of the Syrian refugee girls ages 15–19 were married (UNHCR, UNICEF, and WFP 2018).

The cost of education appears to be one of the main reasons preventing parents from sending their children to school. For many displaced families, the financial cost of education for their children is too high. The cost of transportation, clothing, and expenses for learning materials accumulate; and schooling quickly becomes unaffordable for households. In Lebanon, 39 percent of parents with children ages 6–14 report that the cost of education is the main reason for not enrolling their children in school (UNHCR, UNICEF, and WFP 2018). Thirty-five percent of refugee households reported that they reduced education-related expenditure as a coping

Figure 2.53. **Comparative Enrollment Rates for School-Age Children, Precrisis and Present-Day Syrian Arab Republic and Host Countries**

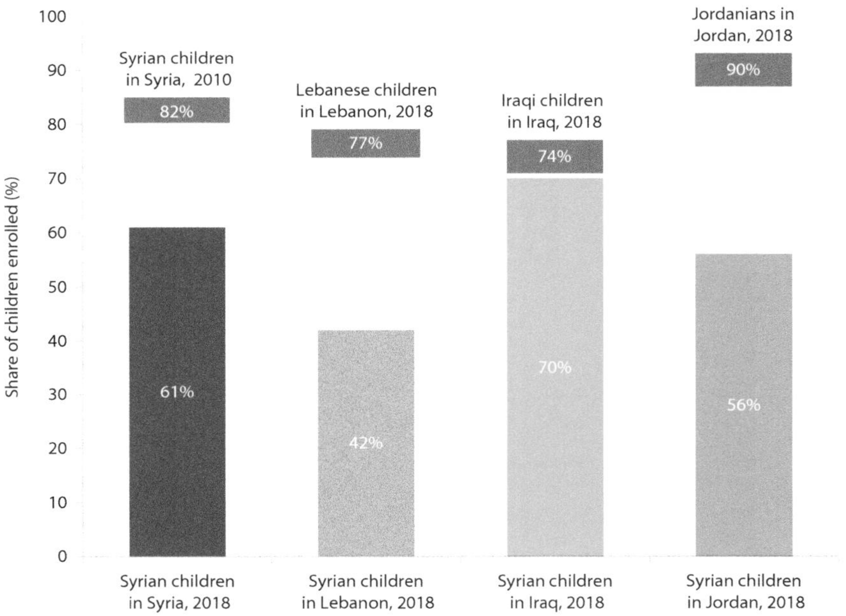

Sources: Data for Syria: estimates rely mainly on the Ministry of Education's Education Management Information System. Data for Iraq, Jordan, and Lebanon: UNICEF calculation based on UNHCR data portal, 3RP monthly updates, and UNICEF Syria Crisis Situation Report.

Note: The enrollment rate of Syrian children in Iraq includes only in-camp children. Out-of-camp children have a significantly lower enrollment rate. 3RP = Regional Refugee & Resilience Plan; UNHCR = United Nations High Commissioner for Refugees; UNICEF = United Nations Children's Fund.

strategy following financial distress. In Iraq, for the age group 13–18, the main reasons for not going to school were also related to the cost of education. An important dynamic in terms of enrollment among Syrian refugees was that they typically did not return to school once they left.

Water and sanitation

Syria's water supply systems before the conflict, like other systems in the MENA region, were characterized as being predominantly urban, modern, and complex. There were high coverage rates and high-quality service prior to 2011. Over 90 percent of urban and 80 percent of rural households had access to piped water in the home. In urban areas per capita water use was in the range of 120–170 liters per day (UNICEF 2017b). Over 95 percent of urban households were also connected to a sewerage network with about 70 percent of wastewater being treated. Even in rural areas 80 percent of households had access to piped water, with only a small minority relying on other sources such as wells, springs, or water tankers. Over 95 percent of rural households also had access to improved toilet facilities (UNICEF 2006).

Urban and rural systems were state-owned, state-managed, and heavily subsidized. They required high operational costs (especially for water pumping) and a mix of qualified human resources working in complex engineering harmony.

However, the precrisis water sector in Syria faced typical sector challenges including inadequate preventive maintenance and challenges in connecting some neighborhoods in rural areas (for example, Idleb) to the public water supply. Most regions experienced regular shortages, and rationing of drinking water was common in major cities, particularly in the summer months. Losses in municipal networks of 30–40 percent were common because of poor maintenance of distribution networks. Illegal connections, low tariffs, and high collection transaction costs meant that cost recovery for drinking water services was consistently low (World Bank 2017). The tariff structure was based on consumption blocks for households and on flat rates for public institutions and productive activities. More than two-thirds of households fell into the lowest block, and less than 4 percent of subscribers were in the highest block of domestic consumption. In 2009, households in the lowest tariff band paid only US$0.06 per cubic meter. Tariffs were set by the central government and applied uniformly throughout the country. Even though they were increased every three years, their levels remained very low for water services, and sewerage charges were negligible.

There were already signs of a deterioration of water services before 2011. The decade running up to the conflict saw a sharp rise in the number of people having to buy water from tankers rather than directly from the utility. This increase points both to the declining ability of utilities to meet demand, and to a proliferation of alternative sources to supplement utility supply. These alternative supplies mark a shift in the structure of service delivery, in which unregulated water from private boreholes form an increasing share of supply.

Conditions in Syria

Violence and conflict have damaged infrastructure, disrupted distribution, and changed patterns of water supply and demand. Shelling, bombing, and ground conflict have destroyed infrastructure installations (intakes, pumping stations, and treatment plants) and caused widespread damage to piped water supply networks. Despite active attempts to keep services running by state and nonstate actors, access to services has deteriorated dramatically in cities that have not been under government control. These cities and the governorates now face a chaotic mix of dilapidated utilities and alternative service delivery arrangements from wells and tanker trucks supported by an array of internal and external actors.

Aleppo has experienced the greatest deterioration in water supply and sanitation (WSS) services of all towns in Syria. Where prior to the conflict Aleppo had near universal coverage, a recent household survey reported that only 3 of 10 households can rely on the water network. Because of widespread damage to the water network and associated infrastructure, 70 percent of households have had to shift to using wells, water tankers, and other local coping mechanisms. Despite many relief actors' efforts to improve access and infrastructure in the city of Aleppo, most WSS infrastructure is only partially functional. The city of Al Bab, also in Aleppo governorate, experienced widespread destruction of WSS infrastructure; in Kobani over 70 percent of the infrastructure was not operational.

In other governorates services have deteriorated sharply (figure 2.54). Network water service coverage has decreased by about 60 percent in Ar-Raqqa, Dar'a, Idleb, and Quneitra. In the governorates of Deir-ez-Zor, Al-Hasakeh, Hama, Homs, and Rural Damascus levels of piped coverage have deteriorated sharply with up

Figure 2.54. **Structure of Water Supply in the Syrian Arab Republic, by Governorate, 2017**

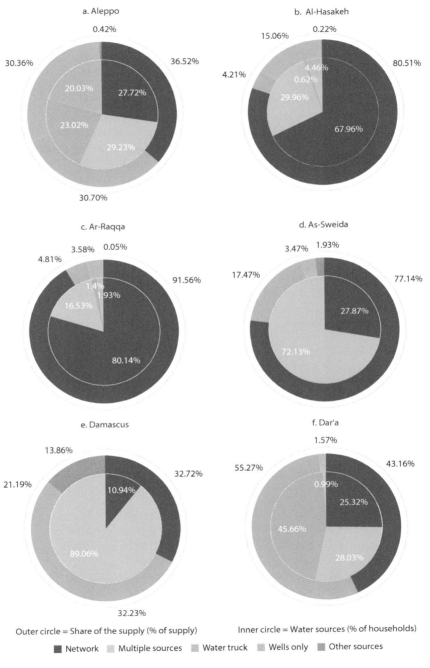

a. Aleppo

0.42%
30.36%
36.52%
20.03%
27.72%
23.02%
29.23%
30.70%

b. Al-Hasakeh

0.22%
15.06%
80.51%
4.46%
0.62%
4.21%
29.96%
67.96%

c. Ar-Raqqa

3.58% 0.05%
4.81%
91.56%
1.4%
1.93%
16.53%
1.93%
80.14%

d. As-Sweida

3.47% 1.93%
17.47%
77.14%
27.87%
72.13%

e. Damascus

13.86%
21.19%
32.72%
10.94%
89.06%
32.23%

f. Dar'a

1.57%
55.27%
43.16%
0.99%
25.32%
45.66%
28.03%

Outer circle = Share of the supply (% of supply) Inner circle = Water sources (% of households)

■ Network Multiple sources Water truck Wells only ■ Other sources

(figure continues next page)

Figure 2.54. *(continued)*

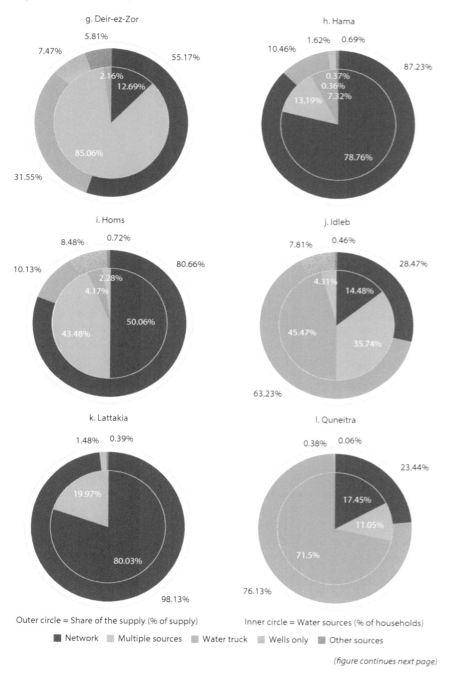

g. Deir-ez-Zor

h. Hama

i. Homs

j. Idleb

k. Lattakia

l. Quneitra

Outer circle = Share of the supply (% of supply)   Inner circle = Water sources (% of households)

■ Network   ■ Multiple sources   ■ Water truck   ■ Wells only   ■ Other sources

(figure continues next page)

139

Figure 2.54. *(continued)*

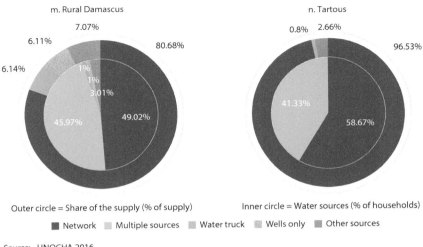

Outer circle = Share of the supply (% of supply)   Inner circle = Water sources (% of households)

■ Network   ▨ Multiple sources   ▨ Water truck   ▨ Wells only   ■ Other sources

Source: UNOCHA 2016.

to one-half of households cut off from access to piped water. Over 30 percent of households across these governorates are now entirely dependent on water provided by trucks, with a further 15 percent dependent on wells and springs. The damage assessment also reported very high levels of destruction and nonfunctionality of WSS infrastructure in the cities of Douma, Idleb, and Al Qusayr.

Alternate sources of drinking water supply, including groundwater wells, tanker trucks, and deliveries by humanitarian agencies, have grown significantly. The increase in alternate nonnetwork sources used by households, such as wells and tankers, is an indication that there is widespread damage to networks. From 2018 UNICEF household survey data, it is clear that the number households able to rely on the water network for water has dropped even since 2017. This finding is particularly true in the North, Northwest, and Southeast of the country. Supply disruptions to besieged areas have left residents reliant on groundwater wells at times. Although much of the rest of the infrastructure was undamaged, reduced functionality is a significant problem for all the assessed cities. The alternative service providers that have sprung up to fill gaps in service delivery supply by tankers expensive (more than US$10 per cubic meter) water of often unregulated quality.

Wells were the most common WSS assets and the most likely to be damaged or destroyed. Of the 413 WSS assets evaluated by the damage assessments across 15 cities, just over a quarter (26 percent) had suffered damage. Most of the damage was to wells, over half of which had been affected. Just under a quarter of all water towers and tanks had also been damaged. Other WSS infrastructure such as water treatment plants, sewage plants, dams, pumping stations, reservoirs, and offices had not sustained much damage; however, many had decreased or no functionality. The main damage reported as at May 2018 is presented in table 2.10.

The state of piped water and sewerage networks, which represent a substantial share of water supply systems, is unknown. The analysis in this report could not assess the damage to water and sewerage networks using remote sensing because

Table 2.10. Total Damage for Water Supply and Sanitation Infrastructure Inventory Numbers

Asset type	Baseline	Completely destroyed	Partially damaged	Unknown	Total damage count	Percentage of damage by asset type
Well	179	11	45	18	56	51
Water tower/tank	163	5	20	4	25	23
Water treatment plant	9	1	5	0	6	6
Sewage treatment plant	6	0	4	1	4	4
Dam	4	0	2	0	2	2
Dike	0	0	0	0	0	0
Levee	0	0	0	0	0	0
Other drainage structure	14	0	2	1	2	2
Pumping station	31	0	10	3	10	9
Storage reservoir	4	1	0	0	1	1
Water/ Sanitation office	3	0	3	0	3	3
Total	413	18	91	27	109	
Percent		4	22	7	26	

Figure 2.55. Damage to Water Supply and Sanitation Infrastructure

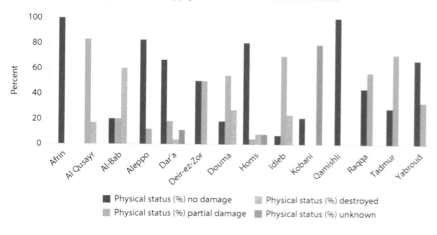

■ Physical status (%) no damage   ▨ Physical status (%) destroyed
▨ Physical status (%) partial damage   ■ Physical status (%) unknown

these networks are underground. In the absence of reliable estimates, the analysis rated damage to specific assets in each city and whether they were functioning (see figures 2.55 and 2.56). Although these assets may not have been directly targeted by violence, the level of nonfunctionality may be the result of the network damage. Equally, the destruction of one treatment plant would render the distribution network nonfunctional.

The water sector is also severely affected by damage to the power infrastructure, which supplies electricity needed to pump water and to run treatment plants. Water

Figure 2.56. Operational Status of Water Supply and Sanitation Infrastructure

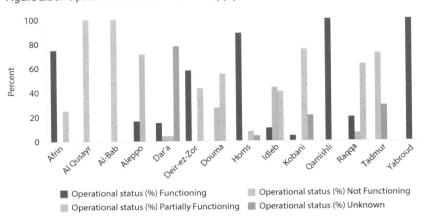

supplied from wells and/or through the distribution network requires pumping; pumping requires electricity. The functionality of water services is therefore directly correlated to the status of the electricity grid and/or the availability of generators and fuel. Lack of electricity was the main reason for water network outages, with damage to pumping stations and piped networks being the second most common reason. Because of this vulnerability, and because wells use much less electricity for water pumping, many cities were forced to develop a backup plan relying on point-source wells, especially during long episodes of public water network outages.

In addition to physical damage, biological and chemical pollution of water sources is also likely. Not much is known about water pollution in Syria. Pollution—especially biological contamination—can follow failure of wastewater treatment plants and increased illegal dumping of septage. Chemical contamination of water sources, flowing into reservoirs and leaching into aquifers, can follow illegal waste dumping, the burning of toxic materials (domestic/industrial), and residues of military munitions. There are reports of discharge of untreated wastewater and sewage, damage to urban sanitation networks, use of chemical agents, and depleted uranium munitions in areas including Damascus, Idleb, and Al-Hasakeh (Oakford 2017). The adoption by IS of small-scale, rudimentary techniques for producing petroleum and *mazout*—a low-quality fuel oil—in Al-Hasakeh and Deir-ez-Zor has led to widespread land pollution that may contaminate critical groundwater supplies (Simpson and Philips 2015; Warrick 2016). With no available data, the impact of these practices has not been assessed yet.

With large-scale displacement, water management systems also suffer from human resource shortages. Many highly educated researchers, water managers, and engineers have left the country, and millions of farmers with expertise in soil and water management were displaced. Although the state administration has managed to retain technicians and employees in dams, pumping stations, and other critical infrastructure, their numbers are greatly reduced. The Ministry of Water Resources—along with other ministries—is understaffed, with a severe shortage of skilled workers and experts. The Ministry reportedly lacks the people and expertise for strategic water resources and investment planning, policy development, fundraising, and project management. Ministries, utilities, and technical organizations (those engaged in water management) are experiencing shortfalls in technical, financial, and administrative capacities, and struggle to maintain basic functions in the areas they are able to reach. There is no effective overall policy making or strategic plan in place for water, WASH, agriculture, or industry, either for the conflict period or any postconflict reconstruction. Many large dams and water sources are either under or threatened by rebel control; however, the government in Damascus has been able to negotiate water releases, where necessary, to maintain supplies. The state's ability to enforce regulations is highly degraded, contributing to the proliferation of illegal wells (Müller et al. 2016). The state's weakened financial and administrative capacity has also been a significant challenge. Highly constrained public finances have limited investment during the conflict and curtailed options for reconstruction. Several interviewees noted that degraded administrative capacity will greatly complicate the identification, selection, and implementation of reconstruction projects, and management of related finance.

With the breakdown of the public water supply systems, informal private providers have filled the large supply gap. Tanker trucks are most concentrated in Idleb and Aleppo governorates, and rarer in Lattakia and Al-Hasakeh where municipal networks are more functional (REACH 2016). Water is most commonly delivered by the truckload, with households often sharing the costs of delivery, and prices are high because traders pass on logistical costs and security risks to consumers. These providers are likely to operate in cartel-like structures, reflecting a prominent aspect of war economy. A market survey in May 2017 found that prices ranged from 250 Syrian pounds (LS) per cubic meter (m^3) in Idleb to LS 1,760 per m^3 in Badama, with median prices highest in Northeast Syria at LS 570 per m^3, greatly exceeding the official tariff (REACH 2017).[40] Most private sector operators are informal, and the water they sell is often untreated or stolen from public networks. State regulation of the price and quality of water for sale has been largely ineffective.

Humanitarian actors and agencies have been active across the country, providing chlorine tablets and water kits and operating water tankers since early in the conflict. As of May 2017, UNICEF reported that its emergency interventions reached 1.1 million people, with a further 3.1 million reached by repair and rehabilitation interventions (UNICEF 2017b). International Crisis Response Group engineers have made critical contributions in collaboration with technicians and engineers from state utilities and water authorities to deliver services in conflict-afflicted areas, including repairs to the Tabqa Dam in early 2017. In many areas, the UN system and NGOs have substantial field organizations and have effectively taken over the delivery of WASH services. In principle, these organizations are well positioned to support postconflict WASH delivery. In practice, however, the missions of humanitarian organizations do not always have the mandate to support the institution building, cost recovery, and long-term sustainability of water utilities.

Overall, despite the efforts of humanitarian actors, surveys confirm that problems with access to water have deepened. The 2017 WASH survey by UNICEF and WHO shows that most households receive less than two hours of water supply per day. Consequently, more than two-fifths of households do not have enough water to meet household needs. Only 36 percent of households receive water primarily from the public network. Others rely on private suppliers, wells, or bottled water. Although access matters, the quality of water supplied is also of concern, because contaminated water can lead to a high burden of infectious disease. The incidence of diarrhea is very high in Syria, with most households reporting at least one member contracting diarrhea in the previous six months. In a sign of the unreliability of

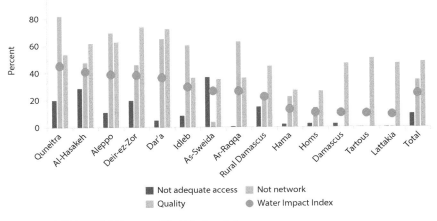

Figure 2.57. Water Deprivation Index in the Syrian Arab Republic, by Governorate, 2017

Source: UNICEF 2017 WASH Survey and World Bank analysis.

Note: "Not adequate access" is a simple average of those experiencing 2 or more consecutive days without water in the past 30 days and those reporting not enough water for their needs in the past 30 days. "Not network" means that piped water is not the main source. "Quality" is a simple average of those differentiating between drinking and nondrinking water and the average time for which the network was not running if a household has piped water. The aggregate Water Impact Index is 0.5 × Not adequate access, 0.3 × Not network and 0.2 × Quality.

existing water, a large share of Syrian households (44 percent) treat drinking and nondrinking water differently.

Many Syrians lack adequate access to piped water or even other basic improved water supplies. Figure 2.57 shows those without adequate access to safe water supplies by governorate, which is an average of those without water for 2 or more consecutive days in the past 30 days and those self-reporting not having enough water (the two measures are very similar in most places). Lack of access is particularly high in As-Sweida (37 percent), Al-Hasakeh (29 percent), and Deir-ez-Zor and Quneitra (both 20 percent). Moreover, even when households have full access, in many places it is not usually from the piped network: most households in Aleppo, Ar-Raqqa, Dar'a, Idleb, and Quneitra are not getting piped water. Finally, the quality of water is also often affected, meaning that the household is treating its drinking water differently from its nondrinking water. This is particularly so in Al-Hasakeh, Aleppo, Dar'a, Deir-ez-Zor, Quneitra, and Tartous. Combining these three indicators (50 percent of inadequate access, 30 percent of nonnetwork, and 20 percent of quality) into an aggregate Water Impact Index shows many regions where the household deprivation index is greater than 25 percent, including Ar-Raqqa (26 percent), As-Sweida (27 percent), Idleb (30 percent), Dar'a (37 percent), Deir-ez-Zor (38 percent), Aleppo (39 percent), Al-Hasakeh (41 percent), and Quneitra (45 percent).

Access to a toilet facility is also a problem, although not as affected as other services. In Ar-Raqqa (27 percent) and Deir-ez-Zor (11 percent), a significant number of households have limited access to a toilet (figure 2.58), where limited access means all or some of the household do not have access to a functioning toilet. Even among households that do have full access, it is sometimes shared or communal,

144

Figure 2.58. Sanitation Deprivation Index in the Syrian Arab Republic, by Governorate, 2017

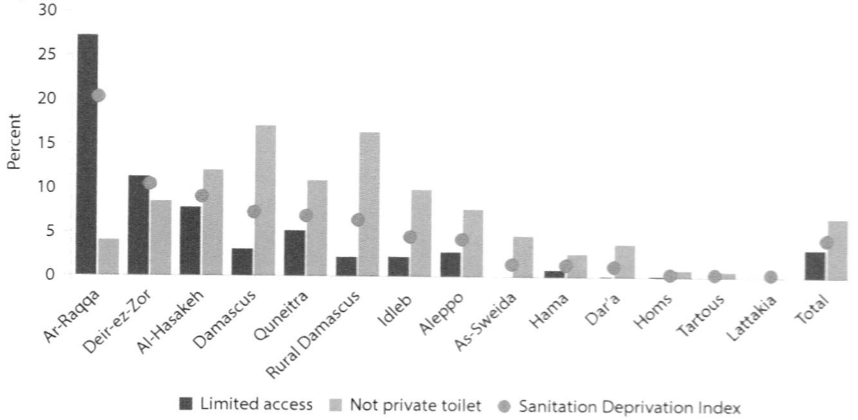

Source: UNICEF 2017 WASH Survey and World Bank analysis.
Note: "Limited access" means either none or not all of the household have access to a functioning toilet; "Not private toilet" means the toilet is shared with other households, communal, or public. The Sanitation Deprivation Index is 0.7 × Limited access + 0.3 × Not private toilet.

especially in Damascus (17 percent), Rural Damascus (16 percent), Al-Hasakeh (12 percent), and Idleb (10 percent). The overall Sanitation Deprivation Index, which weights access by 0.7 and nonprivate by 0.3, indicates that households in Ar-Raqqa fare the worst (20 percent), primarily because of a lack of access. The Index is less than 10 percent in all other governorates, emphasizing that sanitation outcomes are better than for most other dimensions of welfare.

Conditions in countries of asylum

Lebanon has for many years struggled with inadequate water and sanitation services. The state of Lebanon's water sector today is a cumulative reflection of 15 years of civil war, two decades of postconflict underinvestment, and an unprecedented recent influx of refugees from Syria. Lebanon's already fragile water resources are buckling under extreme pressure. Even before the crisis, Lebanon's water governance was undermined by a lack of funds, administrative and technical staffing gaps, incomplete technical data, and weak structural incentives for good integrated water management (including weak tariff collection). Regulatory, legislative, and management initiatives targeted by the 2010 Water Sector Strategy are still incomplete, with capital projects still prioritized over other essential reforms. The sector is still struggling to finance and implement critical mechanisms for water quality and resource management, contingency planning, and supply.

The water sector has suffered from a drastic demand shock. The influx of more than a million displaced Syrians dispersed in host communities has challenged a system where one in five households still lacks even a basic water connection, where networks are fragile and unreliable, and where only 8 percent of sewage is effectively treated. Over 48 percent of water supplied by the public system is lost through leakage. Wastewater networks are extremely poor, and in some areas nonexistent. Over 92 percent of Lebanon's sewage runs untreated directly into watercourses and the sea.

The Ministry of Energy and Water estimates that more than two-thirds of all resources received since 2015 have been to support families displaced from Syria. Fewer Syrian families were able to afford rent in 2016 compared to 2015, which resulted in many evictions and therefore to a proliferation of small informal settlements. The number of informal sites rose within the past year to 4,312, a 34 percent increase in locations and a 30 percent increase in resident families. Needs are also particularly acute in urban settings of host communities where 12 percent of displaced Syrians live in nonresidential buildings, such as worksites, garages, and shops, which are overcrowded and lack basic water and sanitation services. Twenty-three percent of displaced Syrians living in nonresidential buildings reported not having enough water compared to 20 percent in informal settlements and 17 percent in residential buildings. Forty-two percent of displaced Syrians living in nonresidential buildings do not have access to an improved toilet facility (flush toilet or improved latrine) compared to 57 percent in informal settlements and 16 percent in residential buildings (UNHCR, UNICEF, and WFP 2018).

The Lebanon Crisis Response Plan (2017–2020) estimated the cost for reinstating precrisis levels of water supply and sanitation services to host and refugee communities at US\$375 million (UNHCR 2017a). In 2017, more than US\$207 million was channeled to strengthen Lebanon's public sector, an increase of more than 20 percent since 2015. Lebanese institutions have constructed and rehabilitated 280 kilometers (km) of public water supply distribution networks. In supporting government authorities, the UN, donors, and local and international NGOs have implemented programs, projects, and activities so that more vulnerable people in Lebanon are accessing sufficient, safe water for drinking and domestic use with reduced health and environmental impacts from unsafe wastewater management. This effort can only be achieved through strengthening institutional capacities from national to local levels. In 2017, a total of US\$34 million was received, including 2017 tranches of multiyear projects (for water sector–related projects that either were completed in 2017 or are ongoing into 2018), down from US\$38 million in 2016 (UNHCR 2017a).

Jordan is one of the most water-scarce countries in the world. The country relies on both internal groundwater resources and a number of transboundary rivers as well as groundwater aquifers. Notably, the Yarmouk (tributary of the Jordan River) has its sources in southern Syria before entering Jordan. Jordan also relies heavily on fossil groundwater (shared with Saudi Arabia) that is pumped into the Disi pipeline from the south to central Jordan (predominantly Amman) (Swain and Jägerskog 2016). There is no basin-wide agreement covering the whole Jordan basin for transboundary water, but there are agreements on a bilateral basis. Jordan and Syria have an agreement regarding the Yarmouk River although Syria has been abstracting more than the agreement stipulates.[41] The Yarmouk basin includes the city of Dar'a, where civil protests started in 2011. An unexpected outcome of the Syrian crisis has been that the conflict and ensuing migration in Southern Syria has led to an observed increase in the flow of water in the Yarmouk River from Syria to Jordan. The fact that conflict started in southern Syria has led to a decrease in the use of water for agriculture, which has been documented through satellite imagery (Müller et al. 2016).

Jordan's water sector is highly energy intensive, which has led to the accumulation of over US\$2.4 billion of energy-related debt. In Jordan the water sector is a major consumer of energy (13 percent of country's total energy production) because much of the water needs to be pumped to where it is consumed. Escalating energy costs, caused by the cutoff of Egyptian natural gas since 2009 and rising global energy prices, have resulted in the accumulation of US$2.4 billion of debt for the Jordanian water sector. The sector also has high levels (40–50 percent) of nonrevenue water, which is water that is processed but lost to leakage or pilferage before delivery. Agricultural water is subsidized and agricultural irrigation practices are relatively inefficient. Current levels of reuse of treated wastewater are still low, but improvements are being made, many through the improvements and expansions of the As-Samra wastewater treatment plant, which treats most of the wastewater from Amman.

Catering to the water needs of people, citizens, and refugees alike has been a major challenge in Jordan. The Syrian conflict has exacerbated Jordan's problems in the water sector. The challenges include both assistance to the refugee population in camps and the increasing pressure on the infrastructure of the country's WSS services. According to the Jordan Response Plan 2016–2018 the vulnerability in terms of water supply is extremely high, with 70 percent of the population (Jordanian citizens and Syrian refugees) receiving less than the national standard of 100 liters per person per day (JPRSC 2016). The Jordan Response Plan attributes approximately 60 percent of this vulnerability to needs associated with Syrian refugees, thereby demonstrating that water supply challenges existed prior to the Syrian crisis. Currently, water sources in Jordan are overpumped, with high risk of salinization of the resource.

In host communities, sanitation challenges have also increased and the long-term plans for sanitation in large parts of Jordan have become outdated. Treatment plants will soon not be able to cope with the increased sewage load. The Jordanian government has developed a number of proposed interventions to address the short-, medium-, and long-term needs of the sector. In the refugee camps sanitation solutions have largely been put in place; however, for some sites, such as the Zaatari camp, the location of the camp atop a major aquifer has raised concerns about seepage and pollution of the aquifer. Over 60 percent of the population in Jordan is connected to a sewage network, although in parts of northern Jordan (where the concentration of Syrian refugees is the highest) the connection rate is just above 40 percent (JPRSC 2016). This low rate makes the vulnerability of the refugees and host communities in the north higher than in other parts of the country. It should be noted that women are vulnerable, especially refugee women and Jordanian female-headed households. Vulnerability in refugee camps is associated with increased prevalence of gender-based violence connected to the location of water and sanitation facilities.

The Kurdistan Regional Government (KRG) has provided access to publicly provided services, including water, for refugees and IDPs amid economic difficulties. Most refugees and IDPs, together more than a quarter of the region's population, have been integrated into the local population at large, especially in urban areas. Only one-third of the refugees and one-fifth of IDPs are still living in the 42 camps set up throughout the Kurdistan Region of Iraq. They have equal rights with the host population in these communities with regard to access to clean water, electricity, and security. However, the significant demand pressures created by the influx have affected the provision of health, education, and social protection programs to the population in general, as well as the provision of water, waste management, and electricity (WHO 2018). Although this level of settlement is an illustration of the commitment of the KRG to support refugees and IDPs under highly strained circumstances, further improvement in the well-being of the displaced—not to mention helping those still to come—will not be possible without additional resources from the international community and an improvement in economic conditions.

Water and sanitation deprivations can be analyzed for refugees living in Lebanon and Jordan in the same manner as was done across Syrian governorates, but not for those living in the Kurdistan Region of Iraq. Levels of inadequate access to water—defined here as households reporting not enough water—are similar between those living in Lebanon (18 percent) and Jordan (23 percent); however, most refugees in Lebanon are not on the piped water network (74 percent), whereas only 10 percent of those in Jordan are not.[42] Despite the fact that most refugees in Lebanon do not use network water, water quality is good, with less than 10 percent needing to treat their drinking water. The degree of treatment in Jordan is unknown. Even if up to 40 percent of refugees in Jordan were treating water, however, the aggregate water deprivation index for those living in Jordan would still be better (22 percent) than for those living in Lebanon (33 percent) because of the much greater access to piped water; the index could be as low as 14 percent in the best case, in which no one needs to treat water (figure 2.59).

Overall, a comparison between the water access conditions inside Syria and those faced by refugees in countries of asylum paints a mixed picture. Current water and sanitation conditions vary, both between refugees and those still living in Syria, and between different host countries (table 2.11). A greater proportion of refugees lack access to enough water in Jordan (23 percent) and Lebanon (18 percent) than in present-day Syria (10 percent). In Jordan most refugees use piped water, but one-third of those in Syria do not, rising to three-quarters of those in Lebanon. Water quality for those living in Lebanon is much better, with very few having poorer quality water, compared to 48 percent in Syria. Quality information is not

Figure 2.59. Water Deprivation Index for Refugees, by Host Country

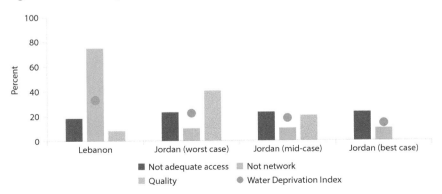

Sources: UNHCR 2017d; UNHCR, UNICEF, and WFP 2018; "Not adequate access" and "Not quality" data for Lebanon from UNHCR 2018a; World Bank analysis.
Note: "Not adequate access" is households reporting not enough water. "Not network" means that piped water is not the main source. "Quality" in Lebanon differentiates between drinking and nondrinking water (having to treat water to drink). "Quality" in Jordan is presented with three different scenarios; best case means no treatment, mid-case means 20 percent treatment, worst case means 40 percent treatment. The aggregate Water Deprivation Index is 0.5 × Not Adequate Access, 0.3 × Not Network and 0.2 × Quality.

Table 2.11. Summary of Water and Sanitation Conditions for Current Syrian Arab Republic and for Refugees, by Host Country, 2017

	Water				Sanitation		
	Inadequate access (%)	Not preferred access (%)	Poorer quality (%)	Water Deprivation Index (%)	Inadequate access (%)	Poorer quality (%)	Sanitation Deprivation Index (%)
Syrian Arab Republic	10	35	48	25	3	7	4
Jordan	23	10	0–40*	14–22*	5	47	18
Lebanon	18	74	8	33	16	28	19

Sources: UNHCR 2017b, 2018b; UNHCR, UNICEF, and WFP 2018; UNICEF and WHO 2017; World Bank analysis.

149

Figure 2.60. Sanitation Deprivation Index for Refugees, by Host Country and Location, 2017

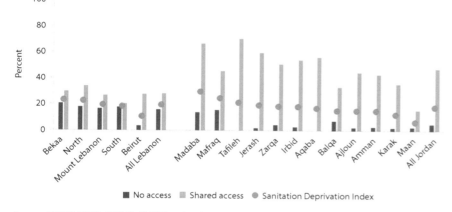

Source: UNHCR 2017b; UNHCR, UNICEF, and WFP 2017; World Bank analysis.
Note: The Sanitation Deprivation Index is 0.7 × Limited Access + 0.3 × Not Private Toilet.

available for Jordan. Taken together, the water deprivation index is lower in Syria (25 percent) than Lebanon (33 percent), but likely lower again in Jordan (14–22 percent, depending on quality scenarios).

With respect to sanitation, those within Syria are clearly less deprived than refugees living in the host countries. The Syrian sanitation deprivation index is only 4 percent, with almost everyone having access to a nonshared latrine. By contrast, the deprivation index is at 18–19 percent in both Jordan and Lebanon; however, although access is high in Jordan, it is often to a shared toilet, whereas one in six refugees in Lebanon does not have access and just over a quarter share access.

The overall sanitation deprivation index is very similar between those living in Lebanon (19 percent) and those in Jordan (18 percent); however, the components of the index differ significantly. Far more refugees in Lebanon are likely to lack access to a toilet (16 percent on average) compared to Jordan (5 percent), but most refugees in Lebanon do not have to share a toilet. Only 28 percent have shared access, compared to nearly half (47 percent) of those living in Jordan (figure 2.60).

Solid waste management

Before the conflict, solid waste services were still under development in Syria. Garbage collection services existed in most urban areas with 80–90 percent of the urban population and 60–90 percent of the rural population provided collection service (Kasparek and Dimashki 2009; SWEEP-Net and GIZ 2010). Most collection services in urban areas were provided by municipal "cleanliness departments" with about 5 percent of the services nationally provided by private companies, including in cities such as Aleppo and Homs. There were 13 constructed landfills in the country with over half of those in operation under the responsibility of the cleanliness departments and some operated by the private sector. The landfills accommodated an estimated 20 percent of waste in the country and had varying levels of control and quality of operation with few fully meeting engineering and operational standards (Kasparek and Dimashki 2009; SWEEP-Net and GIZ 2010). The remainder of the collected waste was disposed of in designated open dumpsites near towns and cities or, to a lesser extent, burned. Only a few areas (specifically Damascus) disposed of medical waste in proper medical waste incinerators; the remainder disposed of medical waste in open dumps and landfills (SWEEP-Net and GIZ 2010). Similarly, construction and demolition waste, which amounted to an estimated 410,000 tons per year,[43] also was commonly disposed of in landfills without special handling (see table 2.12).

Conditions in Syria

The conflict has significantly changed the character and quantity of solid waste to be managed. Municipal solid waste generation has declined because of a

Table 2.12. Preconflict Solid Waste Services in the Syrian Arab Republic, by City

City	Municipal waste generation (thousand tons)	Disposal facilities
Idleb	74	landfill
Aleppo	1,967	landfill
Dar'a	73	landfill
Duma	83	open dump
Homs	602	landfill
Kobani	34	open dump
Ar-Raqqa	203	open dump
Al Qusayr	22	open dump
Menbij	75	open dump
Al Bab	47	open dump
Tadmur	38	open dump
Afrin	27	open dump
Quamishli	170	open dump
Yabroud	19	open dump
Deir-ez-Zor	159	landfill

Source: Based on population estimates per city using 2004 census data and a growth rate of 2.4 percent, and precrisis per capita waste generation rates from Sweep-Net and GIZ 2010. Disposal information based on information from Sweep-Net and GIZ 2010 and presentation of Ministry of Local Administration and Environment in 2006, https://www.slideshare.net/AmirAlboukhari/solidwaste-management-in-syria.

Table 2.13. Solid Waste Management before the Conflict, 2010

	Baseline prior to the conflict
Municipal waste generation	4.5 million tons per year
• Domestic	3.8 million tons per year
• Industrial and commercial	0.7 million tons per year
Construction and demolition waste *	410,000 tons per year
Waste collection	90–100 percent coverage in urban areas
Expenditures on waste collection	LS 1,000–1,600/ton (US$20–32/ton)
Waste disposal	80 percent open dumps 20 percent sanitary landfills
Expenditures on waste disposal	LS 200–400/ton (US$4–8/ton)

Sources: Data from Sweep-Net and GIZ 2010 and presentation of Ministry of Local Administration and Environment in 2006. https://www.slideshare.net/AmirAlboukhari/solidwaste-management-in-syria.
Note: * = national currency; LS = Syrian pound.

combination of lower consumption and depleted commercial activity. Lower overall waste generation is estimated to take place in all conflict-affected cities even in cases where the population has grown, for example in Idleb (24 percent less waste generated) and Al Bab (21 percent less waste generated), and is especially apparent in cities with a significant population decrease, such as Tadmur (100 percent less waste generated) and Al Qusayr (96 percent less waste generated). See table 2.13 for preconflict quantity used as a baseline.

At the same time the conflict has led to large-scale generation of debris. The amount generated is orders of magnitude higher than both the construction and demolition waste generated before the conflict and the municipal waste currently being generated. For example, in Aleppo, analysis of satellite images of damaged buildings suggests an estimated 14.9 million tons of debris (World Bank 2017). Before the conflict it would have taken 200 years to produce the same amount of construction and demolition waste. Similarly, at current generation rates, it would take the population of Aleppo 62 years to produce the equivalent amount of municipal solid waste (see table 2.14).

Government-run solid waste services were immediately affected in conflict areas. The onset of the conflict increased fuel prices and limited the available budget, equipment, and labor, which quickly posed severe constraints on the ability of governments to provide waste services. Access to certain areas was also limited, and this problem was exacerbated in those cities that relied on private contractors who stopped operating in certain areas. For example, in Deir-ez-Zor in 2015, there was an 80 percent reduction (from 45 to 13) in government vehicles available for solid waste collection and a similar labor force reduction of 88 percent (from 300 to 37 workers), meaning that large parts of the city did not have collection service (see table 2.15).

As the conflict continued, waste collection services in many areas were assumed by other groups or not provided at all. Most commonly solid waste collection, where provided, is now undertaken by local councils or directly by local inhabitants. In a sampling of 105 districts in conflict areas in 2017, 57 percent of the districts had collection services provided by local councils, while local inhabitants provided

Table 2.14. Solid Waste Generation and Debris Accumulation Estimates, 2018

City	Estimated municipal solid waste generation in tons per day (% change)	Estimated debris accumulation (tons overall)
Idleb	56 (−24)	607,727
Aleppo	649 (−67)	14,900,000
Dar'a	30 (−59)	1,730,684
Duma	34 (−60)	974,277
Homs	205 (−66)	5,300,000
Kobani	23 (−32)	358,208
Ar-Raqqa	54 (−74)	374,401
Al Qusayr	1 (−96)	246,575
Menbij	41 (−45)	142,302
Al Bab	37 (−21)	81,701
Tadmur	0 (−100)	188,427
Afrin	14 (−51)	1,472
Quamishli	109 (−36)	—
Yabroud	7 (−62)	—
Deir ez Zor	61 (−61)	—

Sources: Based on May 2018 population estimates per city and precrisis per capita waste generation rates adjusted to reduced consumption (53 percent reduction) and commercial activity (42 percent) based on composition of national gross domestic product figures between 2010 and 2015 (World Bank 2017a). Estimates of debris based on building damage assessments (July 2018) using unit debris generation rates derived from an analysis of satellite images from Aleppo and Homs (World Bank 2017a).

Note: — = not available.

Table 2.15. Status of Solid Waste Services at the Height of the Conflict, 2014–15

City	Collection services		Disposal services		
	Reduction in the number of government vehicles (% change)	Reduction in the number of government solid waste workers (% change)	Coll. coverage (% of districts)	Accessibility to official disposal site	Disposal practices
Aleppo	150 to 50 (67)	2,350 to 500 (80)	—	No	Informal dumping grounds in and on fringes of city
Homs	80 to 50 (38)	1,100 to 750 (32)	67	Yes	Official dumpsite
Deir-ez-Zor	45 to 13 (60)	300 to 27 (88)	45	No	Informal and alternatives dumpsites; Euphrates River; in city streets.
Dar'a	4 vehicles remaining	Reported significant decrease	37	No	Improvised dumpsite

Source: UN-Habitat 2014a, 2014b, 2014c, 2014d.
Note: — = not available.

their own services in 25 percent of districts. A survey conducted in six conflict-affected cities showed that most collection services use simple collection equipment and are precarious in their reliability and sustainability, with no reinvestment and a severely limited operational budget (figure 2.61). The quality and coverage of the service has led to significant quantities of litter on streets, on average over 70 percent of the residents indicated there was a presence of litter and piles of garbage.

Solid waste disposal has been impeded by the low coverage and quality of municipal solid waste collection services. The logistical and security challenges of waste transport in some cities also prevents the use of disposal sites established before the conflict, which has resulted in an increase of open dumping within communities (13–17 percent of sampled households in four cities), burning of garbage in communities (0–53 percent of sampled subdistricts in six cities), and a rise in new dumpsites located outside of the urban area (50–100 percent of sampled subdistricts in six cities).

Unsurprisingly, the greatest collapse of solid waste management services is observed in high-conflict areas. Nationally, across 61 districts in 14 governorates, 25 percent of households had neither private nor public access. Of those who did have access to solid waste management services, 81 percent had public access, and 7 percent of them received it less than once a week. Consequently, the Access Index—which weights lack of access at 0.5, nonpreferred access at 0.3 and infrequent access at 0.2—is 19 percent across all districts. Moreover, 32 percent of those with garbage collection said it was not disposed of in formal landfills or open dumpsites (UNICEF 2017 WASH Survey). Combining access and disposal as an aggregate index shows that the greatest solid waste management deprivation was in Ar-Raqqa (53 percent) and Quneitra (52 percent), with Al-Hasakeh (42 percent), Aleppo (38 percent), Dar'a (35 percent), Deir-ez-Zor (41 percent), and Idleb (28 percent) also over 25 percent (figure 2.62). The least deprived governorates are As-Sweida, Damascus, Lattakia, and Tartous.

Figure 2.61. Arrangements for Solid Waste Collection, 2017

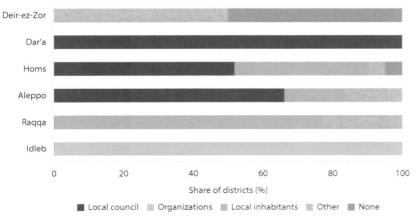

Source: IMU 2017, based on a sampling of districts in each city.

Figure 2.62. Solid Waste Management Deprivation Index, by Governorate, 2017

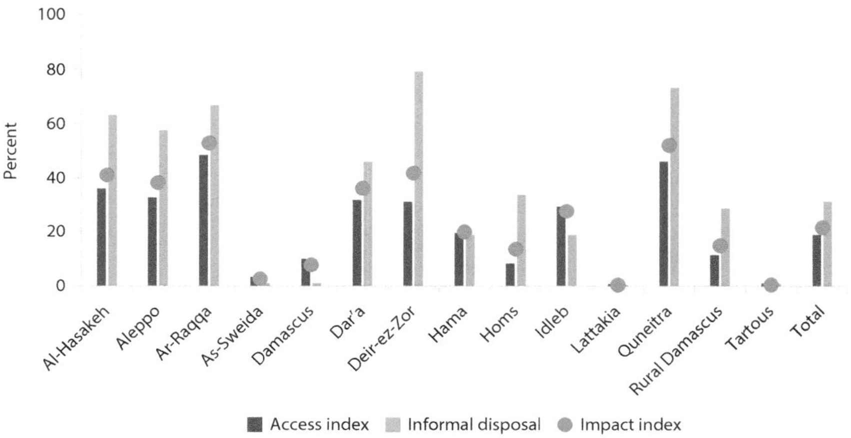

Source: UNICEF 2017 WASH Survey and World Bank analysis.
Note: Access Index is 0.5 × lack of access (neither public nor private), 0.3 × nonpreferred access (nonpublic), and 0.2 × infrequent access (less than once a week). The Aggregate Impact Index or Solid Waste Management Deprivation Index is 0.8 × Access index and 0.2 × informal disposal.

Services to manage debris largely did not exist before the conflict. Facilities to manage construction and demolition debris were very limited, with debris disposed of mainly by being mixed with municipal solid waste in landfills or dumpsites. Debris from armed conflict presents additional challenges in management and processing because of contaminants and unexploded ordinance not found in normal construction and demolition waste. Because of the large quantity, much of the debris has not been cleared and there is little evidence of debris management activities at the scale needed to begin tackling the problem. The available information has indicated that efforts have focused on debris clearance into informal dumps and disposal sites with some efforts at recovery of marketable items.

Conditions in countries of asylum

Access to good garbage collection is very high for refugees living in Lebanon and the Kurdistan Region of Iraq, whereas conditions in Jordan are not known. Refugees in Lebanon clearly enjoy much better access and quality than those still living within Syria, with 95 percent of the population with waste collection service in Lebanon and 25 percent in Syria. The formal public sector is able to provide the collection service in Lebanon, with only 2 percent of the population with service using private or NGO collection (table 2.16) (UNHCR, UNICEF, and WFP 2018). This situation is in contrast to Syria where, with the collapse of municipal services, most of the collection service is provided by NGOs, local councils, or private entities. In the Kurdistan Region of Iraq, more refugees in noncamp settings are covered by municipal garbage collection than are camp residents. Whereas only slightly more than half of residents live in a house where garbage is collected by the municipality or private contractors, virtually all refugees are covered by the services. That refugees live mostly in urban areas in rented dwellings likely explains the discrepancy.

Table 2.16. Garbage Collection for Syrians and Refugees in Lebanon

Location	Share with no garbage collection (%)	Share without public collection, if garbage collected (%)
Syrian Arab Republic	25	19
Lebanon	5	2

Source: UNHCR, UNICEF, and WFP 2018; UNICEF and WHO 2017.

Energy

Even before the conflict, Syria's electricity sector was in urgent need of investment and institutional reform. After experiencing relative stability in the 1990s, Syria's power sector was facing numerous and significant challenges by the mid-2000s including a widening gap between demand and supply that led to frequent load shedding; large network losses, both technical and nontechnical; an insufficient domestic gas supply leading to scarcity and security issues; deteriorating sector profitability necessitating substantial government subsidies; and the struggle to attract private investment to mitigate the demand–supply gap. Considering these challenges, the government of Syria committed to reforming the sector's institutional framework in 2010, with the aim of attracting private financing for generation and distribution in order to improve sectoral efficiencies and address the gap between demand and supply. Before the conflict, the power system was managed by the Public Establishment for Electricity (PEE), which was divided into PEEGT (Generation and Transmission), and PEDEEE (Distribution and Exploitation of Electrical Energy). PEEGT was responsible for transmission including 400-kV (kilovolt) and 230-kV levels, whereas PEDEEE supervised the 66-kV, 20-kV, and 0.4-kV levels. As a result, PEEGT had 230-kV customers, that is, large industries and irrigation. All other customers were under the responsibility of PEDEEE. The conflict led to the breakdown of this institutional mechanism.

Conditions in Syria

Syria's power sector assets suffered relatively limited damage, but nevertheless are largely dysfunctional. The remote-sensing-based assessment covered a total of 1,134 power sector assets across 15 cities. This included 15 power plants, three dams, 56 substations, 1,051 towers, seven transformers, and two administrative offices. Damage incurred by power sector infrastructure and assets in these 15 cities has been significant but relatively limited when compared to other sectors such as housing, education, and health. It is estimated that 7.5 percent of assets are partially damaged, and 5.5 percent of assets are completely destroyed. Although the remaining assets are reported to have no damage (with the exception of about 21 percent with unknown status), only 9.7 percent of assets were fully functioning, 28.7 percent partially functioning, and 14.6 percent not functioning. Because of the restrictions of conducting a remote assessment with only limited data and on-the-ground presence, many assets were unable to be assessed, resulting in an unknown physical and operational status for 20.8 percent and 47.0 percent of assets, respectively. Many of the upstream assets (power plants, dams, substations, and towers) are either not damaged or partially damaged. The transformers seem to be either fully or partially damaged. Some electricity is also supplied by off-grid minigrid solar systems and diesel generators, but it was not possible to quantify these activities (see table 2.17).

155

Table 2.17. Total Power Sector Damage Inventory, by Cities Overall

Facility classification	Precrisis baseline number	Cities TOTAL Postcrisis damage and service data Consolidated damages data for governorate							
		Physical status (number)				Operational status (number)			
		No damage	Partially damaged	Destroyed	Unknown	Functioning	Partially functioning	Not functioning	Unknown
Power Plant	10	5	4	0	1	6	2	2	0
Dam	3	3	0	0	0	3	0	0	0
Substation	56	30	18	6	2	13	15	26	2
Tower	1,051	707	61	51	232	86	307	130	528
Transformer	7	0	2	5	0	0	0	7	0
Admin Office	2	2	0	0	0	1	0	0	1
Total (2018)	1,129	747	85	62	235	109	324	165	531
% Total		66.2	7.5	5.5	20.8	9.7	28.7	14.6	47.0

The low functionality of power sector assets is also driven by shortages of skilled personnel, fuel, and necessary spare parts. Although physical damage to the sector is a key driver of functionality decline, power sector functionality in many cases has been significantly hampered not by damage directly to the asset, but by other factors including, but not limited to, insufficient personnel to operate the assets, damage to interlinked downstream or upstream assets, interruptions due to conflict, the politicization of power, and a lack of fuel supply and availability. For example, the Euphrates Dam in Ar-Raqqa, although physically undamaged, is experiencing impaired power production because only a few hundred qualified staff remain while roughly 2,500 are necessary to keep the dam operating at full capacity. In addition, villages outside of Menbij currently receive only two hours of power from the Tishrin Dam daily, because the lack of machinery and equipment necessary to repair the dam equipment results in low water levels that can only power the dam inefficiently.[44] The city of Kobane, meanwhile, has experienced power interruptions for myriad reasons, not limited to IS's redirection of power from the Tishrin Dam away from Kobani in 2013, and a strike in September 2017 by employees of the Kobani Electricity Committee to protest low wages (Al Jazeera 2015). Furthermore, institutional breakdown has caused delays of much-needed repairs and rehabilitation to sector assets that would restore their functioning. On the fuel supply front, it is the damage to Syria's oil and gas sector that may have resulted in operational breakdowns in the country's power network. The international trade sanctions imposed on the government of Syria have harshly curtailed its ability to both acquire key spare inputs and attract much-needed foreign direct investment to the power sector (World Bank 2017).

A wide gap exists in the availability of electricity across different cities. Table 2.18 shows the divergence of electricity access across the 15 cities covered in this study. Conflict intensive cities and opposition-controlled areas are often deprived of electricity access as their connectivity with other regions is broken. In Idleb, Dar'a, and Douma, electricity access is estimated for less than five hours a day, mostly from diesel generators. In comparison, electricity is available for most of the day in cities with undamaged (or repaired) grids like Deir-ez-Zor, Kobani, and Yabroud.

Conditions in countries of asylum

Increased energy demand due to the influx of Syrian refugees has placed added strain on Lebanon's already-strained power sector. Lebanon was subject to significant load-shedding even before the arrival of Syrian refugees, resulting in supply cuts of roughly 3 hours (12.5 percent) daily in Beirut and up to 12 hours (50 percent) outside the capital, forcing locals to rely on diesel generators on a regular basis. Although 715 megawatts (MW) of total capacity have been added since 2010, the arrival of Syrian refugees necessitates the addition of 486 MW of additional power supply (inclusive of 15 percent technical losses during generation) to cover increased net demand. In total, 3,309,487 people need improved access to electricity. Lebanon currently has a peak demand of 3,400 MW, but only 2,720 MW of installed capacity available at peak supply. Information on energy access and consumption is not available for refugees, but their access is almost certainly better than those currently within Syria. On average, between 2012 and 2016, Lebanese residents had roughly 14 hours daily (58.3 percent) of power consumption available to them, compared to the 9.12 hours a day average in Syria.

Table 2.18. Precrisis and Current City-Level Power Availability

City	Precrisis availability	Current reported availability in hours	Reported rationing information
Aleppo*	1,850 MW prewar capacity (shared)	On average 50 percent or 12 hours, varying significantly by neighborhood; heavy reliance on generators	12–14 hours in areas with power; periodic interruptions, with some areas alternating 2 hours of power then 2 hours rationed
Dar'a	1,764 MW prewar capacity (shared with Damascus)	Approx. 17 percent or roughly 4.5 hours; heavy reliance on generators	Alternating 1 hour on, then 5 hours off while lines are being repaired in Dar'a
Douma	1,870 MW prewar capacity (shared)	Scarce, and completely reliant on generators with all towers and substations destroyed	No power as of July 2018
Homs	1,424 MW prewar capacity (shared)	On average 30 percent or slightly over 7 hours, varying significantly by neighborhood; heavy reliance on generators	6 hours of cut power followed by 2 hours of power as of March 2017
Idleb	544 MW prewar capacity (shared)	Approx. 10 percent or almost 2.5 hours, primarily via generators	Cut off from the national grid
Kobani	630 MW prewar capacity (shared)	Approx. 67 percent or 16 hours, varying with dam water level; roughly 20 percent provided by generators	16 hours, but may vary depending on water level in river (dam)
Ar-Raqqa	990 MW prewar capacity (shared)	Approx. 33–50 percent or 8–12 hours, varying significantly by neighborhood, with some not receiving electricity at all; heavy reliance on generators	2–3 hours of rationing around noon
Menbij	25–40 MW coming in from the dam depending on water level	Approx. 33 percent or 8 hours, with heavy reliance on generators. Some neighborhoods are devoid of electricity.	4:00 p.m to midnight
Qamishli	25 MW provided out of needed 140 MW	Approx. 17 percent or 4 hours, with 72 percent of energy production coming from generators.	Approx. 4 hours per day on average

Sources: World Bank staff calculations based on analysis from local interviews with key informants, Facebook, findings from satellite imagery, and local news sources including Al-Monitor.
Note: MW = megawatt.

Jordan was already an energy-insecure country, importing 96 percent of its total energy consumption; the influx of Syrian refugees has put a substantial strain on service provision (JPRSC 2018). Total annual electricity consumption rose markedly from 4,296 gigawatt-hours in 2009 to 6,560 gigawatt-hours in 2014 (an increase of 34.5 percent), and liquefied petroleum gas consumption increased from 300,000 per annum tonnes to 366,000 p.a. tonnes during the same time period. The government of Jordan forecasted an additional 225MW of energy required between 2016 and 2018 (JPRSC 2016). In November 2017, Jordan established the world's first refugee camp powered by renewable energy. The Azraq solar energy plant, a 12.9-MW solar photovoltaic plant at the Zaatari refugee camp, allowed UNHCR to increase power provision to refugees' homes from 8 hours to the current 14 hours (UNHCR 2018c).

Supply of electricity reflects the inferior living conditions of Syrian refugees in the Kurdistan Region of Iraq. Although all Syrian refugees are connected to the electricity grid, they received only about 9 hours of electricity per day on average, despite living in urban areas. By constrast, residents of Kurdistan received 18 hours of electricity per day.

Transportation

Syria's roadway network expanded rapidly before the conflict, to keep pace with the fast-growing economy and population. In the decade preceding the conflict, the road network grew by 10 percent, with 70 percent of the network being asphalted (map 2.1). This increase was more than matched by an increase in the number of vehicles. Six years of economic reforms, including a reduction in import taxes from more than 250 percent to 50 percent and the introduction of bank credits for purchasing cars, created an unprecedented surge in the number of vehicles on the road. According the Syrian Central Bureau of Statistics, the total number of registered vehicles in Syria increased from 1.2 million in 2006 to 2.1 million in 2010 (World Bank 2017).

Syria's well-developed network of motorways is primarily located in the western half of the country. The motorway system is a divided, multilane highway along the Damascus–Homs–Hama–Aleppo corridor, with extensions to the Mediterranean Ports of Tartous and Lattakia, and to Jordan to the south and Lebanon to the west. At the time violence broke out, the secondary road network was generally in good

Map 2.1. Transport Infrastructure, Syrian Arab Republic

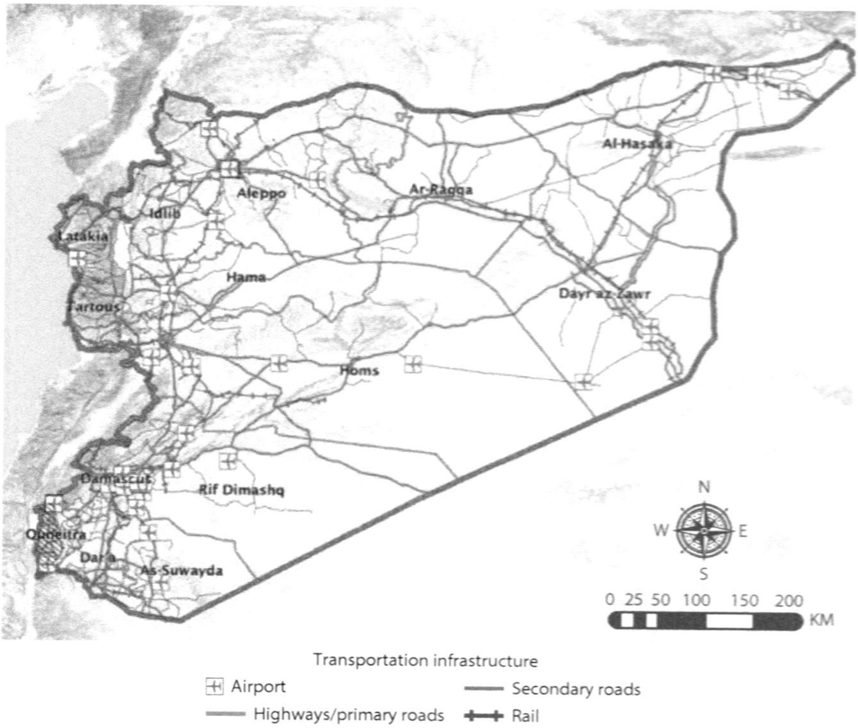

Source: World Bank 2017a.

condition and additional road construction was underway to extend the major highway network to include a link from Lattakia to Aleppo. Motorways and secondary roads have been assigned weight-load limits, and weigh stations operated to limit truck overloading. The eastern part of the country was connected only through two-lane roads because of the sparse population. According to the U.S. Central Intelligence Agency, the total distance of the road network in Syria was 69,837 km, of which 63,060 km was paved (including 1,103 km of expressways).[45] M5 remains the most important motorway in the country. At 474 km in length, it functions as the backbone of the national network, connecting the border with Jordan in the south with Damascus, the capital, and continuing further north to Aleppo, the country's second-largest city. Other cities connected by this motorway are An Nabk, Dar'a, Hama, and Homs (World Bank 2017). The Syria road network was highly affected by the crisis and will be described further in the damage assessment section in this report.

Current Conditions in Syria

Conflict has posed significant challenges to people's road connectivity and accessibility to basic social services, such as healthcare and education. The deterioration of accessibility is mainly attributed to three factors: (a) road damage, (b) damage to social facilities, and (c) population changes in size and distribution. Despite limited data availability it is estimated that about 3,000 km of roads have been damaged in 13 urban areas (map 2.2). Although it is highly likely that the civil war damaged

Map 2.2. Damaged Road Network, Syrian Arab Republic

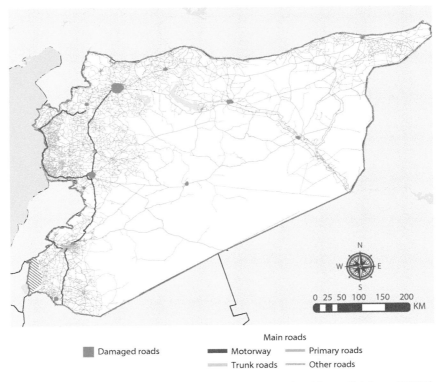

Main roads

☐ Damaged roads   ▬▬ Motorway   ▬▬ Primary roads
                              ▬▬ Trunk roads   ---- Other roads

Source: Open Street Map, World Bank (https://www.openstreetmap.org/search?query=Syria#map=5/34.853).

160

other roads, in other cities as well as in rural areas, data limitations require this analysis to assume that all roads are passable except for the identified damaged roads.

Although Syria's road network was severely damaged during the crisis, the impact of the damage was not homogeneous across governorates. According to recent damage results, eight governorates still present damage in roads and bridges: Aleppo, Dar'a, Rural Damascus, Homs, Al-Hasakeh, Idleb, Ar-Raqqa, and Deir-ez-Zor. Among these eight governorates, 43 percent of the damage is in Aleppo governorate (95 percent of total damage is in the city of Aleppo), and 27 percent is in the governorate of Homs (83 percent of total damage is in the city of Homs). Figure 2.63 represents the share of damaged roads per governorate based on table 2.19. The total number of damaged roads per governorate is calculated as the sum of the damaged roads in the cities where damage data are provided.

The level of damage among the 14 studied cities varies from 0 percent to 80 percent damage. In fact, the damage impact on the cities varies based on the conflict level the city experienced. In addition, reconstruction work started in 2016 in cities with available financial capabilities and strong willingness to reconstruct. The percentage of damaged roads provides insights on the impact on connectivity within the cities, and the total number of kilometers damaged provides a view of the investment needed to reconstruct the damaged roads and bridge segments.

Reconstruction has been actively ongoing in areas with limited or no conflict, and especially in areas where there is a will for reconstruction. Some roads, bridges, and highways have already been reconstructed since 2016 across the different governorates of Syria, with a number of Syrian government investment projects ongoing, including 246 projects in Az Zabadani, 195 projects in Damascus, 170 projects in Hama, 75 projects in Banyas, 75 projects in Tartous, and 56 projects in Lattakia. In addition, comparing the damage assessments of 2017 and 2018 makes it clear that the governorates are moving forward with reconstruction work at different

Figure 2.63. Damaged Roads, Syrian Arab Republic

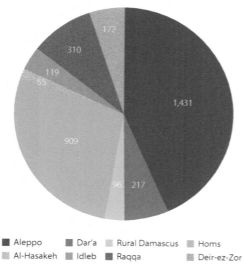

| Aleppo | Dar'a | Rural Damascus | Homs |
| Al-Hasakeh | Idleb | Raqqa | Deir-ez-Zor |

Source: Open Street Map, World Bank.

Table 2.19. Damaged Roads and Percentage Share of Each City

Governorate	City	Roads damaged per city (m)	Bridges damaged (m)	Roads damaged per governorate (m)	Share of total damage (%)
Aleppo	Afrin	5,640		1,431,878	44
	Aleppo	1,352,576	7,027		
	Menbij	53,302			
	Kobani	20,360			
Dar'a	Dar'a	132,259		132,259	4
Rural Damascus	Douma	95,617		95,617	3
Homs	Homs	750,301		909,230	28
	Tadmur	80,458			
	Al-Qusayr	78,471			
Al-Hasakeh	Qamishli	55,425		55,425	2
Idleb	Idleb	119,375		119,375	4
Ar-Raqqa	Ar-Raqqa	310,006	7,027	310,006	10
Deir-ez-Zor	Deir-ez-Zor	172,414		172,414	5

Source: Open Street Map, World Bank (https://www.openstreetmap.org/search?query=Syria#map=5/34.853).

paces, depending on several factors, including security, budget, and willingness to reconstruct. Several bridges have been reconstructed since 2017; however, more bridges were damaged during the same period. The total number of kilometers of damaged bridges in 2017 was 12.6 km; in July 2018 that number reached 14 km. Since 2017, an additional 4.39 km of bridges were damaged in Ar-Raqqa.

Since Aleppo and Homs represent a significant share of this damage, a deeper analysis is warranted. In Aleppo, with a total road network of about 2,700 km, the transport sector has been improving, with nearly 1,800 km of roads experiencing some level of debris removal or repair since January 2017. The current level of potential damage is nearly 1,400 km, a significant decrease from the early 2017 impact assessment of 3,100 km. The affected roads include all road types, from trunk roads to residential roads, with the eastern part of the city remaining the most heavily damaged. In Homs, which accounts for the second-largest share of Syria's road damage, more than 750 km of the nearly 1,100 km of roads are affected by damage. The situation is improving, with about 365 km of roads cleared since January 2017. The central and northern parts of the city remain the most heavily damaged. As in Aleppo, the damage reaches all road types, with more than 50 percent of most road classes being affected, from trunk roads to residential roads.

To assess the implications of this damage for Syrians' connectivity, two measures are used. Indicators to measure the changes in connectivity and accessibility at city level are (a) number of kilometers of roads per person in 2010 and 2018 and (b) proximity to health centers within 30 minutes and proximity to schools within 10 minutes.[46] The analysis focuses on urban areas where data on damage assessment have been provided (see figures 2.64, 2.65, 2.66 and 2.67).

Two factors explain the changes in proximity in a city: (a) changes in road network and functionality of facilities due to damage and (b) change in population

Figure 2.64. Accessible Road Density in Syrian Cities, 2010 vs. 2018

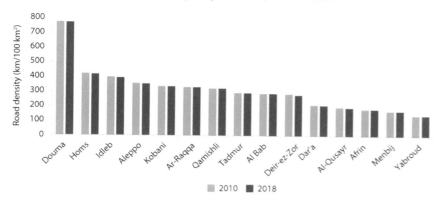

Source: Open Street Map, World Bank.

Figure 2.65. Population Density in Syrian Cities, 2010 vs. 2018

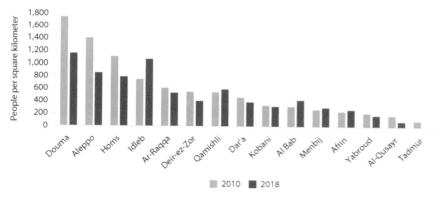

Source: Open Street Map, World Bank.

Figure 2.66. Share of Population within 30-Minute Drive of a Functioning Health Care Facility in Syrian Cities, 2010 vs. 2018

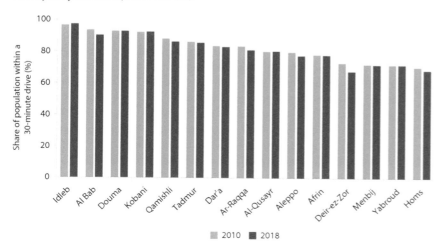

Source: Open Street Map, World Bank.

Figure 2.67. Share of Population within a 10-Minute Drive of a Functioning School in Syrian Cities, 2010 vs. 2018

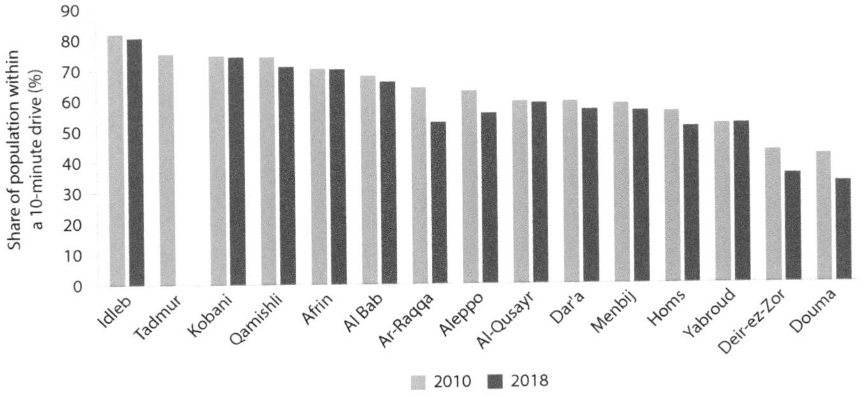

Source: Open Street Map, World Bank.

due to displacement. In cities with high conflict intensity, accessible road density has generally decreased between 2010 and 2018 because of the damage to roads. The density of accessible roads has experienced the highest decreases in severely damaged cities such as Aleppo, Al-Qusayr, Dar'a, Douma, and Homs. The decrease is relative to the percentage of damaged roads per city. Population density has also decreased in affected cities while increasing in less affected cities such as Idleb and Qamishli. Population density therefore provides an indication of how many people have been displaced. Tadmur is an example where the vast majority of the population has fled. Aleppo, Douma, and Homs have also witnessed significant decreases in population, while still having the highest population densities. Al Bab, Idleb, Menbij, and Qamishli have witnessed increases in their population density.

Population movements away from conflict-intensive areas to safer areas partially offset an otherwise drastic impact on proximity. Across the 15 cities studied, about 1.1 million people lacked good physical proximity to health care facilities in 2010; by 2018 the number of people lacking proximity had declined to about 837 thousand because of the overall decline in population in these cities. Compared to preconflict conditions, however, proximity in individual cities, expressed as a share of the population with good access, decreased quite significantly. The highest decrease was observed in the city of Deir-ez-Zor (5.3 percent) from a level that was already relatively low (73 percent) (figure 2.66). Smaller, significant proximity declines are also observed in Aleppo, Ar-Raqqa, and Homs, where roads within the city were significantly damaged and where many of the health care facilities have ceased functioning. In some cities, such as Al-Qusayr, Idleb, and Kobani, accessibility is estimated to have slightly increased. In these cities, damage to roads and health care facilities has been more minor, and population is concentrated in areas that are proximate to health care facilities that remained functioning. The conflict has affected physical proximity to education facilities much more than accessibility to health care services because of the specific distribution of the road damage and because more schools than clinics have become nonfunctional.

Figure 2.68. Accessible Road Density, by Governorate, 2010 vs. 2018

Source: Open Street Map, World Bank.

Figure 2.69. Population Density, by Governorate, 2010 vs. 2018

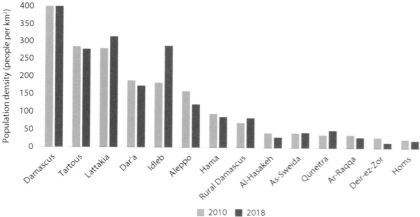

Source: Open Street Map, World Bank.

Governorate-level analysis shows more clearly the dual nature of access indicators (damage and mobility). Figures 2.68 and 2.69 show the results at governorate level. On the mobility side, as discussed above, Idleb, Lattakia, and Rural Damascus experienced significant population increases, which must have generated considerable demand for the road network. On the damage side, available or nondamaged road density dropped substantially in Homs and Aleppo, followed by Ar-Raqqa and Dar'a. In these areas identified from both demand and supply aspects, the needs for road reconstruction are particularly high.

Proximity to a health care facility has been hampered because of damaged roads and closure of hospitals. When health proximity is defined by the share of population with 30-minute access to health care facilities, about 14.9 million people, or 73.8 percent of the total population, are estimated to have proximity to health services in 2018. This share is slightly lower than the 2010 estimate of 74.5 percent.

Figure 2.70. Share of Population within 30-Minute Drive of a Functioning Health Care Facility in Syrian Cities, 2010 vs. 2018

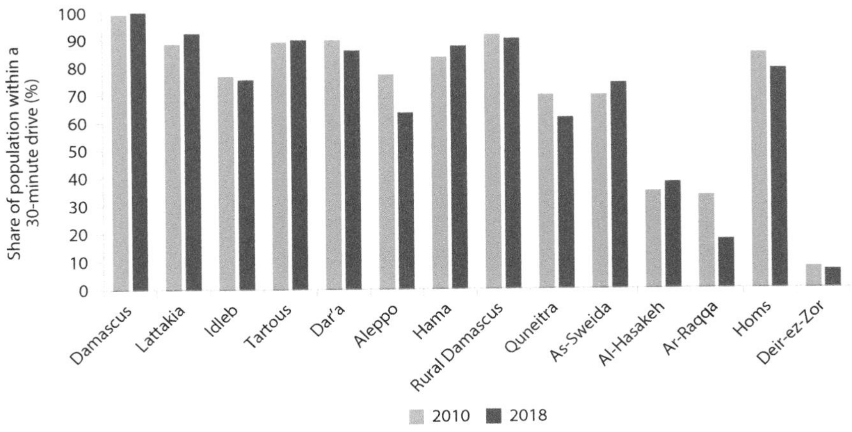

Source: Open Street Map, World Bank.

Although this change in the share is relatively small, it is driven largely by a decline in the total population in Syria; the number of people who have health proximity decreased by over 1 million. Many areas lost health care proximity between 2010 and 2018 (figure 2.70). It is estimated that 5.3 million people were still disconnected from functioning health care facilities in 2018. Health proximity differs substantially across regions; accessibility deteriorated substantially in Aleppo, Quneitra and Ar-Raqqa (figure 2.70). Clearly, proximity tends to be lower where the road network is less developed (that is, road density is lower) (see also map 2.3).

Proximity to school declined from 48.4 percent in 2010 to 44.6 percent in 2018. A similar methodology as in proximity to hospitals was applied for proximity to schools, with a threshold of 10 minutes assumed driving time (figure 2.71). Not surprisingly, school proximity is similar to health proximity: it seems to have deteriorated, particularly in Aleppo, Ar-Raqqa, Idleb, and Homs governorates.

Although transport connectivity is a useful indicator, it is not synonymous with access to services in health care or education. It is important to note that being close to a hospital or school does not necessarily guarantee benefitting from the services offered there. It just shows that transportation per se is not a great determinant of service inaccessibility.

Conditions in countries of asylum

Proximity to schools and hospitals in Syria was among the lowest in the region and has worsened as a result of the conflict. Lebanon has the best proximity to health facilities and schools, followed by Jordan and Iraq. Lebanon's better proximity may be attributed partly to a more complete coverage of available data as mentioned above, but also to the country's high population density, urbanization, and road density. Syria's health proximity is 20 percentage points lower than Lebanon's, and school proximity is merely half of Lebanon's (figure 2.72).

In host countries, transport infrastructure is sufficient to connect residents with services and markets. Especially in Lebanon and Jordan, highly urbanized societies imply relatively good access for residents. In rural areas, access to road infrastructure

Map 2.3. Proximity Maps, Syrian Arab Republic, 2010 vs. 2018

a. Thirty-minute proximity to a functioning health care facility

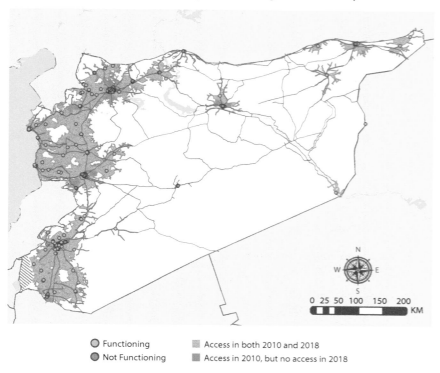

○ Functioning   ▦ Access in both 2010 and 2018
● Not Functioning   ■ Access in 2010, but no access in 2018

b. Ten-minute proximity to a functioning school

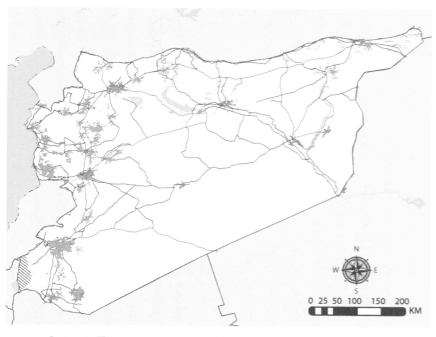

● Schools   ▦ Access in both 2010 and 2018   ■ Access in 2010, but no access in 2018

Source: Open Street Map, World Bank.

Figure 2.71. Share of Population within 10-Minute Drive of a Functioning School in Syrian Cities, 2010 vs. 2018

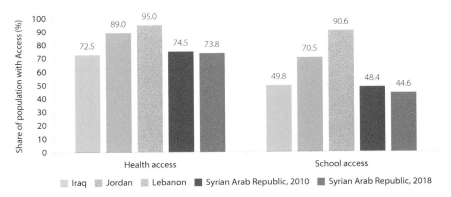

Source: Open Street Map, World Bank.

Figure 2.72. Health and School Connectivity Indicators in the Syrian Arab Republic and Its Neighbors

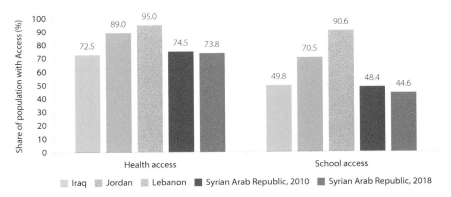

Source: Open Street Map, World Bank.

is high, compared to global benchmarks. Even in Iraq, where the largest share of rural residents lives, the rural access index (the share of population living in 2 km proximity of a road) is estimated at 63 percent. As with Syria, however, such infrastructure access is only part of the issue, because many refugees face policy-driven limitations on their movement and access to transport, which was not possible to measure at this stage.

Concluding Remarks

This chapter assessed the conditions faced by Syrians inside and outside Syria with respect to four dimensions distilled from international experience. For each of the four dimensions (peace, security, and protection; livelihoods and employment; housing, land, and property rights; and access to basic services), several narrower categories were identified and analyzed using multiple sources of data including needs assessments and vulnerability assessments organized by UN agencies, official sources of data, and World Bank assessments of damage and functionality. Data sources lent themselves to comparison between conditions within Syria and those outside Syria in some cases, especially in vulnerability/needs-related issues because they were covered by surveys both in Syria and in host communities, albeit not identically. The data, however, did not always support such comparisons, forcing the analysis to pursue second- or third-best approaches for some issues, such as monetary poverty.

Most Syrians are likely to face extreme poverty both inside and outside of Syria. Before the conflict, the extreme poverty rate ranged from 6 percent in the urban areas of the Coastal region to 20 percent in the rural areas of the Northeastern region in Syria. By 2016, the average extreme poverty rate was estimated to be between 55 and 67 percent depending on various scenarios, indicating a massive jump in poverty with most of those remaining in the country under the extreme poverty line. Poverty rates for refugees are not particularly better, ranging from 51 to 61 percent in Jordan and 37 to 50 percent in Lebanon. Although these estimates are sensitive to assumptions and methodological choices as previously discussed, the standard of living for Syrians living both inside and outside the country is far worse than it was in preconflict Syria.

Other dimensions of welfare and quality of life are in parallel with poverty. Generally, as with monetary poverty, the nonmonetary welfare of Syrians, which includes access to key services and infrastructure, tends to be highest for those refugees living in Lebanon, followed by those living in Jordan, with current welfare for Syrians still living in Syria the worst. This pattern holds on most comparable indicators of health, livelihoods, and core infrastructure, with education and housing being notable exceptions (table 2.20). Female labor force participation is very low in all three countries, but male unemployment is highest in Syria (57.7 percent), followed by Jordan (20.5 percent), and then Lebanon (12.7 percent). More school-age children are enrolled in Syria (61 percent) than in Jordan (56 percent) and Lebanon (42 percent), indicating that on this critical dimension for the future, refugee children are particularly challenged, especially in Lebanon. The picture is also mixed on measures of living standards. Sanitation deprivation is considerably lower in Syria than for refugees in Jordan and Lebanon. Water deprivation is higher in Lebanon than in Syria, where it is higher than in Jordan. Garbage collection is much worse for those in Syria than in Lebanon where there are almost no problems (no information is available for Jordan).

In Syria, deprivation is concentrated in the most conflict-affected governorates even after accounting for major displacement away from these locations. Figure 2.73 summarizes sector-specific deprivation rankings presented throughout the chapter in three broad categories: living standards (water, housing, sanitation, energy, and solid waste), human capital (education and health), and livelihoods (employment and agriculture). Note that the higher the ranking (the lower the number), the worse the relative deprivation. With average rankings of 1.5 and 2.0, Idleb and Ar-Raqqa, respectively, are the most deprived governorates, followed closely by Deir-ez-Zor (3.5), Dar'a (4.3), and Aleppo (4.5). Al-Hasakeh (6.0) also performs badly, but its average is better because of less deprivation on human capital (only eighth worst). The least deprived governorates are consistently Tartous (12.5), Lattakia, and As-Sweida (both 11.5).

Table 2.20. Comparison of Key Indicators in Present-Day Syrian Arab Republic and Host Countries

Factor	Indicator	Syrian Arab Republic	Refugees in Lebanon	Refugees in Jordan
Poverty	Share of households in extreme poverty (%)	55–67	40–53	56–65
Housing	Average share of housing problems (%)	28	44	15
Water	Deprivation Index	25	33	18
Sanitation	Deprivation Index	4	19	18
Garbage	No collection (%)	25	5	—
	Not public collection (%)	19	2	—
Education	School-age enrollment (%)	61	42	56
Health	Infrastructure Index	0.230	0.369	0.291
	Human Resource Index	0.095	0.562	0.612
Employment	Female participation (%)	11.9	12.7	13.1
	Male unemployment (%)	57.7	12.7	20.5
	Female unemployment (%)		2.7	59.9
Transport	Health access (%)	73.8	95.0	89.0
	Education access (%)	44.6	90.6	70.5

Source: All measures are summarized from earlier in the chapter. Refer to earlier sectoral discussions for full sources and notes.
Note: — = not available.

Figure 2.73. Deprivation Rankings, by Governorate and Welfare Channel

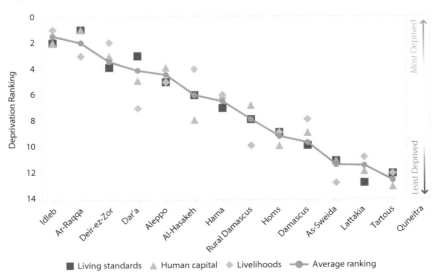

Source: All measures are summarized from earlier in the chapter. Refer to earlier sectoral discussions for full sources and notes.
Note: Rankings for Quneitra are not available because of lack of data for some sectors.

Overall, most Syrian refugees are from the governorates that experienced the greatest incidence of conflict and, by the analysis above, the greatest deprivation. Combining the demographic results from the previous chapter and conflict/ deprivation results from this chapter shows that about one-half of all refugees in Iraq, Jordan, and Lebanon come from the five governorates with the worst deprivation rankings (Idleb, Ar-Raqqa, Deir-ez-Zor, Dar'a, and Aleppo). Another quarter come from the next three worst governorates (Al-Hasakeh, Hama, and Rural Damascus). The only significant outlier is Homs, which sent the second-highest number of refugees yet has the fifth-best deprivation ranking; Damascus has also sent many refugees (139,000) despite having the fourth-best ranking. Thus, for most refugees, the correct benchmark is clearly not the average security and deprivation across Syria but these conditions in already badly hit areas. It is clear for most refugees that, if they were to return to their place of origin, they would face considerable deprivations on all dimensions of welfare.

Given these concerns, the next chapter will take a more granular approach by exploring the relationship between refugee returns and conditions faced by individual refugees at origin and in host countries. The assessments provided in this chapter helped reveal the conditions faced by refugees in countries of asylum and in Syria; however, vast heterogeneities exist across different locations and different refugees. To better understand how the four dimensions of factors discussed so far may influence the return behavior of refugees, these differences need to be accounted for. This is done in chapter 3.

Annex 2A

Health access indicators

Table 2A.1. Health Accessibility Index, 2010

Health Accessibility Index, 2010								2010							
Assets accessible to Syrians	Syria	Hasakah	Aleppo	Ar-Raqqa	As-Sweida	Damascus	Dar'a	Deir-Az Zor	Hama	Homs	Idleb	Lattakia	Quneitra	Rural Damascus	Tartous
Health infrastructure															
Hospitals															
Number of hospitals	462	32	112	11	5	50	15	23	48	42	31	21	1	50	21
Number of hospital beds	26,430	1,358	5,251	841	704	5,104	993	1,035	1,914	2,228	845	1,660	200	2,941	1,356
Health units															
Number of health units	1,826	98	241	73	93	61	106	103	175	225	114	118	59	189	171
Human resources for health															
Physicians	11,305	619	1,746	628	348	731	526	663	1,146	1,173	538	971	212	1,082	922
Nurses and midwives	29,126	1,059	2,386	997	2,340	785	1,668	2,110	2,486	3,978	1,997	3,660	321	2,063	3,276
Financial coverage															
Financial coverage hospitals	1	1	1	1	1	1	1	1	1	1	1	1	1	1	1
Financial coverage primary care	1	1	1	1	1	1	1	1	1	1	1	1	1	1	1
Population of Syrians															
Population of host country (only host country citizens)															
Health infrastructure															
Hospitals															
Number of hospitals per 1,000	0.022	0.021	0.023	0.012	0.014	0.029	0.015	0.019	0.029	0.023	0.021	0.021	0.011	0.018	0.026
Number of hospital beds per 1,000	1.236	0.898	1.079	0.891	1.903	2.91	0.967	0.835	1.176	1.236	0.563	1.647	2.222	1.037	1.701
Normalized no. of hospitals per 1,000	0.451	0.437	0.494	0.14	0.198	0.666	0.232	0.356	0.696	0.503	0.421	0.426	0.123	0.327	0.598

(table continues next page)

Table 2A.1. *(continued)*

Health Accessibility Index, 2010

Assets accessible to Syrians	Syria	Hasakah	Aleppo	Ar-Raqqa	As-Sweida	Damascus	Dar'a	Deir-Az Zor	Hama	Homs	Idleb	Lattakia	Quneitra	Rural Damascus	Tartous
2010															
Normalized number of hospital beds per 1,000	0.316	0.178	0.252	0.175	0.589	1	0.206	0.152	0.292	0.316	0.041	0.484	0.719	0.235	0.506
Health units															
Number of health units per 1,000	0.085	0.065	0.05	0.077	0.251	0.035	0.103	0.083	0.107	0.125	0.076	0.117	0.656	0.067	0.215
Normalized number of health units per 1,000	0.101	0.069	0.045	0.089	0.363	0.022	0.13	0.098	0.136	0.164	0.087	0.151	1	0.072	0.305
Health infrastructure indicator	0.209	0.124	0.148	0.132	0.476	0.511	0.168	0.125	0.214	0.24	0.064	0.318	0.86	0.153	0.406
Human resources for health															
Physicians per 1,000	0.529	0.409	0.359	0.665	0.941	0.417	0.512	0.535	0.704	0.651	0.358	0.963	2.356	0.382	1.157
Nurses and midwives per 1,000	1.362	0.7	0.49	1.056	6.324	0.448	1.624	1.703	1.527	2.206	1.33	3.631	3.567	0.727	4.11
Normalized physicians per 1,000	0.194	0.149	0.129	0.246	0.351	0.152	0.188	0.197	0.261	0.24	0.129	0.359	0.889	0.138	0.433
Normalized nurses and midwives per 1,000	0.202	0.095	0.061	0.153	1	0.055	0.244	0.257	0.228	0.338	0.197	0.567	0.556	0.1	0.644
Human resources for health indicator	0.198	0.122	0.095	0.199	0.675	0.103	0.216	0.227	0.245	0.289	0.163	0.463	0.723	0.119	0.538
Financial coverage															
Financial coverage hospitals	1	1	1	1	1	1	1	1	1	1	1	1	1	1	1
Financial coverage primary care	1	1	1	1	1	1	1	1	1	1	1	1	1	1	1
Financial coverage indicator	1	1	1	1	1	1	1	1	1	1	1	1	1	1	1
Health Accessibility Index	0.404	0.342	0.348	0.366	0.657	0.531	0.388	0.369	0.418	0.442	0.323	0.525	0.86	0.356	0.587

Source: All measures are summarized from earlier in the chapter. Refer to earlier sectoral discussions for full sources and notes.

Table 2A.2. Health Accessibility Index, 2018

Assets accessible to Syrians	Syria	Hasakah	Aleppo	Ar-Raqqa	As-Sweida	Damascus	Dar'a	Deir-Az Zor	Hama	Homs	Idleb	Lattakia	Quneitra	Rural Damascus	Tartous	Lebanon	Jordan	Iraq
									2018									
Health infrastructure																		
Hospitals																		
Number of hospitals	505	31	117	11	6	60	13	28	48	51	34	26	1	58	21	147	116	260
Number of hospital beds	27,667	1,081	4,131	675	724	5,190	1,011	1,392	2,014	2,937	1,092	2,841	200	3,017	1,362	12,555	14,779	44,821
Health units																		
Number of health units	1,585	98	169	73	93	61	25	15	175	225	114	118	59	189	171	900	1,177	2,669
Human resources for health																		
Physicians	5,889	155	481	270	225	1,601	67	13	629	113	180	768	90	127	1,170	13,813	26,019	27,208
Nurses and midwives	12,915	497	716	559	1,019	1,529	280	77	1,593	1,080	630	1,594	132	724	2,485	16,087	14,795	62,795
Financial coverage																		
Coverage hospitals	1	1	1	1	1	1	1	1	1	1	1	1	1	1	1	0.45	0.45	0.45
Coverage primary care	1	1	1	1	1	1	1	1	1	1	1	1	1	1	1	0.65	0.65	0.65
Population of Syrians	20,226,627	1,169,176	3,808,479	869,808	404,872	1,824,931	954,726	713,623	1,439,831	1,449,869	2,363,035	1,138,556	122,575	3,189,742	777,404	976,065	666,596	251,157
Population of host country (citizens)																5,851,479	9,159,302	36,115,649
Health infrastructure																		
Hospitals																		
Number of hospitals per 1,000	0.025	0.027	0.031	0.013	0.015	0.033	0.014	0.039	0.033	0.035	0.014	0.023	0.008	0.018	0.027	0.022	0.012	0.007
Number of hospital beds per 1,000	1.368	0.925	1.085	0.776	1.788	2.844	1.059	1.951	1.399	2.026	0.462	2.495	1.632	0.946	1.752	1.839	1.504	1.232
Normalized number of hospitals per 1,000	0.555	0.604	0.735	0.171	0.239	0.802	0.202	1	0.816	0.873	0.226	0.489	0.031	0.344	0.619	0.448	0.145	–

(table continues next page)

Table 2A.2. *(continued)*

Assets accessible to Syrians	2018																	
	Syria	Hasakah	Aleppo	Ar-Raqqa	As-Sweida	Damascus	Dar'a	Deir-Az Zor	Hama	Homs	Idleb	Lattakia	Quneitra	Rural Damascus	Tartous	Lebanon	Jordan	Iraq
Normalized number of hospital beds per 1,000	0.37	0.189	0.254	0.128	0.542	0.973	0.244	0.608	0.383	0.639	–	0.831	0.478	0.198	0.527	0.562	0.426	0.315
Health units																		
Number of health units per 1,000	0.078	0.084	0.044	0.084	0.23	0.033	0.026	0.021	0.122	0.155	0.048	0.104	0.481	0.059	0.22	0.132	0.12	0.073
Normalized number of health units per 1,000	0.09	0.099	0.037	0.099	0.329	0.02	0.008	–	0.158	0.211	0.043	0.13	0.725	0.06	0.314	0.175	0.156	0.083
Infrastructure indicator	0.23	0.144	0.146	0.114	0.435	0.496	0.126	0.304	0.271	0.425	0.021	0.48	0.602	0.129	0.42	0.369	0.291	0.199
Human resources for health																		
Physicians per 1,000	0.291	0.133	0.126	0.31	0.556	0.877	0.07	0.018	0.437	0.078	0.076	0.675	0.734	0.04	1.505	2.023	2.648	0.748
Nurses and midwives per 1,000	0.639	0.425	0.188	0.643	2.517	0.838	0.293	0.108	1.106	0.745	0.267	1.4	1.077	0.227	3.197	2.356	1.506	1.727
Normalized number of physicians per 1,000	0.104	0.043	0.041	0.111	0.204	0.327	0.02	–	0.159	0.023	0.022	0.25	0.272	0.008	0.565	0.762	1	0.278
Normalized number of nurses and midwives per 1,000	0.085	0.051	0.013	0.086	0.388	0.117	0.03	–	0.161	0.102	0.026	0.208	0.156	0.019	0.497	0.362	0.225	0.26
Human resources for health indicator	0.095	0.047	0.027	0.099	0.296	0.222	0.025	–	0.16	0.063	0.024	0.229	0.214	0.014	0.531	0.562	0.612	0.269
Financial coverage																		
Coverage hospitals	1	1	1	1	1	1	1	1	1	1	1	1	1	1	1	0.45	0.45	0.45
Coverage primary care	1	1	1	1	1	1	1	1	1	1	1	1	1	1	1	0.65	0.65	0.65
Financial coverage indicator	1	1	1	1	1	1	1	1	1	1	1	1	1	1	1	0.55	0.55	0.55
Health Accessibility Index	0.389	0.334	0.33	0.331	0.542	0.554	0.319	0.402	0.425	0.478	0.267	0.547	0.604	0.318	0.593	0.462	0.436	0.304

Note: – = not available.

Table 2A.3. Water Sectors

City	Status of networked facilities
Afrin	The Local Council of Afrin city, with Turkish support, was able to rehabilitate several water network pipelines, in addition to reactivating the main water station. As a result, the public water network and the supply of most neighbourhoods of the city was reactivated in mid-2018. While restoration is still in progress, water is continuously provided, with some occasional delays between pumping periods. Previously, the cost of a 24-barrel water tank was about LS 3500 (US$3.5 m³).
Al-Bab	Following widespread damage, the water network was rebuilt and is 90 percent ready to use. However, since it was taken over, Syrian government authorities have been blocking the water line toward Al-Bab city, from A'ayn Al-Baydaa station near the Euphrates River within their territories.
Aleppo	Widespread destruction has damaged network assets leaving only 30 percent of households able to depend on the network. Humanitarian actors invested heavily in a network of wells during the siege of Aleppo. While this was a critical safety net during the siege, it has changed the structure of the service delivery—possibly irreversibly. Aleppo has a water treatment plant (WTP) and a wastewater treatment plant (WWTP): Al-Khafsa Water Treatment Plant supplies drinking water to 3.5 million people, including all residents of the city of Aleppo, and produces around 18,000 m³ of drinking water per day. The plant is located to the east of Aleppo near Lake Assad, a dammed portion of the Euphrates River, and consists of two facilities, one smaller and one larger, likely representing the initial station (the smaller) and more recent additions to increase the plant's output. Water travels from the plant through 90 kilometers of pipelines to supply the main water pumping stations in the city of Aleppo (Sulayman al-Halabi and Bab al-Nayrab), a journey that takes roughly 20 hours. The damage to this WTP impacted the water supplied to Al-Bab's city. The sewage water treatment plant located in the Ar-Ramouseh Industrial District, is functioning, but the physical status of the plant is unknown.
Dar'a	The water supply network in Dar'a has suffered severe damage and is nonfunctional as a result of sustained conflict leaving 65 percent of people without access to the network. Dar'a has a WTP and a WWTP: Dar'a's existing WTP is not functioning, but local media report that repairs/construction are in progress and will cost LS 1.4 billion (and may take approximately seven months to complete). It is expected to be completed in October 2018 and will be able to treat 1,200 m³ per day of water. The WWTP in Dar'a had been damaged in fighting and was no longer functioning. Government-affiliated reports in December 2016 and February 2017 confirm the station is still damaged, with electricity outages and continued fighting in the area making repairs to, and completion of, the station difficult. No repairs are reported to have occurred in 2018. Even prior to the Syrian conflict, local municipal authorities stated that the treatment plant did not have capacity to treat sewage.
Deir ez-Zor	In the populated neighbourhoods of Al-Joura, Al-Qusoour, and Harabesh, the water network didn't incur any substantial damage and is still functioning properly, yet nearly half of households are not receiving network water. As for the unpopulated neighborhoods,[a] the network has seen major damage that rendered it out of service. The nature of damage varies from one neighborhood to another, based on the rate at which each neighborhood was targeted. Water Establishment announced restoration of functionality of its main pumping station that was rehabilitated when electricity returned to the city in May 2018. The water pumped daily increased from 1000 cubic meters to 1400 cubic meters and is expected to be at 2400 cubic meters, depending on the stability of electricity. A one-megawatt diesel engine was also installed at the facility that allows the pump to remain operational in case of power failure.

(table continues next page)

Table 2A.3. *(continued)*

City	Status of networked facilities
	Deir ez-Zor had 10 functional water purification plants until 2011, constructed during different time periods. The main WTP is the Al-Basel Plant (capacity max: 1,200m³/day; practical: 600m³/day). This plant started operating in 2007 and could cover the city's water needs. Recent problems related to the endurance of the water conveyance pipes between the plant and the water tanks prevent the plant from functioning. This plant is out of service with damage of 90 percent as estimated by government officials. The estimated cost for repair is about US$2.6 million. Six treatment plants need partial maintenance with repairs estimated at US$200,000 and the three remaining plants are functioning.
Douma	The Local Council reported repairs to the city's sewage and water networks in April 2018. The Barada pipeline has been partially functioning since the beginning of 2011, due to shelling. Douma has a WTP and a WWTP: Al-Fija Spring Treatment and Pumping Station, located in Ayn al-Fija (25 km northwest of Damascus), also served the Douma area but was destroyed in 2013. Local reporting indicates that wells have been constructed in the Ayn al-Fija area as an alternative water source, however diminishing water level because of the lack of rainfall is increasing the water deficit in surrounding areas (including Douma). Adra WWTP was the main wastewater treatment facility for all of Damascus and its suburbs. It is located approximately seven miles northeast of Douma. Due to its proximity, wastewater from Douma was likely sent to this plant but when Douma was cut off from the Damascus water network in 2012, it likely also was cut off from this plant. The facility was destroyed in 2013 as a result of bombing. Adra wastewater treatment facility has been partially operational since 2011 because of shelling.
Homs	Needs assessments reports claim that Homs residents have consistent availability of potable water, but water quantity has been less than fully sufficient to address household needs, resulting in additional expenditures and trade-offs in household budgets. However, most local communities have reported disruptions to sewerage services, including "blocked connections to sewage" and inability to empty septic tanks. Several repair and reconstruction projects are reportedly ongoing in Homs, including replacement of sewage lines, sanitation system repair, and replacement of street water lines. WASH infrastructure in Homs is undergoing extensive reconstruction and repair, with improved physical integrity at approximately 38.5 percent of all facilities. This is in contrast with significant conflict-related disruptions to water access examined in the previous assessments.
Idleb	The proportion of pipelines affected in the water network does not exceed 8 percent. The water networks appear in good condition and are able to meet necessary demands for the required use. However, the networks require constant maintenance in order to address issues that result from pumping and continuous operations. A majority of the WSS infrastructure is not operating at full capacity, and access to water appears largely dependent on donors and aid organizations. As a result only 40 percent of households are able to depend on the network for water. Most of the neighborhoods have similar access to water, depending heavily on alternative nonnetwork sources. Houses with multiple floors often have difficulties with accessing water, because many pumping operations only extend as far as the ground floor and do not have the capacity to reach the second or third floor or higher. The average expenditure on water in Idleb is reportedly above the national average, at 6 percent of household income.
Kobane	There is a project underway to repair the sewage system and to repave the streets. NGOs are also fundraising to help rehabilitate the water networks throughout Kobane. Only one WTP is located in the Kaniya Murside neighbourhood. The plant is not damaged, but it is not functioning.

(table continues next page)

177

Table 2A.3. *(continued)*

City	Status of networked facilities
Manbij	The Water Directorate is responsible for repairing works and maintenance of the water pipelines in the Self Administration's territories in Manbij city and its countryside. It is important to note that the Manbij Water Directorate implemented a project in June 2018 to replace asbestos pipelines in the Manbij water network.
Qamichli	Water is generally supplied to citizens through the main water network. In some areas, especially in summer, citizens are required to pay LS 500 per barrel or dig wells in order to get water. Despite the great population pressure and increasing numbers of IDPs, the electricity, water, and other services have not had major repairs and experienced significant service disruptions; however, no new projects have been initiated to cover these developing needs. In addition to the three old water stations which supply drinking water to the entire city (the stations of Awijah, Halaliya, and Jagjag), there is a large collection of artesian wells that civilians dug because these stations were unable to supply the entire city with water, which obliges residents to get water through tanks or sometimes dig manual or artesian wells. Some neighborhoods located in the eastern part of Qamishli City lack water entirely during the summer. The residents of these neighborhoods are supplied with water by tanks, and, in particular, the Qanat Al- Suez neighborhoods experience a severe water deficit. Except for these neighborhoods, the others have a stable water supply. Some northern parts of Qamishli City are supplied by the Safan Dam, which is located in Derik "Malikia" district.
Ar-Raqqa	According to local authorities, damage and cracks are estimated to affect no less than 45 percent of the total water network system, but because most of it is underground the exact damage cannot be clearly pinpointed. As a result, both local authorities and residents are engaged in simultaneous repairs of the water lines, for example of the main line 600, another two lines 300 km west of the city, and one line 60 km east of the city. As part of a new initiative called "The rehabilitation of basic services in the city of Ar-Raqqa," water sanitation workers repair the sewage and water pipes. There is one WTP located between the two bridges, to the south of the Euphrates River. It provides most neighborhoods in the city and ten neighboring villages with clean drinking water. The Reconstruction Committee supervised its maintenance after being funded by the Euphrates Program to operate the station and to provide salaries for employees and some machinery and accessories needed for the station to continue working. The Dbsi Afnan Water Plant in the Western Ar-Raqqa countryside, which services suburbs of Ar-Raqqa city, is currently undergoing repairs. The sewage treatment plant, located to the east of the city near Al-Qarmid Factory (Brick Factory), is partially damaged and not functional.
Yabroud	Water is generally supplied to citizens through the main water network by the Self Administration authorities. All water wells and reservoirs are functioning properly with no damage. Maintenance to these water facilities is provided by the Yabroud Water Unit of the Water Foundation, and all neighborhoods are provided with water services equally. Over the past two years, the Yabroud Water Unit has been providing regular maintenance and repairs of the water networks and well system within the city. In addition to repairs, the Water Unit has conducted regular testing of tap water quality as it was recently (June–July 2018) affected by sand at the bottom of the wells. Notably, as of July 2018, the Water Unit conducted full rehabilitation of the main pumping line for the city, drastically improving availability of running water in the city.

Note: IDP = internally displaced person; LS = Syrian pound; m^3 = cubic meter; NGO = nongovernmental organization; WASH = water, sanitation, and hygiene; WSS = Water Supply and Sanitation; WTP = water treatment plant; WWTP = wastewater treatment plant.

a. The length of the network in the unpopulated neighborhoods is estimated at 3,000 km, with dimensions that range between 5 and 100 cm. Based on the estimated cost (before 2011), the total cost of installing 1 linear meter is US$30, including the price of the pipe, along with its accessories, transportation, excavating work, protection materials, backfilling works, and so on.

Notes

1. Additional concerns include future protection of women and their children who were married in religious or tribal courts outside of government-controlled areas and the possibility that these will not be recognized in the future because often there is no formal documentation process (Syrian Center for Legal Research 2018; see also Zabel 2016).

2. Information in this section comes from the Syrian Ministry of Transport. For more information see http://www.mot.gov.sy/web/main.php.

3. UN Comtrade Database, United Nations, New York (accessed September 2018), https://comtrade.un.org/.

4. The conflict reduced the number of state collection centers from approximately 140 before the conflict broke out to 22 in 2015, according to data from the General Organization for Cereal Processing and Trade in Hoboob.

5. For more information on the "Jordan Program for Results" project, see the Competitive Industries and Innovation Program website at www.theciip.org/content/jordan.

6. World Bank (2017) estimates about 3.1 million to 3.2 million job losses across the country, using underlying data from the Syria Center for Policy Research.

7. Figures pertain to government-controlled regions that make up most of the population.

8. Jordan Labor Code, 1996. Eligibility criteria and the process for obtaining a work permit are not specified in the law but are detailed in a series of regulations.

9. According to MOL letter dated June 7, 2015, (Ref. No L/1/6868) and MOL letter dated March 1, 2016, (Ref. No. L/1/2389).

10. The work permit does not guarantee good working conditions or social security benefits. Many non-Jordanian workers argue that the sponsors of work permits exploit them, refusing to release them from employment or threatening to turn them over to the police. See ILO 2017a.

11. Circular 98/2017 dated March 16, 2017, (Ref. No. TM/1/1/481) clarifies the open professions in the agriculture sector, and a letter dated June 14, 2017, clarifies the open professions in the manufacturing sector. Closed sectors include administrative and accounting professions; literary professions including printing and secretary professions; warehouse professions; sales; decoration professions; electrical work; car maintenance and mechanics; drivers' professions; security guard and office boys; medical professions; engineering; hair-dressing; and education

12. A circular was issued on April 5, 2016; another circular issued on July 3, 2016, extended this for an additional three months and exempted Syrian workers from work permit fees, additional amounts due in accordance with Bylaw 67 for 2014, and revenue stamp fees. A circular issued December 24, 2016, clarified that audit fees, verification fees, pledge fees, and authorization fees would be collected. A later circular exempting Syrian workers from work permit fees was issued on December 10, 2018.

13. Instructions for 2012 Article 11 state that non-Jordanian workers can obtain their dues from the Social Security Corporation when they leave the country permanently. If the worker has been paying into Social Security but does not have a work permit, he must pay work permit fees retroactively for the duration of his subscription (see also letters dated July 7, 2013; February 8, 2016; and April 14, 2016). However, refugees often do not consider this a guaranteed mechanism.

14. The following cases apply: (a) workers in the agriculture sector whose permits have expired can move from an employer to another in the agriculture sector, (b) workers in the agriculture sector whose permits are still valid can move from an employer to another in the agriculture sector if they have permission of the original employer, (c) workers in sectors other than agriculture whose permits have expired can move from an employer to another in any sector, (d) workers in the construction sector whose permits are still valid can move from an employer to another in the construction sector if they have permission of the original employer, and (e) workers in sectors other than agriculture and construction whose permits are still valid can move from an employer to another in any sector if six months have passed since the permit was issued and if they have the permission of the original employer. The case of workers in the agriculture sector was revised to require the original employer's permission.

15. MOL letter dated May 22, 2016 (Ref. No. L/1/6751).

16. Circular 249/2017 dated July 23, 2017 (Ref. No. TM/1/1/13997).

17. A circular issued on November 13, 2017, slightly improves intersectorial mobility for Syrians by allowing mobility from the agriculture, bakeries, and support services sectors to other sectors once an existing work permit has expired; it also allows Syrians to change employers without clearance from their previous employer once an existing work permit has expired.

18. Another West Asia–North Africa Institute survey conducted in 2017 but with a small sample size of 501 also estimated employment of men at 50 percent. The JLPMS survey conducted in 2016 estimated that 36 percent of men were working, whereas an ILO survey in 2014 put employment of men at 20 percent.

19. The figures are similar to JLMPS data, which show that 96 percent of Syrian refugee women were inactive (Krafft et al. 2018).

20. The Agreement for Economic and Social Cooperation and Coordination Between the Lebanese Republic and the Syrian Arab Republic, signed in 1993, affirmed the freedom of movement for Lebanese and Syrians between their two countries, as well as their citizens' right to work in Lebanon or Syria according to each country's labor code.

21. It should be noted that Syrians fleeing the conflict are not recognized as refugees in Lebanon and are treated according to general regulations applicable to all Syrian nationals. Lebanon has not ratified the 1951 Refugee Convention relating to the Status of Refugees, and protection mechanisms for refugees are considered weak. However, the Universal Declaration of Human Rights, which is included in the Lebanese Constitution, binds Lebanese to "the right to seek asylum." In practice, the Lebanese government rarely arrests, prosecutes, or detains irregular refugees.

22. Data are from REACH (2015), but figures on agriculture employment are not very different from those in UNHCR (2017c).

23. UNDP reports estimate poverty lines adopting cost-of-basic-needs methodology. The approach estimates expenditure necessary to acquire enough food intake for adequate calorie requirement, augmented by minimum cost necessary for nonfood expenditure. Three main measures of poverty are (a) abject poverty, defined as the share of population whose expenditure lies below the food poverty line; (b) extreme poverty, defined as the share of population whose per capita expenditure is less than the cost of food plus expenditure on absolute minimum essential nonfood goods; and (c) overall poverty, defined as the share of population whose per capita expenditure is less than the cost of food and a reasonable minimum expenditure on nonfood items. See UNDP (2011) for more detail.

24. For ease of exposition, the discussion focuses on extreme poverty. Poverty incidence was also estimated at a higher poverty line. The interpretations are qualitatively the same with the two poverty rates.

25. Each region consists of the following governorates: South—Damascus, Rural Damascus, Dar'a, As-Sweida, and Quneitra; Northeast—Idleb, Aleppo, Ar-Raqqa, Deir-ez-Zor, and Al-Hasakeh; Central—Homs and Hama; Coastal—Tartous and Latakkia.

26. The elasticity of poverty with respect to growth in per capita consumption and inequality (measured by the Gini coefficient) is estimated on historical data, giving the percentage change in poverty when mean per capita consumption changes by 1 percent (keeping the distribution unchanged) and when inequality changes by 1 percent (keeping the mean expenditure constant). In the past, owing to the shallowness of poverty, the growth and distribution elasticity of poverty in Syria was quite high. For the purpose of the 2017 analysis, elasticities from the most recent period were used (2004–07), when growth elasticity was −2.911 and distribution elasticity was 3.046. Next, the latest available poverty rate and estimates of GDP per capita growth rates are used, with baseline poverty estimated from the Household Income and Expenditure Survey 2006–07 (HIES 06-07, https://microdata.worldbank.org/index.php/catalog/69) (12.3 percent). The estimates of real GDP and total population are combined with an assumed pass-through between GDP per capita growth and per capita expenditure growth of 1.

27. VAF samples only the refugee population outside of camps in Jordan. Thus, these findings can be extrapolated only to that segment of the refugee population.

28. This is the lower poverty line, which is the food poverty line augmented by an allowance for expenditure on essential nonfood goods.

29. Regression-based PPP exchange rate was used for Jordan instead of the direct estimates reported by the International Comparison of Prices (ICP). In eight countries, the 2011 PPPs were outliers because they showed a large difference in inflation implied by the 2005 and 2011 PPPs and domestic consumer price index. There were also concerns over the coverage and quality of ICP price collection in four countries, Jordan included. Therefore, the PPP conversion rate for these countries is estimated from a regression model that predicts PPP on the basis of macroeconomic explanatory variables. Please refer to Atamanov et al. (2018) for more details.

30. For more information on the 3RP, visit http://www.3rpsyriacrisis.org/.

31. Data are from World Bank Development Indicators (database), (accessed September 2018), databank. worldbank.org/source/world-development-indicators.

32. For more information about Institute of Health Metrics and Evaluation's (IHME) Syria assessment, see the IHME website at http://www.healthdata.org/syria.

33. The lower number is from Save the Children, and the higher number is from the Syrian American Medical Association.

34. Data from World Health Organization, 2018.

35. However, Iraq, Jordan, and Lebanon do not have official policies that currently provide health coverage to refugees from national budgets and coverage to date is mainly provided through donors and UN agencies; therefore, the results from the latest UN surveys, including VASyR in Lebanon and VAF in Jordan, are used to estimate the extent to which financial coverage is provided to Syrian refugees in host countries. Responses from the surveys indicate that, in relation to primary health care, approximately 65 percent of respondents did not see financial coverage as a barrier to accessing services. In contrast, when it comes to hospital care, 45 percent of respondents did not indicate financial coverage as a barrier to accessing services. Using the population sizes for 2010 and 2018, precrisis and current access ratios are calculated for each governorate within Syria. Similarly, the population size in host countries (considering the population size of Syrian refugees in those countries), current access ratios within Syria are compared to access ratios in Iraq, Jordan, and Lebanon.

36. In the Syrian education system, early childhood education (preprimary) is available for children ages 3 to 5, but it is not compulsory and is provided on a fee-paying basis (WES 2016). Syria has a 12-year basic and secondary education system (9 years of basic education, which is mandatory, and 3 years of secondary education, which is offered at general secondary schools or seven technical/vocational schools).

37. Children can be enrolled in primary school or in secondary school (both general and vocational education track). Only enrollment in public schools, which represents most schooling in Syria, is considered. Generally, 97 percent of all basic education schools in Syria are public; the remaining 3 percent are private. Children not enrolled in public schools are considered out of school even if they may receive some kind of nonformal education.

38. The impact of conflict on child labor has been widely analyzed both theoretically and empirically in the recent literature, generally finding that conflict increases child labor. See, for example, Di Maio and Nandi (2013) for West Bank and Gaza, Kofol and Ciarli (2017) for Afghanistan, and Rodriguez and Sanchez (2012) for Colombia. The child labor model of Basu and Van (1998) is built on the luxury axiom, which posits that children work when their family cannot meet their basic needs otherwise, regardless of how large or small the return to child labor is.

39. Child labor was defined as working at least one day in the previous 30 days.

40. Wartime currency devaluation and inflation makes conversion of Syrian pounds misleading. In 2017, LS 2.00 was worth US$1.18, but in 2011 it was worth US$5.40, which more accurately reflects the real cost to Syrian people. In 2011 equivalents, LS 570 is worth US$12.26, and LS 1,760 is worth US$37.84. Reach assumes that a household of six requires 2.8 m³ of water per month for basic survival needs. The official domestic tariff is stepped. Up to 3 m³ per month is free, 3–8 m³ is LS 7.00, 8–13 m³ is LS 15.00, with further steps to a maximum of LS 60.00 for over 60 m³ per month.

41. There are actually three agreements from 1953, 1987, and 2012 in relation to the Yarmouk River between Jordan and Syria.

42. Note that the VAF data for Jordan exclude those in camps.

43. Based on characterization of waste in 2004 national strategy that indicates 9.1 percent of municipal solid waste is demolition waste.

44. Information from local interviews.

45. For more information on Syria's transportation system, see CIA website at https://www.cia.gov/library /publications/the-world-factbook/geos/sy.html.

46. A smaller time threshold is used for schools because many students walk to school; the 10-minute driving distance is equivalent to about 7 to 13 km, depending on type of road.

References

Al Jazeera. 2015. "Fears of the Collapse of the Aleppo Dam in Aleppo." *Al Jazeera Net*, December 29. https://www .aljazeera.net/news/arabic/2015/12/29/حلب-بريف-تشرين-سد-انهيار-من-مخاوف.

Al-Tamimi, Aymenn Jawad. 2015. "The Archivist: Unseen Islamic State Financial Accounts for Deir az-Zor Province." *Pundicity*, October 5. http://www.aymennjawad.org/17916/the-archivist-unseen-islamic-state-financial.

Atamanov, Aziz, Dean Jolliffe, Christoph Lakner, and Espen Beer Prydz. 2018. "Purchasing Power Parities Used in Global Poverty Measurement." Global Poverty Monitoring Technical Note 5, World Bank, Washington, DC.

Basu, Kaushik, and Hoang Pham Van. 1998. "The Economics of Child Labor." *American Economic Review* 88 (3).

Beegle, K., J. De Weerdt, J. Friedman, and J. Gibson. 2012. "Methods of Household Consumption Measurement through Surveys: Experimental Results from Tanzania." *Journal of Development Economics* 98 (1): 3–18.

CARE. 2016. "On Her Own: How Women Forced to Flee from Syria Are Shouldering Increased Responsibility as They Struggle to Survive." CARE International UK, London.

Central Administration of Statistics. 2010. "Multiple Indicators Cluster Survey 2009." Central Administration of Statistics, Beirut, Lebanon.

Central Bureau of Statistics. 2007. "Labor Force Survey." Central Bureau of Statistics, Damascus, Syrian Arab Republic.

———. 2009. "Labor Force Survey." Central Bureau of Statistics, Damascus, Syrian Arab Republic.

Central Intelligence Agency. 2019. "CIA World Factbook: Syria." Washington, DC. https://www.cia.gov/library /publications/the-world-factbook/geos/sy.html.

Competitive Industries and Innovation Program. 2017. "Mobilizing Syrian Diaspora for New Markets and Investments for Syrian Refugees." World Bank, Washington, DC. https://www.theciip.org/content/jordan.

Cunial, Laura. 2016. "Housing Land and Property (HLP) in the Syrian Arab Republic." Briefing Note, Norwegian Refugee Council, Oslo, June 7.

Di Maio, Michele, and Tushar K Nandi. 2013. "The Effect of the Israeli-Palestinian Conflict on Child Labor and School Attendance in the West Bank." *Journal of Development Economics* 100 (1): 107–16.

Economic Research Forum. 2016. "Jordan Labor Market Panel Survey, JLMPS 2016." Economic Research Forum, Giza, Egypt.

Euro-Mediterranean Human Rights Network. 2013. "Violence against Women, Bleeding Wound in the Syrian Conflict." Euro-Mediterranean Human Rights Network, Copenhagen.

FAO (Food and Agriculture Organization of the United Nations), IFAD (International Fund for Agricultural Development), UNICEF (United Nations Children's Fund), WFP (World Food Programme), and WHO (World Health Organization). 2018. *The State of Food Security and Nutrition in the World 2018. Building Climate Resilience for Food Security and Nutrition*. Rome: FAO.

Forni, Nadia. 2001. "Land Tenure Systems Structural Features and Policies." Food and Agricultural Organization of the United Nations, Italian Ministry of Agriculture and Agrarian Reform, Damascus, March.

Freihat, Moath. 2014. "Syrian Refugees in Jordan: Economic Risks and Opportunities" Arab Reporters for Investigative Journalism, January 26. https://en.arij.net/report/syrian-refugees-in-jordan-economic-risks -and-opportunities.

Guha-Sapir, D., B. Schlüter, J. M. Rodriguez-Llanes, L. Lillywhite, and M. H. R. Hicks. 2018. "Patterns of Civilian and Child Deaths due to War-Related Violence in Syria: A Comparative Analysis from the Violation Documentation Center Dataset, 2011–16." *The Lancet Global Health* 6 (1): e103-e110.

HLRN (Housing and Land Rights Network). 2011. "Systematic Housing and Land Rights Violations against Syrian Kurds." NGO Submission to the UN Human Rights Council, Universal Periodic Review of Syrian Arab Republic Twelfth Session of the UPR Working Group, October 13–14, Habitat International Coalition's Housing and Land Rights Network.

Howden, Daniel, Charlotte Alfred, and Hanna Patchett. 2017. "The Compact Experiment." *Refugees Deeply*, December 13. https://www.newsdeeply.com/refugees/articles/2017/12/13/the-compact-experiment.

HRGJ (Human Rights and Gender Justice). 2016. "Human Rights Violations against Women and Girls in Syria." Paper submitted at United Nations Universal Periodic Review of the Syrian Arab Republic 26th Session of the UPR Working Group of the Human Rights Council. https://www.madre.org/sites/default/files/PDFs /Syria%20UPR%20 submission%20Final.pdf.

ILO (International Labour Organization). 2017a. "Work Permits and Employment of Syrian Refugees in Jordan: Towards Formalising the Work of Syrian Refugees." ILO Regional Office for Arab States, Beirut.

———. 2017b. "A Challenging Market Becomes More Challenging: Jordanian Workers, Migrant Workers and Refugees in the Jordanian Labour Market." ILO Regional Office for Arab States, Beirut.

IMU (Information Management Unit). 2017. "DYNAMO: Syria Dynamic Monitoring Report." Issue 6 (February), Assistance Coordination Unit, Syria. https://reliefweb.int/sites/reliefweb.int/files/resources/ACU-IMU -DYNAMO-6-EN.pdf.

JRPSC (Jordan Response Platform for the Syria Crisis). 2016. "Jordan Response Plan for the Syria Crisis 2016–2018." Ministry of Planning & International Cooperation, Hashemite Kingdom of Jordan.

———. 2018. "Jordan Response Plan for the Syria Crisis 2018–2020." Ministry of Planning & International Cooperation, Hashemite Kingdom of Jordan.

Jordan Department of Statistics. 2016. Amman. http://dosweb.dos.gov.jo/labourforce/employment-and -unemployment.

Kasparek, Max, and Marwan Dimashki. 2009. "Country Environmental Profile for the Syrian Arab Republic." Final Report of the Delegation of the European Commission to Syria, April.

Kelley, C. P., S. Mohtadi, M. A. Cane, R. Seager, and Y. Kushnir. 2015. "Climate Change in the Fertile Crescent and Implications of the Recent Syrian Drought." *Proceedings of the National Academy of Sciences* 112 (11): 3241–46.

Kherallah, M., T. Alahfez, Z. Sahloul, K. D. Eddin, and G. Jamil. 2012. "Health Care in Syria before and during the Crisis." *Avicenna Journal of Medicine* 2 (3): 51–53. http://doi.org/10.4103/2231-0770.102275.

Kofol, Chiara, and Tommaso Ciarli. 2017. "Child Labor and Conflict: Evidence from Afghanistan." ZEF Discussion Papers on Development Policy No. 240, Zentrum für Entwicklungsforschung, Bonn. https://www.econstor .eu/bitstream/10419/180189/1/zef_dp_240.pdf.

Krafft, Caroline, Maia Sieverding, Colette Salemi, and Caitlyn Keo. 2018. "Syrian Refugees in Jordan: Demographics, Livelihoods, Education, and Health." ERF Working Paper No. 1184, Economic Research Forum, Giza, Egypt.

Kurdistan Regional Statistics Office. 2016. "The Results of the Labor Force Survey in Kurdistan Region Second Half of 2015." http://www.krso.net/files/articles/221117014510.pdf.

Luce, E. 2014. "Evolution of WFP's Food Assistance Programme for Syrian Refugees in Jordan." *Field Exchange*, Issue 48, November. https://www.ennonline.net/fex/48/evolution.

Müller, M. F., J. Yoon, S. M. Gorelick, N. Avisse, and A. Tilmant. 2016. "Impact of the Syrian Refugee Crisis on Land Use and Transboundary Freshwater Resources." *Proceedings of the National Academy of Sciences* 113 (52): 14932–37.

NRC (Norwegian Refugee Council). 2017. "Reflections on Future Challenges to Housing, Land and Property Restitution for Syrian Refugees." Briefing Note, NRC, Oslo, January. https://www.nrc.no/globalassets/pdf /briefing-notes/icla/final-hlp-syrian-refugees-briefing-note-21-12-2016.pdf.

Oakford, Samuel. 2017. "The United States Used Depleted Uranium in Syria." *Foreign Policy*, February 14. http:// foreignpolicy.com/2017/02/14/the-united-states-used-depleted-uranium-in-syria/.

PAX and TSI (The Syria Institute). 2013. "No Return to Homs: A Case Study on Demographic Engineering in Syria." PAX, Utrecht, and TSI, Washington, DC.

REACH. 2015. "Multi-Cluster Needs Assessment for Internally Displaced Persons Outside of Camps: Kurdistan Region of Iraq." REACH Initiative, Geneva. http://www.reachresourcecentre.info/system/files /resource-documents/reach_irq_report_multi_cluster_needs_assessment_of_idps_outside_camps _february_2015.pdf.

———. 2016. "Northern Syria Market Monitoring Exercise: January–August 2016 Overview." Cash-Based Responses Technical Working Group, REACH Initiative, Geneva. http://www.reachresourcecentre.info /system/files/resource-documents/reach_syr_marketmonitoring_trendsanalysis_janaug2016.pdf.

———. 2017. "Syria Community Profiles Update: June 2017" REACH Initiative, Geneva. http://www.reach resourcecentre.info/system/files/resource-documents/reach_syr_factsheet_community_profiles _update_june2017.pdf.

Rodriguez, Catherine, and Fabio Sanchez. 2012. "Armed Conflict Exposure, Human Capital Investments, and Child Labor: Evidence from Colombia." *Defence and Peace Economics* 23 (2): 161–84.

Sarris, A. 1995. *A Policy Framework for Agricultural Development Strategy in Syria*. Volumes 1 and 2. Report to the Food and Agriculture Organization of the United Nations, project TSS-1.

Sayigh, Yezid. 2016. "Clausewitz in Syria." Carnegie Middle East Center, Beirut, October 14. https://carnegie-mec .org/2016/10/14/clausewitz-in-syria-pub-64761.

SCLSR (Syrian Center for Legal Studies and Research). 2018. "Factors affecting Syrian Female Minors' Arranged Marriages as a Wide-spread Phenomenon." October 19. https://sl-center.org/?p=613&lang=en.

SCPR (Syrian Center for Policy Research). 2015. "Alienation and Violence: Impact of Syria Crisis Report." SCPR, Damascus, Syria. https://www.unrwa.org/sites/default/files/alienation_and_violence_impact_of_the _syria_crisis_in_2014_eng.pdf.

———. 2016. "Confronting Fragmentation! Impact of Syrian Crisis Report." SCPR, Damascus, Syria.

Shami, Muntasir. 2019. "Institutional Change and Entrepreneurship: The Impact of Incremental Change, Change due to Conflict, and Social Change Captured by Migration." PHD thesis, Aston University. https://ethos .bl.uk/OrderDetails.do?uin=uk.bl.ethos.774134.

Simpson, C., and M. Philips. 2015. "Why ISIS Has All the Money It Needs." *Bloomberg Business*, November 19. https://www.bloomberg.com/news/articles/2015-11-19/why-u-s-efforts-to-cut-off-islamic-state-s-funds -have-failed?cmpid=BBD111915_BIZ.

Swain, A., and A. Jägerskog. 2016. *Emerging Security Threats in the Middle East: The Impact of Climate Change and Globalization*. Lanham, MD: Rowman and Littlefield Publishers.

SWEEP-Net (Regional Solid Waste Exchange of Information and Expertise Network in Mashreq and Maghreb Countries) and GIZ (Deutsche Gesellschaft für Internationale Zusammenarbeit GmbH). 2010. "Country Report on the Solid Waste Management in Syria." GIZ, Bonn; and SWEEP-Net, on behalf of the German Federal Ministry for Economic Cooperation and Development, Tunis.

Syrian Ministry of Labour. 2018. "Syrian Refugee Unit Work Permit Progress Report August 2018." Monthly Progress Report, September 5. https://data2.unhcr.org/en/documents/download/66061.

UNDP (United Nations Development Programme). 2005. *Human Development Report 2005—International Cooperation at a Crossroads: Aid, Trade, and Security in an Unequal World*. New York: UNDP.

———. 2011. *Human Development Report—Sustainability and Equity: A Better Future for All*. New York: UNDP.

UN-Habitat (United Nations Human Settlements Programme). 2013. "Emergency Response to Housing, Land and Property Issues in Syria." Housing, Land and Poverty Briefing Note, January 30, UN-Habitat, Nairobi.

———. 2014a. "City Profile Aleppo. Multi Sector Assessment." UN-Habitat, Nairobi. https://unhabitat.org /city-profile-aleppo-multi-sector-assessment/.

———. 2014b. "City Profile Dar'a. Multi Sector Assessment." UN-Habitat, Nairobi. https://unhabitat.org /city-profile-daraa-multi-sector-assessment/.

———. 2014c. "City Profile Deir-ez-Zor. Multi Sector Assessment." UN-Habitat, Nairobi. https://unhabitat.org /wpdm-package/deir-ez-zour-city-profile/.

———. 2014d. "City Profile Homs. Multi Sector Assessment." UN-Habitat, Nairobi. https://unhabitat.org /city-profile-homs-multi-sector-assessment/.

———. 2016. "Urban Community Profiling Survey." UN-Habitat, Nairobi.

UNHCR (United Nations High Commissioner for Refugees). 2017a. "Support to Public Institutions in Lebanon under the Lebanon Crisis Response Plan (LCRP 2017–2020): 2017 Results." Government of Lebanon and UNHCR. https://data2.unhcr.org/en/documents/download/64658.

———. 2017b. "Jordan Vulnerability Assessment Framework: 2017 Population Survey Report." UNHCR, Geneva.

———. 2017c. "Multi-Sector Needs Assessment: Iraq." UNHCR, Geneva.

———. 2017d. "Multi-Sector Needs Assessment: Syria." UNHCR, Geneva.

———. 2018a. "Fourth Regional Survey on Syrian Refugees' Perceptions and Intentions on Return to Syria: Egypt, Iraq, Jordan, and Lebanon." UNHCR, Amman, Jordan.

———. 2018b. "Support to Public Institutions in Lebanon under the Lebanon Crisis Response Plan (LCRP 2017–2020): 2018 Update." Government of Lebanon and UNHCR.

———. 2018c. "UNHCR Jordan Fact Sheet—February 2018." Geneva: UNHCR. https://data2.unhcr.org/en/documents/download/62241.

UNHCR, UNICEF (United Nations Children's Fund), and WFP (World Food Programme). 2017. "Vulnerability Assessment of Syrian Refugees in Lebanon—VASyR 2018." Geneva: UNHCR.

UNICEF (United Nations Children's Fund). 2006. "Multiple Indicator Cluster Survey: Jordan." http://mics.unicef.org/surveys.

———. 2009. "Multiple Indicator Cluster Survey: Lebanon."

———. 2012. "Multiple Indicator Cluster Survey: Jordan."

———. 2017a. "Running on Empty: The Situation of Syrian Children in Host Communities in Jordan." UNICEG Jordan, Amman. https://data2.unhcr.org/en/documents/download/60270.

———. 2017b. "Water Utilities Management during Crisis." Workshop presentation, Marseille.

———. 2018. "An Overview of Children's Protection Needs in Syria." Whole of Syria Child Protection Area of Responsibility, UNICEF.

UNICEF (United Nations Children's Fund) and WHO (World Health Organization). 2017. "Water Supply, Sanitation and Hygiene (WASH) Joint Monitoring Program." https://washdata.org/data.

United Nations. 2018. "Children and Armed Conflict. Report of the Secretary-General." United Nations General Assembly Security Council, May 16. United Nations, New York.

UNOCHA (United Nations Office for the Coordination of Humanitarian Affairs). 2016. "Needs Population Monitoring Round 5." UNOCHA, New York and Geneva. https://www.humanitarianresponse.info/en/operations/whole-of-syria/assessment/needs-and-population-monitoring-round-5-report.

———. 2017. "Humanitarian Needs Overview: Syrian Arab Republic." UNOCHA, New York and Geneva.

———. 2018. "Humanitarian Needs Assessment Programme: Syrian Arab Republic." UNOCHA, New York and Geneva.

Unruh, J. D. 2016. "Weaponization of the Land and Property Rights System in the Syrian Civil War: Facilitating Restitution?" *Journal of Intervention and Statebuilding* 10 (4): 453–71.

U.S. Department of State. 2015. "Syria 2015 Human Rights Report." U.S. Department of State, Washington, DC. https://2009-2017.state.gov/j/drl/rls/hrrpt/humanrightsreport/index.htm?year=2015&dlid=252947.

Verme, Paolo, Chiara Gigliarano, Christina Wieser, Kerren Hedlund, Marc Petzoldt, and Marco Santacroce. 2016. *The Welfare of Syrian Refugees: Evidence from Jordan and Lebanon.* Washington, DC: World Bank.

WANA (West Asia–North Africa Institute). 2017. "Refugee Labour Inclusion: Turkey and the Kurdistan Region of Iraq." WANA Institute, Royal Scientific Society, Amman, Jordan.

Warrick, J. 2016. "Satellite Photos Show Islamic State Installing Hundreds of Makeshift Oil Refineries to Offset Losses from Airstrikes." *Washington Post*, July 13. https://www.washingtonpost.com/news/worldviews/wp/2016/07/07/satellite-photos-show-isis-installing-hundreds-of-makeshift-oil-refineries-to-offset-losses-from-air-strikes/?tid=a_inl.

WES (World Education Services). 2016. "SYRIA: Educational Profile." World Education Services. https://wenr.wes.org/2016/04/education-in-syria.

WHO (World Health Organization). 2018. "WHO Providing Health Care to Syrian Refugees in and outside the Camps." Press Release. http://www.emro.who.int/irq/iraq-news/syrian-refugees-in-iraq.html.

World Bank. 2009. "The Status and Progress of Women in the Middle East and North Africa." Washington, DC: World Bank.

————. 2017a. *The Toll of War: The Economic and Social Consequences of the Conflict in Syria*. Washington, DC: World Bank.

————. 2017b. "Syria Damage Assessment of Selected Cities: Aleppo, Hama, and Idlib." Phase III. World Bank, Washington, DC.

Zabel, J. 2016. "Untying the Knot: Child Marriage in Situations of Armed Conflict." Political Science Honors Project, Macalester College, St. Paul, MN.

CHAPTER 3

The Anatomy of Returns to Date

Returns to the Syrian Arab Republic have been low relative to the total refugee population but more than 100 thousand (103,090 between 2015 and mid-2018) returned, nevertheless. These returnees (and millions of nonreturnees) provide an opportunity to investigate the factors that have contributed to return decisions so far.

This chapter estimates the importance of the four broad factors distilled from international experience in shaping the mobility of Syrian refugees so far. To do so, it uses empirical tests to identify generalized (population-wise) effects of each factor on actual return behavior and uses machine-learning techniques such as decision trees and boosted trees to capture localized (group-wise) effects, which enables better understanding of the complexity of return.

To complement the analysis of actual returns, the study also investigates willingness to return by employing new surveys of refugees, including nonregistered ones.

CHAPTER 3

The Anatomy of Returns to Date

Unlike an initial forced displacement, voluntary and spontaneous return is, at least to a certain extent, a rational/economic/multidimensional decision. Violence-induced displacement often takes place quickly, allowing no lead time for preparation and planning. The threat to the lives of individuals and their families overrides any economic concerns in that short period of time, and, although the nature of flight may differ across different socioeconomic groups, society as a whole is affected by the shock across all subgroups. In comparison, voluntary return decisions, assuming no direct coercion, are made gradually. Refugees, to a certain extent, act differently in this case: they compare their options—such as staying in their current location, returning to their country of origin, or moving to a third location. Because these options typically change over time, many refugees move several times after the initial displacement.

The complexity surrounding refugee returns renders a systematic analysis daunting. Factors that influence the well-being of refugees in host communities, country of origin, or a third location can all influence their return decisions. Like other economic actors, refugees compare their current and future quality of life in all locations that are within reach. They face many more constraints than an ordinary person, however, including numerous economic, social, cultural, judicial, psychological, and institutional factors, all of which interact in a convoluted web. In such unconventional conditions, no single factor becomes the sole reason explaining refugee mobility decisions. For these reasons, and because of the absence of comprehensive data, the literature on returns is thin and confined to descriptive case studies. Quantitative evidence and empirical analyses of refugee returns beyond limited aspects of individual cases are virtually absent.

Descriptive evidence suggests a nuanced and nonlinear pattern of return that may look inconsistent at first sight. It is common to see cyclical return movements and considerable secondary movement (after return) as refugees seek out optimal solutions to their immediate reintegration challenges. Although structural considerations such as security, livelihoods, and potential reintegration are key to return decisions, what these considerations really mean to individual refugees differs significantly depending on asset ownership, business and education opportunities in exile, recognition of school diplomas and certificates, recognition of civil registration (birth and death certificates, marriage, and inheritance), health considerations, state of the house or dwelling in the home country (whether or not it was destroyed), security, and accessibility. For a relatively urbanized refugee population, the longer the exile, the more they establish economic and social links (networks), and the more complicated returns may become. In the end, refugees rarely return in the same way as they arrived—either quantitatively (in the same numbers, at the same time) or qualitatively (to original places of origin, or to former occupations). Return takes place in varied and staggered shapes, occurring on different scales, at different times to different places, especially in the absence of a full peace accord/political settlement. It is often spontaneous, sporadic, and opportunistic rather than controlled and predictable.

Understanding the relative importance of key factors entails a quantitative approach. Facing the daunting task of making sense of the complexity surrounding return behavior makes it necessary to impose a logical structure onto the problem in order to reflect upon refugee returns effectively. When "everything matters" it is difficult to prioritize policies to help relax some of the constraints faced by refugees. To analyze the relative importance of various factors that explain the mobility of refugees, a framework within which different factors can be classified and ranked must be considered. In practical terms, this entails limiting the number of factors considered in the analysis. To that effect, this chapter adopts the classification of factors provided by international experience, described in the previous chapters, to analyze the return of Syrian refugees to date. In particular, a "push and pull factors" framework is used to classify the data and rely on insights from economic theory to reduce the dimensionality of the data, that is, by eliminating redundancies across variables.

The analysis in this chapter comprises a suite of methods that aim to shed light on the complexity of returns that have taken place until now. Subsequent sections here provide a brief descriptive summary of return behavior, presenting unidimensional comparisons between returnees and nonreturnees. Several empirical tests are presented to identify the generalized (population-wise) effects of each factor on return behavior. Next considered is an approach based on machine learning to identify the localized (group-wise) effects of various factors. Finally, a few extensions are considered where specific issues, like conflict dynamics and return perceptions, are analyzed in more detail.

Return Trends at First Sight

The knowledge of returns presented here comes from the Profile Global Registration System (ProGres) database, compiled by the United Nations High Commissioner for Refugees (UNHCR) to record each person of concern who approaches it.[1] ProGres is a limited administrative database, which may leave out some forcibly displaced people if they are not registered, and it includes a broad set of demographic characteristics for each recorded individual. It also contains information about the kinship of individuals within each "case" (that is, familial relationships of everyone within a case to the principal applicant, ranging from members of the nuclear family to extended family, such as in-laws, aunts, and uncles).[2] The UNHCR registration system effectively functions like a civil register, because the status of each entry is updated in subsequent contacts after the initial registration. Therefore, although information on arrival, registration, and return dates is fixed because they are onetime events, other information like occupation, marital status, and location of asylum may change over time.

UNHCR records show a small, but nonnegligible, number of returns to Syria from its Mashreq neighbors. The data used in this analysis cover all persons of concern in the Mashreq—mainly Iraq, Jordan, and Lebanon—who have registered with UNHCR up to March 2018, accounting for more than 2.4 million people.[3] Of this group, roughly 103,000, or less than 2 percent, have been recorded as returned to Syria, but this overall figure marks notable differences in returns across countries of asylum. By 2018, almost 10.8 percent of the refugees in Iraq, 6.6 percent of the refugees in Jordan, but less than 2 percent of those in Lebanon have returned to Syria.

Refugees also stayed for different durations in different countries of asylum. Refugees in Lebanon stayed longer than the refugees in the other two countries included in the study (figure 3.1, panel a). The average returnee from Lebanon remained in that country for almost 1.5 years more than peers from Iraq and 10 months more than those from Jordan. Using a separate metric, a simple pairwise comparison across countries shows that a Syrian refugee who sought asylum in Iraq was far more likely to return to Syria within a year than peers from the other two countries of this study. One may consider differences in arrival year as a driving factor in explaining such differences in duration of stay, that is, if refugees arrived earlier in one country, then they will stay longer. The first chapter, however, showed that this explanation is not likely. The relative distribution of arrival times is very similar across all three countries covered in this study. There are also no meaningful differences between male and female durations of stay at first sight (figure 3.1, panel b). Thus, we must look elsewhere for an explanation.

Age is an important parameter in the decision to return. When sheer return numbers are considered, the two biggest age groups for the returnee population are 15–19 and 20–24 years of age, followed by the two subsequent age groups in third and fourth places. Together, individuals between 15 and 34 years old represent 40 percent of the returnees (figure 3.2, panel a). However, when returnee and nonreturnee population age distributions are compared, these numbers show an underrepresentation of children, youth, and young adults in the returnee population and an overrepresentation of older adults and seniors. In fact, the share of individuals above the age of 55 is more than twice the size of the share of the same age group in the general refugee population. This observation provides some support to the hypothesis that older individuals would be more willing to return to their country of origin. This willingness may be driven by numerous factors, including difficulty in adapting to a new cultural or economic system, lesser concerns about military conscription for seniors, and concerns about maintaining asset ownership that requires the official owner to be present—in most cases this owner would be an older adult.

Family size is also an important correlate of return: single persons and smaller families are more likely to return. The marriage status of refugees does not seem to have influenced the decision to return: the distributions for returnees and refugees are almost identical. In a pairwise comparison between returnees and nonreturnees, however, having at least one child is correlated with a lower likelihood of return: only 73 percent of the returnees have children, compared to 85 percent of the refugee population in the study. Indeed, the average case size for the returnees is 5.0, compared to 5.3 for the entire sample (figure 3.2, panel b). As panel b of

Figure 3.1. Duration of Asylum, by Country and Gender, as of March 2018

a. Distribution of the duration of stay, by country

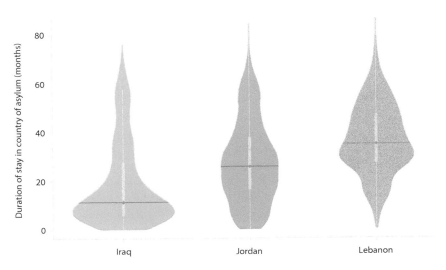

b. Distribution of the duration of stay, by gender

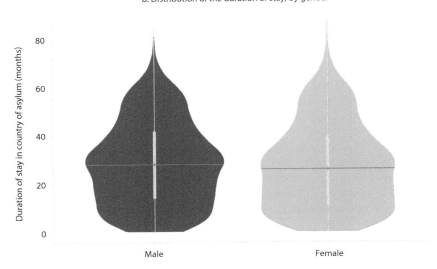

Source: Profile Global Registration System database, World Bank staff calculations.
Note: The violin plot figures show the distribution of values. The red lines in the middle show the median value, the vertical long lines show the full range of observations, and the thicker portions of the vertical line show where 50 percent of the observations are observed. The areas to the right and left of the vertical line (mirror images) show the actual distribution, smoothed.

figure 3.2 shows, in comparison to nonreturnees, smaller households are overrepresented in the returnee population. Although the underlying mechanisms behind this outcome could be very complex, one driver of such outcome could be family reunification, where individuals and small families decide to go back after the rest of the family fails to leave the country of origin.

Figure 3.2. Age and Family Size Distribution, Returnees vs. Nonreturnees

a. Returnees vs. nonreturnees, by age distribution

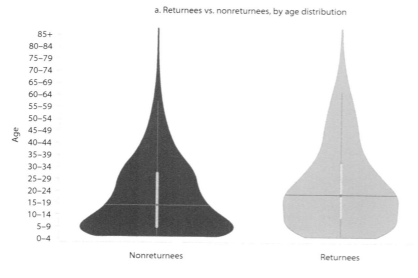

b. Returnees vs. nonreturnees, by family size

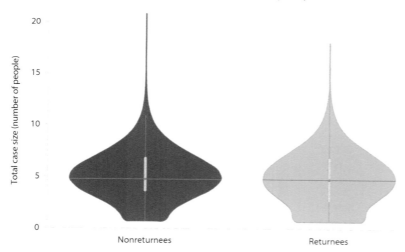

Source: Profile Global Registration System database, World Bank staff calculations.
Note: The violin plot figures show the distribution of values. The red lines in the middle show the median value, the vertical long lines show the full range of observations, and the thicker portions of the vertical line show where 50 percent of the observations are observed. The areas to the right and left of the vertical line (mirror images) show the actual distribution, smoothed.

On average, returnee adults have fewer years of education than nonreturnee adults. Although, at first glance, it appears that returnees have more years of schooling than their peers who did not choose to return (figure 3.3, panel a), a large segment of the refugees are children of school age who are less likely to return than adults. Therefore, the distribution of education should be considered for adults only. When children are excluded, returnees have less education than nonreturnees on average (figure 3.3, panel b). In fact, individuals with no schooling represent

Figure 3.3. Education Profile of Returnees and Nonreturnees

a. Returnees vs. nonreturnees, by level of education

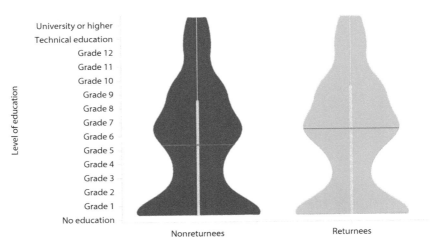

b. Returnees vs. nonreturnees, by level of education (adults only)

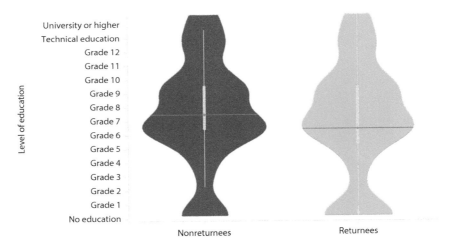

Source: Profile Global Registration System database, World Bank staff calculations.
Note: The violin plot figures show the distribution of values. The red lines in the middle show the median value, the vertical long lines show the full range of observations, and the thicker portions of the vertical line show where 50 percent of the observations are observed. The areas to the right and left of the vertical line (mirror images) show the actual distribution, smoothed.

about 19 percent of the adult returnee population, whereas the same category represents less than 12 percent of the nonreturnee population.

The simple exploration of returnee and nonreturnee differences provided in this section should not be overinterpreted. The picture provided by pairwise comparisons of returnee and nonreturnee populations is incomplete, and numerous potential confounding factors need to be controlled for a more conclusive assessment of the factors that drive return. The education example discussed above, where not controlling for age could lead to a wrong conclusion that returnees are more educated than nonreturnees, points to a common pitfall. Many outcomes regarding the differences between returnee and nonreturnee populations can be driven by factors that are not obvious at first sight. These factors may include the differences between socioeconomic conditions of refugees before arrival, conditions at their locations of origin, and conditions they face in different host countries. Thus, they need to be accounted for before the analysis could suggest effects of specific factors on return. The next section will do that.

Disentangling the Drivers of Return

To better characterize the drivers of return to date, mixed sources of data on conditions in Syria and the main countries of asylum—Jordan and Lebanon—are used.[4] The team did not have access to a comprehensive longitudinal record of the conditions faced by refugees in countries of asylum and potential return locations in Syria. To offset this problem, a pragmatic approach that combines different sources and types of data has been adopted.

- For *conditions in countries of asylum*, consistent measures of push factors were developed from a series of representative household surveys of registered refugees conducted in both Jordan and Lebanon during the 2015–17 period: the Vulnerability Assessment (VAF) in Jordan and the Vulnerability Assessment of Syrian Refugees in Lebanon (VASyR) (UNHCR 2015, 2017a; UNHCR, UNICEF, and WFP 2018).[5] These household surveys assessed refugee needs at the case, household, and individual levels, in such areas as access to water and sanitation, and poverty and food coping strategies. An important shortcoming of these surveys is the limited sample size: whereas the registration data provide information for about 2.4 million refugees, the vulnerability surveys cover only a few thousand in each round, defined at the case level. To take advantage of a larger dataset for accuracy, the case-level data from the vulnerability surveys were aggregated geographically using the lowest available administrative subdivision.[6] This approach enabled a robustness check to be conducted by using inference from a larger, individual-level dataset.

- For *conditions in Syria*, it was not possible to acquire a comparable and geographically comprehensive time series on living conditions or access to services. Instead, the analysis draws on a UNHCR-led Multi-Sector Needs Assessment (MSNA), which conducted key informant interviews in more than 5,000 communities in all 14 governorates in 2017 (UNHCR 2017b). This information was subsequently aggregated to the district level and used as a proxy for access to publicly provided goods and services. In addition, a monthly dataset comprising conflict dynamics was compiled using information from secondary sources (including the Carter Center, Institute of War, and University of Maryland). These data provide a record of verified conflict-driven casualties, area control, and key conflict events (skirmishes, air strikes, and the like) from January 2011 until August 2018.

The study has taken additional steps to remove doubts regarding the objectivity of data. In addition to testing the ideas with several samples (for example, the entire population, only case-level data, and country-specific analyses), which are described in subsequent sections, the study also considered mitigating potential issues with the data. The data sources described above, especially the ones regarding the conditions in countries of asylum, may potentially suffer from a few biases. First, the sampling may be biased, that is, the vulnerability survey participants are not representative of the broader population of registered refugees. Second, because the vulnerability survey participants are chosen only from those who are registered, results based on this sample may not be representative of the entire displaced Syrian community in countries of asylum. This problem is particularly likely if registered refugees are self-selected; certain types of refugees prefer not to register or are unable to register for some reason. Third, in certain cases, responses to vulnerability surveys may be biased. Because UNHCR is both an aid agency and the agency that conducts the vulnerability surveys, participants may have incentives to reflect a more vulnerable profile to directly or indirectly influence the amount of aid they would receive even if their responses do not have any direct influence on their qualification for aid.

To capture the livelihood conditions of unregistered refugees,[7] and to provide a comparison between responses to surveys conducted by different agencies, a limited household survey was conducted in Jordan and Lebanon over a two-month period in July–August 2018. To ensure comparability with the ProGres database and the VAF and VASyR surveys, comparable information was collected for heads of Syrian refugee households, including demographic characteristics, livelihood conditions, and work status in the host countries. In addition, the survey included questions on participants' livelihoods and employment in Syria prior to the conflict as well as vignettes to elicit the refugees' opinions on how likely a hypothetical refugee family would be to return. For the latter, the details of the scenario presented to a given individual respondent were randomly varied. Data were collected for an overall sample of 950 refugees in each country, including both registered and unregistered refugees.[8] Given the relatively high incidence of unregistered/unrecorded refugees in Lebanon,[9] existing sampling frames could be used to capture both populations, with quotas placed to ensure that the requisite number from each subgroup was interviewed in each geographic region. Because the incidence of unregistered refugees was reported to be much lower in Jordan, using existing sampling frames was not practicable. Instead, door-to-door surveys were combined with a snowball methodology for both registered and unregistered Syrian refugees to capture the required number of responses in both groups.

Building on the international experience described in previous chapters, four main categories of push and pull factors are used to classify data. The first category—peace, security, and protection—includes factors that influence the perception of security in the refugee's home location in Syria (table 3.1). These factors include an index on the total number of conflict events that have occurred since the refugee's arrival in the host country. For returnees this series ends at the individual's return date to Syria; for others, March 2018, the last time the researchers' version of the ProGres database was updated, is used as a cutoff date. In addition, information on area control and change of control one or three months prior to return (or March 2018), respectively, is also used. The second category of push and pull factors focuses on the livelihood situations of refugees in the countries of both asylum and origin. This category is proxied for by how food insecure households are. Data are much more limited for housing, land, and property rights—the third category—and often confined to anecdotal evidence.

An indicator for whether a case lives in a camp is used to proxy for access to shelter in countries of asylum.[10] Last, access to basic services can be measured directly for both country of asylum and country of origin through household and key informant surveys, respectively.

The selection of indicators reflects challenges in measuring the push and pull factors. Two data conditions limit a more comprehensive approach. First, in certain cases, reliable data series are absent altogether. For instance, information on access to employment is absent for both the countries of asylum and the countries of origin. Most refugee employment is informal, and refugees refrain from revealing this so as not to lose assistance or be subjected to legal repercussions. Thus, proxy indicators are often used to replace missing or unreliable data. For example, food insecurity, one of the few variables measured consistently across countries and over time, is used as a proxy for living conditions. The second problem is the time dimension of the data. Return is a dynamic process, that is, it takes place over time, depending on conditions that change; however, the ProGres database is largely cross-sectional—a characteristic driven by its social registry nature. In addition, the time series information on push and pull factors needs to be matched to the return date for returnees, which is not always possible with available data. In those cases, the most recent information is used as a proxy. Often only one year of information is available, especially for conditions within Syria.

What matters and what does not: Generalized effects

To assess the relative importance of various factors in explaining return, the analysis first runs a linear probability model using data on actual returns. With a binary dependent variable (return or no-return), the linear probability model employed here estimates the probability of return using a range of control or independent variables, including all the push and pull factors listed in table 3.1 as well as demographic and socioeconomic characteristics and registration information. In addition, fixed effects for the year of arrival as well as for location in the country of asylum are included. A technical discussion on the specification of this approach is provided in box 3.1. A robustness check of the specification is performed by using a logit model (shown in annex 3A), with remarkably similar results.

Results are cross-verified by using three datasets, each with its own strengths and weaknesses. The first dataset is based on UNHCR's ProGres, conflict dynamics, and the Syria MSNA, and covers the Mashreq region, including Iraq, Jordan, and Lebanon, comprising more than 2.16 million records.[11] Because vulnerability assessments are available only for refugees in Jordan and Lebanon (through VAF and VASyR, respectively), they are excluded from the first dataset, which supports only analyses focusing on demographic characteristics, registration information, and conditions in Syria. The second dataset adds the vulnerability surveys for Jordan and Lebanon to incorporate conditions in host communities; however, because most individuals in ProGres are not covered in vulnerability surveys, an imputation is needed. To this effect, the case-level host community conditions in the vulnerability surveys are aggregated at the lowest possible geographic unit, and those values are imposed for all ProGres cases that are recorded in corresponding areas. This approach helps exploit the additional information provided by the VAF and VASyR, but it restricts attention to Jordan and Lebanon. Finally, to avoid

Table 3.1. Push and Pull Framework Used in the Empirical Analysis

Push and pull factors	Variables used in the analysis for		Notes
	Location in country of asylum	Location in country of origin	
Peace, security, and protection	—	• Index on total conflict events during stay in host country, for example, low-intensity conflict, artillery, and air strikes. (Source: World Bank data not publicly available) • Change in control during three months prior to departure (Source: World Bank data not publicly available) • Armed group, who is in control of the area 1 month prior to departure. (Source: World Bank data not publicly available) • Security is a primary concern (UNHCR 2017b)	No comparable data are available on security and protection for the main host countries.
Livelihoods and access to employment	• Number of meals a household eats in a day (UNHCR 2015, 2017a; UNHCR, UNICEF, and WFP 2018) • Index on food insecurity, including how many days per week an average household needs to borrow food or reduce the number of meals or portion sizes. (UNHCR 2015, 2017a; UNHCR, UNICEF, and WFP 2018)	• The price of 1 kilogram of unsubsidized and subsidized bread (UNHCR 2017b) • Malnutrition is a serious concern in the community (UNHCR 2017b)	No comparable data are available on access to employment for Syrian Arab Republic or in the host countries. We use data on food availability to proxy for livelihood conditions.
Housing, land, and property (HLP) rights	• Case lives in a refugee or transit camp (ProGres)	—	No systematic data were found on HLP in Syria.

Note: — = not available. ProGres = Profile Global Registration System.

using any imputations, the third dataset restricts the analysis to those refugees who were covered by the vulnerability surveys. This approach allows more variation at the case level, but it significantly reduces the sample size to slightly over 42,500. Overall, each approach has merits and shortcomings, but together they present a convincing case.

The analysis first focuses on the effects of refugees' socioeconomic characteristics and their registration status in the host communities. Overall, the number of variables used to describe the socioeconomic characteristics, refugee registration status, and push and pull factors is too large to present in a single table.

BOX 3.1

Specification of Baseline and Robustness Check Estimations

When studying refugee returns, the dependent variable is binary, that is,

$Y = \{0$ if a refugee is still in the country of asylum as of March 2018
$\quad\{1$ if a refugee has returned from the country of asylum to the Syrian Arab Republic

Binary outcome models can estimate the probability that $y = 1$ as a function of the regressors, x, where $p = pr\,[y = 1 | x] = F(x'\beta)$.

There are three different binary outcome models depending on the assumed functional form of $F(x'\beta)$.

1. The *linear probability model* (LPM) assumes that $F(x'\beta)$ is linear, that is,

   $F(x'\beta) = x'\beta$ and $p = pr\,[y = 1 | x] = x'\beta$, with constant marginal effects

   $\partial p / \partial x_j = \beta_j$ for the jth for the independent regressor.

2. The *logit model* assumes that $F(x'\beta)$ follows the cumulative distribution function of the logistics distribution, where

   $F(x'\beta) = \Lambda(x'\beta) = e^{x\beta}/(1+e^{x\beta})$ with marginal effects

   $\partial p / \partial x_j (e^{x\beta}/(1+e^{x\beta})\beta_j$ for the jth independent regressor.

Concerns have been raised about the use of an LPM with binary regressors, given that it yields biased and inconsistent estimates and that its fitted values are not restricted to the unit interval. However, the LPM generally performs well in estimating marginal effects, especially if the functional form is not known. Compared to the logit and probit models, it yields similar results, especially with datasets that have a large sample size, and performs better when many dummy regressors are presented—both of which are the case in this analysis. It is also computationally simpler.

For these reasons, the analysis in this chapter uses the LPM for the main results, estimating this equation:

Probability $y_{ilm} = 1|x)$

$$= \beta_0 + \beta_1 \times characteristics_i + \beta_2 \times registration_i + \beta_2 \times peace_m$$
$$+ \beta_3 \times livelihood_{coal} + \beta_4 \times livelihood_{coom} + \beta_5 \times camp_l + \beta_6 \times$$
$$services_{coal} + \beta_7 \times services_{coam} + \mu_l + \eta_{it} + \varepsilon_{ilm}$$

where y_{ilm} has a value of zero if refugee i is still in location l in the country of asylum as of March 2018 and 1 if refugee i from home location m has returned to Syria. In the equation, *characteristics_i* measures refugee i's demographic characteristics; *registration_i* measures refugee i's refugee information; *peace_m* measures the security sitation in refugee i's home

(box continues next page)

199

BOX 3.1. *(continued)*

district m in Syria; *livehood_coa$_l$* and *livehood_coo$_m$* measure the livehood sitations in location l in the country of asylum and home location m in the country of origin, respectively; *camp$_l$* is a dummy equal to 1 if location l in the country of asylum is a camp; *services_coa$_l$* and *services_coa$_m$* measure access to basic services in location l in the country of asylum and home location m in the country of origin, respectively; μ_l are country of asylum fixed effects; η_{it} are fixed effects for the year t refugee i arrived in the country of asylum; and ε_{ilm} is the error term.

To test the robustness of the results of this LPM-based analysis, annex 3A presents the results for the logit model. Consistent with the argument above, it yields marginal effect estimates that are very similar to those of the LPM in terms of their significance, sign, and magnitude.

Therefore, the results are discussed in three stages: table 3.2 shows the results for socioeconomic characteristics and refugee registrations status, table 3.3 shows the results pertaining to conditions in Syria (pull factors), and table 3.4 shows the results on conditions in host communities (push factors). Although, the characteristics are not shown explicitly in all tables for ease of exposition, they are still controlled for.

The analysis of demographic characteristics suggests that return has so far happened in stages with select family members—singles, males, and non-nuclear-family members—more likely to return to Syria. Table 3.2 shows the demography- and registration-related results from the linear probability model specification. Column (1) shows the results for the Mashreq dataset, whereas the next two columns limit the analysis to Jordan and Lebanon with column (2) using geographical aggregates and column (3) using case-level data only. Adult men are generally more likely to return to Syria than women. Moreover, marital status plays a role in the return decision, with singles being 2.7 percentage points more likely to return to Syria compared to the omitted category of married refugees for the Mashreq dataset, a result that is statistically significant at the 1 percent level. Comparable results, both in terms of magnitude and statistical significance, are obtained for the two Jordan and Lebanon datasets. (Because this is the case for most of the other coefficients as well, the subsequent discussion will focus on the interpretation of the Mashreq results unless otherwise indicated.) In contrast, widowed refugees are 1.6 percentage points less likely to return (significant at the 1 percent level). In addition, principal applicants are 4.5 percentage points less likely to return, whereas members of the immediate and extended family are 14 and 12 percentage points, respectively, more likely to return than the nuclear family (all coefficients are significant at the 1 percent level).[12] This finding is in line with findings from international experience, which suggests that families send single, male members, especially those who are not nuclear family members, back to the country of origin to assess the situation on the ground while the rest of the case remains in the country of asylum.

Higher education has been associated with lower likelihood of return. The results in table 3.2 suggest that the refugee's education level matters, with higher levels of

Table 3.2. The Effects of Demographic Characteristics and Registration Status on Return

Dependent variable: Refugee returned to Syrian Arab Republic (No = 0; Yes = 1)			Mashreq	Jordan and Lebanon add host country factors using	
				Geographical aggregates	Case–level information only
Category	Variable	Omitted category	(1)	(2)	(3)
Demographic characteristics	Single	Married	0.027 ***	0.024 ***	0.024 ***
			(0.00060)	(0.00060)	(0.0038)
	Widowed	Married	−0.016 ***	−0.013 ***	−0.016
			(0.0020)	(0.0020)	(0.011)
	Other marital status	Married	−0.013 ***	−0.0071 ***	−0.012 *
			(0.0010)	(0.0011)	(0.0066)
	Age 20–44	Age 0–19	0.035 ***	0.034 ***	0.034 ***
			(0.00059)	(0.00060)	(0.0040)
	Age 45–59	Age 0–19	0.054 ***	0.054 ***	0.049 ***
			(0.00085)	(0.00086)	(0.0052)
	Age 60+	Age 0–19	0.059 ***	0.066 ***	0.088 ***
			(0.0014)	(0.0014)	(0.0093)
	Female	Male	−0.0064 ***	−0.0047 ***	−0.0046 ***
			(0.00024)	(0.00024)	(0.0013)
	Principal Applicant	Case Member	−0.045 ***	−0.042 ***	−0.031 ***
			(0.00043)	(0.00041)	(0.0022)
	Extended family	Nuclear family	0.12 ***	0.11 ***	0.12 ***
			(0.0027)	(0.0029)	(0.018)
	Immediate family	Nuclear family	0.14 ***	0.14 ***	0.17 ***
			(0.0022)	(0.0024)	(0.015)
	Primary education	No education	0.0029 ***	−0.000068	0.0032 *
			(0.00035)	(0.00034)	(0.0018)
	Secondary education	No education	−0.017 ***	−0.014 ***	0.00022
			(0.00057)	(0.00057)	(0.0033)
	University education	No education	−0.025 ***	−0.022 ***	−0.0026
			(0.00083)	(0.00084)	(0.0051)
	Case has children	Case has no Children	0.062 ***	0.059 ***	0.041 ***
			(0.00089)	(0.00086)	(0.0045)
	Case size		−0.030 ***	−0.024 ***	−0.012 ***
			(0.00022)	(0.00020)	(0.0011)
	Special need	No Special need	−0.0021 ***	−0.0021 ***	−0.0044 ***
			(0.00030)	(0.00030)	(0.0015)
Registration status	Enrolled for assistance	Asylum seeker	−0.0031 ***	−0.0043 ***	−0.0060 **
			(0.00064)	(0.00060)	(0.0030)
	Refugee	Asylum seeker	−0.0029 ***	0.0012	0.0047
			(0.0011)	(0.0013)	(0.0081)
	Registration lag, months		−0.0015 ***	−0.0014 ***	−0.00078 ***
			(0.000020)	(0.000020)	(0.00011)
Push and pull factors controlled?	Country of asylum		Yes	Yes	Yes
	Country of origin		Yes	Yes	Yes
Other controls	Ethnicity and religion		Yes	Yes	Yes
	Constant		Yes	Yes	Yes
Fixed effects	Arrival year		Yes	Yes	Yes
	Country of asylum		Yes	Yes	Yes
	Observations		2,162,865	1,851,135	42,655
	R-squared		0.218	0.245	0.156

Note: Significance level: * = 10 percent, ** = 5 percent, *** = 1 percent.

201

Table 3.3. The Effects of Conditions in the Syrian Arab Republic (Pull Factors) on Return

Dependent variable: Refugee returned to Syria (0 = No; 1 = Yes)			Mashreq	Jordan and Lebanon add host country factors using	
				Geographical aggregates	Case-level information
Pull factor	Variable	Omitted category	(1)	(2)	(3)
Peace, security, and protection	Dread factor		−0.00082 *** (0.0000061)	−0.00078 *** (0.0000060)	−0.00045 *** (0.000028)
	Change in control		0.18 *** (0.0033)	0.23 *** (0.0068)	0.21 *** (0.063)
	Control: Not government of Syria	Control: Government of Syria	0.036 *** (0.00060)	0.028 *** (0.00057)	0.017 *** (0.0026)
	Security a concern?		−0.0032 *** (0.00049)	−0.0067 *** (0.00049)	−0.0070 *** (0.0023)
Livelihoods and access to employment	Price for 1 kilogram (kg) of bread (subsidized)		0.000051 *** (0.0000028)	0.000029 *** (0.0000028)	0.000015 (0.000015)
	Price for 1 kg of bread (unsubsidized)		0.0000018 (0.0000026)	0.000013 *** (0.0000025)	0.0000073 (0.000012)
	Malnutrition: Moderate problem	Malnutrition: No problem	0.015 *** (0.00050)	0.012 *** (0.00049)	0.0096 *** (0.0023)
	Malnutrition: Serious problem	Malnutrition: No problem	0.032 *** (0.00080)	0.025 *** (0.00078)	0.015 *** (0.0034)
Infrastructure and services	Basic services a concern?		−0.022 *** (0.00056)	−0.017 *** (0.00057)	−0.0095 *** (0.0025)
	Health/education a concern?		−0.0081 *** (0.00047)	−0.010 *** (0.00044)	−0.010 *** (0.0023)
Push factors controlled?	Conditions in country of asylum		Yes	Yes	Yes
Other controls	Demographic characteristics		Yes	Yes	Yes
	Registration status		Yes	Yes	Yes
	Constant		Yes	Yes	Yes
Fixed effects	Arrival year		Yes	Yes	Yes
	Country of asylum		Yes	Yes	Yes
	Observations		2,162,865	1,851,135	42,655
	R-squared		0.218	0.245	0.156

Note: Significance level: * = 10 percent, ** = 5 percent, *** = 1 percent.

education being associated with a lower probability of return. Having a university degree reduced the likelihood of return by 2.5 percentage points, and having a secondary degree by 1.7 percentage points, relative to having no education (both coefficients are significant at the 1 percent level). Although these results may seem intuitive at first sight, this is likely to be misleading. Because skilled refugees are not allowed to work formally in skilled jobs in Lebanon and Jordan, the difference in return likelihood should not immediately be correlated with opportunity cost of leaving the country of asylum. It may, instead, be related to limited differences in financial wealth (for example, more-skilled people may have more savings) and

Table 3.4. The Effects of Conditions in Countries of Asylum (Push Factors) on Return

Dependent variable: Refugee returned to Syrian Arab Republic (0 = No; 1 = Yes)			Mashreq	Jordan and Lebanon add host country factors using	
				Geographical aggregates	Case-level information
Push factor	Variable	Omitted category	(1)	(2)	(3)
Livelihoods and access to employment	Number of meals per day			0.15*** (0.0020)	0.00016 (0.00060)
	Food insecurity index			−0.031 *** (0.00083)	−0.00078 (0.00092)
Housing, land, and property rights	Case lives in a camp	Case does not live in a camp	0.056 *** (0.0013)	0.093*** (0.0016)	0.14 *** (0.028)
Infrastructure and services	Access to basic service index			0.0050*** (0.00087)	−0.0011 (0.00084)
Pull factors controlled?	Conditions in country of origin		Yes	Yes	Yes
Other controls	Demographic characteristics		Yes	Yes	Yes
	Registration status		Yes	Yes	Yes
	Constant		Yes	Yes	Yes
Fixed effects	Arrival year		Yes	Yes	Yes
	Country of asylum		Yes	Yes	Yes
	Observations		2,162,865	1,851,135	42,655
	R-squared		0.218	0.245	0.156

Note: Significance level: * = 10 percent, ** = 5 percent, *** = 1 percent.

lower transaction costs (for example, more-skilled people may communicate or navigate better in host communities).

Refugees' legal status in host countries has important influences on the return decision, because it reflect refugees' opportunity costs. A small group of refugees has been selected for resettlement to a third country.[13] This group is found to be 0.3 percentage points less likely to return to Syria than refugees who are not selected (the omitted category), a result that is statistically significant at the 1 percent level. Similar figures are found for refugees in Lebanon who receive assistance but are not formally registered as refugees or asylum seekers. Interestingly, the results also suggest that refugees who delay registration upon arrival are less likely to return; a one-standard-deviation increase in the time elapsed between arrival and registration reduces the likelihood of return by 1.3 percentage points (significant at the 1 percent level). Registration seems to be driven, at least in part, by how well-off the refugees are financially. In fact, the survey conducted for this study, covering both registered and unregistered refugees in Jordan and Lebanon, shows that unregistered refugees report higher incomes, are less likely to be in debt, and have engaged in fewer poverty-coping strategies than their registered counterparts (see annex 3A). Thus, a registration delay could indicate that the refugees are not in immediate need of assistance and are in a better economic position in the host country, which might discourage return.

Next, pull factors are analyzed. Having discussed the effects of demographic aspects of refugees and their registration status on their return decisions, attention now turns to a more conventional push and pull analysis. Table 3.3. shows the estimations for conditions in Syria (pull factors). The factors related to demographic and registration status are still controlled for, but those results are compressed for visual clarity.

Security is one of the most important determinants of return, but it is manifested via a complex set of conditions. The sense of security is based not only on current conditions but also on the likelihood of future events. To reflect this multi-dimensional nature of security, the analysis uses several variables for measuring the peace, security, and protection in the home locations of refugees. These variables include an aggregate measure of the number of conflict events (dread factor), which includes tank/artillery strikes, air strikes/bombing, and reported use of chemical weapons. These results are aggregated for the period between the arrival date of refugees in the country of asylum and their return dates (if not yet returned, then March 2018). The other indicators include a control change indicator variable, which shows if there was a change in control in the home district prior to return, and a controlling group dummy, which shows the conflict actor that is in control of the district. These indicators, in turn, provide a more complete picture of current and future likelihood of violent events.

Refugees are less likely to return to districts with intensive conflict and more likely to return to districts after a takeover of control. The security situation in the country of origin (measured at the district level) seems to play an important role in determining the probability of return. Overall, refugees are less likely to return to areas that have experienced intense conflict, but more likely to return to those that have seen a change in control: a one-standard-deviation increase in the dread variable reduces the likelihood of return by 4.5 percentage points, a result that is statistically significant at the 1 percent level. Refugees are 18 percentage points more likely to return to Syria if there has been a change in control in the three months prior to return (significant at the 1 percent level).[14] This effect is one of the largest (in magnitude) found in the overall study, and it confirms that security is more than the absence of violence. A factor that further confirms this point is the refugees' revealed choice of returns to areas controlled by different parties to the conflict. On average, returns have been 3.6 percentage points more likely to areas not controlled by the government of Syria (the omitted category) with the coefficient being statistically significant at the 1 percent level.[15]

Low provision of education, health, and basic services in Syrian districts provides an effective deterrent against return. Table 3.3 shows that concerns about access to basic services (such as the provision of electricity, fuelwood, and so forth) and education and health services provide a consistently negative effect on the likelihood of return across all specifications. Refugees are 2.2 percentage points less likely to return if access to basic services is a primary concern in their home district (significant at the 1 percent level). Similar results are obtained for concerns about limited access to public health and education, but the coefficient is much smaller. In terms of livelihood conditions, higher prices for subsidized bread increase the likelihood of return though only marginally—a one-standard-deviation increase makes return 0.4 percentage point more likely for the Mashreq dataset (significant at the 1 percent level), but this result cannot be replicated in case-level analysis. Last, higher levels of malnutrition are associated with a higher likelihood of return. This result may seem counterintuitive but could capture location-specific characteristics, especially if refugees return to locations that are not under government control and thus potentially face more severe food shortages. However, it is not possible to control for home location fixed effects that would allow a look at how changes in malnutrition and food prices within a given locality affect the return decision, because the MSNA data have only cross-sectional variation for 2017.

Focusing next on conditions in countries of asylum, estimations suggest nonlinear effects. Overall, findings do not support the common perception that, if refugees face bad living conditions in host communities, they will be more likely to go back. The relationship between host community living conditions and return is more complex. The results reported in table 3.4 suggest the opposite in some scenarios. For example, on the one hand, refugees who experience better living conditions in the country of asylum, as measured by their access to basic services or the number of meals consumed per day (or lower levels of food insecurity), are more likely to return. Refugees are 15 percentage points more likely to return if they consume an extra meal per day, a result that is statistically significant at the 1 percent level for the Lebanon and Jordan dataset using geographical aggregates as shown in column (2). Similarly, a one-standard-deviation increase in food insecurity decreases the likelihood of return by 1.8 percentage points (significant at the 1 percent level). Households that are more food secure are likely to have other resources available that can help facilitate their return to Syria. In addition, better access to publicly provided basic services—such as access to piped water and a latrine—increases the likelihood of return though the magnitude is small. On the other hand, if the case lives in a camp, there is a 5.6-percentage-points greater likelihood to return for the Mashreq dataset, a result that is statistically significant at the 1 percent level across all three samples. These nonlinearities indicate that a more flexible approach might be needed to analyze the push and pull factors of refugee return, which is further explored in the subsequent section using machine learning.

Dodging complexity: Localized effects

An important element of complexity in refugee returns is the fact that, although generalizations are indicative, they hide important nuances. The estimation techniques used in the previous section provide a transparent approach to test the relative importance of individual factors that help explain the return decision. Their effects, however, are evaluated globally (that is, for all levels of a specific factor, unless otherwise specified).[16] For instance, improvements in security may matter a lot for the return decision when large-scale violence (such as intense armed conflict) takes place, but not when a "normal" level of violence (such as crime) takes place. Moreover, these magnitudes might also depend on other characteristics of refugees—for certain subgroups of refugees, the effects might be different. Because the nature of this relationship is unknown at the outset, it is not possible to set up the estimation model accordingly. Therefore, there is sufficient rationale to consider some atheoretical (for example, no assumptions about the model selection) approaches to explore some of these nuances.

Machine-learning techniques provide a flexible way to identify the drivers of return with no prior knowledge about functional forms or cutoff values. By not restricting attention to a linear functional form, machine-learning techniques help model basically any type of interaction, without the need for the modeler to identify the variables that might be interacting. Thus, these techniques can model complex, nonlinear relationships and allow interactions between predictors; however, they also have drawbacks. First, because they often have high variance, refitting a decision tree after a small change to the training data could lead to different results. Second, they often do not have the same predictive power as other models like neural networks, random forest, or boosted trees. Considering these drawbacks, this analysis first adopts a decision tree approach to take advantage of the trees' interpretability, and then tests the trees' robustness by employing random forests. A more technical discussion of this approach is provided in box 3.2.

Given the structure of data, a decision tree approach is followed in two steps. First, analyze the conditions in Syria by using all 2.2 million observations at the individual level; second, add host country conditions by using about 49,000 case-level observations. In both cases, demographic characteristics of refugees are taken into consideration. Because information about conditions in the country of asylum is unavailable for all 2.2 million refugees, a truncated dataset is used when analyzing those issues. As in the previous section, this is done by using case-level data. Thus, there is a trade-off between the two options: the first option takes advantage of a much larger dataset but suffers from a narrower scope, whereas the second option takes advantage of a wider scope but suffers from a smaller sample. Finally, because returnees constitute less than 2 percent of all refugees, to enhance the estimations a random selection of nonreturnees was used to construct an estimation sample where returnees constitute one-third of the sample. Thus, return likelihoods are magnified quantitatively, but the qualitative results regarding splits and relationship hierarchy are indicative.

An interesting nexus between family ties, conflict intensity, and returns is detected: in places with intensive conflict, returnees are mainly non-nuclear-family members of refugee cases. Figure 3.4 shows the results of the two-step estimations. Both panels show that, when the conflict intensity, measured by cumulative dread factors, is high, returnees are mostly members of a case who are not within the nuclear family of the case head. Overall, the case-level analysis shows that only 14 percent of nuclear family members return, whereas 74 percent of those who are not members of the nuclear family return in this specific sample. The returns of nuclear family members become even less likely under high-intensity conflict. For instance, in the case-level analysis, only 3 percent of nuclear family members return when the dread factor is greater than 92 (the left-most path from top to bottom of the case-level tree in figure 3.4). In comparison, within the group of non-nuclear-family members, 88 percent return when the dread factor is less than 52 (the rightmost path) and 67 percent return when the dread factor is greater than 51 and the individual is older than 55 years (the path that is second from the right). These findings provide some support for anecdotal evidence that suggests senior relatives go back, despite an active conflict, for family reunification, identifying return conditions, or watching property against appropriation risk.

Adding age, economic livelihood, and education level makes clearer the complexity of return dynamics with numerous subgroups. In addition to suggesting that mostly individuals who are not nuclear family members of cases return if the location of origin has high conflict intensity, the case-level results also provide

BOX 3.2.

Machine Learning Algorithms: Decision Trees and Boosted Trees

The idea behind the tree-fitting algorithm is simple and relies on sequentially dividing the observations into smaller groups, which are called regions. For a response Y and a predictor from series $X_1, X_2, ..., X_n$, a split is made by using a cut-point value: both the splitting variable and the cut-point value are chosen by the algorithm via optimization, as further explained here. If the splitting variable is numerical, the cut-point is a threshold value: the observations are split in two groups, above and below the threshold. With categorical variables, the cut-point is given by the values that the variables admit. Then the first split is made, and observations are split in two regions. Observations in each region are then further split in two regions, and the process continues until a stopping rule is reached. When the algorithm stops splitting, what is left are J distinct and nonoverlapping regions: each training observation will fall in one and only one region. The response is finally predicted to be as constant over each region. Summing up, fitting a binary classification tree involves two main steps:

- First, stratify or segment the predictor space—that is, all possible values of the predictors $X_1, X_2, ..., X_n$—into J regions.

- Second, assign the same predicted class to each observation that falls into a specific region R_j by simply looking at the most commonly occurring class among training observations in the region. The predicted probability for all observations in class R_j is intuitively given by the proportion of training observations belonging to the positive class.

Single trees are often called weak learners because, by being small, they feature high bias and, by themselves, are not good predictors of the response. Having high bias, however, inevitably means that they have low variance.

Boosted trees are tree-based ensemble methods that involve producing multiple trees that are then combined to yield a single prediction. Combining many trees can result in improvements in prediction accuracy and can lead to a reduction in variance, with only a small cost in terms of ease of interpretation. In boosting, individual trees are fit sequentially, and each tree leverages the information learned by previously grown trees. Although boosted trees cannot be easily visualized like a decision tree, they still have built-in variable importance measures. In general terms, the algorithm relies on the following steps:

1. At each iteration, instead of using the outcome Y as the response, fit a decision tree to the residual from the model (in the first iteration, because there is no model, the prediction is set equal to 0 and $r = Y$); each tree is called a "weak learner," and it should be a small tree.

(box continues next page)

207

BOX 3.2. *(continued)*

2. Add the weak learner to the model and update the residuals.

3. Start a new iteration.

In this study, decision tree algorithms are first employed to explore the nonlinear form of relationship between push and pull factors and return patterns in data. Then a boosted tree algorithm is used to test the robustness of results based on decision trees.

Figure 3.4. Decision Tree Algorithm Results

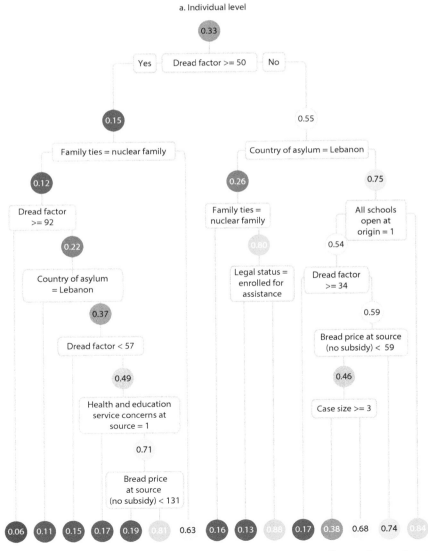

a. Individual level

(figure continues next page)

Figure 3.4. *(continued)*

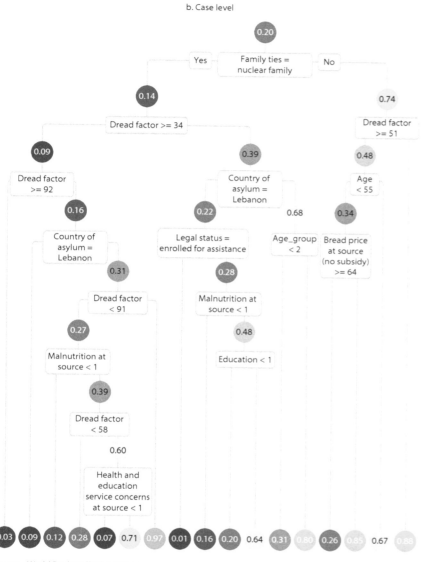

b. Case level

Source: World Bank staff calculations.
Note: Analysis based on 2,391,275 observations for panel a and 48,774 observations for panel b. Both analyses include conditions in the countries of asylum.

some nuances with respect to age and education characteristics of refugees. Of those individuals from areas with high conflict intensity (dread factor > 51), non-nuclear-family members who are younger than 55 are more likely to return (85 percent) if unsubsidized bread prices are less than 64.00 Syrian pounds (LS) in their original location. In comparison, if bread prices are greater than LS 64.00, the return likelihood of the same group is low (26 percent). Similarly, nuclear

Figure 3.5. Boosted Trees: Relative Influences with Two Datasets (Common Factors Highlighted)

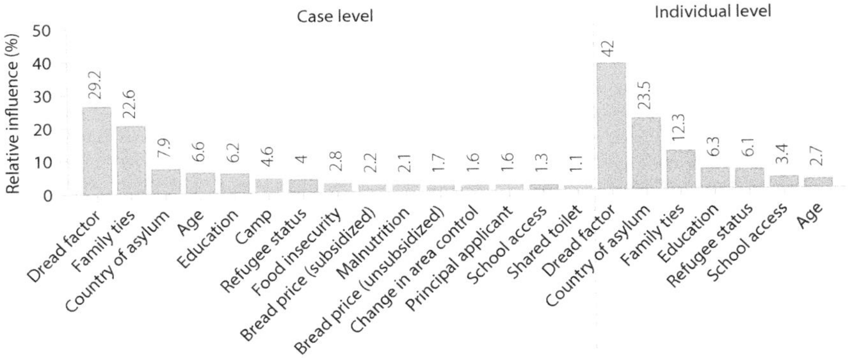

Source: World Bank staff calculations.

family members from relatively low-intensity conflict areas who have malnutrition concerns and reside in Lebanon are more likely to return if they have some education (64 percent) and less likely to return if they have less education (20 percent). Finally, nuclear family members who came from relatively low-intensity conflict areas and reside in either Iraq or Jordan are more likely to return if they are 10 years of age or older.

Overall, the factors that influence return most consistently are conflict intensity, family ties, the country of asylum, and refugees' age, education, and legal status. To assess the robustness of individual-level and case-level analysis and analyze the similarities between the two approaches, boosted-tree algorithms were run. Figure 3.5 shows the results. Overall, because the case-level analysis includes additional variables (conditions in countries of asylum), the number of factors that influence returns is larger; however, all six factors that have more than 1 percent influence in the individual-level analysis also have comparable levels of influence in the case-level analysis. Moreover, although the magnitudes of their influence cannot be compared quantitatively across the two approaches, the factors are similarly ordered (dread factor is the highest ranked, and the same top three factors drive about 60 percent or more of variation in both cases).

Special Issues in Return

This analysis has, at this point, focused on providing a nuanced but broad overview of the mobility calculus used by refugees. Both the generalized effects discussed in the first section and the localized effects discussed in the previous section focused on putting all our information together and understanding the relative importance of different factors in explaining the spontaneous returns that have taken place so far. The following subsections will analyze three issues more deeply: (a) the relationship between conflict events and return, (b) the effect of refuge duration on return, and (c) a more detailed account of family ties and return.

Conflict events and return

The preceding analysis has provided strong evidence that peace and security in Syria are major pull factors for refugee returns, a finding that is further confirmed by using different proxies for the conflict as presented in table 3.5. In particular, the intensity of the conflict, as measured by the so-called dread factor or the number of conflict events in the home location during exile, has been identified as one of the main determinants of refugee returns. To test the robustness of this baseline result for the entire dataset (replicated in column (1) in table 3.5), an alternative measure for conflict intensity is used in column (2)—the total number of casualties during the refugee's time in exile. Like the dread factor, a higher number of casualties is associated with a lower probability of return, with a one-standard-deviation increase reducing the likelihood to return by 1.6 percentage points (significant at the 1 percent level). Moreover, it is important to note that the coefficient of the dread factor is unchanged as additional conflict variables are included in columns (3) and (4), further illustrating the robustness and importance of the conflict intensity proxy.

A refugee's return decision is influenced not only by actual conflict events but also by his or her perception of the conflict. Individuals vary in their risk aversion, with some individuals willing to tolerate higher levels of conflict. To capture this risk aversion, the dread factor is measured *prior* to the refugee's arrival in the country of asylum (that is, the number of conflict events that occurred in the home location while the refugee was still in Syria). Refugees who left after only a few conflict events are likely more risk averse than those who stayed longer (though early leavers may also have access to resources or family abroad). Consistent with the risk interpretation, we find that refugees who had a higher tolerance for risk are also more likely to return, though the magnitude of the effect is small—a refugee is 0.07 percentage point more likely to return for a one-standard-deviation increase in this new dread factor variable (significant at the 1 percent level).

The risk of being drawn into the actual fighting seems to be less of a push factor. There is some conflicting anecdotal evidence on whether young men are more likely to return to Syria. On the one hand, they are the likely choice for the family to send ahead to check the situation on the ground. On the other hand, they are at a higher risk of being drawn into the fighting. Our empirical results suggest that men are indeed less likely to return to areas with a high intensity of fighting, but this effect is largest for the oldest (more than 60 years) age cohort. However, overall adult men are more likely to return to conflict areas than children, suggesting that the need to verify living conditions and the status of family property is greater than the fear of being drawn into the conflict.

Duration of refuge

Until now, all refugees have been treated the same, no matter at which point they arrived in the country of asylum; however, there could be systematic differences across refugees based on their duration of refuge. First, recent arrivals are likely to be in a more precarious and transitory situation because they have not yet had an opportunity to establish themselves in the host community. More-tenured refugees will, in contrast, have had an opportunity to integrate and adjust, possibly by finding work, sending their children to school, and finding housing. Both situations

Table 3.5. The Effects of Conflict on Return

Dependent variable: Refugee returned to Syrian Arab Republic (0 = No; 1 = Yes)		Mashreq			
Variable	Omitted category	(1)	(2)	(3)	(4)
Dread factor		−0.00077 *** (0.0000064)		−0.00077 *** (0.0000064)	−0.00077*** (0.0000064)
Change in control		0.15 *** (0.0032)	0.11 *** (0.0036)	0.15 *** (0.0033)	0.15 *** (0.0032)
Control: Not government of Syria	Control: Government of Syria	0.037 *** (0.00062)	0.025 *** (0.00060)	0.037 *** (0.00062)	0.033 *** (0.00071)
Security a concern?		−0.0040 *** (0.00049)	0.0047 *** (0.00049)	−0.0039 *** (0.00049)	−0.0041 *** (0.00049)
Casualties, in thousands			−0.0000028 *** (0.000000039)		
Dread factor (before arrival in asylum country)				0.000024 *** (0.0000079)	
Dread factor × Female					−0.0000048 (0.0000050)
Dread factor × Age 20–44	Dread factor × Age 0–19				−0.00018 *** (0.0000069)
Dread factor × Age 45–59	Dread factor × Age 0–19				−0.00016 *** (0.000012)
Dread factor × Age 60+	Dread factor × Age 0–19				−0.00058 *** (0.000025)
Dread factor × Age 20–44 × Female	Dread factor × Age 0–19 × Female				0.000024 *** (0.0000084)
Dread factor × Age 45–59 × Female	Dread factor × Age 0–19 × Female				−0.00019 *** (0.000017)
Dread factor × Age 60+ × Female	Dread factor × Age 0–19 × Female				−0.00040 *** (0.000033)
Age 20–44	Age 0–19	0.047 *** (0.00070)	0.048 *** (0.00072)	0.047 *** (0.00070)	0.045 *** (0.00071)
Age 45–59	Age 0–19	0.078 *** (0.0010)	0.080 *** (0.0010)	0.078 *** (0.0010)	0.074 *** (0.0011)
Age 60+	Age 0–19	0.069 *** (0.0016)	0.071 *** (0.0016)	0.069 *** (0.0016)	0.057 *** (0.0016)
Female	Male	0.0042 *** (0.00027)	0.0044 *** (0.00027)	0.0042 *** (0.00027)	0.0037 *** (0.00030)
Age 20–44 × Female	Age 0–19 × Female	−0.020 *** (0.00053)	−0.021 *** (0.00054)	−0.020 *** (0.00053)	−0.019 *** (0.00057)
Age 45–59 × Female	Age 0–19 × Female	−0.048 *** (0.00095)	−0.048 *** (0.00097)	−0.048 *** (0.00095)	−0.051 *** (0.0010)
Age 60+ × Female	Age 0–19 × Female	−0.025 *** (0.0017)	−0.025 *** (0.0018)	−0.025 *** (0.0017)	−0.029 *** (0.0019)

(table continues next page)

Table 3.5. *(continued)*

Dependent variable: Refugee returned to Syrian Arab Republic (0 = No; 1 = Yes)		Mashreq			
Variable	Omitted category	(1)	(2)	(3)	(4)
Push and pull factors controlled?					
Conditions in country of origin		Yes	Yes	Yes	Yes
Conditions in country of asylum		Yes	Yes	Yes	Yes
Other controls					
Demographic characteristics		Yes	Yes	Yes	Yes
Registration status		Yes	Yes	Yes	Yes
Constant		Yes	Yes	Yes	Yes
Fixed effects					
Arrival year		Yes	Yes	Yes	Yes
Country of asylum		Yes	Yes	Yes	Yes
Observations		2,012,143	2,012,143	2,012,143	2,012,143
R-squared		0.198	0.176	0.198	0.200

Note: Significance level: * = 10 percent, ** = 5 percent, *** = 1 percent.

could discourage return but for very different reasons. If the situation is too dire for either group—for example, if tenured refugees fail to establish a viable livelihood in the country of asylum or recent arrivals suffer severe food insecurity—it might provide a powerful push factor for tenured refugees. Second, recent arrivals are most likely less willing to return, given that they have left Syria only a few months back. In fact, return rates for recent arrivals are considerably lower at 0.76 percent compared to 3.85 percent for tenured refugees.

To explore whether there are differences in return decisions between recent arrivals and tenured refugees, the baseline regression is rerun for the sample of recent arrivals and tenured refugees separately. For this analysis, recent arrivals are defined as refugees who arrived in the country of asylum between March 2017 and March 2018, whereas more-tenured refugees arrived prior to March 2017. The results for recent arrivals and tenured refugees are presented in table 3.6 for the Mashreq region in columns (1) and (2), respectively. Because conditions in the host country could provide an important push factor, the same regressions are also run for the Jordan and Lebanon dataset (using geographical aggregates to measure host country factors) and are shown in columns (3) and (4), respectively.

Return decisions of recent arrivals and tenured refugees are largely determined by the same factors, but their living conditions in the country of asylum matter differentially, further magnifying the nonlinearity of these effects. The effects of demographic characteristics and a refugee's registration status on the likelihood of return are very similar across both groups and samples, which is why they are not reported in table 3.6.[17] The main difference in results for the Mashreq sample is for those refugees living in a camp. Recent arrivals are 2.5 percentage points less likely to return to Syria if they live in a camp, whereas more-tenured refugees are 5.8 percentage points more likely to return (both significant at the 1 percent level).

Table 3.6. The Effects of Duration of Stay on Return

Dependent variable: Refugee returned to Syrian Arab Republic (0 = No; 1 = Yes)			Mashreq		Jordan and Lebanon add host country factors using geographical aggregates	
Category	Variables	Omitted category	Recent arrivals	Tenured refugees	Recent arrivals	Tenured refugees
			(1)	(2)	(3)	(4)
Peace, security, and protection	Dread factor		−0.00019 *** (0.000013)	−0.00083 *** (0.0000062)	−0.000041 *** (0.0000066)	−0.00079 *** (0.0000060)
	Change in control		−0.019 *** (0.0032)	0.19 *** (0.0034)	−0.000059 (0.00044)	0.24 *** (0.0068)
	Control: Not government of Syria	Control: Government of Syria	−0.00048 (0.00096)	0.038 *** (0.00063)	0.0013 *** (0.00035)	0.030 *** (0.00060)
	Security a concern?		−0.0020 *** (0.00056)	−0.0034 *** (0.00052)	0.00074 *** (0.00025)	−0.0070 *** (0.00053)
Livelihoods and access to employment	Price of 1 kilogram (kg) of bread (subsidized)		0.000029 *** (0.0000027)	0.000052 *** (0.0000030)	−0.00000076 (0.0000012)	0.000032 *** (0.0000030)
	Price of 1kg of bread (unsubsidized)		−0.000029 *** (0.0000039)	0.0000031 (0.0000027)	0.0000032 ** (0.0000016)	0.000012 *** (0.0000026)
	Malnutrition: Moderate problem	Malnutrition: No problem	0.0056 *** (0.00086)	0.015 *** (0.00053)	0.00027 (0.00032)	0.012 *** (0.00052)
	Malnutrition: Serious problem	Malnutrition: No problem	0.0041 *** (0.00077)	0.033 *** (0.00085)	0.00052 * (0.00030)	0.026 *** (0.00084)
	Number of meals per day				−0.0014 *** (0.00036)	0.15 *** (0.0020)
	Food insecurity index				0.000045 (0.00017)	−0.032 *** (0.00088)
Housing, land, and property rights	Case lives in a camp	Case does not live in a camp	−0.025 *** (0.0032)	0.058 *** (0.0013)	0.012 *** (0.0028)	0.093 *** (0.0016)
Infrastructure and services	Basic services a concern?		−0.0014 ** (0.00063)	−0.023 *** (0.00059)	0.00015 (0.00025)	−0.017 *** (0.00060)
	Health/ education a concern?		0.0034 *** (0.00082)	−0.0090 *** (0.00050)	−0.00043 ** (0.00018)	−0.011 *** (0.00047)
	Access to basic service index				−0.000081 (0.00042)	0.0064 *** (0.00090)
Other controls	Demographic characteristics		Yes	Yes	Yes	Yes
	Registration status		Yes	Yes	Yes	Yes
	Constant		Yes	Yes	Yes	Yes
Fixed effects	Arrival year		Yes	Yes	Yes	Yes
	Country of asylum		Yes	Yes	Yes	Yes
	Observations		130,878	2,031,987	101,045	1,750,090
	R-squared		0.077	0.227	0.012	0.252

Note: Significance level: * = 10 percent, ** = 5 percent, *** = 1 percent.

Because recent refugees are likely to first find shelter in a camp, it is not surprising that this group is less likely to return after having just arrived in the country of asylum. In contrast, more-tenured refugees who are still in a camp after more than one year might be pushed to return to Syria given their difficulty in getting established in the host community. This result, however, is not confirmed for Jordan, where recent arrivals who live in a camp are more likely to return (there are no refugee camps in Lebanon). This result should be interpreted with caution, because only a small number of recent arrivals returned from Jordan (166 out of 20,429 refugees).

Food insecurity also has a differential impact on return decisions of recent arrivals. The baseline results have suggested that greater food security is associated with a higher likelihood of return. This result is replicated for the tenured refugees in the Jordan and Lebanon sample in column (4), for both the number of meals and the food insecurity index. The opposite is the case for recent arrivals, where one more meal per day reduces the likelihood of return by 0.14 percentage point, an effect that is small in magnitude but highly significant at the 1 percent level.

Confirming the earlier results, recent arrivals are also less likely to return to areas now controlled by the government of Syria. The results for tenured refugees in both samples (column (2) for the Mashreq and column (4) for Jordan and Lebanon) are in line with the baseline results of this analysis, suggesting that refugees are more likely to return to Syria if there has been a change in control and if this control now rests with an actor other than the government of Syria. Between 2017 and 2018, however, most of these changes of control have been back to the government of Syria. It is, thus, not surprising that recent arrivals are 1.9 percentage points less likely to return for the Mashreq dataset if there has been a recent change in control, a result that is statistically significant at 1 percent. Given that this variable now captures which actor is in control, the other control variable loses significance.

Gender and family ties

Because return seems to happen in several stages, it is important to understand the decision-making process at the case level. That is, when refugees consider the possibility of returning to Syria, they do not make this decision in isolation, but rather jointly with other members of the same case. A case is typically made up of the nuclear family, (that is, a husband and wife and their children), with at times additional members from the immediate or extended family. The case will likely first decide whether the entire case should return to Syria or whether only one or two family members should be sent ahead to assess the situation on the ground.[18] Next, a decision needs to be made about which member(s) of the case should return. To shed more light on this decision-making process, the analysis needs to be expanded to explain return decisions not at the individual but at the case level, which is the focus of this section.

Return patterns vary significantly across countries of asylum with case-level returns being much more common in Iraq and Jordan than in Lebanon. Two-thirds of all returnees, or nearly 59,000 people, returned with their entire case. These cases are typically small, with an average of 4.6 family members. By contrast, the average size of cases with individual returns is significantly larger, at 6.7 individuals on average, whereas the average size of a nonreturnee case is 5.0 individuals. Case-level returns are most common from Jordan and Iraq (89 percent and 85 percent of all returns, respectively).

For Lebanon, however, the pattern is the reverse with 89 percent of all returns involving individual family members only.

To further disentangle how households make return decisions, demographic characteristics are aggregated to the case level. That is, for each case the share of individuals who are, for example, single, who fall into a specific age category, or who are part of the extended family is computed. Then a linear probability model is run to determine how these case-level characteristics determine the probability of the entire case returning to Syria. A comparable analysis is carried out to estimate which factors determine the probability of only some family members returning while the rest of the case remains in the country of asylum. Like the prior analysis, controls are introduced in both regressions for push and pull factors as well as for country of asylum and year fixed effects. These results are suppressed in tables 3.7 and 3.8 for visual clarity, which show the results for the case-level differences and conditions in the country of asylum, respectively.

Interestingly, most of the case-level characteristics are similar across both types of returns. In fact, the results for the Mashreq and the Jordan/Lebanon sample mimic many key findings on individual return decisions. For instance, cases with a larger share of singles are more likely to return, whereas the opposite is true for households with a larger proportion of widows. Similarly, cases with more immediate or extended family members are more likely to return both as a case and as individuals.

One key factor that distinguishes cases where the entire family returns from those where only some family members return is the case's age composition. First, the probability of only some family members returning is higher if the household has a greater share of adults. For example, a one-standard-deviation increase in the proportion of family members aged 20–44 drives up the likelihood to return by 1.8 percentage points with similar magnitudes for the older cohorts, results that are statistically significant at the 1 percent level. In contrast, a larger share of adults is associated with a lower probability of the entire case returning. This finding is in line with international experience, which suggests that refugees adopt complex return strategies, where one or two adult members of a refugee household return informally from the host countries for short periods to assess the scope for a more permanent return of the entire household. A greater share of adults in a given household makes following this strategy more feasible.

How registration status influences returns differs between household-level returns and individual-level returns. Refugee cases are more likely to return if they are not registered, potentially indicating more limited international protection for the household in the country of asylum, while the opposite is true for instances where only a few family members return to Syria. In a related fashion, individual-level returns are also less likely when a large share of their cases is considered for resettlement to a third country, which reduces the need to explore the current situation in the home location.

Living conditions in the country of asylum also have differential, nonlinear effects on return type as shown in table 3.9. For the entire case, return is less likely the greater its food insecurity—a one-standard-deviation increase in food insecurity decreases the likelihood of return by 1.6 percentage points, a result that is statistically significant at the 1 percent level for the Jordan and Lebanon dataset using

Table 3.7. The Effects of Case-Level Differences on Types of Return

Category	Variable	Omitted variable	A few case members returned (0 = No; 1 = Yes)	Entire case returned (0 = No; 1 = Yes)	A few case members returned (0 = No; 1 = Yes)	Entire case returned (0 = No; 1 = Yes)
Dependent variable			Entire Mashreq		Jordan and Lebanon using geographical aggregates	
			(1)	(2)	(3)	(4)
Demographic and socioeconomic characteristics	% Single	% Married	0.0041 *** (0.00057)	0.029 *** (0.0010)	0.0063 *** (0.00070)	0.023 *** (0.00094)
	% Widowed	% Married	−0.0012 (0.0027)	−0.043 *** (0.0032)	−0.0059 ** (0.0029)	−0.029 *** (0.0033)
	% Other marital status	% Married	−0.012 *** (0.00098)	−0.031 *** (0.0016)	−0.012 *** (0.0011)	−0.024 *** (0.0016)
	% Age 20–44	% Age 0–19	0.046 *** (0.0013)	−0.084 *** (0.0016)	0.051 *** (0.0015)	−0.068 *** (0.0015)
	% Age 45–59	% Age 0–19	0.065 *** (0.0016)	−0.064 *** (0.0018)	0.072 *** (0.0018)	−0.052 *** (0.0017)
	% Age 60+	% Age 0–19	0.061 *** (0.0017)	−0.057 *** (0.0021)	0.068 *** (0.0019)	−0.039 *** (0.0020)
	% Female	% Male	0.0036 *** (0.00059)	0.0034 *** (0.00092)	0.0035 *** (0.00070)	0.011 *** (0.00087)
	% Extended family	% Nuclear family	0.29 *** (0.0082)	0.11 *** (0.0056)	0.29 *** (0.0087)	0.084 *** (0.0054)
	% Immediate family	% Nuclear family	0.28 *** (0.0042)	0.035 *** (0.0027)	0.29 *** (0.0046)	0.031 *** (0.0027)
	% Primary education	% No education	0.0020 *** (0.00068)	−0.0071 *** (0.00085)	0.00062 (0.00077)	−0.0098 *** (0.00080)
	% Secondary education	% No education	−0.0020 ** (0.00083)	−0.033 *** (0.0012)	−0.0027 *** (0.00098)	−0.030 *** (0.0011)
	% University education	% No education	−0.0024 *** (0.00090)	−0.038 *** (0.0015)	−0.0033 *** (0.0011)	−0.034 *** (0.0013)
	Case has children	Case has no children	0.045 *** (0.00090)	0.022 *** (0.00082)	0.047 *** (0.00099)	0.027 *** (0.00082)
	Case size		−0.0024 *** (0.00014)	−0.034 *** (0.00022)	−0.0021 *** (0.00016)	−0.027 *** (0.00021)
	% Special need	% No special need	−0.0037 *** (0.00051)	−0.020 *** (0.00071)	−0.0058 *** (0.00060)	−0.017 *** (0.00069)
Registration information	% Enrolled for assistance	% Asylum seeker	−0.028 *** (0.00070)	0.0081 *** (0.00092)	−0.024 *** (0.00082)	0.021 *** (0.00097)
	% Refugee	% Asylum seeker	−0.0083 *** (0.0018)	0.0090 *** (0.0014)	−0.0089 *** (0.0022)	0.014 *** (0.0017)
	Average registration lag		−0.00058 *** (0.000017)	−0.0016 *** (0.000024)	−0.00061 *** (0.000021)	−0.0014 *** (0.000025)
Push and pull factors controlled?						
Conditions in country of origin			Yes	Yes	Yes	Yes
Conditions in country of asylum			Yes	Yes	Yes	Yes

(table continues next page)

Table 3.7. *(continued)*

Category	Variable	Omitted variable	A few case members returned (0 = No; 1 = Yes)	Entire case returned (0 = No; 1 = Yes)	A few case members returned (0 = No; 1 = Yes)	Entire case returned (0 = No; 1 = Yes)
	Dependent variable		Entire Mashreq		Jordan and Lebanon using geographical aggregates	
			(1)	(2)	(3)	(4)
Other controls						
Ethnicity and religion			Yes	Yes	Yes	Yes
Constant			Yes	Yes	Yes	Yes
Fixed effects						
Arrival year			Yes	Yes	Yes	Yes
Country of asylum			Yes	Yes	Yes	Yes
Observations			632,397	632,397	523,307	523,307
R-squared			0.074	0.217	0.080	0.234

Note: Significance level: * = 10 percent, ** = 5 percent, *** = 1 percent.

Table 3.8. The Effects of Conditions in Country of Asylum on Types of Return

Category	Variable	Omitted variable	A few case members returned (0 = No; 1 = Yes)	Entire case returned (0 = No; 1 = Yes)	A few case members returned (0 = No; 1 = Yes)	Entire case returned (0 = No; 1 = Yes)
	Dependent variable		Mashreq		Jordan and Lebanon using geographical aggregates	
			(1)	(2)	(3)	(4)
Livelihoods and access to employment	Number of meals per day				0.011 *** (0.0017)	−0.00087 (0.00095)
	Food insecurity index				0.028 *** (0.0010)	−0.044 *** (0.00091)
Housing, land, and property rights	Case lives in a camp	Case does not live in a camp	0.0066 *** (0.00078)	0.076 *** (0.0014)	0.0079 *** (0.00094)	0.14 *** (0.0018)
Infrastructure and services	Access to basic services				−0.00033 (0.00089)	−0.0061 *** (0.00095)
Push and pull factors controlled?						
Conditions in country of origin			Yes	Yes	Yes	Yes
Other controls						
Demographic characteristics			Yes	Yes	Yes	Yes
Registration status			Yes	Yes	Yes	Yes
Constant			Yes	Yes	Yes	Yes
Fixed effects						
Arrival year			Yes	Yes	Yes	Yes
Country of asylum			Yes	Yes	Yes	Yes
Observations			632,397	632,397	523,307	523,307
R-squared			0.074	0.217	0.080	0.234

Note: Significance level: * = 10 percent, ** = 5 percent, *** = 1 percent.

Table 3.9. The Effects of Individual-Level Differences on Types of Return

Dependent variable	A few case members returned (0 = No; 1 = Yes)	Entire case returned (0 = No; 1 = Yes)	A few case members returned (0 = No; 1 = Yes)	Entire case returned (0 = No; 1 = Yes)
	Mashreq		Jordan and Lebanon using geographical aggregates	
Variable	(1)	(2)	(3)	(4)
A few case members returned to Syria Arab Republic = 1		−0.038 *** (0.0051)		−0.058 *** (0.0055)
Single	0.027 *** (0.0006)	0.015 *** (0.0005)	0.024 *** (0.0006)	0.01 *** (0.0005)
Single # = 1 if other case member(s) returned to Syria = 1		0.11 *** (0.0046)		0.13 *** (0.0049)
Widowed	−0.016 *** (0.0020)	−0.015 *** (0.0015)	−0.013 *** (0.0020)	−0.011 *** (0.0015)
Widowed # = 1 if other case member(s) returned to Syria = 1		−0.04 ** (0.0180)		−0.04 ** (0.0200)
Other	−0.013 *** (0.0010)	−0.0095 *** (0.0008)	−0.0071 *** (0.0011)	−0.00 *** 5 (0.0008)
Other # = 1 if other case member(s) returned to Syria = 1		0.02 *** (0.0064)		0.032 *** (0.0068)
Age 20–44	0.035 *** (0.0006)	0.016 *** (0.0005)	0.034 *** (0.0006)	0.012 *** (0.0004)
Age 20–44 = 1 # = 1 if other case member(s) returned to Syria = 1		0.19 *** (0.0044)		0.21 *** (0.0047)
Age 45–59	0.054 *** (0.0009)	0.029 *** (0.0007)	0.054 *** (0.0009)	0.026 *** (0.0007)
Age 45–59 = 1 # = 1 if other case member(s) returned to Syria = 1		0.18 *** (0.0057)		0.2 *** (0.0061)
Age 60+	0.059 *** (0.0014)	0.022 *** (0.0011)	0.066 *** (0.0014)	0.024 *** (0.0011)
Age 60+ = 1 # = 1 if other case member(s) returned to Syria = 1		0.3 *** (0.0076)		0.32 *** (0.0082)
1 if female = 1	−0.0064 *** (0.0002)	−0.0062 *** (0.0002)	−0.0047 *** (0.0002)	−0.0043 *** (0.0002)
1 if female = 1 # = 1 if other case member(s) returned to Syria = 1		−0.003 (0.0025)		−0.0059 ** (0.0027)
Extended family = 1	0.12 *** (0.0027)	0.03 *** (0.0016)	0.11 *** (0.0029)	0.022 *** (0.0014)
Extended family = 1 # = 1 if other case member(s) returned to Syria = 1		0.42 *** (0.0092)		0.43 *** (0.0100)
Immediate family = 1	0.14 *** (0.0022)	0.0095 *** (0.0014)	0.14 *** (0.0024)	0.0033 ** (0.0013)
Immediate family = 1 # = 1 if other case member(s) returned to Syria = 1		0.46 *** (0.0055)		0.46 *** (0.0061)
Push and pull factors controlled?				
Conditions in country of origin	yes	yes	yes	yes
Conditions in country of asylum	yes	yes	yes	yes
Other controls				
Demographic characteristics	yes	yes	yes	yes
Registration status	yes	yes	yes	yes
Constant	yes	yes	yes	yes
Observations	2,162,865	2,162,865	1,851,135	1,851,135
R-squared	0.218	0.307	0.245	0.354

Note: Significance level: * = 10 percent, ** = 5 percent, *** = 1 percent.

geographical aggregates (column (4)). By contrast, food security has nonlinear effects on the case decision to send only a few family members back. An extra meal increases the likelihood to return by 1.1 percentage points (column (3), significant at the 1 percent level); however, a one-standard-deviation increase in the food insecurity index also increases the likelihood to return of selected family members by 1.1 percentage points (also significant at the 1 percent level). This finding could reflect the fact that more precarious living conditions in the asylum country push some refugee families to send individual members back to Syria to assess to what extent the situation in the home location is better. At the same time, more well-off households might want to explore possibilities for rebuilding livelihoods or reclaiming assets and property in Syria.

Perceptions of Return

The analysis so far has analyzed the drivers of return to date; however, only a very small fraction of refugees have returned to Syria. In particular, the analysis is limited in two key dimensions. First, the refugees who have already returned may be motivated to return by very different factors than the refugees who have so far chosen to stay. Spontaneous returns during an active conflict are probably very different in terms of composition, timing, and purpose than returns after a stabilization period. Therefore, this analysis provides some insights into the decision-making process of only certain types of refugees. Second, the analysis of the existing data does not allow us to predict how refugees will react to changes in circumstances not yet observed in the real world. For instance, the future concerns and expectations of refugees about the broader political economy of Syria will likely be different from those in 2011–19.

This section begins to consider future returns by analyzing return intentions through a vignettes survey. Return intentions of refugees are often studied by means of interviews, focus group discussions, and perception surveys; but these approaches may be prone to cognitive challenges. First, simple manipulations, such as ordering words or questions in certain ways or presenting problems in different scales, can affect how people respond to questions. In addition, the participants may not spend enough mental effort to remember or think, or they may not want to reveal answers that they deem socially undesirable. In order to avoid the pitfalls of a simple intentions survey, a vignettes survey was employed; refugees' opinions were elicited on how likely a hypothetical refugee family would be to return, and randomization of details across participants was relied on to reduce the likelihood of introducing systematical biases into the findings. Box 3.3 provides more details about this approach.

The first analysis looks at variations in responses to opportunities for exercising skills in the host communities and to varying property conditions in Syria. Table 3.10 shows the structure of the first vignette exercise. In this case, there are four key variants of the description of the family's economic situation in the country of asylum (physician in Syria now working as a janitor, physician in Syria now working as a physician, miner in Syria now working with a permit, or miner in Syria now working without a permit). There are also three variants on how long the security situation in their hometown has stabilized (6 months, 9 months, or 12 months). Therefore, the regression includes five dummy variables capturing the vignette scenarios. To interpret these coefficients, we need to refer to the omitted category. For example, the coefficients "physician in Syria now working as a physician," "miner in Syria now working

BOX 3.3.

Vignette Analysis

In a survey of 900 Syrian refugees in Jordan and Lebanon, the details of the scenario or vignette presented to a given individual respondent were randomly varied. Some refugee families are certainly more predisposed to wanting to return than others. Describing hypothetical scenarios, but ones that hit fairly close to home, and varying key factors within those scenarios should help identify what factors are important to many refugee families when deciding whether to return.

All respondents in all vignettes were asked "How likely is this family to return to the Syrian Arab Republic in the next two months?" The respondent could answer using a Likert scale, with options ranging from "very likely" to "very unlikely." For the analysis described here, we use an indicator that is equal to 1 if a respondent says the family is either very likely or likely to return, and 0 if the respondent says neutral, unlikely, or very unlikely.

Each respondent was presented with three vignettes, where key aspects of the scenarios were randomly varied across respondents. These three vignettes were designed to probe the impact of different push and pull factors on the refugees' return decision, allowing researchers to go beyond the data limitations of the above analysis. That is, the vignettes explored the impact on return decisions not only of security but also of employment prospects in both the country of asylum and Syria, the status of property in the home community, and the availability of financial assistance. In particular, the first vignette probes three questions: first, whether the ability to work in the host country affects the return decision and moreover if the ability to work is more or less important among highly skilled workers; second, whether the length of time that security has been stabilized in the origin community affects the return decision; and, third, whether financial assistance, and the level of that assistance, affects the return decision.

The second vignette has two key aspects of the scenario that vary across respondents. The first varies if the wife of a refugee family from Syria, now living in either Lebanon or Jordan (the country was matched to the country where the respondent was currently residing), was working as a housekeeper or stayed home to take care of the family. The second aspect varied the opportunities of the husband of the family to get work back in the home community in Syria. The vignette also sought to understand how a family may decide to send some but not all family members to return and elicits the likelihood of each family member to return.

The third and final vignette varied what information a hypothetical family in either Lebanon or Jordan had about its home back in Syria. A respondent was told that a family's house in Syria was either destroyed or intact and unoccupied. The information was provided to the family either by a resident of the village or by family members who remained in their village in Syria.

(box continues next page)

221

BOX 3.3. *(continued)*

The responses to the vignettes are analyzed using a linear probability model:

$$y_i = \alpha + \beta_1 \, VignetteScenario_i + \gamma Jordan + \epsilon_i,$$

where y_i is an indicator variable equal to 1 if the respondent *i* reported that the family depicted in the vignette was very likely or likely to return to Syria in the next two months. The variable *Jordan* equals 1 if the respondent resides in Jordan and 0 if the respondent currently resides in Lebanon. The different scenarios are captured by either a dummy variable *VignetteScenario_i* or a series of dummy variables. β_1 captures how changes in a refugee family's conditions—either in the country of asylum or back in Syria—affect the perception that the refugee will return to Syria.

Table 3.10. The First Vignette: Occupation and Security

	All	Jordan only	Lebanon only
	(1)	(2)	(3)
Physician in the Syrian Arab Republic now working as a physician	−0.055 *	−0.021	−0.089 *
	(0.032)	(0.045)	(0.046)
Miner in Syria now working without a permit	−0.103 ***	−0.096 **	−0.109 **
	(0.032)	(0.045)	(0.045)
Miner in Syria now working with a permit	−0.050	−0.008	−0.089 *
	(0.032)	(0.046)	(0.045)
9 months of security	0.033	0.052	0.016
	(0.027)	(0.039)	(0.039)
12 months of security	0.008	0.058	−0.045
	(0.028)	(0.039)	(0.040)
Respondent resides in Jordan	−0.145 ***		
	(0.023)		
Observations	1,900	950	950
Mean: Physician working as janitor and 6 months of security	0.497	0.375	0.590
Standard deviation	0.501	0.487	0.494
Test: Physician, physician = Miner, no permit [p-value]	0.129	0.084	0.667
Test: Miner, no permit = Miner, with permit [p-value]	0.093	0.045	0.653
Joint test of significance of occupation vars [p-value]	0.015	0.110	0.071

Note: Significance level: * = 10 percent, ** = 5 percent, *** = 1 percent.

without a permit," and "miner in Syria now working with a permit" should all be interpreted as changes in the reported likelihood of the family's return relative to the scenario where the husband/father is working as a janitor after having been a physician in Syria, which serves as the reference category. Column (1) shows the analysis with all respondents, whereas column (2) uses data only from respondents in Jordan and column (3) uses data only from Lebanon.

Working in jobs that are less skill-intensive than one's original profession is perceived to be a catalyst for return. Column (1) of the table shows that about one-half of all respondents indicate that they think the family is "very likely" or "likely" to return (henceforth referred to as just "likely to return") to Syria when the father/husband is depicted as a physician from Syria who now works as a janitor in Lebanon or Jordan. On average, about 50 percent of respondents thought that a family where the father/husband was working as a janitor in Lebanon, despite having been a doctor in Syria prior to the conflict, would likely return if there had been six months of security in their hometown. Compared to this benchmark, the scenario where the father/husband can work as a physician makes it 5.5 percentage points less likely, an 11 percent decline, that the family would return. This difference is statistically significant at the 10 percent level. If the father/husband had been a miner in Syria and is now working without a permit, the family is believed to be 10 percentage points less likely to return (significant at the 1 percent level). The miner in Syria who is working with a permit is 5 percentage points more likely to return than a miner who is working without a permit. This difference is at the margin of statistical significance at the 10 percent level.[19]

The aversion to "skill-downgrade" is stronger among respondents in Lebanon. Column (1) shows that, overall, respondents in Jordan (whose scenarios depicted refugees who also lived in Jordan) are less likely to say that the hypothetical family is likely to return. This finding motivates doing the same analysis separately for the Jordan and Lebanon samples. Column (2) presents the results of the same regression but for only the Jordan subsample and column (3) uses only the Lebanon data. The finding that the scenario where the husband/father who had been a miner in Syria and is now working without a permit is less likely to return than a scenario where the husband/father was previously a physician but is now working as a janitor is robust for both subsamples. In Jordan, however, we do not observe any differences among the scenarios—physician working as janitor, physician working as physician, and miner working with permit. In Lebanon, the analysis shows that the physician currently working as a janitor is the most likely to return, with all other scenarios being about 10 percentage points less likely to return. This finding suggests that, for respondents in Lebanon, the gap in the type of work someone was doing in Syria versus the type of work that individual can find in Lebanon is a factor in the return decision. Blue collar work with or without a permit is not an important factor.

In Jordan, providing permits does not make refugees want to stay more. As column (2) shows in table 3.10, only 28 percent of respondents indicated that a worker without a permit would be likely to return to Syria, compared to 37 percent of workers who have a permit. When combined with the results from actual return analyses discussed in this chapter (which showed that those who are more well-off are more likely to return), this result shows that having a permit may in fact allow a refugee family to save up more money to fund its return home.

Security conditions appear to affect return intentions with no lag. Across all specifications, there is essentially no observed effect of a longer period in which the hypothetical family's hometown has been conflict free, that is, 6 months of no violence appears to have a similar effect on the return decision as 9 months and 12 months. This finding suggests that, at least intention-wise, return can take place relatively rapidly if it happens when the conditions are right.

Assistance-related results paint a complex nexus of human psyche and economic factors: refugees do not embrace financial factors in discussing mobility, but those factors still play a role. Table 3.11 focuses on how information on cash assistance for return influences the perception of whether a hypothetical family will in fact return. Column (1) looks at the full sample, column (2) is only for Jordan, and column (3) is only for Lebanon. Comparing the overall means, it is striking that there is no increase in the likelihood that respondents say the family will return with the introduction of the information about the US$2,000 cash assistance. In the vignette that mentions nothing about external assistance, about 50 percent of respondents indicated the family would likely return. When US$2,000 per person is introduced, however, that number is only 46 percent. Nevertheless, being offered less money is associated with a lower likelihood to return to Syria (about 8 percentage points). This overall effect is driven by the Lebanon subsample, where the lower assistance level means a 16-percentage-point reduction in the likelihood a respondent says the hypothetical family will return.

Turning next to the third vignette, the results show that access to schools in Syria is an important determinant of return perceptions. The third vignette is analyzed by comparing the scenario in which the wife is working and schools in Syria are open and well-resourced to the other three scenarios as illustrated in table 3.12. The first column shows responses to the question of whether the entire family is likely to return in the next two months, and the following columns ask about individual family members, as described in the table in the row "Who migrates?" The responses show that refugees do not consider female labor force participation an important factor in the return decision; however, schools not being open in Syria significantly reduces the probability that a respondent thinks the family (and individual family members) will return. The benchmark likelihood is 43 percent, and this likelihood is reduced to 25 percent if schools in Syria do not have resources to pay teachers their full salaries. In this scenario, having open schools matters both for the children—who are enrolled in school—and because the father/husband was a school teacher in Syria. We do not observe dramatically different patterns for the return decisions for the individual family members versus the entire family.

The fourth vignette shows that refugees' ability to reclaim nondestroyed houses in Syria is a key determinant of return intentions. This vignette focuses on the conditions of the family's house and whether other family members remain in the

Table 3.11. The Second Vignette: Assistance

	Mashreq	Jordan	Lebanon
	(1)	(2)	(3)
Respondent resides in Jordan	−0.139 ***		
	(0.022)		
US$1,000 cash assistance per returnee	−0.082 ***	−0.005	−0.156 ***
	(0.022)	(0.031)	(0.032)
Observations	1,900	950	950
Mean: US$2,000 cash assistance per returnee	0.457	0.373	0.540
Standard deviation	0.498	0.484	0.499

Note: Significance level: * = 10 percent, ** = 5 percent, *** = 1 percent.

Table 3.12. The Third Vignette: Conditions in the Syrian Arab Republic and Family Returns

	Migration Profiles				
	(1)	(2)	(3)	(4)	(5)
Wife not working	0.012	0.004	0.021	0.012	0.027
	(0.022)	(0.021)	(0.021)	(0.021)	(0.021)
Schools poor resources	−0.187 ***	−0.188 ***	−0.143 ***	−0.142 ***	−0.130 ***
	(0.021)	(0.021)	(0.021)	(0.021)	(0.021)
Respondent resides in Jordan	−0.063 ***	−0.143 ***	−0.099 ***	−0.096 ***	−0.089 ***
	(0.022)	(0.021)	(0.021)	(0.021)	(0.021)
Who migrates?	Entire family	Father/ Husband	Wife/ Mother	Older daughter	Younger daughter
Observations	950	950	950	950	950
Mean: Wife is working and schools in Syria open	0.433	0.440	0.357	0.357	0.337
Standard deviation	0.496	0.497	0.480	0.480	0.473

Note: Significance level: * = 10 percent, ** = 5 percent, *** = 1 percent.

225

Table 3.13. The Fourth Vignette: Condition of House or Dwelling in the Syrian Arab Republic

	(1)
Family says house intact	0.020
	(0.028)
Neighbor says house destroyed	−0.224 ***
	(0.028)
Family says house destroyed	−0.229 ***
	(0.028)
Respondent resides in Jordan	−0.009
	(0.020)
Observations	1900
Mean: Neighbor says house is intact	0.381
Standard deviation	0.486

Note: Significance level: * = 10 percent, ** = 5 percent, *** = 1 percent.

home village. In this scenario, 38 percent of respondents indicate that the family is likely to return to Syria if it finds out from its neighbors in Syria that its house is intact (table 3.13). This rate is the same if the family in Syria tells the refugee family its house is intact. The destruction of the family's house, however, reduces the likelihood of returning home by 22–23 percentage points. In this case, no significant difference is observed between Jordan and other host countries in responses.

These vignettes do not cover all factors that influence refugees' decisions; however, they provide a useful introduction to a more forward-looking analysis of return. Refugees who have thus far returned to Syria may be motivated by very specific reasons that are less relevant for refugees who have so far stayed in their country of asylum. This survey helps uncover factors that may influence the decisions among the clear majority of refugees who have not returned to Syria. In the next chapter, the analysis will investigate more formally the possible paths of future conditions in Syria, and how those may influence the return behavior.

Concluding Remarks

In this chapter, the analysis estimated the importance of the four broad factors distilled from international experience in shaping the mobility of Syrian refugees so far. Returns to Syria have been low relative to the total refugee population; nevertheless, more than 100 thousand (103,090 between 2015 and 2018) have returned. These returnees (and nonreturnees) provide an opportunity to investigate the factors that have contributed to return decisions so far. For this investigation, the analysis uses empirical tests including linear probability and logit models to identify generalized (population-wise) effects of each factor on return behavior and uses machine-learning techniques like decision trees and boosted trees to capture localized (group-wise) effects, which enable better capture of the complexity of return. Finally, novel surveys of refugees, including nonregistered ones, are employed to analyze the willingness to return. The use of vignette scenarios (for example, not asking refugees directly about their own return but presenting them with scenarios about hypothetical refugee profiles, and randomizing the scenarios across participants) lessens some important biases that often plague return-intentions surveys, such as cognitive problems (for example, responses being shaped by social/political pressure).

Results show that the actual returns to date are of a special kind, in both their scale and composition, that are generally different from large-scale returns. Overall, the estimations of generalized effects show that demographic characteristics like family ties, age, and marital status are important determinants of return. Empirical results in this study confirm the findings from international experience that refugee return is a complex process. Although this analysis cannot verify the cyclical and transitory nature of some return behavior (because these data do not lend themselves to such an exercise), the nuances of who returns and under what conditions are identified.

- Refugees who are single, or male, or not members of a nuclear family have been more likely to return. Generalized results (applicable to the entire Syrian refugee population in Iraq, Jordan, and Lebanon) show that singles are 2.7 percentage points more likely to return than married refugees, male members are 0.6 percentage points more likely to return than females, and extended family members are 12 percentage points more likely to return than nuclear family members. This pattern varies greatly across countries of asylum with individual returns being very common in Lebanon (89 percent of all returns). In contrast, case-level returns are much more common in Iraq and Jordan, making up more than 85 percent of all returns. "Case" here refers to UNHCR's registration system of "refugee case" where a group of refugees, often families with relatives, is headed by the case-head. It should also be noted that frequent back-and-forth movements of refugees between Lebanon and Syria have been reported, and these movements may not be captured completely by the official return statistics.

- With intensive conflict in home locations in Syria, returnees are more narrowly selected from a specific profile of refugees. Using the machine-learning algorithm with a return-augmented sample (by randomly choosing a smaller sample from nonreturnees) elaborates on more complex dynamics. In this biased sample, overall, only 14 percent of nuclear family members return, whereas

74 percent of non-nuclear-family members return in this specific sample. The returns of nuclear family members become even less likely under high-intensity conflict. For instance, only 3 percent of nuclear family members return when the dread factor (tank, artillery, and air strikes) has been high in the district of origin in Syria. In comparison, within those in the group of non-nuclear-family members, 88 percent return when the dread factor is low, and 67 percent return when the dread factor is moderate, and the non-nuclear-family member is older than 55 years of age. These findings provide some support for the anecdotal evidence that suggests senior relatives go back—despite an active conflict—for family reunification, to identify return conditions, or to watch property against appropriation risk.

Results also show that, while "pull factors" in Syria have unambiguous effects on return behavior, "push" factors in countries of asylum have mixed implications. Findings confirm international lessons regarding dominance of country of origin effects. This study, however, finds no evidence for any suggestion that, if refugees face bad living conditions in host communities, they will be more likely to go back. The relationship between host community living conditions and return is complex, as shown below.

- Security in Syria is one of the most important determinants of return. Figure 3.5 shows that security, along with demographic aspects, is one of the most important determinants of return, a result that is consistent across specifications. Refugees are found to be less likely to return to districts with a history of intensive conflict. A one-standard-deviation increase in the dread factor reduces the likelihood to return by 4.5 percentage points; however, by itself the absence of violence is not sufficient, and the party in control is equally critical. Estimations show that refugees are 3.6 percentage points more likely to return if the district of origin is not controlled by the government of Syria. Similarly, a takeover of control (by any group) increases the likelihood of return by 18 percentage points. Thus, security is not only a backward-looking factor (conflict history) but also a forward-looking one (future exposure to violence and possible tensions).

- Low provision of education, health, and basic services in Syria provides an effective deterrent against return. Other things being equal, concerns about access to basic services, education, and health provide a consistently negative effect on the likelihood of return across all specifications. Refugees are 2.2 percentage points less likely to return if access to basic services (electricity, fuelwood, and so forth) is a primary concern in their home district. Similar results are obtained for limited access to public health and education, but the coefficients are smaller.

- Better living conditions and access to services in countries of asylum do not reduce the likelihood of return on the low end of the distribution. Results regarding living conditions (such as food security) and access to services (such as education) show that refugees' living conditions and access to services in countries of asylum have nonlinear effects on the likelihood of return. For instance, refugees are 15 percentage points more likely to return if they consume an extra meal per day (Lebanon and Jordan dataset with geographical aggregation). Similarly, a one-standard-deviation increase in food insecurity decreases the likelihood to return by 1.8 percentage points. Although higher education has been associated with lower likelihood of return at secondary and tertiary levels (for example, having a university degree reduced the likelihood of return by 2.5 percentage points, and having a secondary degree reduced it by 1.7 percentage points), having a primary education increased this likelihood by 0.3 percentage points relative to having no education.

Surveys detected a complex nexus of human psyche and economic factors: refugees do not embrace financial issues in discussing mobility, but those issues still matter. Responses to vignette surveys provided predictable results regarding the role of assets in returns. About 38 percent of respondents indicated that their family would likely return to Syria if they find out from their neighbors in Syria that their house is intact, but the destruction of the family's house reduces the likelihood of return by 22–23 percentage points. Responses to hypothetical scenarios of financial assistance, however, were rather unexpected. Positive responses to a fictional return scenario decreased from 50 percent to 46 percent when a hypothetical amount of US$2,000 cash assistance was introduced in the scenario.[20] Interestingly, however, a scenario with less money (US$1,000) is still associated with a lower likelihood to return to Syria by about 8 percentage points as compared to the scenario with more money (US$2,000). Thus, somewhat paradoxically, cash assistance reduced the positive return responses, but more assistance still triggered more positive responses than less assistance.

The future mobility of Syrian refugees could be different from their past mobility. In many ways, the return that has happened so far has been undertaken in specific circumstances, that is, during an active conflict, with specific motives like protecting property. Going forward, however, both the circumstances and the motives are likely to be different. To capture these concerns, the analysis in the next chapter considers scenario-based simulations.

Annex 3A

Survey response comparison

In this section, we compare responses to questions posed to refugees in both the VAF and the VASyR, administered by UNHCR, and in our own survey implemented by a third party. The sample from our survey includes only registered refugees from Jordan and Lebanon, to allow for more accurate comparisons. Differences we observe stem from two main reasons: (a) a change in time or (b) bias arising from the fact that refugees may respond differently (the direction of the bias could go different ways) to survey questions when an aid organization is administering the question. There is no way to separate these two explanations; however, because we have VAF and VASyR surveys from multiple years, table 3A.1 shows the data for each year.

Table 3A.1 combines data from the VAF and the VASyR in the years 2015 and 2017 and combines Lebanon and Jordan from the survey data in 2018. In parentheses are standard deviations. The column titled p-value shows whether the means in the 2018 column are statistically different from those in the 2017 column. This test was chosen because the years are closest to each other, in an attempt to minimize—though surely not eliminate—differences resulting from changes over time.

We focus on measures related to coping with poverty. In all surveys, respondents were asked whether they had to engage in a number of activities, all of which

Table 3A.1. Comparison of Refugees in VAF, VASyR, and Survey Data, All Countries

	All			N	p-value
	2015	2017	2018		
Had to do the following to cope with poverty:					
Sell household goods	0.291	0.282	0.495	19,149	0.000
	(0.454)	(0.450)	(0.500)		
Reduce consumption of essentials	0.454	0.532	0.815	19,149	0.000
	(0.498)	(0.499)	(0.389)		
Spend savings	0.370	0.364	0.656	19,149	0.000
	(0.483)	(0.481)	(0.475)		
Buy food on credit	0.656	0.706	0.748	19,149	0.005
	(0.475)	(0.456)	(0.434)		
Stop sending children to school	0.150	0.103	0.267	19,150	0.000
	(0.357)	(0.304)	(0.443)		
Send children to work	0.034	0.055	0.192	19,150	0.000
	(0.182)	(0.229)	(0.394)		
Send children to beg	0.019	0.027	0.025	19,149	0.579
	(0.136)	(0.163)	(0.155)		
Engage in dangerous or exploitative work	0.183	0.120	0.126	19,149	0.519
	(0.386)	(0.324)	(0.332)		
Received food voucher assistance	0.753	0.601	0.402	19,148	0.000
	(0.431)	(0.490)	(0.490)		
Has piped water	0.602	0.486	0.762	19,148	0.000
	(0.489)	(0.500)	(0.426)		
Has toilet	0.977	0.856	0.842	15,273	0.124
	(0.151)	(0.351)	(0.365)		
Average meals per day	2.138	2.107	2.509	19,140	0.000
	(0.780)	(0.957)	(0.642)		
Number of times reduced meals	2.727	2.351	1.112	19,139	0.000
	(2.753)	(2.832)	(1.596)		

Sources: UNHCR 2015, 2017a; UNHCR, UNICEF, and WFP 2018.
Note: VAF = Vulnerability Assessment Framework; VASyR = Vulnerability Assessment of Syrian Refugees; N = number of observations.

would ideally be avoided, in order to deal with a shortage of food or money since they arrived in their country of asylum. The 2018 data show much higher rates of households reporting engaging in poverty-coping strategies, ranging from selling household goods to reducing consumption of essentials. Notably, the 2018 data show a higher rate (27 percent) of households reporting that they had to stop sending their children to school than in the 2015 and 2017 data (15 percent and 10 percent, respectively), with a corresponding increase in the percentage of households that report having to send their children to work. Fortunately, however, we do not observe an increase in the percentage of households that have to resort to sending their children to beg, which is 2–3 percent of households in all surveys.

A smaller fraction of households reports receiving food voucher assistance, decreasing from 60 percent in 2017 and 75 percent in 2015 to 40 percent in 2018. Comparisons for Jordan and Lebanon are shown separately. The largest change is in Jordan, where in 2018 only 45 percent of the respondents reported receiving food assistance in the form of a voucher, compared to 93 percent and 91 percent, respectively, for 2015 and 2017.

In contrast to the coping strategy results—which suggest refugees are struggling more in the 2018 survey, either because of deterioration in time or different reporting—their ability to eat regular meals has improved. The average meals per day was 2.5 in the 2018 survey compared to 2.1 in 2015 and 2017. Consistent with this finding, households report having to reduce meals less often. In all three years, respondents were asked, "In the last seven days, how many times has the household had to reduce the number of meals eaten per day?" Respondents answered 1.1 in the 2018 data, whereas in 2015 and 2017 the average was 2.7 times and 2.3 times respectively. This is a large difference.

Table 3A.2 focuses only on Jordan, comparing the VAF to the survey data collected by the team in 2018. In Jordan, across almost all the measures of coping with poverty,

Table 3A.2. Comparison of Refugees in VAF, VASyR, and Survey Data, in Jordan

	Jordan			*N*	*p*-value
	2015	**2017**	**2018**		
Had to do the following to cope with poverty:					
Sell household goods	0.235 (0.424)	0.340 (0.474)	0.557 (0.497)	5,679	0.000
Reduce consumption of essentials	0.148 (0.356)	0.546 (0.498)	0.849 (0.358)	5,679	0.000
Spend savings	0.398 (0.490)	0.445 (0.497)	0.685 (0.465)	5,679	0.000
Buy food on credit	0.356 (0.479)	0.619 (0.486)	0.740 (0.439)	5,679	0.000
Stop sending children to school	0.073 (0.259)	0.105 (0.307)	0.246 (0.431)	5,679	0.000
Send children to work	0.009 (0.094)	0.075 (0.263)	0.174 (0.379)	5,679	0.000
Send children to beg	0.005 (0.068)	0.042 (0.200)	0.006 (0.078)	5,679	0.000
Engage in dangerous or exploitative work	0.531 (0.499)	0.304 (0.460)	0.148 (0.355)	5,679	0.000
Received food voucher assistance	0.929 (0.256)	0.912 (0.283)	0.454 (0.498)	5,678	0.000
Has piped water	0.940 (0.238)	0.900 (0.300)	0.857 (0.350)	5,679	0.001
Has toilet	0.966 (0.182)	0.951 (0.216)	0.926 (0.262)	5,679	0.007
Average meals per day	2.495 (0.541)	2.103 (1.208)	2.382 (0.597)	5,679	0.000
Number of times reduced meals	2.908 (2.689)	2.152 (2.684)	1.093 (1.655)	5,671	0.000

Sources: UNHCR 2015, 2017a; UNHCR, UNICEF, and WFP 2018.
Note: VAF = Vulnerability Assessment Framework; VASyR = Vulnerability Assessment of Syrian Refugees; *N* = number of observations.

we observe an increase in reports of having to engage in each strategy over time, increasing from 2015, 2017, and then 2018; however, reports of being engaged in dangerous or exploitative work declined significantly in 2018 compared to earlier years. We also observe fewer households reporting access to piped water and having a toilet in the 2018 sample, though the differences are fairly small in magnitude even if statistically significant. The trend in food consumption is a little different than discussed with the full sample. Respondents report far fewer incidents of reducing their meals in the last week, but there is a different pattern over time for reported average meals per day. In 2015 households reported on average 2.5 meals per day, going down to 2.1 in 2017, and then rising again to 2.4 in 2018.

Table 3A.3 examines only Lebanon, including VASyR data from 2015–17 compared to the survey data from 2018. The p-value continues to compare only 2018 to 2017. In the Lebanon data, a striking change in the 2018 data compared to earlier years

Table 3A.3. Comparison of Refugees in VAF, VASyR, and Survey Data, in Lebanon

	Lebanon					
	2015	2016	2017	2018	N	p-value
Had to do the following to cope with poverty:						
Sell household goods	0.316 (0.465)	0.307 (0.461)	0.250 (0.433)	0.404 (0.491)	13,470	0.000
Reduce consumption of essentials	0.593 (0.491)	0.534 (0.499)	0.524 (0.499)	0.764 (0.425)	13,470	0.000
Spend savings	0.358 (0.479)	0.363 (0.481)	0.319 (0.466)	0.616 (0.487)	13,470	0.000
Buy food on credit	0.793 (0.405)	0.616 (0.486)	0.754 (0.430)	0.760 (0.428)	13,470	0.794
Stop sending children to school	0.185 (0.388)	0.118 (0.322)	0.102 (0.303)	0.298 (0.458)	13,470	0.000
Send children to work	0.046 (0.209)	0.031 (0.174)	0.045 (0.207)	0.218 (0.413)	13,470	0.000
Send children to beg	0.025 (0.157)	0.018 (0.135)	0.019 (0.137)	0.051 (0.220)	13,470	0.000
Engage in dangerous or exploitative work	0.024 (0.154)	0.021 (0.142)	0.018 (0.133)	0.096 (0.294)	13,470	0.000
Received food voucher assistance	0.673 (0.469)		0.429 (0.495)	0.327 (0.470)	13,470	0.000
Has piped water	0.449 (0.497)	0.340 (0.474)	0.257 (0.437)	0.624 (0.485)	13,468	0.000
Has toilet	0.982 (0.134)	0.889 (0.314)	0.656 (0.475)	0.719 (0.450)	9,594	0.000
Average meals per day	1.975 (0.817)	1.865 (0.837)	2.109 (0.784)	2.696 (0.659)	13,461	0.000
Number of times reduced meals	2.645 (2.778)	2.208 (2.708)	2.461 (2.906)	1.138 (1.509)	13,468	0.000

Sources: UNHCR 2015, 2017a; UNHCR, UNICEF, and WFP 2018.
Note: VAF = Vulnerability Assessment Framework; VASyR = Vulnerability Assessment of Syrian Refugees; N = number of observations.

is the percentage of households reporting that they had to stop sending their children to school (30 percent compared to 10–19 percent in previous years) and having to send their children to work (22 percent compared to 3–5 percent in previous years). We also observe a steady decline in the percentage of households reporting receiving food assistance in the form of a voucher in Lebanon between 2015, 2017, and 2018.

Registered vs. unregistered refugee responses: Sampling bias

The data from UNHCR include only refugees who are registered (or recorded in Lebanon after 2015). There are, however, refugees in both Lebanon and Jordan who are not registered with UNHCR. In the survey, both registered and unregistered refugees were interviewed in Lebanon and Jordan. In this annex section, we provide some summary statistics comparing characteristics of different refugees. A refugee household is considered "registered" in Jordan if the refugee who was the primary respondent to the survey indicates that he or she is registered, and the registration is current. The refugee is "unregistered" if he or she never registered, has an expired registration, or was registered only in a refugee camp (and no longer resides in the camp). In Lebanon, a refugee is registered if he or she either has a current registration or is recorded for assistance. A refugee is treated as unregistered if he or she has an expired registration or was never registered or recorded.

In table 3A.4 we observe some differences across registered and unregistered refugees, though most of the differences are fairly small. Note that the figures in parentheses are standard deviations, and the column titled "p-value" demonstrates whether the differences between registered and unregistered refugee households are statistically different from one another. The registered sample has a higher fraction of female-headed households (27 percent vs. 22 percent). This difference is found in Lebanon; in Jordan, however, the percentage of female-headed households is similar in registered and unregistered households. Registered households are also larger—on average, 6.5 individuals compared to 4.6 individuals in unregistered households. There is no difference in whether the household head had a skilled occupation in Syria prior to the conflict. Those who are registered are a bit less likely to report that their home in Syria is intact (10 percent compared to 17 percent). This finding may suggest that registered refugees plan to stay in their country of asylum for longer if their home has been affected by the war. This difference, however, is not dramatically large.

Overall, in the sample, monthly food expenditure is the same in registered and unregistered refugee households; however, in Lebanon specifically, registered households report higher food expenditure than unregistered households. This difference could reflect the benefits of the UNHCR assistance received by registered households. These households are also larger, however, so per capita consumption is lower among the registered than the unregistered. Registered households are also slightly more likely (84 percent vs. 78 percent) to be in debt than unregistered households. This difference may reflect higher need, which also motivated them to register with UNHCR. Overall both types of households consume about 2.5–2.6 meals per day. In Jordan, unregistered refugees consume a slightly higher number of meals on average per day (2.48 vs. 2.38).

Table 3A.4. Comparison of Registered and Unregistered Refugees

	All				Jordan				Lebanon			
	Registered	Unregistered	N	p-value	R	NR	N	p-value	R	NR	N	p-value
Female-headed household	0.267 (0.443)	0.218 (0.413)	1,900	0.015	0.257 (0.437)	0.240 (0.428)	950	0.577	0.282 (0.451)	0.204 (0.403)	950	0.005
Household size	5.603 (2.492)	4.604 (2.577)	1,846	0.000	5.689 (2.346)	5.368 (2.334)	949	0.050	5.469 (2.698)	4.126 (2.608)	897	0.000
Skilled occupation in Syrian Arab Republic	0.234 (0.423)	0.227 (0.419)	1,716	0.534	0.273 (0.446)	0.284 (0.452)	803	0.749	0.183 (0.387)	0.198 (0.399)	913	0.575
Condition of Syrian home: Unaffected/intact	0.095 (0.293)	0.166 (0.373)	1,900	0.000	0.082 (0.274)	0.147 (0.354)	950	0.002	0.113 (0.317)	0.178 (0.383)	950	0.005
Monthly household income in country of asylum	299 (224)	332 (265)	1,846	0.148	266 (181)	285 (211)	920	0.167	345 (266)	360 (290)	926	0.417
Monthly food expenditure in country of asylum	213 (123)	212 (118)	1,851	0.303	198 (124)	207 (117)	927	0.310	234 (117)	215 (118)	924	0.016
Monthly rent expenditure in country of asylum	174 (106)	161 (111)	1,851	0.097	181 (80)	170 (77)	940	0.036	162 (135)	156 (128)	911	0.496
Reduced consumption of essentials: Have never done	0.180 (0.384)	0.248 (0.432)	1,900	0.013	0.146 (0.354)	0.180 (0.385)	950	0.183	0.229 (0.421)	0.288 (0.453)	950	0.038
Household currently in debt	0.839 (0.367)	0.784 (0.411)	1,894	0.016	0.858 (0.349)	0.817 (0.388)	950	0.098	0.812 (0.391)	0.765 (0.424)	944	0.081
Average meals per day	2.509 (0.642)	2.595 (0.648)	1,887	0.325	2.382 (0.597)	2.480 (0.620)	950	0.020	2.696 (0.659)	2.665 (0.655)	937	0.474

Note: N = number of observations.

On net, this analysis suggests that certain factors may influence refugees' legal status within their country of asylum. Do these differences affect the inference we can make from the earlier analysis? They are fairly small in magnitude but statistically significant. Although it is impossible to fully answer that question, given we can't undertake the analysis with comparable data that include unregistered refugees, we can analyze the responses to the vignettes by whether the refugees were registered or not. The tables in the next section suggest that the responses of refugees of either status are very similar.

Robustness checks of the linear probability model: logit model

To allow for possible nonlinearities in the underlying distribution of our data, we test the robustness our baseline results by estimating a logit model. As discussed earlier in the chapter, linear probability models with binary regressors yield biased and inconsistent estimates and do not restrict the fitted values to the unit interval; however, they typically yield similar results to a logit or probit model, especially with datasets that have a large sample size and in specifications that include many dummy regressors. We confirm that this is the case in this context, by estimating a logit model for the two Jordan and Lebanon datasets.[21] These results are presented in table 3A.5 with the baseline specification shown in column (1) and the average marginal effects estimates of the logit model shown in column (2) for the dataset using geographical aggregates to measure host country factors.[22] The corresponding columns for the case-level data are columns (3) and (4), respectively. We find that the average marginal effects estimates are largely of similar sign, magnitude, and significance as those of the linear probability model.

Robustness checks of the linear probability model: country of origin fixed effects

To further test the robustness of the baseline results of the linear probability model presented in tables 3.2, 3.3, and 3.4, we control for time-invariant characteristics of the refugee's home location. That is, we include country of origin fixed effects at the subdistrict level in the baseline specification, which will control for all factors that do not vary over time—such as preconflict ethnic composition, cultural factors, or institutional characteristics—but that could determine return behavior.[23] Fixed effects absorbed all time-invariant information, so the variables from the MSNA Syria survey are dropped from the regression because this information is available only for one time period. This analysis is presented for the entire dataset in column (2) and for the Lebanon and Jordan datasets (using geographical aggregates) in column (4) of table 3A.6. For comparison, the baseline results for both datasets are reproduced in columns (1) and (3), respectively. We find that the results are robust to the inclusion of country of origin fixed effects, with the coefficients largely of a similar magnitude, sign, and significance level.

Table 3A.5. The Linear Probability Model with Country of Origin Fixed Effects

Dependent variable: Refugee returned to Syrian Arab Republic (0 = No; 1 = Yes)			Jordan and Lebanon, add host country factors using			
			Geographical aggregates		Case-level information only	
Category	Variables	Omitted variables	Linear probability model	Average marginal effects	Linear probability model	Average marginal effects
			(1)	(2)	(3)	(4)
Demographic and socioeconomic characteristics	Single	Married	0.024*** (0.00060)	0.0081*** (0.00029)	0.024*** (0.0038)	0.012*** (0.0020)
	Widowed	Married	−0.013*** (0.0020)	0.00041 (0.0012)	−0.016 (0.011)	−0.000022 (0.0092)
	Other marital status	Married	−0.0071*** (0.0011)	0.0026*** (0.00035)	−0.012* (0.0066)	−0.00017 (0.0017)
	Age 20–44	Age 0–19	0.034*** (0.00060)	0.020*** (0.00030)	0.035*** (0.0040)	0.018*** (0.0017)
	Age 45–59	Age 0–19	0.054*** (0.00086)	0.026*** (0.00041)	0.049*** (0.0052)	0.026*** (0.0025)
	Age 60+	Age 0–19	0.066*** (0.0014)	0.032*** (0.00050)	0.088*** (0.0093)	0.039*** (0.0030)
	Female	Male	−0.0047*** (0.00024)	−0.0037*** (0.00018)	−0.0046*** (0.0013)	−0.0042*** (0.0011)
	Principal applicant	Case member	−0.042*** (0.00041)	−0.025*** (0.00024)	−0.031*** (0.0022)	−0.024*** (0.0016)
	Extended family	Nuclear family	0.11*** (0.0029)	0.032*** (0.00058)	0.12*** (0.019)	0.027*** (0.0031)
	Immediate family	Nuclear family	0.14*** (0.0024)	0.025*** (0.00036)	0.17*** (0.015)	0.023*** (0.0018)
	Primary education	No education	−0.000068 (0.00034)	0.0014*** (0.00022)	0.0032* (0.0018)	0.0039*** (0.0013)
	Secondary education	No education	−0.014*** (0.00057)	−0.0016*** (0.00032)	0.00019 (0.0033)	0.0036* (0.0020)
	University education	No education	−0.022*** (0.00084)	−0.0031*** (0.00047)	−0.0026 (0.0051)	0.0022 (0.0030)
	Case has children	Case has no children	0.059*** (0.00086)	0.025*** (0.00028)	0.041*** (0.0045)	0.024*** (0.0021)
	Case size		−0.024*** (0.00020)	−0.014*** (0.000093)	−0.012*** (0.0011)	−0.0095*** (0.00064)
	% special need	% no special need	−0.0021*** (0.00030)	−0.0022*** (0.00017)	−0.0044*** (0.0015)	−0.0040*** (0.0011)
Registration information	Enrolled for assistance	Asylum seeker	−0.0043*** (0.00060)	−0.022*** (0.00046)	−0.0059* (0.0030)	−0.011*** (0.0021)
	Refugee	Asylum seeker	0.0012 (0.0013)	−0.0044*** (0.0011)	0.0046 (0.0081)	0.0075 (0.0100)
	Registration lag, months		−0.0014*** (0.000020)	−0.00048*** (0.000022)	−0.00078*** (0.00011)	−0.00053*** (0.00013)

(table continues next page)

235

Table 3A.5. *(continued)*

Dependent variable: Refugee returned to Syrian Arab Republic (0 = No; 1 = Yes)			Jordan and Lebanon, add host country factors using			
			Geographical aggregates		Case-level information only	
Category	Variables	Omitted variables	Linear probability model	Average marginal effects	Linear probability model	Average marginal effects
			(1)	(2)	(3)	(4)
Peace, security, and protection	Dread factor		−0.00078*** (0.0000060)	−0.00035*** (0.0000038)	−0.00045*** (0.000028)	−0.00032*** (0.000020)
	Change in control		0.23*** (0.0068)	0.043*** (0.0017)	0.21*** (0.063)	0.046*** (0.0054)
	Control: Not government of Syria	Control: Government of Syria	0.028*** (0.00057)	0.010*** (0.00023)	0.017*** (0.0026)	0.0093*** (0.0015)
	Security a concern?		−0.0067*** (0.00049)	−0.0012*** (0.00025)	−0.0070*** (0.0023)	−0.0031** (0.0015)
Livelihoods and access to employment	Price of 1 kilogram (kg) of bread (subsidized)		0.000029*** (0.0000028)	0.000011*** (0.0000018)	0.000015 (0.000015)	−0.0000019 (0.000013)
	Price of 1 kg of bread (unsubsidized)		0.000013*** (0.0000025)	0.000016*** (0.0000014)	0.0000072 (0.000012)	0.000023** (0.0000093)
	Malnutrition: Moderate problem	Malnutrition: No problem	0.012*** (0.00049)	0.0049*** (0.00025)	0.0096*** (0.0023)	0.0072*** (0.0016)
	Malnutrition: Serious problem	Malnutrition: No problem	0.025*** (0.00078)	0.0091*** (0.00048)	0.015*** (0.0034)	0.0081*** (0.0030)
	Number of meals per day		0.15*** (0.0020)	0.015*** (0.00056)	0.00016 (0.00060)	−0.00056 (0.00078)
	Food insecurity index		−0.031*** (0.00083)	−0.0053*** (0.00039)	−0.00078 (0.00092)	−0.00081 (0.00063)
Housing, land, and property rights	Case lives in a camp	Case does not live in a camp	0.093*** (0.0016)	0.010*** (0.00032)	0.14*** (0.028)	0.017*** (0.0026)
Infrastructure and services	Basic services a concern?		−0.017*** (0.00057)	−0.0084*** (0.00034)	−0.0095*** (0.0025)	−0.0033* (0.0019)
	Health/education a concern?		−0.010*** (0.00044)	−0.0053*** (0.00028)	−0.010*** (0.0023)	−0.0038** (0.0019)
	Access to basic service index		0.0050*** (0.00087)	0.0097*** (0.00041)	−0.0010 (0.00084)	−0.00038 (0.00068)
Other controls	Ethnicity and religion		Yes	Yes	Yes	Yes
	Constant		Yes	Yes	Yes	Yes
Fixed effects	Arrival year dummies		Yes	Yes	Yes	Yes
	Country of asylum dummies		Yes	Yes	Yes	Yes
	Observations		1,851,135	1,851,135	42,588	42,588

Note: Significance level: * = 10 percent, ** = 5 percent, *** = 1 percent.

Table 3A.6. The Linear Probability Model with Country of Origin Fixed Effects

Category	Variables	Omitted variables	Mashreq (1)	Mashreq (2)	Jordan and Lebanon, add host country factors using geographical aggregates (3)	Jordan and Lebanon, add host country factors using geographical aggregates (4)
Demographic and socioeconomic characteristics	Single	Married	0.027*** (0.00060)	0.024*** (0.00055)	0.024*** (0.00060)	0.021*** (0.00054)
	Widowed	Married	−0.016*** (0.0020)	−0.014*** (0.0019)	−0.013*** (0.0020)	−0.012*** (0.0020)
	Other marital status	Married	−0.013*** (0.0010)	−0.012*** (0.00094)	−0.0071*** (0.0011)	−0.0068*** (0.00096)
	Age 20–44	Age 0–19	0.035*** (0.00059)	0.030*** (0.00054)	0.034*** (0.00060)	0.029*** (0.00054)
	Age 45–59	Age 0–19	0.054*** (0.00085)	0.049*** (0.00078)	0.054*** (0.00086)	0.048*** (0.00077)
	Age 60+	Age 0–19	0.059*** (0.0014)	0.054*** (0.0012)	0.066*** (0.0014)	0.059*** (0.0013)
	Female	Male	−0.0064*** (0.00024)	−0.0047*** (0.00022)	−0.0047*** (0.00024)	−0.0036*** (0.00022)
	Principal applicant	Case member	−0.045*** (0.00043)	−0.040*** (0.00039)	−0.042*** (0.00041)	−0.036*** (0.00036)
	Extended family	Nuclear family	0.12*** (0.0027)	0.11*** (0.0025)	0.11*** (0.0029)	0.098*** (0.0026)
	Immediate family	Nuclear family	0.14*** (0.0022)	0.13*** (0.0020)	0.14*** (0.0024)	0.12*** (0.0021)
	Primary education	No education	0.0029*** (0.00035)	0.0065*** (0.00033)	−0.000068 (0.00034)	0.0036*** (0.00032)
	Secondary education	No education	−0.017*** (0.00057)	−0.0061*** (0.00053)	−0.014*** (0.00057)	−0.0066*** (0.00052)
	University education	No education	−0.025*** (0.00083)	−0.013*** (0.00078)	−0.022*** (0.00084)	−0.013*** (0.00078)
	Case has children	Case has no children	0.062*** (0.00089)	0.055*** (0.00079)	0.059*** (0.00086)	0.051*** (0.00077)
	Case size		−0.030*** (0.00022)	−0.027*** (0.00019)	−0.024*** (0.00020)	−0.021*** (0.00018)
	% special need	% no special need	−0.0021*** (0.00030)	−0.0012*** (0.00028)	−0.0021*** (0.00030)	−0.0014*** (0.00028)
Registration information	Enrolled for assistance	Asylum seeker	−0.0031*** (0.00064)	−0.017*** (0.00070)	−0.0043*** (0.00060)	−0.013*** (0.00069)
	Refugee	Asylum seeker	−0.0029*** (0.0011)	0.0018* (0.0011)	0.0012 (0.0013)	0.0023* (0.0012)
	Registration lag, months		−0.0015*** (0.000020)	−0.00095*** (0.000019)	−0.0014*** (0.000020)	−0.00094*** (0.000020)

(table continues next page)

237

Table 3A.6. *(continued)*

Category	Variable	Omitted variable	Dependent variable: Refugee returned to Syrian Arab Republic (0 = No; 1 = Yes) — Mashreq		Jordan and Lebanon, add host country factors using geographical aggregates	
			(1)	(2)	(3)	(4)
Peace, security, and protection	Dread factor		−0.00082*** (0.0000061)	−0.0030*** (0.000018)	−0.00078*** (0.0000060)	−0.0033*** (0.000021)
	Change in control		0.18*** (0.0033)	0.39*** (0.010)	0.23*** (0.0068)	0.41*** (0.012)
	Control: Not government of Syria	Control: Government of Syria	0.036*** (0.00060)	0.060*** (0.0032)	0.028*** (0.00057)	0.014** (0.0060)
	Security a concern?		−0.0032*** (0.00049)		−0.0067*** (0.00049)	0.0058 (0.0047)
Livelihoods and access to employment	Price of 1 kilogram (kg) of bread (subsidized)		0.000051*** (0.0000028)		0.000029*** (0.0000028)	0.00069*** (0.000080)
	Price of 1 kg of bread (unsubsidized)		0.0000018 (0.0000026)		0.000013*** (0.0000025)	−0.00026*** (0.000031)
	Malnutrition: Moderate problem	Malnutrition: Not a problem	0.015*** (0.00050)		0.012*** (0.00049)	0.025*** (0.0070)
	Malnutrition: Serious problem	Malnutrition: Not a problem	0.032*** (0.00080)		0.025*** (0.00078)	0.033*** (0.0082)
	Number of meals per day				0.15*** (0.0020)	0.12*** (0.0017)
	Food insecurity index				−0.031*** (0.00083)	−0.022*** (0.00081)
Housing, land, and property	Case lives in a camp	Case does not live in a camp	0.056*** (0.0013)	0.052*** (0.0012)	0.093*** (0.0016)	0.085*** (0.0014)
Infrastructure and services	Basic services a concern?		−0.022*** (0.00056)		−0.017*** (0.00057)	0.041*** (0.0064)
	Health/education a concern?		−0.0081*** (0.00047)		−0.010*** (0.00044)	0.016*** (0.0049)
	Access to basic service index				0.0050*** (0.00087)	0.0077*** (0.00083)
Other controls	Ethnicity and religion		yes	yes	yes	yes
	Constant		yes	yes	yes	yes
Fixed effects	Arrival year		yes	yes	yes	yes
	Country of asylum		yes	yes	yes	yes
	Country of origin		no	yes	no	no
	Observations		2,162,865	2,162,865	1,851,135	1,851,135
	R-squared		0.218	0.312	0.245	0.350

Note: Significance level: * = 10 percent, ** = 5 percent, *** = 1 percent.

Notes

1. For information about the ProGres database, see https://undatacatalog.org/dataset/progres.

2. A case is the unit of individuals, often relatives but not necessarily limited to kinship groups, which is headed by the principal applicant through whom the interaction with UNHCR is maintained.

3. The "closed cases" (for example, those refugees who were resettled to third countries but not those who returned) are dropped from the dataset.

4. Note that Turkey is left out of the study altogether because even demographic data for refugees have not been accessible. Iraq is left out of the push and pull factor analysis because survey data on conditions in that country were not accessible at the time of the preparation of this report.

5. The VAF (Jordan) was conducted in 2015 and 2017, and the VASyR (Lebanon) was conducted annually during the 2015–17 period. Variables were selected on the basis of the availability of consistent measures both across countries and over time.

6. For Jordan, data are aggregated to administrative level 1 (governorate); for Lebanon, data are aggregated to administrative level 2 (district).

7. For the purposes of this survey, Syrian refugees with expired registrations were also considered unregistered.

8. In Lebanon, 450 registered and 500 unregistered Syrian refugees were interviewed. In Jordan, 650 registered and 300 unregistered refugees were interviewed.

9. UNHCR stopped registering refugees in 2015 at the request of the government of Lebanon.

10. It is important to note that there are no refugee camps in Lebanon.

11. Because of missing locational information, some observations were dropped.

12. *Nuclear family* includes the spouse and children of the principle applicant; *immediate family* is defined as the parents, siblings, children of siblings, nephews, and nieces of the principle applicant; and *extended family* includes in-laws, grandchildren, grandparents, and other blood and nonblood relatives of the principle applicant. The vast majority of the refugee population is part of a nuclear family (96.5 percent), whereas immediate and extended families make up 2.6 percent and 1.0 percent, respectively. However, return probabilities are much higher for the latter, with 22.1 percent of immediate and 12.6 percent of extended family members returning to Syria as compared to only 3.1 percent of nuclear family members.

13. This study uses the term "refugee" to denote all forcibly displaced Syrians who reside in a country of asylum.

14. Change in control over a given district does not occur often. The mean of the dummy variable is 0.009 with a standard deviation of 0.094.

15. The analysis also includes a security perception variable at the district of origin. The signs of regression coefficients are not consistent across the three datasets being used, which may be explained by the possibility that this indicator is a perception-based indicator that is based on key informant responses, and not consistently measured across different geographical units.

16. This is particularly the case for linear probability models. In logit/probit-based estimations, level-specific variations in the marginal effects of a specific regressor can be observed over its range of support. In those cases, however, the levels of other regressors are fixed at a specific level (often at their mean values), and repeating the analysis for all ranges is not practicable. In contrast, Classification and Regression Trees (CART) allow simultaneous observations of localized marginal effects for multiple variables in a systematic manner.

17. In particular, the coefficients for recent arrivals are remarkably similar in terms of both magnitude and sign to those of the more-tenured refugees for both samples. Because of the significantly smaller sample size of recent arrivals, however, a few coefficients lose significance although the main results remain significant.

18. For the returns where only a subset of case members leaves for Syria, 70 percent of the time only one family member returns, and 15 percent of the time two individuals return.

19. See "Test: Miner, no permit = Miner, with permit," which provides the *p*-value of the test of whether the coefficient on "Miner in Syria now working no permit" is statistically different from the coefficient on "Miner in Syria now working with permit."

20. Please note that enumerators emphasized the fictional nature of this question.

21. The logit model for the entire Mashreq dataset does not converge.

22. Given the large number of dummy regressors, marginal effect at the means is difficult to interpret in this context, which is why we report average marginal effects instead.

23. Because we do not have subdistrict-level information for the refugees, we replace the subdistrict information with district or governorate information before creating the fixed effects.

References

UNHCR (United Nations High Commissioner for Refugees). 2015. "Vulnerability Assessment Framework: Baseline Survey." UNHCR Jordan, Amman. https://data2.unhcr.org/en/documents/download/45570.

———. 2017a. "Jordan Vulnerability Assessment Framework: 2017 Population Survey Report." UNHCR, Geneva. https://data2.unhcr.org/en/documents/download/65404.

———. 2017b. "Multi-Sector Needs Assessment: Syria." UNHCR, Geneva. https://www.humanitarianresponse .info/en/operations/stima/assessment/msna-2017.

UNHCR, UNICEF (United Nations Children's Fund), and WFP (World Food Programme). 2018. "Vulnerability Assessment of Syrian Refugees in Lebanon—VASyR 2018." Geneva: UNHCR. https://data2.unhcr.org/en /documents/download/67380.

CHAPTER 4

Return Simulations

The future mobility of Syrian refugees will likely be different from their past mobility. In many ways, the returns that have happened so far have been undertaken in specific circumstances, that is, during an active conflict, with specific motives like protecting property. Going forward, both the circumstances and motives are likely to change.

Considering these potential changes, the analysis in this chapter develops scenario-based simulations that characterize different degrees of improvement in security and service provision in the Syrian Arab Republic. Given the complexity of these two concepts (for example, security requires more than the sheer absence of violence), the analysis employs indexes that comprise multidimensional descriptions of these conditions, and location-specific scenarios regarding their future evolution.

CHAPTER 4

Return Simulations

The future mobility of Syrian refugees will likely be different from their past mobility. Chapter 3 shows the complexity of return dynamics that have taken place to date. In many ways, returns so far have been undertaken in specific circumstances, for example, during an active conflict, or with specific motives, such as protecting property. Going forward, however, both circumstances and motives are likely to change. The intensity of conflict has begun to decrease in certain areas, and the nature of concerns regarding protection of property is shifting from a simple takeover toward more institutionalized risks, as encapsulated in fears surrounding Law No. 10. Thus, many parties to the conflict and forced displacement may expect future returns to be at a different scale and composition than those realized so far. Although there were no signs of such change at the time of this report's preparation, the analysis in this chapter investigates the plausibility of such expectations by performing a forward-looking exercise.

The analysis of future refugee mobility is, however, complicated by major uncertainties surrounding key drivers of mobility in the future. Although a significant reduction in hostilities is expected in the coming years for the first time since the onset of the conflict, a "positive peace" in which all constituents feel safe is absent. The possibility of some fighting and large-scale displacement in and around Idleb, and in the Northeast, cannot be dismissed. In addition, important dimensions of safety, other than sheer absence of violence, are yet to be fulfilled. There are widespread social tensions, including ethno-sectarian aspects, retribution against communities that have allegedly sided with another fighting camp, and institutional punitive practices like appropriation of assets, arrest, military conscription, and predatory practices involving the use of unreasonable civil documentation requirements. Similarly, much uncertainty exists regarding living standards going forward. With largely degraded administrative and financial capacity, it is unclear at what speed the provision of services like electricity, water, roads, education, and health will recover. Together, these factors provide a highly unpredictable path for quality of life in Syria in the future.

This chapter develops a scenario-based approach to analyzing the future mobility of Syrian refugees by using a simulation model. To complement the inferences based on international and Syrian experiences so far, and to perform policy analyses based on various realizations of outcomes that are not captured in data, the analysis builds on the model developed for *The Toll of War: The Economic and Social*

Consequences of the Conflict in Syria (World Bank 2017), with amendments that are required to capture the specific issues regarding refugee mobility. These issues include attachment to the home location and valuation of conflict and amenities. The underlying features of the simulation model are discussed below, and more technical descriptions of the model and its calibration are provided in annex 4A.

It is important to emphasize that this report focuses solely on refugees' own rational choices; other options such as forced repatriation are renounced and not analyzed. Refugees are not people who are "out of place and to be returned." They have the full biological and cognitive facilities to assess their options, and they act rationally given their resources and constraints. Other parties, including the international community, host country governments, and the government of the source country, can influence those resources and constraints; but they can neither prevent refugees from reassessing the situation nor prevent them from acting accordingly. In technical terms, it is the refugee who undertakes the optimization decision, not the other parties. Therefore, to estimate the potential impact of a policy action, it is necessary to understand how the refugees would react to the proposed changes. These reactions are discussed in subsequent sections.

Taking Uncertainty into Consideration

A bottom-up scenario-based approach was developed to study the responsiveness of refugee movements to shifting conditions in Syria. To avoid making strong, top-down assumptions regarding the complex and unpredictable political economy dynamics surrounding the Syrian conflict, the analysis described here pursues a pragmatic micro-approach. This involves building scenarios for two prominent pull factors: security and infrastructure. To do so, eight underlying conditions are analyzed for every governorate in Syria (14 overall): political influence/control, administrative capacity, social tensions, reconstruction priority, rule of law, legal/procedural complexity of return, financial capacity, and the region's connectivity with other regions. By using observations and expert assessments regarding these conditions, three possible future paths for security and infrastructure are generated for each governorate.

Figure 4.1 shows these three paths for security and infrastructure separately. In panel a, an insecurity index is developed. The historical series are based on actual conflict events across governorates, which are then extrapolated in three different trajectories by using a subset of the eight underlying conditions for each of the 14 governorates. In the figure, the future scenarios are represented by different colors (lines show governorate averages). Both historical and forward-looking elements are normalized by using the average conflict event numbers across governorates between 2012 and 2017. Panel b shows the distributions of an infrastructure index across governorates for the preconflict level, the current (early 2018) level, and the level five years out—with three possible outcomes for the latter. Index values show the status of infrastructure assets by using education and health sector assets as proxies, which are normalized by preconflict averages across Syria. Overall, the security and infrastructure dimensions are characterized by the following three forward-looking paths:

1. ***Baseline environment***: This case presents a "business as usual" situation where conflict dynamics follow the most recent trends and security conditions improve gradually in most areas; however, social tensions largely prevail. Similarly,

Figure 4.1. Security and Infrastructure Scenarios

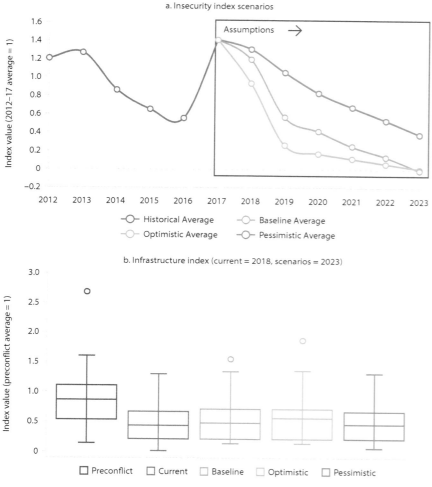

a. Insecurity index scenarios

Legend:
—O— Historical Average —O— Baseline Average
—O— Optimistic Average —O— Pessimistic Average

b. Infrastructure index (current = 2018, scenarios = 2023)

☐ Preconflict ☐ Current ☐ Baseline ☐ Optimistic ☐ Pessimistic

Note: In panel a, each data point in a given year shows the index value for a specific governorate. Historical series are single valued, and projections provide three values for each governorate (baseline, optimistic, and pessimistic). Index values are normalized with 2012–17 averages of all governorates. In panel b, each box-whisker plot shows the distribution of facility numbers across Syrian governorates. Index values are normalized with preconflict averages across governorates. Boxes show the positions of governorates between Q1 and Q3, and the parallel lines within boxes show median values. The whiskers include observations within 1.5 times the interquartile range (IQR) distance from the box (Q1 − 1.5 × IQR, Q3 + 1.5 × IQR). Dots are outliers from this range.

damaged infrastructure is gradually rebuilt in key strategic areas; however, these efforts are handicapped by financial and administrative capacity constraints. In aggregate terms, the insecurity index decreases from 1.40 in 2017 to 0.15 in 2023. In the meantime, 16 percent of the currently damaged infrastructure is rebuilt or fixed in the entire country, but the reconstruction ratio varies from 3 percent to 32 percent in different areas.

2. **Optimistic environment**: In comparison to the baseline scenario, this one presents a more rapid deescalation from conflict and faster easing of social tensions

across the country. With access to additional finance and technical assistance, the country undertakes a greater effort to reconstruct damaged infrastructure and restore publicly provided goods and services. Overall, the insecurity index decreases from 1.40 to 0.07 between 2017 and 2023, and about 30 percent of the currently damaged infrastructure is rebuilt or fixed during the same period. With greater capacity of rebuilding, the reconstruction ratio is more divergent across different locations than the baseline: 5 percent in the lowest case and 48 percent in the highest.

3. ***Pessimistic environment***: This scenario considers the slowest gradual deescalation of conflict across the country, which in turn fuels further social conflict and grievances. Protracted tensions will limit financial and administrative capacity that can be spared for rehabilitation projects more than the other scenarios. The insecurity index decreases from 1.40 in 2017 to 0.54 in 2023. The average reconstruction ratio remains at 5 percent of the current damage across the country, with significant disparities between the highest reconstruction at 14 percent and the lowest at 2 percent.

It is important to note that *these environments do not project future events*; they are merely assumptions that allow the study of the mobility of refugees under different conditions. It is impossible to make predictions about security or reconstruction in an active conflict situation. Thus, the environments developed here are not predictions of future events. They only provide benchmarks to study the mobility responses of refugees, and the analysis is agnostic about the likelihood of such outcomes. Overall, the suggested interpretation of these scenarios is as follows: if conditions specified by a scenario hold, then the corresponding results generated by the analysis are to be expected; however, it is not possible to assess if those conditions will hold or not.

A Simulation Approach to Analyzing Mobility

The analysis in this section uses a dynamic mobility model with perfect foresight to study the potential reactions of Syrian refugees to changes in security and service restoration. As in the model used in *The Toll of War: The Economic and Social Consequences of the Conflict in Syria* (World Bank 2017), at the core of the simulation model lie rational agents who compare alternative locations to choose a mobility/immobility path that maximizes their expected lifetime welfare (figure 4.2). For instance, other things being equal, higher wages in a certain location can attract people from other locations. Unlike the previous model, in this case the model features "attachments" to the home country, which have some intrinsic components for which an explanation is not attempted (for example, subjective feelings for the home country). Two components of these attachments are estimated: insecurity (decreases attachment) and amenities like publicly provided services (increase attachment). Overall, it is more likely that agents will move to a location from other locations if the wages are higher and it is more secure and more amenities are available. The simulations here, therefore, build on these two dimensions. Box 4.1 provides more details about the modeling framework, and annex 4A presents the technical details like calibration.

To account for heterogeneity among refugees, the analysis considers two types of refugees. Previous chapters discussed the characteristics of refugees that

Figure 4.2. Structure of the Simulation Model

a. Before conflict

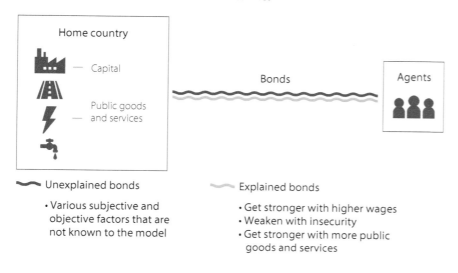

Unexplained bonds

- Various subjective and objective factors that are not known to the model

Explained bonds

- Get stronger with higher wages
- Weaken with insecurity
- Get stronger with more public goods and services

b. Conflict

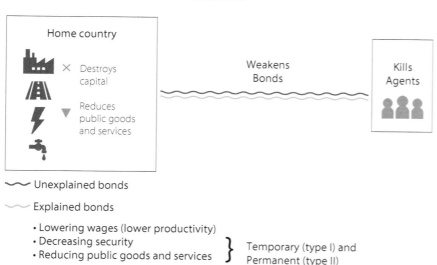

Unexplained bonds

Explained bonds

- Lowering wages (lower productivity)
- Decreasing security
- Reducing public goods and services

} Temporary (type I) and Permanent (type II)

generate a vast degree of heterogeneity among refugee populations: gender, age, occupation, family structure, location of origin, location of refuge, income/wealth status, refugee registration status, ethnicity, religious orientation, political orientation, military service status, and so forth—all of which differ across refugees; thus, thousands of different factors could be used to classify individuals. Because it is not possible to take these numerous dimensions of information into account in simulations, these simulations consider two types of refugees: Type I and Type II, who differ primarily by their history. More specifically, Type II refugees would suffer

BOX 4.1.

Simulation Model

The simulation model builds on *The Toll of War: The Economic and Social Consequences of the Conflict in Syria* (World Bank 2017) and extends it in various aspects, including the characterization of conflict and migration both within and outside the Syrian Arab Republic. The model comprises 14 regions (governorates) within Syria, neighbor countries (Iraq, Jordan, Lebanon, and Turkey), and the rest of the world to account for out-migration. Agents decide to live and work in a region on the basis of wages and amenities provided in the region, including safety, and the cost of moving between regions. Agents take their expectations about the future into account and compare options in all regions as well as countries before deciding to move or stay. Because of an individual-specific random utility component, similar agents can make different decisions. The model takes into account projections of security, amenities, reconstruction of capital, possible subsidies and transfers, and other relevant measures prepared by experts and forecasts the decisions of current and potential refugees.

Wages: Agents take wages into account, in addition to other factors such as safety, when deciding to move or stay. Wages are affected by the number of agents in a region. As the number of workers declines, and labor becomes scarcer, the marginal product of labor increases because it is the standard in most economic models. Destruction of capital, however, reduces the availability of fixed production factors and factor productivity, so wages can decline endogenously as conflict intensifies even if the supply of labor declines at the same time.

Amenities: Agents' instantaneous utility includes a component for amenities in addition to wages. Amenities account for nonpecuniary factors that influence agents' decisions and can be potentially more important than wages. Amenities have two main components: (a) perception of safety and (b) provision of public goods.

Safety: The perceived safety is a function of casualties in a given region. We assume that there are two types of agents. For Type I agents, the perceived safety is a function of current casualties only. For Type II agents, the perceived safety is a function of both current and past casualties. More specifically, Type I refugees are more likely to return after safety improves compared to Type II refugees, because they are not influenced by past casualty levels.

Public goods: The provision of public goods such as education, health care, road infrastructure, public transportation, social security, water and electricity distribution, and other factors can affect refugee return and migration decisions. Provision of public goods, hence amenities, declines with conflict and increases with reconstruction.

(box continues next page)

BOX 4.1. *(continued)*

Other factors that affect mobility: The agents pay a moving cost if they decide to move. The moving cost is larger if an agent decides to move outside Syria. Agents are rational and form expectations about the future. Agents are not myopic; therefore, they take the future stream of wages and amenities into account after discounting them.

Policy interventions: Policy makers can influence agents' decisions by reducing conflict, improving safety, providing public goods, reducing moving costs through subsidies, or giving unconditional transfers to people in Syria. At that point, agents' decisions join with policy interventions to determine the number of refugees and their welfare in Syria. Because the policy maker must operate within a constrained budget, it is useful to analyze implications of different policy scenarios for welfare and refugee return.

from a permanent welfare effect from their exposure to conflict once they return to Syria, but Type I refugees do not. In other words, Type II refugees' current welfare is affected by their history of conflict and service destruction in their hometown. This effect can be interpreted as a permanent psychological trauma or political affiliation that will keep reducing their life quality if they return. Type I refugees consider only current conditions and do not suffer from such persistent effects. Although this structure is far from representing the complexity in sufficient detail, it helps us to analyze how each factor may influence the return decision in isolation.

Unless otherwise noted, Syrian borders are assumed to be closed inside out. Considering the current conditions on the ground, where all movements of Syrians to neighboring countries are highly restricted, the main simulations in this chapter assume that Syrians within Syria, including returnees, are not able to emigrate. This condition is also known by refugees outside of Syria in advance, that is, if they decide to return, they do it despite knowing that they will be unable to move out even if they want to in the future. Additional simulations show how results would differ if such border closures were not implemented.

The Role of Security and Service Restoration

Simulations show that improvements in security conditions and services are key drivers of return. Figure 4.3 shows the simulation results in comparison to the baseline environment, that is, how return would change from its trajectory under the baseline environment if security and service restoration took either the optimistic path or the pessimistic one instead of the baseline path. Thus, if the insecurity index is reduced from 1.40 now to 0.07 (optimistic environment) in five years, instead of 0.15 (baseline environment), and if 30 percent of the infrastructure is rebuilt (optimistic environment) instead of 16 percent (baseline environment), then returns would be 4.9 percent higher than in the baseline environment in the same time frame. In contrast, if the insecurity index decreases to only 0.54 and only 5 percent of the infrastructure is rebuilt, as in the case of the pessimistic environment, then the returns would be about 9.8 percent less than the baseline.

Service restoration is more effective in mobilizing refugees when security is less of an issue. To better understand the distinct roles played by improving security conditions and service restoration, these effects are introduced separately. This is done by first introducing different security paths as specified in the baseline, optimistic, and pessimistic environments, and then adding the service restoration in the second step. Figure 4.4 shows the results by using the baseline outcomes as benchmark. When only security improvements are considered, the optimistic path features 1.9 percent more returns than the baseline environments in five years. This ratio more than doubles to reach 4.9 percent when service restorations are involved (second blue group in the figure). In comparison, the gap between "security only" and "security + service restoration" cases is smaller when the pessimistic

Figure 4.3. Returns under Optimistic and Pessimistic Environments

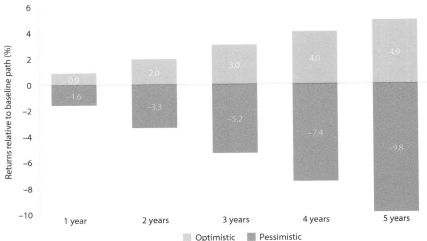

Source: Original World Bank staff calculations for this publication.

Figure 4.4. The Effect of Service Restoration on Returns

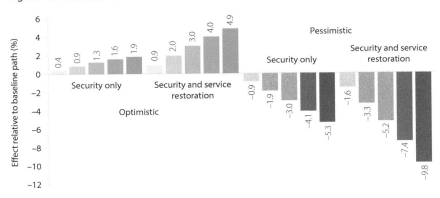

Source: Original World Bank staff calculations for this publication.

Figure 4.5. Return, by Types of Refugees

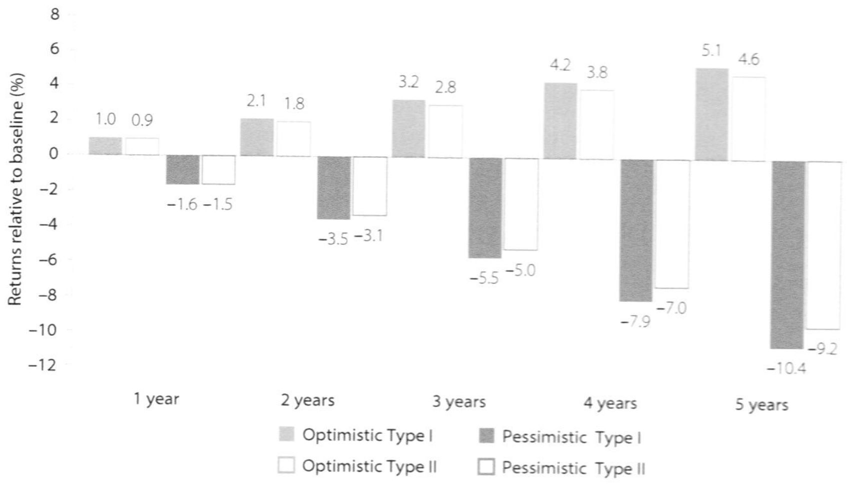

Source: Original World Bank staff calculations for this publication.

scenario is compared with the baseline scenario. The pessimistic insecurity path, by itself, reduced returns by 5.3 percent as compared to the baseline path. When differences between service restoration rates are also accounted for, this gap widens to 9.8 percent, nearly double. Another way to evaluate this is to analyze how much additional returns can be generated by service restoration in different security conditions. In this case, service restoration by itself increases returns by 26 percent in the pessimistic scenario. This effect increases to 48 percent and 62 percent in the baseline and optimistic scenarios, respectively. Some of these differences are driven by the fact that there is simply more restoration as scenarios get better. There are diminishing marginal effects of service restoration within a given scenario, for example, the first kilometer of road, water well, or hour of electricity is more effective than the second one, and the second one more than the third one, and so on; however, the effect of the first service restoration unit in a good security environment is greater than the effect of the first unit in a bad security environment. The same goes for the second unit, third unit, and so on.

Type II refugees (those with higher costs) are both less mobile than Type I refugees within each scenario and less responsive to shifts across scenarios. Type II refugees are about 4 percent less likely to return than Type I refugees in the baseline, 5.3 percent in the optimistic environment, and 2.3 percent in the pessimistic environment over the five-year period covered here. The differences between these lags across scenarios are also visible in figure 4.5. The return "lead" of optimistic scenario over baseline is more pronounced for Type I refugees. Similarly, the "lag" of pessimistic scenario is also more pronounced for Type I refugees. Thus, Type-II refugees are not only less likely to return in a given environment but also less likely to respond to changes in environment.

The Role of Resource Allocation

To further investigate the mobility responses of refugees, the analysis considers alternative resource allocation scenarios. As refugees' mobility decisions may also be influenced by other policy-driven conditions, this study analyzes relative effectiveness of alternative uses of financial resources. More specifically, for each of the three environments specified above (baseline, optimistic, and pessimistic), the study investigates if certain ways to allocate resources other than service restoration may be more conducive to return. To this end, the following options are used:

- *Transfers*: In each environment, the estimated environment-specific cost of service restoration is distributed equally on a per capita basis within Syria, in the form of cash transfers, including to the returnees. This distribution continues for five years until the money is depleted; no service restoration is performed.

- *Subsidies*: In each environment, the estimated environment-specific cost of service restoration is used to subsidize the return of refugees to Syria, in the form of reductions in mobility costs and cash transfers to the returnees. Because the Syrians inside Syria are not subsidized, the returned receive a larger transfer in this case. This distribution continues for five years until the money is depleted; no service restoration is performed.

Results show that, on average, mobility subsidies are the most effective in mobilizing refugees, but the least desirable from a welfare perspective. Table 4.1 shows that returns under the subsidy scheme can exceed those under the service restoration scheme by about 29 percent, 45 percent, and 60 percent for pessimistic, baseline, and optimistic environments, respectively. Intuitively, for refugees, subsidies provide a more direct, exclusive, and thus larger benefit associated

Table 4.1. Returns and Welfare under Transfer or Subsidy Schemes, as Compared to Service Restoration (Percent, Cumulative)

Returns and welfare (% deviation from service restoration case)						
		RETURN				
		1 year	2 years	3 years	4 years	5 years
Baseline environment	Transfers	−0.1	−0.7	−1.6	−2.9	−4.8
	Subsidies	9.1	17.9	26.6	35.5	45.0
Optimistic environment	Transfers	0.7	0.4	−0.7	−2.6	−5.2
	Subsidies	14.0	26.6	38.3	49.3	60.3
Pessimistic environment	Transfers	−0.1	−0.4	−0.7	−1.1	−1.7
	Subsidies	5.6	11.1	16.6	22.5	28.8
		WELFARE				
		1 year	2 years	3 years	4 years	5 years
Baseline environment	Transfers	−4.1	−4.6	−5.1	−5.6	−6.2
	Subsidies	−6.9	−7.1	−7.4	−7.6	−7.8
Optimistic environment	Transfers	−4.0	−4.8	−5.7	−6.5	−7.4
	Subsidies	−8.6	−9.0	−9.2	−9.5	−9.7
Pessimistic environment	Transfers	−2.5	−2.7	−3.0	−3.2	−3.5
	Subsidies	−4.0	−4.1	−4.2	−4.4	−4.5

with returns. In comparison, the benefits of service restoration are shared by all Syrians and, thus, diluted from the refugee's perspective. The difference between the two schemes is the most prominent in the optimistic environment, where a larger financial resource is either shared among returnees (subsidies) or diluted by means of service restoration. The downside of the subsidy allocation is low welfare achievement within Syria. With no service restoration or reconstruction of capital stock, and a greater return of refugees, the average Syrian is worse off by about 10 percent in the optimistic environment, and by 4.5 percent and 7.8 percent in the pessimistic and the baseline environments, respectively, in five years.

Transfers, by themselves, are less effective than subsidies and service restoration in mobilizing refugees; they are also inferior in terms of welfare. Transfer schemes, where the financial resources that would otherwise be used for service restoration are distributed in equal installments for everybody in Syria over five years, generate less mobilization than the other schemes. By the end of five years, returns under transfers are 4.8 percent, 5.2 percent, and 1.7 percent less than those under service restoration for the baseline, optimistic, and pessimistic environments, respectively. This result is interesting because it shows that, although refugees may be tempted by the prospect of a small transfer, once they are back such transfers do not present a durable solution over the long term, compared to service restoration. This issue is most clearly seen in the optimistic scenario, where in the first few years, returns under the transfer scheme are marginally higher (0.7 percent in the first year and 0.4 percent in the second year) than those under the service restoration case. This effect does not last long, and by the fifth year returns under the service restoration scheme dominate the one under transfers by more than 5 percent. In welfare terms, transfers provide a slightly better outcome in Syria than mobility subsidies because a larger group of individuals benefits from transfers, and fewer refugee returns work in favor of wages in this case. Welfare outcomes under service restoration dominate both transfers and subsidies in all environments.

These results could be magnified as more details are considered. The simulation results presented here are partially driven by certain modeling assumptions that make this computationally heavy exercise possible; however, researchers here believe that the qualitative results would prevail, and the quantitative effects would be magnified in certain cases and weakened in others as further details are considered. For example, one implication of the money-metric utility specification is that cash receipts (that is, wages, transfers, and subsidies) are substitutes for publicly provided services (such as electricity and roads). A more realistic assumption would consider more ordered structure of preferences (that is, a minimum level of services is needed before income can be useful). Introducing such an assumption would reinforce the welfare comparisons between service restoration, transfer, and subsidy schemes, but weaken the superiority of subsidies in mobilizing refugees.

The Role of Border Policies

Border policies have two opposite effects in these simulations: more Syrians move out when borders are open, but at the same time more displaced Syrians move in. In all environments (baseline, optimistic, and pessimistic) the living standards in Syria continue to be below standards in host countries. Although insecurity diminishes gradually over time, and services are restored to different extents across governorates, Syria continues to be largely insecure and service-deprived in comparison to other economies. On the one hand, these conditions translate into further displacement when allowed by border policies. Some Syrians move to safer areas that have better service access. On the other hand, the ability to move out again gives better incentives for already displaced Syrians to return. This result is obviously more relevant when the future paths of security and service provision suffer from large uncertainties, but it would still hold, albeit to a smaller degree, even in the absence of such aggregate uncertainty. This follows from the fact that, even if there is no aggregate uncertainty, there are still individual-level uncertainties, so rational agents prefer the ability to move if warranted.

Simulations show that the difference open borders can make is more pronounced in negative environments, both for outflows and inflows. Figure 4.6 shows that in the pessimistic path about 1.8 percent more Type II refugees would return to Syria over five years in net terms if borders were open. In comparison, the differences are at 0.9 percent in the baseline environment and 0.7 percent in the optimistic environment. These returns are, however, in parallel with greater outflows of Syrians: compared to the closed border case, the net outflow of Type I refugees would be at 34.5 percent, 14.4 percent, and 9.9 percent in pessimistic, baseline, and optimistic environments, respectively. Note that, in the beginning of the simulations (year 0), the simulations assume that all Type II refugees are in exile (half of the refugee population) and all Syrians in Syria are Type I. Thus, the movement of Type II refugees can also be used as a proxy for gross returns of Type I, albeit in an imperfect manner as previous analysis showed that the mobility of Type II refugees is less elastic than that of Type I refugees.

Figure 4.6. The Effect of Border Opening on Returns, by Environment

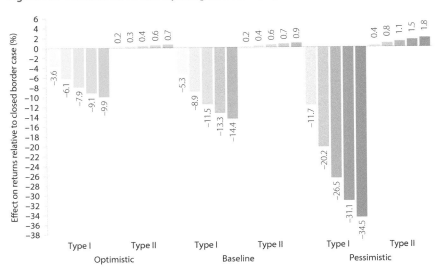

Concluding Remarks

Despite daunting challenges, the analysis in this chapter attempted to study possible mobility patterns of Syrian refugees in the medium term. Previous chapters in this report showed that the returns of Syrian refugees to date have been limited and specific in nature, reflecting transitory coping strategies rather than durable solutions. Thus, they have limited implications for understanding large-scale returns that may happen when the conditions are right. The analysis in this chapter produced conjectures regarding the transition from a limited and selective mobility pattern to broader mobility dynamics, depending on different degrees of improvement in security and service provision in Syria. Given the complexity of these two concepts (for example, security requires more than the sheer absence of violence), the analysis employed index values that comprise multidimensional descriptions of these conditions, and location-specific scenarios regarding their future evolution. Overall, given the high degrees of complexity and uncertainty surrounding mobility of refugees, no analysis can claim precision and completeness; nevertheless, the methodology developed in this chapter enables conjecture on dynamics of refugee mobility depending on assumptions in a systematic and transparent manner.

The analysis showed that, for service restoration in Syria to be effective in mobilizing refugees, it needs to be accompanied by improving security conditions. In addition to simulating refugee returns under overall baseline, optimistic, and pessimistic conditions, the analysis in this chapter also introduced improvements in security and service access separately under these conditions to better understand the distinct roles played by these factors. Results showed that service restoration acts like a greater multiplier for returns in better security conditions. For instance, service restoration by itself increases returns by 26 percent in the pessimistic scenario. This effect increases to 48 percent and 62 percent in the baseline and optimistic scenarios, respectively. Thus, the difference-making potential of service sector restoration goes together with improvements in security. This result supports the observations from chapters 2 and 3, which showed that security is the most important driver of return (both in refugees' perceptions and their revealed preferences as observed from the actual returns that have taken place).

Results also show that using limited resources for trying to maximize the return of Syrian refugees is inefficient from a welfare perspective for Syrians. Some returns are welfare improving; they take place spontaneously, and assistance for such returns can also be welfare improving. There is a trade-off, however, after a certain level. To study this trade-off, the analysis considered three extreme cases: in each of the security conditions (baseline, optimistic, and pessimistic), money can be used (a) to restore services, (b) to transfer cash to all Syrians, or (c) to subsidize the return of refugees. Simulations show that, on average, mobility subsidies are the most effective in mobilizing refugees, but the least desirable from a welfare perspective. In comparison, the benefits of service restoration are shared by all Syrians and, thus, diluted from refugees' perspective. The difference between the two schemes is the most prominent in the optimistic environment, where a larger financial source is either shared among returnees (subsidies) or diluted by means of service restoration. The downside of the subsidy allocation is low welfare achievement for Syrians in Syria.

Annex 4A

Key features of the model

Regions and mobility:

- In the model, there are 14 regions within Syria and 5 regions outside Syria. The regions are Syrian governorates, plus Iraq, Jordan, Lebanon, Turkey, and the rest of the world.

- The agents choose a region to live and work in every period. If they choose to move, they face a moving cost. The moving cost parameter has a fixed and a random component.

- Workers' instantaneous utilities include wages determined by market conditions and a subjective nonpecuniary term capturing the security conditions and available amenities.

- We consider two agent types: Type I and Type II. The agent type determines how each agent is affected by conflict; otherwise all agents within the same region are identical.

- We abstract away from education, gender, age, and other agent characteristics for computational simplicity.

Amenities:

- We assume that agents have a nonpecuniary component in their utility. The region-specific nonpecuniary utility component is a function of conflict events (casualty) and provision of public goods.

- Type I agents care only about the current levels of casualty and public goods.

- Type II agents will be affected by the historical levels of casualty and public goods.

- Note that both Type I and Type II agents are rational, but only Type II agents have a disutility based on experience (for example, trauma, social tensions, political exclusion, and so on).

Capital and productivity:

- We assume that the potential capital levels are fixed in each region. The capital levels are calibrated to match the destroyed infrastructure.

- We allow the total factor productivity to recover either with decreasing conflict events or as the infrastructure is rebuilt.

Introduction of notation

Subscripts and superscripts:

- i: Region superscript, $i = 1, 2, \ldots, N + M$

- N: Number of regions in Syria

- M: Number of regions outside Syria, that is Iraq, Jordan, Lebanon, Turkey, and the rest of the world.

- s: Agent type, or $s = 1$ or $s = 2$
- t: Time subscript
- τ: Time subscript to indicate the most intensive conflict period

Parameters:

- α: Cobb-Douglas production function labor share parameter
- v: Regional moving cost shock (") scale parameter
- β: Intertemporal discount factor
- δ: Conflict discount factor for type II workers
- γ_0, γ_1, and γ_2: Parameters in the amenity function
- C^{ij}: Moving cost friction from region i to region j
- C_1: Moving cost friction for internal migrants (part of C^{ij})
- C_2: Moving cost friction for international migrants (part of C^{ij}).

Exogenous variables:

- A_t^i: Total factor productivity in region i
- K_t^i: Amount of intact capital
- d_t^i: Casualty per capita
- q_t^i: Provision of public goods (schools, hospitals, and so on)

Endogenous variables:

- y_t^i : Output in region i
- $L_{s,t}^i$: Number of type s workers in region i
- L_t^i : Total number of workers in region i
- w_t^i : Real wage of workers in region i
- $\eta_{s,t}^i$: Nonpecuniary utility of type s agents in region i
- $u_{s,t}^i$: Instantaneous utility of type s agents in region i
- $U_{s,t}^i$: Present discounted utility of type s agents in region i
- $V_{s,t}^i$: Expected discounted utility of type s agents in region i
- $m_{s,t}^{i,j}$: Probability of moving from region to region for a type worker.

Random shocks:

- ε_t^i: Regional moving cost shock (Gumbel with scale v). These shocks are individual. Specific and independent and identically distributed random with no memory.

The model

Assume that there are $N + M$ regions. We assume first that N regions are inside Syria and regions from $N + 1$ to $N + M$ to are outside Syria. Agents choose a region in

257

every time period on the basis of current wages, public goods, security, and expectations about the future. We will assume that wages in Syria are a function of capital and labor. The amenities in Syria will be a function of public goods and security. The capital and total factor productivity will be determined by the undamaged infrastructure. The wages and amenities outside Syria will be constant. The agents are rational, and they form expectations about the future.

Production and wages:

The output in region i is equal to

$$y_t^i = A_t^i \left(L_t^i \right)^\alpha \left(K_t^i \right)^{1-\alpha},$$

where $L_{a,t}^i$ is the number of active workers, $K_{a,t}^i$ is the amount of active capital, and A_t^i is the productivity parameter. Then the wage equation is

$$w_t^i = \alpha A_t^i \left(L_t^i \right)^{\alpha-1} \left(K_t^i \right)^{1-\alpha}.$$

We assume that A_t^i is proportional to the intact (undamaged) infrastructure in region i, but otherwise fixed. We take K_t^i as exogenous and do not model investment or depreciation.

Amenities:

We assume that amenity level in region i, expressed as η_t^i, is a function of safety (that is, casualty) and public good provision. We assume that the current level of safety and public good provision, as well as the history, matters for the amenity levels. More precisely, we will consider two agent types: Type I agents, indexed as $s = 1$, will consider only the current security and public good levels, whereas Type II, indexed as $s = 2$, will take a weighted average of current and historical security and public good levels. The piecewise amenity function is

$$\eta_{s,t}^i = \begin{cases} \gamma_0 + \gamma_1 d_t^i + \gamma_2 q_t^i & \text{for } s = 1 \\ \gamma_0 + \gamma_1 \left(d_t^i + [1-\delta] d_\tau^i \right) + \gamma_2 \left(\delta q_\tau^i + [1-\delta] q_\tau^i \right) & \text{for } s = 2 \end{cases},$$

where d_t^i is the deaths per capita and q_t^i is a measure of public good provision. The time index t denotes the period with highest number of casualties, and is the current period.

Note that the history term in agents' utility function does not mean that some agents are irrational or myopic. Some agents have region-specific disutility associated with past conflict and casualty.

Agents:

The number of type s agents in region i is denoted as $L_{s,t}^i$. The total number of workers is equal to

$$L_t^i = \sum_s L_{s,t}^i.$$

The instantaneous utility of a worker is equal to

$$u_{s,t}^i = w_t^i + \eta_{s,t}^i.$$

In each period, workers decide to move to another region or to stay. After the decision the agent faces a moving cost $C^{i,j} + \varepsilon_t^j$, *where* $C^{i,j}$ is the fixed component and ε_t^j is the random component. We assume the following structure for C:

$$C^{i,j} = \begin{cases} 0, & i = j \\ c_1, & (i \neq j) \wedge (i \leq N) \wedge (j \leq N), \\ c_2, & (i \neq j) \wedge (i > N) \vee (j > N) \end{cases}$$

where $c_1 > c_2$. In other words, agents migrating within Syria face a lower moving cost compared to international migrants:

$$L_{s,t}^i = \sum_i \left(m_{s,t-1}^{ij} L_{s,t-1}^i \right),$$

where $m_{s,t-1}^{ij}$ is the proportion of agents moving from i to j. The value of an agent is equal to

$$U_{s,t}^i = w_t^i + \eta_{s,t}^i + E_{t,\varepsilon} \max_j \left(\beta U_{s,t+1}^i - C^{i,j} - \varepsilon_t^i \right),$$

where $U_{s,t}^i$ is the present discounted utility, and β is the intertemporal discount factor. If we define and assume that $V_{s,t} = E_\varepsilon U_{s,t}^i$ is distributed Gumbel with scale parameter v, then the expected value function becomes

$$V_{s,t} = w_t^i + \eta_{s,t}^i + \beta E_t V_{s,t+1}^i - v \log m_{s,t}^{i,i}.$$

The probability of moving for inactive workers is defined as

$$m_{s,t}^{i,j} = \frac{\beta E_t V_{s,t+1}^j - C^{i,j}}{\sum_k \left(\beta E V_{s,t+1}^k - C^{i,k} \right)}$$

Data

We use different time series from the Syrian Central Bureau of Statistics (CBS) for the period 2010 to 2016. This data source provides information on the population, number of workers, and wages inside Syria before and during the crisis. Household expenditure data from the CBS and informal wage estimates from the World Food Programme are also used to complement our dataset of salaries across governorates. Data regarding labor allocations and wages in host countries have been taken from the United Nations High Commissioner for Refugees and the International Labour Organization.

Data on the number of casualties and the public goods provision come from The Syrian Martyrs Revolution Database, and the CBS. The former collects data on the number of people killed as result of the conflict, and the latter presents estimates of the number of public goods before the crisis, such as the number of health care facilities, housing, schools, and so on, for the period 2002 to 2010.

Solution algorithm

The solution algorithm relies on the existence of a fixed point and has two components: (a) solution of the initial steady state and (b) solution of the transition.

Also, we need to calibrate unknown parameters of the model that cannot be taken as given. We use different moments from the observed data to do that.

Initial steady state:

Guess the value $V_{s,1}^i$ and labor allocation $L_{s,0}^i$ arrays. Consider the parameters of the model as given:

- Calculate wages given $L_{s,0}^i$ and $K_{s,0}^i$ using the wage equation derived from the production function $V_{s,1}^i$.

- Calculate probability of industry change given $V_{s,1}^i$

- Calculate location moving probabilities.

- Calculate new implied value $V_{s,1}^i$.

- Calculate implied labor allocations given the guessed labor allocation and moving probabilities.

- Continue until the guessed values and labor allocation ($V_{s,1}^i$ and $L_{s,0}^i$) are equal to the implied values and labor allocations.

- Because the value functions of agents are concave, a fixed point exists and the solution is unique once the implied and guessed values are equal to each other.

Transition:

This procedure is like the steady state solution. Rather than guessing a value for a single time, we need to guess the entire time series. We do not need to guess labor allocations for periods after $t = 0$; we only need to observe the initial ones. More details are presented in Artuç, Chaudhuri, and McLaren (2008).

Calibration strategy:

There is no available information for some parameters in the model, $\eta_{s,t}^i, C_1,$ and C_2. To obtain estimations on those parameters, we take the discount factor, the scale parameter, and the labor share in the production function as given, and calibrate moving costs and amenities matching observed data and model simulation results for labor allocations and mobility patterns inside Syria—that is average outflows between governorates, and average outflows from governorates to host countries, with the same moments obtained in the simulations.

Calibration results

Parameters for the extreme value distribution v, the discount factor β, the labor share α, and the pessimistic discount factor τ:

$v = 100$

$\beta = 0.95$

$\alpha = 0.70$

$\tau = 0.90$ (it means only 10 percent discount)

Moments:

Average outflows between governorates = 2.0 percent

Average outflows from governorates to host countries = 0.1 percent

Calibrate for the moving cost between governorates C_1 and the moving cost between governorates and host countries C_2. We assume the latter as the cost of moving between host countries too.

$C_1 = 6.3457$

$C_2 = 6.8083$

Table 4A.1. Results for Etas in Calibrations Normalizing ROW to Zero

Region\Year	2010	2011	2012	2013	2014	2015	2016
Aleppo	3.626	3.928	3.928	3.928	3.928	3.486	3.486
Al-Hassakeh	3.634	3.508	3.508	3.508	3.508	3.892	3.892
Ar-Raqqa	3.666	3.880	3.880	3.880	3.880	3.272	3.272
As-Sweida	3.577	3.778	3.778	3.778	3.778	3.479	3.479
Damascus	3.272	3.638	3.638	3.638	3.638	3.460	3.460
Dar'a	3.497	3.638	3.638	3.638	3.638	3.783	3.783
Deir-ez-Zor	3.756	3.894	3.894	3.894	3.894	3.559	3.559
Hama	3.655	4.171	4.171	4.171	4.171	3.575	3.575
Homs	3.605	3.542	3.542	3.542	3.542	3.719	3.719
Idleb	3.746	3.806	3.806	3.806	3.806	3.273	3.273
Lattakia	3.438	3.982	3.982	3.982	3.982	3.236	3.236
Quneitra	3.473	2.936	2.936	2.936	2.936	3.456	3.456
Rural Damascus	3.509	4.476	4.476	4.476	4.476	3.364	3.364
Tartous	3.413	4.371	4.371	4.371	4.371	3.379	3.379
Iraq	3.556	4.769	4.769	4.769	4.769	3.741	3.741
Jordan	3.877	4.933	4.933	4.933	4.933	3.822	3.822
Lebanon	3.783	5.321	5.321	5.321	5.321	3.726	3.726
ROW	0	0	0	0	0	0	0
Turkey	3.145	3.745	3.745	3.745	3.745	3.499	3.499

Note: ROW = rest of world.

Projection of etas:

$$\widehat{\eta_t} = \eta_{2010}^{s.s} + \hat{\theta}\left[\hat{\delta_1}\left(\log schools_t - \log schools_{2010}^{s.s.}\right) \right.$$
$$\left. + \hat{\delta_2}\left(\log health_t - \log health_{2010}^{s.s.}\right)\right] + \hat{\gamma}\log casualties_t ,$$

where correlations are obtained from the ordinary least squares (OLS) estimations in tables 4A.2, 4A.3, and 4A.4.

Table 4A.2. OLS Estimations before Conflict, 2010

Variables	(1) eta_pre_conflict	(2) eta_pre_conflict
log_cost_dwellings	0.0619*** (0.00392)	0.0267 (0.125)
Constant		0.326 (1.152)
Observations	14	14
R-squared	0.950	0.004
Year fixed effect	N	N
Region fixed effect	N	N

Note: N = no and Y = yes; OLS = ordinary least squares. Standard errors in parentheses.
* p < 0.1, ** p < 0.05, *** p < 0.01

Table 4A.3. OLS Estimations before Conflict, 2002–10

Variables	(1) log_cost	(2) log_cost	(3) log_cost	(4) log_cost	(5) log_cost	(6) log_cost	(7) log_cost	(8) log_cost
log_health	0.468** (0.194)	0.170*** (0.0221)	0.161*** (0.0198)	0.282*** (0.0725)	0.0796 (0.0867)	0.457** (0.197)	0.797*** (0.134)	0.976*** (0.112)
log_schools	0.962*** (0.135)	−0.0673*** (0.0185)	−0.0667*** (0.0165)	0.0618 (0.0536)	0.0409 (0.0534)	0.919*** (0.139)	0.694*** (0.0819)	0.597*** (0.0686)
Constant		8.782*** (0.0897)	8.786*** (0.0814)	7.293*** (0.399)	8.372*** (0.557)			
Observations	126	126	126	126	126	126	126	126
R-squared	0.994	0.357	0.526	0.582	0.709	0.994	1.000	1.000
Year fixed effect	N	N	Y	N	Y	Y	N	Y
Region fixed effect	N	N	N	Y	Y	N	Y	Y

Note: N = no and Y = yes; OLS = ordinary least squares. Standard errors in parentheses.
* p < 0.1, ** p < 0.05, *** p < 0.01

Table 4A.4. OLS Estimations during Conflict, 2014 and 2016

Variables	(1) change_eta	(2) change_eta	(3) change_eta	(4) change_eta
log_casualties	−0.0458*** (0.0114)	−0.00596 (0.0392)	−0.00613 (0.0405)	−0.0413** (0.0151)
Constant		−0.278 (0.261)	−0.274 (0.293)	
Observations	28	28	28	28
R-squared	0.372	0.001	0.001	0.377
Year fixed effect	N	N	Y	Y
Region fixed effect	N	N	N	N

Note: N = no and Y = yes; OLS = ordinary least squares. Standard errors in parentheses.
* p < 0.1, ** p < 0.05, *** p < 0.01

References

Artuç, Erhan, Shubham Chaudhuri, and John McLaren. 2008. "Delay and Dynamics in Labor Market Adjustment: Simulation Results." *Journal of International Economics* 75 (1): 1–13.

World Bank. 2017. *The Toll of War: The Economic and Social Consequences of the Conflict in Syria.* Washington, DC: World Bank.